Keep this book. You will
need it and use it throughout
your career.

UNDERSTANDING HOSPITALITY ACCOUNTING II

Educational Institute Courses

Introductory

INTRODUCTION TO THE HOSPITALITY INDUSTRY
Third Edition
Gerald W. Lattin

AN INTRODUCTION TO HOSPITALITY TODAY
Second Edition
Rocco M. Angelo, Andrew N. Vladimir

TOURISM AND THE HOSPITALITY INDUSTRY
Joseph D. Fridgen

Rooms Division

FRONT OFFICE PROCEDURES
Fourth Edition
Michael L. Kasavana, Richard M. Brooks

HOUSEKEEPING MANAGEMENT
Margaret M. Kappa, Aleta Nitschke, Patricia B. Schappert

Human Resources

HOSPITALITY SUPERVISION
Second Edition
Raphael R. Kavanaugh, Jack D. Ninemeier

HOSPITALITY INDUSTRY TRAINING
Second Edition
Lewis C. Forrest, Jr.

HUMAN RESOURCES MANAGEMENT
Robert H. Woods

Marketing and Sales

MARKETING OF HOSPITALITY SERVICES
Revised Edition
Christopher W. L. Hart, David A. Troy

HOSPITALITY SALES AND MARKETING
Second Edition
James R. Abbey

CONVENTION MANAGEMENT AND SERVICE
Leonard H. Hoyle, David C. Dorf, Thomas J. A. Jones

MARKETING IN THE HOSPITALITY INDUSTRY
Third Edition
Ronald A. Nykiel

Accounting

UNDERSTANDING HOSPITALITY ACCOUNTING I
Third Edition
Raymond Cote

UNDERSTANDING HOSPITALITY ACCOUNTING II
Third Edition
Raymond Cote

BASIC FINANCIAL ACCOUNTING FOR THE HOSPITALITY INDUSTRY
Raymond S. Schmidgall, James W. Damitio

MANAGERIAL ACCOUNTING FOR THE HOSPITALITY INDUSTRY
Third Edition
Raymond S. Schmidgall

Food and Beverage

FOOD AND BEVERAGE MANAGEMENT
Second Edition
Jack D. Ninemeier

QUALITY SANITATION MANAGEMENT
Ronald F. Cichy

FOOD PRODUCTION PRINCIPLES
Jerald W. Chesser

FOOD AND BEVERAGE SERVICE
Anthony M. Rey, Ferdinand Wieland

HOSPITALITY PURCHASING MANAGEMENT
William P. Virts

BAR AND BEVERAGE MANAGEMENT
Lendal H. Kotschevar, Mary L. Tanke

FOOD AND BEVERAGE CONTROLS
Third Edition
Jack D. Ninemeier

General Hospitality Management

HOTEL/MOTEL SECURITY MANAGEMENT
Raymond C. Ellis, Jr., Security Committee of AH&MA

HOSPITALITY LAW
Third Edition
Jack P. Jefferies

RESORT MANAGEMENT
Second Edition
Chuck Y. Gee

INTERNATIONAL HOTEL MANAGEMENT
Chuck Y. Gee

HOSPITALITY INDUSTRY COMPUTER SYSTEMS
Second Edition
Michael L. Kasavana, John J. Cahill

MANAGING FOR QUALITY IN THE HOSPITALITY INDUSTRY
Robert H. Woods, Judy Z. King

Engineering and Facilities Management

FACILITIES MANAGEMENT
David M. Stipanuk, Harold Roffman

HOSPITALITY INDUSTRY ENGINEERING SYSTEMS
Michael H. Redlin, David M. Stipanuk

HOSPITALITY ENERGY AND WATER MANAGEMENT
Robert E. Aulbach

UNDERSTANDING HOSPITALITY ACCOUNTING II

Third Edition

Raymond Cote, CPA, CCP

EDUCATIONAL INSTITUTE
American Hotel & Motel Association

Disclaimer

This publication is designed to provide accurate and authoritative information in regard to the subject matter covered. It is sold with the understanding that the publisher is not engaged in rendering legal, accounting, or other professional service. If legal advice or other expert assistance is required, the services of a competent professional person should be sought.

   —*From the Declaration of Principles jointly adopted by the American Bar Association and a Committee of Publishers and Associations*

The author, Raymond Cote, is solely responsible for the contents of this publication. All views expressed herein are solely those of the author and do not necessarily reflect the views of the Educational Institute of the American Hotel & Motel Association (the Institute) or the American Hotel & Motel Association (AH&MA).

Nothing contained in this publication shall constitute a standard, an endorsement, or a recommendation of the Institute or AH&MA. The Institute and AH&MA disclaim any liability with respect to the use of any information, procedure, or product, or reliance thereon by any member of the hospitality industry.

©Copyright 1988, 1991, 1997
By the EDUCATIONAL INSTITUTE of the
AMERICAN HOTEL & MOTEL ASSOCIATION
1407 South Harrison Road
P.O. Box 1240
East Lansing, Michigan 48826

The Educational Institute of the American
Hotel & Motel Association is a nonprofit
educational foundation.

Printed in the United States of America
1 2 3 4 5 6 7 8 9 10 01 00 99 98 97

Library of Congress Cataloging-in-Publication Data
Cote, Raymond.
   Understanding hospitality accounting II / Raymond Cote. — 3rd ed.
      p. cm.
   An expanded version of: Understanding hospitality accounting I.
   Includes index.
   ISBN 0-86612-135-8 (pbk.)
      1. Hospitality industry—Accounting.   I. Cote, Raymond.
   Understanding hospitality accounting I.   II. Title.
   HF5686.H75C63   1996
   657'.837—dc20   96-35894
                                                          CIP

Contents

About the Author

Raymond Cote is a Professor in the Accounting Department at Johnson & Wales University in Providence, Rhode Island. He has taught undergraduate courses in accounting and graduate courses in financial management, finance, and international accounting. Professor Cote has also served as the university's faculty exchange representative at Les Roches, an international hotel management school in Switzerland. During his six-month assignment at Les Roches, he designed and implemented a hospitality financial management course that he taught to 180 students from around the world.

Raymond Cote

Professor Cote holds a bachelor of science and a master of science degree, both in business administration, from Suffolk University in Boston, Massachusetts. A certified public accountant and a certified computer professional, his additional professional credentials include Accreditation in Accountancy by the American Council for Accountancy and Enrolled Agent as issued by the Internal Revenue Service.

Professor Cote has written three textbooks: *Understanding Hospitality Accounting I* (Educational Institute of the American Hotel & Motel Association, 1987, 1991, 1995), *Understanding Hospitality Accounting II* (Educational Institute of AH&MA, 1988, 1991, 1997), and *College Business Math* (P.A.R. Incorporated, Educational Publishers, 1984, 1985, 1987, 1988). Prior to his academic career, he owned a certified public accounting firm and also held positions in private industry as an accountant, controller, and Vice President of Management Information Services. His hospitality industry experience includes having been the chief accountant for a national food service and lodging corporation, serving as a public-sector accountant for food service and lodging clients, and owning and managing a food and beverage operation in Florida. He is the Past President of the Chamber of Commerce of North Smithfield, Rhode Island, and a former Vice President and Director of Education for the Florida Accountants Association.

Preface

This text is the second in a series consisting of *Understanding Hospitality Accounting I* and *Understanding Hospitality Accounting II*. The series was developed around the philosophy that hospitality managers, professionals, and students are users of accounting information, not bookkeepers or accountants. This third edition maintains that philosophy and remains true to the original text's user-friendly approach.

Where appropriate, references are made to the *Uniform System of Accounts and Expense Dictionary for Small Hotels, Motels, and Motor Hotels,* published by the Educational Institute of the American Hotel & Motel Association (AH&MA), and to the pronouncements of the Financial Accounting Standards Board (FASB) and the American Institute of Certified Public Accountants (AICPA).

The series addresses the unique needs of the hospitality industry. These texts are written in a style that is easily understandable, yet authoritative and comprehensive. The series helps the reader develop a professional business vocabulary and acquire the necessary accounting knowledge to be a successful manager. The modular, step-by-step presentation of material in the texts makes hospitality accounting easier to understand while delivering thorough coverage of important topics.

The first book in the series, *Understanding Hospitality Accounting I,* presents the accounting concepts and procedures that are the foundation for understanding the processing of hospitality financial data and the accounting cycle.

Understanding Hospitality Accounting II has been extensively revised in order to fill the gap between basic accounting and managerial accounting texts. This text covers such areas as specialized accounting for hotel revenue and expenses; periodic inventory accounting for food and beverage areas; hospitality payroll accounting; intangible assets; accounting for inventory, property, and equipment; financial information systems; hotel departmental financial statements; the income statement, balance sheet, and statement of cash flows; analysis of financial statements; and interim and annual reports.

This third edition of *Understanding Hospitality Accounting II* includes many new topics and extensive improvements.

One noteworthy addition is a specialized chapter on how to read interim and annual reports.

Many other chapters have been updated. For example, the information on depreciation now includes the Modified Accelerated Cost Recovery System (MACRS), a depreciation method mandated by the Internal Revenue Service.

A new chapter on financial information systems covers computer technology, accounting systems, and uniform systems of accounts.

The payroll chapter has been revised to include Medicare and Social Security tax provisions, as well as additional or updated payroll tax forms. Forms 941 and 940 are illustrated, accompanied by instructions and deposit rules. Comprehensive information on the reporting of tip income by employees and employers in accordance with IRS Publication 531 has also been included.

The former chapter on the statement of cash flows has been replaced with a new one based on several years of research and classroom testing.

The coverage of financial statements has also received new treatment. Departmental statements, the income statement, and the balance sheet are now discussed in separate chapters.

Because ratio analysis can be difficult to understand, its coverage has been divided into two chapters: one analyzing the income statement and another analyzing the balance sheet.

The chapter on periodic inventory accounting has been rewritten and simplified.

This third edition also contains new problems, expanded review questions, and new end-of-chapter, self-study review quizzes, which provide the reader with an opportunity to check his or her knowledge of important topics. The review quiz answer key assists the reader by providing the answers and related text references. In addition, new exhibits have been added to improve readability and comprehension. The key terms listed in each chapter are defined in the glossary at the back of the text, as are additional important terms.

I extend my gratitude to those individuals—industry professionals, hospitality educators, and members of professional associations—who give so much to the field of hospitality accounting. The success of this text, or any other text, is made possible only through the contributions of these dedicated individuals.

Many professionals and students have contributed to the success of the first and second editions and to the betterment of this edition. Many thanks are owed to the students and accounting faculty of Johnson & Wales University, who participated in field tests and offered constructive comments. Their input was especially helpful in the design of the text and scope of its coverage. Special thanks are due to the Chairman of the Accounting Department, Professor Louis Piccirilli, CPA, for his interest and cooperation in the success of this text.

My sincere thanks must also be given to the adopters of this text; without them, this book would not be possible.

With deep gratitude, I would also like to recognize and extend my appreciation to the following professors at Johnson & Wales University who, as reviewers of certain chapters of the third edition, gave their valuable time and provided salient recommendations: Maureen Bessette, CPA; Helen Davis, CMA; Guenther DerManelian, CPA; Mary Kathryn Gardner, CPA; A. Donald Hebert; Robert Lizotte; Carmine Marabello, CPA; and Robert W. Ragsdale, CPA.

Special thanks are also extended to the staff of the Educational Institute of AH&MA and the various committees composed of hospitality executives, educators, and accountants who gave their time and effort to review the original manuscript.

Raymond Cote, CPA, CCP
Providence, Rhode Island

Dedication: To all mothers and fathers who provide their children with the love, inspiration, and righteousness needed to succeed in their personal lives—especially to my dear mother and father, Alice E. Cote and Raymond E. Cote, two wonderful people whom I will forever cherish. In their memory, I dedicate this text with love, honor, and gratitude.

Study Tips for Users of
Educational Institute Courses

Learning is a skill, like many other activities. Although you may be familiar with many of the following study tips, we want to reinforce their usefulness.

Your Attitude Makes a Difference

If you want to learn, you will: it's as simple as that. Your attitude will go a long way in determining whether or not you do well in this course. We want to help you succeed.

Plan and Organize to Learn

- Set up a regular time and place for study. Make sure you won't be disturbed or distracted.

- Decide ahead of time how much you want to accomplish during each study session. Remember to keep your study sessions brief; don't try to do too much at one time.

Read the Course Text to Learn

- *Before* you read each chapter, read the chapter outline and the learning objectives. Notice that each learning objective has page numbers that indicate where you can find the concepts and issues related to the objective. If there is a summary at the end of the chapter, you should read it to get a feel for what the chapter is about.

- Then, go back to the beginning of the chapter and *carefully* read, focusing on the material included in the learning objectives and asking yourself such questions as:

  —Do I understand the material?

  —How can I use this information now or in the future?

- Make notes in margins and highlight or underline important sections to help you as you study. Read a section first, then go back over it to mark important points.

- Keep a dictionary handy. If you come across an unfamiliar word that is not included in the textbook glossary, look it up in the dictionary.

- Read as much as you can. The more you read, the better you read.

Testing Your Knowledge

- Test questions developed by the Educational Institute for this course are designed to measure your knowledge of the material.

- End-of-the-chapter Review Quizzes help you find out how well you have studied the material. They indicate where additional study may be needed. Review Quizzes are also helpful in studying for other tests.

- Prepare for tests by reviewing:

  —learning objectives

  —notes

  —outlines

  —questions at the end of each assignment

- As you begin to take any test, read the test instructions *carefully* and look over the questions.

We hope your experiences in this course will prompt you to undertake other training and educational activities in a planned, career-long program of professional growth and development.

Chapter Outline

Revenue Centers
    Categories of Revenue Centers
    Revenue Centers and Financial Reports
    Minor Revenue Centers
Fundamental Revenue Concepts
    Revenue Accounts
    Net Revenue
    Gross Profit
Trade Discounts
Cash Discounts
    ROG
    EOM
    Transportation Charges
Recording Invoices and Discounts
    Gross Method
    Net Method
Internal Control for Food and Beverage
  Sales
    Guest Checks
    Debit and Credit Cards
    Guest Charges
    Accounting for Charged Tips
Accounting Personnel and Front Office
  Functions
    The Accounts Receivable Clerk
    The Cashier
    The Night Auditor
    A Summary of Front Office Accounting
Cash and Data Collection

Learning Objectives

1. Define revenue centers, identify examples of revenue centers in a hospitality business, and explain their roles in financial reporting. (pp. 4–6)

2. Define revenue accounts, identify examples of revenue accounts for a hospitality business, and explain net revenue and gross profit. (pp. 6–9)

3. Identify what is meant by trade discounts and cash discounts, and explain their relevance to a hospitality business. (pp. 9–12)

4. Describe two methods for recording invoices involving discounts and two procedures for recording cash discounts. (pp. 12–15)

5. Explain the common internal control forms and procedures involved in food and beverage sales. (pp. 15–20)

6. Describe the difference between the guest ledger and the city ledger. (pp. 20–22)

7. Identify three front office personnel who report to the accounting department, and describe the roles they play in providing hospitality accounting information. (pp. 22–26)

8. Describe the system used for cash and data collection in a hospitality business. (pp. 26–31)

Hotel Revenue Accounting

I$_N$ ACCOUNTING, there is an important distinction between the terms "revenue" and "income." Revenue is an exchange process represented by sales of merchandise, sales of services, and/or interest and dividends. It results from a business transaction, which is the exchange of goods, property, or services for cash or an account receivable (a promise to pay by the customer).

In a hotel,* the major sources of revenue are rooms department sales and food and beverage department sales. Additional hotel revenues come from other operating departments, interest from savings and money market accounts, dividends from investments, concessions fees, commissions, and discounts earned for timely payment of invoices from suppliers. Because the largest source of revenue is sales, accounting professionals frequently use the terms "revenue" and "sales" synonymously.

Income is the result of revenue being greater than all the hotel's expenses. Income can be shown as:

$$\text{Revenue (sales)} - \text{All expenses} = \text{Income}$$

A hotel's generation of revenue requires good control procedures to record and process transactions involving cash, credit cards, and accounts receivable. Documents associated with revenue accounting provide internal control benefits for both the operation and its employees. All employees appreciate sound internal control procedures; such procedures allow employees to prove that they are performing their duties with efficiency and integrity.

In addressing the topic of revenue accounting and controls, this chapter will answer such questions as:

1. How does revenue accounting for operated departments differ from accounting for leased departments?

2. What is the relationship of net revenue to gross profit?

3. How are purchase discounts handled in the accounting records?

4. What front office activities are performed by accounting department personnel?

5. How are computers used in modern property management systems?

---

*As it is used here, hotel is a broad generic term for all types of lodging operations including luxury hotels, motels, motor inns, and inns.

This chapter presents various **revenue centers** and revenue accounts used by hospitality properties. The recommendations given by the Committee on Financial Management of the American Hotel & Motel Association (AH&MA) form the basis for the revenue accounts discussed here. Operated and leased departments are discussed in terms of how the results of their operations are presented on financial statements.

Purchase discounts receive comprehensive coverage through explanations of the gross and net methods. Revenue and nonrevenue procedures for the treatment of discounts are also discussed.

The role of internal control forms for revenue in an accounting system is explained through discussion and examples. In addition, the relationship between the front office and the accounting department is examined.

Finally, since a hotel generates cash and revenue from many remote activities and departments, the fundamentals of cash and data collection at a central source are important topics of discussion.

Revenue Centers

For purposes of financial reporting and data collection, departments may be classified as revenue centers or support centers. Simply stated, revenue centers generate revenue through sales of products and/or services to guests; revenue centers are also referred to as operated departments. Support centers provide services to revenue centers. For ease of discussion, we will use the terms "center" and "department" interchangeably.

Categories of Revenue Centers

Revenue centers may be further categorized as major revenue centers and minor revenue centers. The two major revenue centers are:

- Rooms
- Food and beverage

The scope of minor revenue centers will vary depending on the type and size of the hotel. The following are classified as minor revenue centers:

- Telephone
- Gift shop
- Newsstand
- Valet
- Laundry
- Barbershop or beauty salon
- Recreation

Some of these minor departments operate in the public areas of the hotel, and their goods or services are available to the general public; these departments generally accept only cash or credit cards. Certain minor departments are for the exclusive use of registered guests, who may charge bills to their room accounts.

Revenue Centers and Financial Reports

The design of a financial information system will determine the number of individual reporting areas at a particular establishment. Most operated departments issue financial reports known as supporting schedules or departmental income statements. For example, a separate departmental income statement is produced for the rooms, food and beverage, and telephone departments. Some operated departments are considered incidental operations because their sales volumes and operating expenses are not significant. These departments may together form a single financial reporting category called Other Operated Departments.

For purposes of financial reporting, some hotels separate the food and beverage department into two individual reporting centers: restaurant and lounge. However, this split may not be practical if these centers share costs and personnel.

Each revenue department receives credit for its share of sales regardless of where the sales are made. For example, any food or beverages sold to guests in their rooms would be reported by the food and beverage department, not the rooms department.

A hospitality establishment may use more than one account for food sales in order to isolate the separate contributions of various segments of its operations. For instance, food sales accounts may be set up for each of the following areas:

- Dining room
- Coffee shop
- Banquets
- Room service (food sales)
- Lounge (food sales)

Similarly, separate accounts to record sales of beverages (alcoholic drinks) may be established for the following areas:

- Bar
- Dining room
- Banquets
- Room service (beverage sales)

Minor Revenue Centers

Minor revenue centers perform functions vital to the operation of a hospitality establishment. Any minor revenue center that is hotel-operated requires a specific section in a hotel's chart of accounts to properly record sales, cost of sales, payroll, and other applicable operating expenses.

The functions associated with some minor revenue centers, rather than being performed by hotel-operated departments, may instead be leased to a **concessionaire.** This arrangement is common for barbershops and beauty salons as well as laundry and valet services. Separate income statements are not produced for concessions leased by the hotel because concessions are not hotel-operated departments. The income derived from leased shops or services appears on a hotel's schedule of **rentals and other income.** The responsibility area addressed by this schedule is considered another revenue center.

Telephone. The telephone department is responsible for providing telephone services for the hotel and its guests. If an electronic communications system is not installed, charges to guests for billable calls must be entered on a log or voucher. These charges must be promptly forwarded to the accounts receivable clerk in the front office. (In fact, any services which guests may charge to their room accounts will require a system to communicate such billings promptly to the accounts receivable clerk.)

Laundry. Laundry services for guests may be performed by the hotel or by an outside laundry. If the work is done by an outside laundry, the hotel usually receives a commission based on charges to the guests. The income from commissions will appear on the hotel's schedule of rentals and other income.

Other Minor Departments. Valet services may include pressing, cleaning, and repairing guests' clothes, as well as shoe shining. This service area may be hotel-operated or handled by a local vendor.

Similarly, a hotel barbershop, beauty salon, or newsstand may be either hotel-operated or leased to a concessionaire. These types of shops often transact business on a cash-only basis; such transactions do not require any provisions for charges to guests' accounts.

A recreation department oversees the use of such facilities as swimming pools, health clubs, golf courses, and tennis courts. These facilities may be free to registered guests or available at an extra charge. Such facilities may be hotel-operated or leased to a concessionaire.

Fundamental Revenue Concepts

As noted earlier, the definition of a business transaction is *the exchange of goods, property, or services for cash or a promise to pay.* Revenue results from the sales of goods and services to guests in exchange for cash or a promise to pay. The amount of a sale is exclusive of any sales taxes or tips.

The realization principle states that a sale is recognized only after services and/or products have been delivered and accepted. It is at this point—called the *point of sale*—that a sale should be recognized, regardless of the method by which the customer pays.

Deposits for services or products to be provided in the future do not constitute sales. For example, the receipt of a $500 deposit from a customer to reserve banquet facilities cannot be recorded as a sale because the services and products have not yet been delivered. The receipt of cash under such circumstances represents a liability broadly categorized as unearned revenue.

The receipt of a deposit results in a debit (increase) to the cash account and an offsetting credit to another account. The account to be credited depends on the accounting system used by the hotel. It may be Accounts Receivable, Banquet Deposits, or some other appropriate account. Generally, accounts of this type are summarized and shown as a liability on the balance sheet. They may appear as Unearned Revenue, or Deposits and Credit Balances.

Revenue Accounts

The revenue accounts used by a hotel depend on the type of business activities it conducts, the size of the business, and the amount of detailed information that management requires in its financial reporting system.

Definitions of the following revenue accounts comply with the recommendations of the Committee on Financial Management of the American Hotel & Motel Association.

Room Sales. Rentals of guestrooms and apartments are credited to this account. Separate charges for housekeeper or linen service should be included. If meals are included in the room rate, a distinction should be made between rooms and food to properly account for room and food sales.

Room Allowances. This is a contra-revenue account which represents rebates and refunds allowed after room sales were initially recorded.

Hospitality businesses sometimes grant these and other types of **allowances** to guests in the interest of maintaining good customer relations. Most allowances involve disputed charges, price adjustments, correction of overcharges, and adjustments for unsatisfactory service.

Food Sales. Sales of food and non-alcoholic beverages served with meals are credited to this account. There may be several food sales accounts classified by facility (for example, dining room, room service, lounge, and banquets).

Employees' meals and officers' checks should be excluded from the food sales account. Officers' checks are guest checks signed by a hotel's corporate officers in lieu of payment for food and beverages.

Sales of grease, bones, and other kitchen by-products are credited to cost of sales, not to this revenue account.

Food Allowances. This is a contra-revenue account which represents rebates and refunds allowed after food sales were initially recorded.

Beverage Sales. Beverage sales may be separated into wines, liquor, beer, or any other category helpful in sales analysis and inventory control. Beverage sales may be further classified according to source, such as dining room, room service, banquets, and lounge. Officers' checks should be excluded from this revenue account.

Beverage Allowances. This is a contra-revenue account which represents rebates and refunds allowed after beverage sales were initially recorded.

Other Income—Food and Beverage Department. The other income—food and beverage account is used to record sales of merchandise not related to food and beverage service. Sales recorded to this account are for sales of items *not* sold from vending machines. For example, the dining room may sell items such as gum, cigars, cigarettes, candy, and novelty items. The lounge may sell peanuts, popcorn, and other snack items. Cover and minimum charges should also be recorded to this account.

These miscellaneous departmental sales are excluded from Food Sales and Beverage Sales to permit a gross profit analysis, i.e., comparisons of the sales of food and beverages against their respective costs.

Telephone Sales. Revenue received from guests for use of telephone services and any commissions earned from pay phones are included in this account. Sales may be classified as local calls, long-distance calls, service charges, and commissions.

Telephone Allowances. This is a contra-revenue account which represents rebates and refunds allowed after sales were initially recorded.

Other Accounts for Income Earned by the Hotel. This is a general revenue classification consisting of many different revenue accounts; the revenue associated with this classification is not credited to any specific department. For purposes of financial reporting, a hotel's other income is treated as coming from a separate revenue center.

Items fitting this classification will appear on a hotel's schedule of rentals and other income. These items include:

- Interest income
- Dividend income
- Rental income (stores, offices, and clubs)
- Concessions income
- Commissions income
- Vending machines income (less the cost of merchandise sold)
- Cash discounts earned (purchase discounts)
- Salvage income

Minor gain or loss on sale of fixed assets may also appear on a hotel's schedule of rentals and other income. If the total gain or loss is significant, however, it should be separately shown on the hotel's summary income statement.

Net Revenue

Net revenue is not a bookkeeping account for revenue. It is a term that represents sales less allowances. Net revenue reflects the billable activities of a facility. For example, assume that room sales total $100,000 and room allowances total $1,500. The net revenue on room sales realized by the rooms department would be $98,500. For financial statement purposes, this is shown as follows on the rooms department income statement:

Revenue	
Room Sales	$100,000
Room Allowances	1,500
Net Revenue	$ 98,500

The term "net revenue" is sometimes referred to as net sales. This net amount is significant in financial statement analysis because it is used as a common divisor in computing percentage relationships of various items to net sales.

Gross Profit

Like net revenue, **gross profit** is not a bookkeeping account; rather, it is a line item on financial statements. It is a term that represents net revenue less cost of sales. Gross profit reflects the profit made on the sale of merchandise before deducting any expenses associated with operating a facility.

The calculation of gross profit depends in part on the type of department in question. Some departments may be described as merchandising facilities. Merchandising facilities sell goods or products and, therefore, have cost of sales expenses.

The rooms department is not a merchandising facility. Therefore, its net revenue and gross profit are identical. If a rooms department has a net revenue figure of $75,000, then its gross profit also equals $75,000.

By contrast, the food and beverage department *is* a merchandising facility. Assume its food sales are $80,450, food allowances $450, and cost of food sold $25,000. The gross profit for food sales would appear on the departmental income statement as follows:

Revenue	
Food Sales	$80,450
Food Allowances	450
Net Revenue	$80,000
Cost of Food Sold	25,000
Gross Profit	$55,000

A department's gross profit must be sufficient enough to cover payroll and other operating expenses and produce a departmental income. The total of all the departmental incomes in turn must be large enough to cover undistributed expenses and fixed charges in order to produce a net income for the hotel.

Trade Discounts

Trade discounts are reductions to those prices indicated on a vendor's price list. Vendors sometimes use trade discounts as a convenience in making price changes without printing new catalogs or price lists.

Trade discounts are never recorded as such. The amount paid is entered without indicating that it is a trade discount. Trade discounts do not depend upon payment within a given time period.

Vendors' invoices normally show the gross amount, trade discount, and net billing; therefore, computation of trade discounts is generally not required. For example, kitchen equipment with a list price of $5,000 purchased at a 40% trade discount will be billed at a net invoice price of $3,000. The purchase of this asset is recorded as $3,000. Any applicable cash discounts are computed on the $3,000 net price.

Exhibit 1   Explanation of Discount Terms

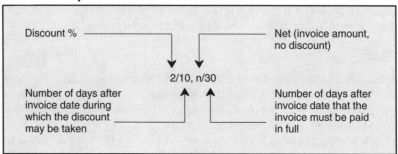

Cash Discounts

Some vendors offer a discount for payment of an invoice before its due date. Early collection from customers provides a vendor with one clear benefit: better cash flow to cover expenditures or to make investments. To encourage prompt payment, vendors may offer an incentive called a **cash discount,** also referred to as a purchase discount.

Unlike trade discounts, cash discounts depend upon payment *within a specified time period.* Cash discount terms are usually shown in abbreviated form such as 2/10, n/30. This format is interpreted in Exhibit 1.

For example, a $100 invoice dated October 16 with cash discount terms of 2/10, n/30 may be paid anytime between October 16 and October 26 to take advantage of the 2% discount. If payment is made during the discount period, the amount of the check in payment of this invoice is $98, computed as follows:

Invoice amount	$100
2% cash discount	− 2
Check amount	$ 98

This example uses terms of payment called ordinary dating. The payment period under ordinary dating payment terms begins with the date of an invoice. Cash discounts can also be given under other payment terms. Some vendors modify the discount terms by adding a suffix such as ROG (receipt of goods) or EOM (end of month) to the discount format. This suffix changes the date of the discount period, and initiates a form of extended dating.

ROG

The term "ROG" (receipt of goods) means the cash discount ending period is computed from the date goods are received—not the invoice date. This form of dating is used by vendors when goods are delivered a relatively long time after the invoice has been sent. Assume an invoice is dated March 5 with terms of 2/10, n/30 ROG. If the goods are received on March 10, the discount period is from March 10 to March 20.

To illustrate this concept further, review the following example. Assume a delivery of goods is received on August 15. The invoice amount for merchandise is

$700, the invoice date is August 2, and terms are 1/10, n/30 ROG. Payment is made on August 24; the 1% cash discount is good until August 25. The payment is calculated as follows:

Invoice amount (merchandise)	$700
1% discount	− 7
Check amount	$693

EOM

The term "EOM" (end of month) signifies that the cash discount period begins after the end of the month in which the invoice is dated. If an invoice is dated June 8 with terms of 2/10, n/30 EOM, the discount period ends on July 10. The determination is simple: the month of the invoice date in this case is June; there are ten discount days and the following month is July; therefore, the discount period is good until July 10.

As a further example, assume an invoice is dated May 25, terms are 4/15, n/30 EOM, and the invoice amount for merchandise is $600. Since the month of the invoice is May, the cash discount period extends to June 15. If the payment is made on or before June 15, it is calculated as follows:

Invoice amount (merchandise)	$600
4% discount	− 24
Check amount	$576

According to business practice, if an invoice with EOM terms is dated on or after the 26th day of a month, the cash discount period extends to the *second* month after the month of the invoice date. In essence, the invoice is treated as if it were dated for the beginning of the next month. Thus, any invoices dated May 26 through the end of the month are treated as if they were June 1 billings. The discount period will therefore extend into July.

For example, assume an invoice is dated May 26, credit terms are 4/15, n/30 EOM, and the invoice amount is $600. The month of the invoice is May but the date is on the 26th day of the month. In this case, the invoice is treated as a June 1 billing; the cash discount period extends to July 15 (15 days into the next month of the billing period). If the payment is made any time up to July 15, it is calculated as follows:

Invoice amount (merchandise)	$600
4% discount	− 24
Check amount	$576

Sometimes, the abbreviation "Prox." is used in offering extended dating terms. Prox. stands for *proximo,* which means "next month" in Latin. The procedures for computing discounts with credit terms of Prox. are identical to those used for EOM.

Transportation Charges

Discounts on freight charges are generally not permitted. Cash discounts should be calculated on the invoice amount exclusive of any freight (delivery) charges. For example, assume a $271.95 invoice consisting of merchandise ($250.00) and freight charges ($21.95) is dated October 17 with discount terms of 2/10, n/30. If payment is made during the discount period, it is calculated as follows:

Invoice amount	$271.95
Cash discount (2% × $250)	− 5.00
Amount of check	$266.95

Recording Invoices and Discounts

A small hospitality business will usually record invoices only as they are paid. If financial statements are required, the accountant will prepare an adjusting journal entry for all unpaid invoices to comply with the matching principle. This procedure, while acceptable for a small business, is not good management practice for larger hospitality companies because of its poor internal control.

In a small restaurant, the owner or manager does the ordering, verifies the receipt of the product, and authorizes the invoice for payment; in fact, he or she might actually write the check. In a large hotel or restaurant operation, each of these functions is performed by different individuals.

Large hospitality businesses process all invoices through an accounts payable system or voucher register system as they are received, regardless of when the invoices are to be paid. A voucher system is a system for controlling accounts payable and payments with the objective of safeguarding cash. In a payables or voucher system, the invoice is immediately recorded upon receipt regardless of whether it is to be paid now or at a future date. The entry is always a debit to a specific account for the purchase and a credit to Accounts Payable.

Specific name of account
Accounts Payable

Some invoices involve discounts. There are two methods in accounting that are used to record these invoices:

- Gross method

- Net method

The *gross method* records the full amount of purchase to Accounts Payable; the discount is recorded only upon actual payment of the invoice.

The *net method* anticipates that the discount will be taken and records the net amount (amount after discount) to Accounts Payable immediately upon receipt of the invoice. The net method can be used only by hospitality businesses that have ample cash flow and are in a position to pay all discount invoices within the time period required to take advantage of the discount terms.

The difference between the gross method and net method can be shown as follows:

Upon Receipt of Invoice	Gross Method	Net Method
Full amount is recorded without any discount	x	
Net amount is recorded anticipating discount		x

In addition to selecting a method for recording invoices, management must decide how to treat discounts for financial statement reporting purposes. The treatment of discounts is an important decision. For example, assume that food provisions are purchased for the restaurant operation of a hotel. Should the food cost be reduced by the discount or should the discount be recorded as other income of the hotel?

To answer this question, let's analyze why suppliers offer discounts. A supplier offers a discount as an incentive to receive payment within a timely period. However, the cost of this incentive has been "built into" the selling price; the discount is considered a cost of doing business. Therefore, the price paid after the discount really reflects the true price. It is likely that if the supplier did not have to offer a discount, the selling price might be lower.

There are two procedures for the recording of **cash discounts**:

- Revenue procedure
- Nonrevenue procedure

The *revenue procedure* records the discount as other income for the hotel in an account called *Cash Discounts Earned*. The Cash Discounts Earned account appears on a hotel's schedule of rentals and other income. Advocates of the revenue procedure believe that cash discounts are earned from the availability of funds and the proper management of cash and payment of accounts payable. The revenue procedure is recommended in the *Uniform System of Accounts and Expense Dictionary for Small Hotels, Motels, and Motor Hotels* published by the Educational Institute of the American Hotel & Motel Association.

The *nonrevenue procedure* treats the discount as a reduction of the cost of the item originally purchased. Advocates of the nonrevenue procedure believe that a department should be charged only for the net cost of a purchase since it represents a true cost.

Regardless of the procedure used, the treatment of the discount produces the same net income for the hotel; the only difference between the procedures is which department will get credit for the discount.

The procedure for recording discounts does not depend on whether the gross method or net method of recording invoices is used; either method may employ the revenue or nonrevenue procedure. The gross and net methods relate to the amount recorded to accounts payable. The discount procedures relate to which account will get the credit for the cash discount. The difference between the revenue and nonrevenue treatment of discounts can be shown as follows:

	Revenue	Nonrevenue
Discount is recorded in Cash Discounts Earned	x	
Discount is used to reduce purchase cost		x

Gross Method

The gross method (also called the gross recording method) is a popular way to record invoices in the hospitality industry. The invoice is recorded at the full purchase price. The discount is not anticipated; it is recorded only when the invoice is timely paid and the actual discount is taken. The supporting principle for this method is that the hotel does not always know whether sufficient cash will be available for all discounts to be realized.

Recording an Invoice Upon Receipt. Assume that an invoice for the purchase of $500 of uniforms has just been received. The invoice is dated March 1 with terms of 2/10, n/30. Under the gross method, the journal entry to record the invoice is:

Uniforms	500	
Accounts Payable		500

The discount will not be recorded until the invoice is timely paid. Remember that the treatment of discounts can be either revenue or nonrevenue.

Revenue treatment of discount. The earlier example of the uniform purchase and the recording of the invoice as a $500 credit to Accounts Payable is used here to demonstrate the revenue procedure for the recording of discounts. Assume the invoice is timely paid to take advantage of the 2% discount; the discount of $10 (2% × $500) allows the $500 liability to be discharged with a cash outlay of only $490. Under the revenue procedure, the entry is:

Accounts Payable	500	
Cash		490
Cash Discounts Earned		10

Nonrevenue treatment of discount. The example of the uniform purchase and the recording of the invoice as a $500 credit to Accounts Payable is again used here. Assume the invoice is timely paid to take advantage of the 2% discount; under the nonrevenue procedure, the entry is:

Accounts Payable	500	
Cash		490
Uniforms		10

The nonrevenue procedure requires referencing the original account charged for the purchase so that the cash discount can be properly credited to the correct account.

Net Method

A major disadvantage of the gross method is that it does not reveal the amount of discounts that are lost because of poor cash flow or poor management of the payments operation. Another criticism of the gross method is that the accounts payable amount could be inflated for a hospitality business that is able to continually take most or all cash discounts within its normal accounts payable cycle.

The net method is suitable for those hospitality businesses that want to measure discounts lost and generally have the funds available to take advantage of cash discounts. (The net method is also referred to as the net purchases recording method.) In the net method, the cash discount is anticipated; that is, the hospitality business assumes that when the invoice will be paid funds will be available to take advantage of the cash discount. Therefore, upon receipt of an invoice, the amount recorded is the purchase minus any potential discount. Upon payment, any discounts lost are recovered and recorded to an expense account called Discounts Lost.

Recording an Invoice Upon Receipt. To illustrate the net method, we will again use the invoice for the purchase of $500 of uniforms, dated March 1 with terms of 2/10, n/30. Under the net method, it is anticipated that the $10 discount will definitely be taken when the invoice is paid; the discount is "netted" upon receipt of the invoice. The journal entry to record the invoice is:

Uniforms	490	
Accounts Payable		490

If the invoice is timely paid within the discount period, the entry to record the payment is:

Accounts Payable	490	
Cash		490

If the invoice is not timely paid within the discount period, the entry to record the payment is:

Accounts Payable	490	
Discounts Lost	10	
Cash		490

Internal Control for Food and Beverage Sales

Cost control through proper handling of cash discounts is only one of the critical factors important to profitable operations. Sales control is an equally important requirement for profitability. Sales control relates to the set of controls and forms designed to enable management to monitor the revenue of a business. Sales control makes certain all sales are recorded and that all sales are made at the correct prices.

The audit of restaurant sales is accomplished by reviewing guest checks, servers' signature books, cashiers' documents, and cash register readings. The actual audit procedures for internal control purposes depend on the size of the establishment, its operating procedures, the design of its forms, and the use of automated equipment.

Allowances should be entered on an allowance voucher such as the sample form shown in Exhibit 2. Before these vouchers are processed, the amounts appearing on them must be approved by an employee designated by management.

Discussion of detailed control procedures is best reserved for specialized courses such as front office and food and beverage control. However, in learning hospitality accounting concepts, one should have a fundamental knowledge of procedures associated with the following:

- Guest checks
- Servers' signature books
- Debit and credit cards
- Guest charges

Exhibit 2   Sample Allowance Voucher

464856	ALLOWANCE

DEPARTMENT

DATE   19

NAME   ROOM OR ACCT. NO.

	DATE	SYMBOL	AMOUNT

DO NOT WRITE IN ABOVE SPACE

EXPLANATION

AMERICAN HOTEL REGISTER CO., NORTHBROOK, IL 60062-7798
AHW 4211   SIGNED BY

Source: American Hotel Register Company.

- Front office operations
- Daily room reports
- Housekeepers' reports

Guest Checks

The **guest check** (Exhibit 3) serves a dual purpose: it initiates the food and beverage order taken from the guest, and eventually represents the invoice given to the guest. Guest checks are prenumbered and usually tinted so that any erasure can be detected. Guest checks are also called servers' checks.

There are a wide variety of procedures associated with the internal control of guest checks. One procedure is to keep them in locked storage, in numerical order, and issue them to servers when servers report for duty. Under this system, each server receives a specified quantity of consecutively numbered checks. As the checks are issued, the server's identification number or name is entered in a servers' signature book (Exhibit 4), along with an entry recording the first and last numbers of the checks issued. The server then signs the book and must account for the checks at the end of his or her shift.

When the server goes off duty, unused checks are returned and the last check number issued by the server is recorded. Unused checks are filed in numerical order and may be re-issued or taken out of circulation. Any outstanding checks should be

Exhibit 3   Sample Guest Check

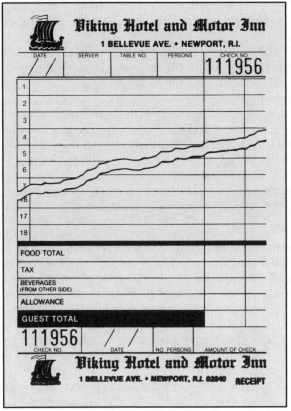

Courtesy of the Viking Hotel and Motor Inn

Exhibit 4   Sample Servers' Signature Book

		CHECKS ISSUED			Last Check Used	CHECKS RETURNED			Total	Missing
Svr. No.	Signature	From	To	Total Issued		Unused	Void	Per Cashier		

SERVERS' SIGNATURE BOOK   Date: _____ 19 ____

accounted for under internal control procedures. Properly approved voided checks must also be submitted and substantiated for validity. The management policy regarding lost checks varies from operation to operation, and may depend upon state payroll laws.

The income auditor compares the servers' signature book to the checks returned to the cashier. In this way, the income auditor ensures that all used checks listed in the book have been recorded as sales.

Servers' checks may be in duplicate to provide a control at the point an order is taken. In a duplicate system, the guest's order is recorded on a special check which simultaneously produces a duplicate. Food can be ordered by the server from the kitchen only with this duplicate. The prenumbered duplicates are retained in the kitchen and later compared with guest checks from the cashier's station to determine whether all sales have been recorded and paid.

There are other types of control systems as well, but any control system must fit the particular needs of an operation. A good control system is one that achieves its objective with a minimum of delay and interference with customer service.

Cash Control in the Dining Room. When a guest has finished dining, the server must price and total the guest check unless that function has been automatically performed by point-of-sale equipment. The server receives payment from the guest and delivers the guest check and payment to the cashier.

The cashier keys each item listed on the check into the register. The register tallies each item and imprints the total on the check for verification with the server's total. The cashier also keeps a record of checks charged to room numbers; amounts from these guest checks are communicated promptly to the front office for posting to guest accounts.

At the end of a shift, the cashier's cash drawer and supporting documents are accounted for. Cash register readings are taken and summarized. The cash, credit card vouchers, room charges, and any miscellaneous paid outs are then reconciled with the cash register readings using a daily cashiers report.[1]

Cash Control in the Lounge. Internal control for beverage sales presents a greater challenge than internal control for dining room sales. The same person (a bartender) may take the customer's order, prepare and serve the drink, receive the cash, and record the sale. While no universal system of beverage control can be described, there are common procedures and rules found throughout the hospitality industry.

One common procedure is to require the bartender to ring each sale as it is made. Since the bartender also acts as the cashier, a safeguard is necessary to prevent the reuse of checks after they have been paid. One such safeguard is to require the bartender to insert each paid check into a locked box.

The control of cash and cashiering functions has great importance to sales control. Cashiering procedures should require that the cash register drawer never remain open, even for a short period of time. An operation that has cocktail servers in the lounge should not allow servers to first pay the bartender in cash and then collect from customers. This procedure may tempt servers to overcharge customers.

Controlling guest checks in the lounge operation is similar to controlling guest checks in the dining room operation. If for some reason it is totally impractical to use guest checks, the register should have a receipt tape which is given to the customer in lieu of a guest check.

Bartenders should not be allowed to take register readings or reconcile their own cash at the end of their shifts. Special procedures are necessary to guard against "voids" and "no sale" rings that may allow embezzlement. The reconciling for beverage sales may be prepared on a form similar to the daily cashiers report which can be custom-designed for a particular operation.

Automated beverage dispensing systems provide a new dimension in the control of liquor sales. Since these systems are costly, however, they are not justifiable for all operations.

Debit and Credit Cards

Debit or ATM cards possess an important characteristic that sets them apart from credit cards. The use of a debit card results in an instant reduction of the cash balance in the cardholder's bank account. The customer's funds are immediately transferred and deposited into the checking account of the hospitality business. Therefore, debit card transactions are treated like cash and processed similarly.

In comparison, the use of a credit card does not immediately affect the cardholder's bank account. Rather, the credit card company pays the retailer, and later the cardholder pays the credit card company upon receipt of a monthly statement. The popular credit cards are MasterCard, VISA, Discover, American Express, Carte Blanche, and Diners Club. Their treatment by a hospitality business depends on whether the card is classified as a bankcard.

MasterCard and VISA are called bankcards because a business may deposit the credit card drafts directly into its checking account just like cash and personal checks. These cards are very popular in the hospitality industry because a business has instant access to the funds. There is no waiting period. *Therefore, a sale made to a guest using a bankcard is recorded as a cash transaction.*

A business may deposit Discover credit card drafts directly into its bank account. However, unlike the procedure used with bankcards, the bank only grants use of the funds after the drafts are approved by Discover. This approval may be granted as quickly as within 24 hours. In any case, a credit card deposit cannot be recorded as cash if the bank does not treat it like cash. Therefore, in cases where such approval is required, the credit card sale is recorded as an account receivable.

American Express, Carte Blanche, and Diners Club represent nonbank credit cards. Sales made to guests using a nonbank credit card or a "house" credit card are treated as accounts receivable transactions. In the case of nonbank credit cards, businesses must forward copies of credit card drafts and wait to be reimbursed. "House" credit cards require that the business bill the customer directly before funds can be collected. Exhibit 5 is a sample American Express draft.

Guest Charges

Certain guests may have charge privileges (i.e., open accounts) with the business. They may purchase services or products by merely signing a guest check or invoice. These transactions are recorded as accounts receivable transactions. The business then sends the customer a bill or statement requesting payment. Open account

Exhibit 5 Sample American Express Draft

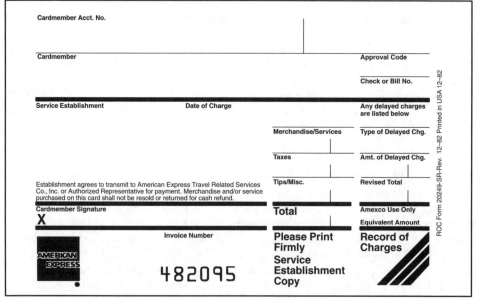

Source: American Express Company.

privileges may include extended credit terms whereby the hotel sends a monthly statement to the guest.

Accounting for Charged Tips

When a guest pays the server a cash tip, no accounting procedures are required since the tip is made directly to the server. Instead of paying the server a cash tip, however, a guest using a credit card or charge account may enter a tip on the credit card draft or guest check.

When tips are entered on credit card drafts or guest checks, the business becomes involved. In a sense, it is now acting as a collection agent for the server; charged tips are a liability of the business until the server is paid. Ultimately, the business will collect the tip portion from the credit card company or, in the case of guest charges, from the guest.

A tip policy should be established to provide a consistent accounting treatment for tips. For instance, a tip policy may state that the credit card fee applicable to the tip portion should not be deducted from the server's tip. A tip policy should also outline when a server will be paid his or her charged tips. Depending on a company's tip policy, a server may be paid for charged tips immediately or only at the end of the shift.

Accounting Personnel and Front Office Functions

The most visible area in a property is the front office, the initial contact point between guests and hotel personnel. It is the center of activities for processing guest

Exhibit 6　Sample Guest Folio

MCP ® MOORE BUSINESS FORMS, INC. † PATENTED SPEEDISET®　R

24961

ROOM　　DEPART.

RATE　　TO FOLIO NO.

NO. PARTY

ARRIVE　　ADVANCED DEPOSIT　AMT.

CLERK

Newport

THE VIKING

Hotel and Motor Inn

The Center of Everything

Remarks

Signature [Direct Bill]

Courtesy of the Viking Hotel and Motor Inn

reservations, arranging guest accommodations, providing information, checking out guests, and maintaining the guest ledger.

The guest ledger comprises individual records for each of the hotel's registered guests. During a guest's stay, the front office is responsible for summarizing all guest charges for goods and services and recording guest payments. These summaries are made on guests' records, called folios, which collectively compose the guest ledger. Exhibit 6 presents a sample **guest folio.**

Guest ledger accounting, also referred to as front office accounting, includes the accumulation of guest charges, credits, and payments. There are two accounts receivable subsidiary ledgers for recording guest transactions: the guest ledger and the city ledger. The guest ledger is the accounts receivable subsidiary ledger for guests who are still registered at the hotel. It is maintained by room number in the front office.

By comparison, the city ledger is the accounts receivable subsidiary ledger for all nonregistered guests. The billings for guests who have checked out and charged

Exhibit 7   Sample Charge Voucher

```
097261                    MISCELLANEOUS CHARGE


                                    DEPARTMENT _____
                                    DATE_____ 19_____

   NAME                                    ROOM OR ACCT. NO.
   _____

          DATE         SYMBOL        AMOUNT
   _____




   _____
                    DO NOT WRITE IN ABOVE SPACE

   EXPLANATION _____

   _____

   _____


   AMERICAN HOTEL REGISTER CO., NORTHBROOK, IL 60062-7798
   AHW 4208                               SIGNED BY _____
```

Source: American Hotel Register Company.

their bills are transferred from the guest ledger to the city ledger. The city ledger is maintained alphabetically in the accounting department.

The accounting department is responsible for recording the results of front of-fice activities, maintaining the city ledger, accounting for credit card receivables, paying vendors, handling payroll, preparing financial statements, budgeting, and other accounting functions. The controller, as head of the accounting department and member of the executive committee, is responsible for timely communication of financial information, participation in decision-making, interpretation of pro-posals, forecasting (short-term), and budgeting (long-term). Other responsibilities of accountants may include controlling and monitoring revenues, providing man-agement advisory services, communicating to various departments, and organiz-ing financial control systems.

Accounts receivable clerks, cashiers, and the night auditor report to the accounting department. These three categories of front office personnel play significant roles in providing hospitality accounting information.

The Accounts Receivable Clerk

The accounts receivable clerk posts charges to guest accounts for food, beverages, and other miscellaneous charges. These guest charges are represented by charge vouchers, which are prenumbered for internal control purposes. Since the precise time a guest will check out is not known, it is important that all vouchers be posted immediately. Exhibit 7 presents a sample charge voucher; charges may occur for

Exhibit 8   Sample Automated Telephone Voucher

Date	Time	Room No.	Telephone No.	State	Duration	Charge
↓	↓	↓	↓	↓	↓	↓
10/27	10:46	0101	15175551276	MI	5.3	03.27
10/27	11:12	0028	6833600	RI	10.7	01.32
10/27	11:14	0072	13136764829	MI	7.4	04.25
10/27	11:25	0129	16143933882	OH	22.5	13.47
10/27	11:26	0053	6834731	RI	12.4	01.92

telephone use, laundry and valet services, and incidentals charged to the guest's folio.

The use of computerized systems is rapidly changing the form of many charge vouchers. For example, recent progress in automating the telephone department has permitted direct entry of charges to the guest folio, supported by a log of guest charges or an automated voucher as shown in Exhibit 8.

The Cashier

The cashier receives payments from guests and, if allowed, will make payments on behalf of guests for such items as theater tickets, COD charges, and other incidental charges. The cashier may also be permitted to cash personal checks as a convenience to guests. The cashier is supplied with a fixed sum of money called a *bank,* usually maintained on an imprest system. With an imprest system, an accounting is made of receipts and payments at the end of each shift, and the bank is restored to its original, fixed amount.

The Night Auditor

The night auditor is primarily responsible for entering all room charges, and insuring that all vouchers have been accounted for and properly posted to each guest folio. One method of determining room charges is to examine the room rack. The room rack may be a card index system, which is constantly updated to reflect occupied and vacant rooms. When a guest registers, a multi-part form is prepared. Part of this form is a room card showing the room number, room rate, and number of guests. This room card is then inserted in the room rack.

In the evening, the room rack contains forms for only those *registered* guests remaining for the night who are to be charged for rooms. A list of rooms occupied by registered guests can be prepared from the room rack; this list is called a **daily room report** (Exhibit 9). As a convenience, the rates per room may be preprinted on the daily room report.

The daily room report is compared to the **housekeeper's report** (Exhibit 10), which is prepared from information supplied by individual housekeepers. This procedure identifies skippers and sleepers. A **skipper** is a guest who leaves the hotel without paying for charges incurred. A **sleeper** is a vacant room that is believed to be occupied because the room rack slip or registration card was not

Exhibit 9   Sample Daily Room Report

DAILY ROOM REPORT

Date: *March 2* 19 *X2*
Floor: 1

No.	Rate S/D	No. of Guests	Code	Room Charge
101	60/80	2		80.00
102	60/80		V	
103	55	1	S	40.00
104	60/80	2		80.00
105	75/95	2		95.00
106	75/95	2		95.00
107	60/80		OOO	
108	70		V	
109	60/80	2	C	—
110	55	1	E	55.00
111	55	1	H	—

C: Complimentary   E: Tax Exempt
H: House Staff   OOO: Out of Order
S: Special Rate   V: Vacant

Exhibit 10   Sample Housekeeper's Report

HOUSEKEEPER'S REPORT   Date: *November 14* 19 *X2*

Status Codes

LCO: Late Check-Out   OOO: Out of Order
V: Vacant   X: Occupied

Room	Status Code	Room	Status Code	Room	Status Code	Room	Status Code
101	V	201	X	301	X	401	X
102	V	202	X	302	X	402	X
103	X	203	X	303	X	403	V
104	X	204	X	304	X	404	V
105	X	205	X	305	V	405	X
106	X	206	X	306	V	406	X
107	OOO	207	V	307	V	407	V
108	V	208	V	308	X	408	V
109	X	209	X	309	X	409	X
110	X	210	X	310	X	410	X
111	X	211	V	311	X	411	X

Exhibit 11   Sample Front Office Cash Receipts and Disbursements Journal

NAME	Room No.	CASH RECEIPTS			CASH DISBURSEMENTS				
		Bank dr	Guest dr	City dr	Guest dr	City dr	Other Amount (dr)	Account	Bank cr

FRONT OFFICE CASH RECEIPTS AND DISBURSEMENTS JOURNAL   Date: _____ 19 ___

removed from the rack when the previous guest departed. A major purpose of the housekeeper's report is to detect errors or intentional omissions from room sales. This report should be forwarded directly to the income auditor, not the front office.

Another duty of the night auditor is to verify food and beverage charges made by guests and charged to their rooms. This is accomplished by comparing the *transfer-in total* with the totals transferred out by the restaurant and lounge. Voucher charges from other departments are verified in a similar manner.

Overcharges and errors in guest billings are corrected by the use of allowance vouchers, which are posted to a separate allowance journal. This journal may affect either the guest ledger or the city ledger, depending on the status of the guest.

A Summary of Front Office Accounting

When front office personnel post transactions to the guest ledger, they perform a part of the accounting process. The design and form of the journals used in the front office depend on the accounting system and the hotel's size, and whether the procedures are manual, semi-automated, or computerized.

When the front office receives cash from guests, this acts as a debit to the house bank. When the front office pays out cash, the result is a credit to the bank. Either of these transactions may affect the guest or city ledgers. Receipts and payments of cash are recorded on a front office cash receipts and disbursements journal (Exhibit 11), which is verified by the night auditor and forwarded to the general cashier.

Each evening, the night auditor enters the daily room charge on each guest folio. As part of the audit process, all charge and allowance vouchers are sorted in numerical sequence and accounted for. The night auditor verifies that they have been posted correctly to the guest folios. As necessary, unposted vouchers are posted to the appropriate folios by the night auditor.

After all postings are completed, the night auditor prepares a **daily transcript** report (Exhibit 12) which summarizes all activity posted to the guest ledger.

Exhibit 12   Sample Daily Transcript Report

DAILY TRANSCRIPT REPORT											Date: _____ 19 _____	
Room No.	Previous Balance	CHARGES TO GUEST FOLIO						CREDITS TO GUEST FOLIO				Ending Balance
		Room	Tax	Restaurant	Lounge	Telephone	Other	Payment	Allowances	Transfer to City Ledger		

Cash and Data Collection

Each operated department generates its individual daily cashiers report as an internal control procedure to reconcile revenue and receipts. These daily cashiers reports (one from each operated department) require a summary at a central point to control and verify sales, receivables, and bank deposits.

All cashiers (including those from the front office, restaurant, bar, and other operated departments) must compute their net receipts, place them in an envelope along with a cashier's deposit slip (Exhibit 13), and forward the envelope to the general cashier. (Sometimes the deposit slip form is printed directly on the envelope itself.)

The general cashier confirms the contents of each cashier's deposit envelope in the presence of the cashier. After confirmation is complete, the general cashier prepares a general cashier's deposit summary (Exhibit 14). This summary should list each operating department separately and by shift.

Note the column on the general cashier's deposit summary report labeled "due back" (sometimes called "due bank"). At the end of a shift, the house bank is *due back* any dip in the imprest of the house bank. A dip, also known as a difference, results when the front office pays out more cash in a day than it receives. For instance, with prior approval, the front office may cash checks for guests or make cash advances. Keep in mind that sales involving credit cards or checks do not add to the cash (actual currency) of the house bank.

Using a form similar to the one shown in Exhibit 14, the general cashier is allowed to take cash from the total receipts of the day and settle the due backs before depositing funds in the checking account of the business. Some hotel controllers prefer that all receipts of the day be deposited intact into the checking account of the business and that the cashier draw an exchange check for the due backs.

An income auditor confirms the sales and cash as reported by each department. After the audit is completed, the income auditor summarizes all sales and other pertinent data on a daily report of revenue, which usually forms the basis for the daily entry in a sales journal. The form and content of the daily report of revenue will depend on the amount of information management requires on a daily

Exhibit 13   Sample Cashier's Deposit Slip

CASHIER'S DEPOSIT SLIP		
DATE		
CASHIER		
DEPARTMENT		
TIME A.M. P.M. TO A.M. P.M.		
	AMOUNT	✓
CURRENCY		
FIFTIES & OVER		
TWENTIES		
TENS		
FIVES		
ONES AND TWOS		
COINS		
DOLLARS		
HALF-DOLLARS		
QUARTERS		
DIMES		
NICKELS		
PENNIES		
PETTY CASH VOUCHERS		
TOTAL CASH ENCLOSED		
REGULAR CHECKS		
TRAVELER'S CHECKS		
TOTAL DEPOSITS		
NET RECEIPTS		
DUE BACK		
FOR RESTAURANT CASHIERS		
TOTAL CASH/CHECKS		
LESS TIPS		
NET DEPOSIT OR (DUE BACK)		

basis. Exhibit 15 presents a portion of a daily report of revenue. Additional items of this particular report not shown in the exhibit include the following: debits, guest and city ledgers, rentals and other income, accounts payable, room statistics, food

Exhibit 14 Sample General Cashier's Deposit Summary

GENERAL CASHIER'S DEPOSIT SUMMARY					Date: _____ 19 ____	
Station	BREAKDOWN FROM ENVELOPES				Due Back	Cash Deposit to Checking Account
	Cash	Checks	MC/VISA	Total		
Front Office						
AM						
PM						
Night						
Subtotal						
City Ledger						
Total						
Restaurant						
Bar						
Gift Shop						
Recreation						
Garage						
Total						

statistics, and other information such as amounts of officers' checks and employee meals.

Information from the daily report of revenue may be used to prepare a departmental revenue report and a summary **sales and cash receipts journal.** The departmental revenue report is basically a sales log. It is individually prepared for each department, but is not used for input to the general ledger. The main purpose of the departmental revenue report is to summarize data that will be useful to management. Exhibit 16 presents a sample departmental revenue report for a main dining room. At the end of the month, the columns of each departmental revenue report are totaled and various sales analysis reports and statistics are prepared from the information.

Information from the daily report of revenue, daily transcript report, general cashier's deposit summary, and other documents is used to prepare a summary sales and cash receipts journal (Exhibit 17), which is the input journal to the general ledger. At the end of the month, the columns are totaled and posted to the general ledger. Exhibit 18 shows a possible route for the flow of forms presented previously.

The summary sales and cash receipts journal shown in Exhibit 17 is designed for a small hotel. In this example, operated departments are not allowed to pay vendors out of the cash drawer; all petty cash payments are routed through the front desk. A larger operation will require a more extensive journal to provide

Exhibit 15   Sample Daily Report of Revenue

SHERATON GRAND ON CAPITOL HILL	DAILY REPORT—REVENUE JOURNAL								FRS NO. 283

DAY   DAY OF   Date _____ 19 _____

SECTION I—REVENUE	ACCT. NO.	TODAY	ALLOW TODAY	NET TODAY	NET TO DATE THIS MONTH	POST	FORECAST TO DATE THIS MONTH	LAST YEAR TO DATE THIS MONTH
ROOMS—TRANSIENT—REG.	009 001 000							
TRANSIENT—GROUP	009 003 000							
PERMANENT	009 004 000							
EXTRA EARNINGS	009 005 000							
AIRLINES	009 006 000							
TOTAL ROOMS REVENUE								
FOOD—THE CAFE	030 019 000							
ROOM SERVICE	030 011 000							
SIGNATURE ROOM	030 020 000							
THE BAR	030 021 000							
WINE BAR	030 022 000							
MINI BAR	030 023 000							
HOSPITALITY	030 024 000							
SUB-TOTAL OUTLETS								
BANQUETS—LOCAL	030 029 001							
BANQUETS—GROUP	030 029 002							
MISC. S&W—TAX	030 199 001							
—NON TAX	030 199 002							
MISC. INC.—TAX	030 199 003							
—NON TAX	030 199 004							
PUBLIC RM. RENTAL	030 199 005							
TOTAL FOOD REVENUE								
BEVERAGE—THE CAFE	050 019 000							
ROOM SERVICE	050 011 000							
SIGNATURE ROOM	050 020 000							
THE BAR	050 021 000							
WINE BAR	050 022 000							
MINI BAR	050 023 000							
HOSPITALITY	050 024 000							
SUB-TOTAL OUTLETS								
BANQUETS—LOCAL	050 029 001							
BANQUETS—GROUP	050 029 002							
CASH BAR	050 030 000							
MISC. S&W—TAX	050 199 001							
—NON TAX	050 199 003							
MISC. INC.—TAX	050 199 003							
—NON TAX	050 199 004							
TOTAL BEVERAGE REVENUE								
MINOR OPERATED DEPARTMENT								
TELEPHONE—LOCAL	061 081 001							
L/DISTANCE	061 081 002							
TOTAL TELEPHONE								
GUEST LAUNDRY	061 082 000							
GUEST VALET	061 083 000							
PARKING	061 084 000							
CONCIERGE SALES	061 088 000							
TOTAL MINOR REVENUE								
RENT & OTHER INCOME								
TOTAL REVENUE								

Exhibit 16   Sample Departmental Revenue Report

Date	Day	Breakfast	Lunch	Dinner	Total Food	Liquor	Other	Total Revenue

MAIN DINING ROOM

Exhibit 17   Sample Summary Sales and Cash Receipts Journal

SUMMARY SALES AND CASH RECEIPTS JOURNAL   Month:_____

Date	Checking Account dr	Guest Ledger dr	City Ledger dr	Room Sales cr	Food Sales cr	Telephone Sales cr	Sales Tax cr	OTHER Amount cr	Account

management with useful information on financial statements. For example, the sales accounts may be expanded as follows:

Food Sales	Beverage Sales	Telephone Sales
Dining Room	Lounge	Local
Lounge	Dining Room	Long-Distance
Banquets	Banquets	Service Charges
Coffee Shop		

An allowances journal (Exhibit 19) is generally only necessary in manual accounting systems. Automated accounting systems are capable of adjusting the proper account when the allowance voucher is processed. If an allowances journal is used, the monthly totals are posted to the general ledger. Observe that columns are assigned debits and credits in an opposite manner to those of the summary sales and cash receipts journal. Hotels using this form would require that any cash refunds be processed through the disbursements procedure.

Exhibit 18   Sample Flowchart of Reports

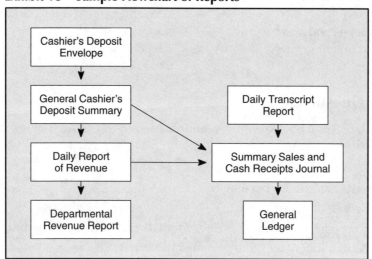

Exhibit 19   Sample Allowances Journal

						Room	Food	Telephone		OTHER	
DATE	NAME	Voucher	Room	Guest Ledger	City Ledger	Sales Allowance	Sales Allowance	Sales Allowance	Sales Tax	Amount	Account
		Number	Number	cr	cr	dr	dr	dr	dr	dr	

Endnotes

1. For further information on daily cashiers reports, see Raymond Cote, *Understanding Hospitality Accounting I*, 3d ed. (East Lansing, Mich: Educational Institute of the American Hotel & Motel Association, 1995), Chapter 9.

Key Terms

allowances
cash discount
concessionaire
daily room report

daily transcript
gross profit
guest check
guest folio

housekeeper's report

net revenue

other income—food and beverage

rentals and other income

revenue

revenue center

sales and cash receipts journal

skipper

sleeper

trade discount

Review Questions

1. Which revenue bookkeeping account is used to record each of the following activities?

   a. Sales of coffee, tea, and milk

   b. Sales of alcoholic beverages

   c. Rentals of guestrooms

   d. Price adjustment on a food tab, granted because of a customer's complaint

   e. A complimentary room provided to a guest

   f. Room service: sale of food

2. Which bookkeeping account is credited for each of the following activities? (Assume a debit to cash.)

   a. Sales of gum and novelty items in the dining room

   b. Interest income

   c. Sales of grease and bones from the kitchen

   d. Separate charges for housekeeping or linen service

   e. Concessions fees

3. What are the two major methods for recording invoices and treating cash discounts?

4. Which internal control document is used to record each of the following activities?

   a. Guest checks issued to servers

   b. Price adjustments

   c. Detection of errors or intentional omissions from room sales

   d. Issuance of food by the kitchen to the server

5. Which bookkeeping account is debited for each of the following activities? (Assume a credit to a sales account.)

   a. Payment by personal check

   b. Payment by a bankcard

   c. Payment by a nonbank credit card

   d. Guest signs the tab using open account privileges

6. Which accounts receivable subsidiary ledger(s) will be affected by the following situations? Specify whether the posting will be a debit or a credit.

   a. Sale of a room to a registered guest who will stay for several days
   b. Payment by a registered guest
   c. A guest who checks out and charges his or her bill with an American Express card
   d. A company that rents a conference room on an open account

7. Which member of the front office is responsible for each of the following functions?

   a. Posting of food and beverage guest charges to the guest ledger
   b. Posting of room charges to the guest ledger

8. Which departments are responsible for maintaining each of the following ledgers? In what sequence are the ledgers maintained?

   a. City ledger
   b. Guest ledger

Problems

Problem 1

Specify whether each of the following statements is true (T) or false (F).

_____ 1. Rooms, food and beverage, and marketing are revenue centers.

_____ 2. Food sold in the course of room service is credited to Room Sales.

_____ 3. Other Income—Food Department and Other Income on the schedule of rentals and other income are the same items.

_____ 4. If food sales are $2,000 and food allowances are $25, then net food sales are $1,975.

_____ 5. If food sales are $2,000, food allowances are $25, and cost of food sold is $600, then gross profit is $1,375.

_____ 6. The gross method refers to a method for recording discounts.

_____ 7. The nonrevenue procedure refers to a procedure for recording invoices.

_____ 8. A sale to a guest using a credit card such as VISA is recorded to Accounts Receivable.

Problem 2

Indicate on which statement the following sales will occur:

	Beverage	Food	Rentals and Other Income
1. Commission from vending machine company	_____	_____	_____
2. Cash discounts earned	_____	_____	_____
3. Coffee, tea, milk	_____	_____	_____

Problem 3

A $200 invoice for storeroom food provisions is received with terms of 2/10, n/30. The invoice is paid within the discount period. What is the amount of the cash discount?

Problem 4

A hospitality operation purchases new tables and chairs at a list price of $12,000 and a trade discount of 25%. What amount will be recorded in the Furniture and Equipment account?

Problem 5

Give the latest date that the discount may be taken for each of the following invoices:

   a. Dated April 27, terms 3/15, n/30 EOM
   b. Dated April 20, terms 2/10, n/30 ROG, goods received May 31
   c. Dated September 26, terms 5/10, n/11 Prox.

Problem 6

Calculate the amount of the check remitted to pay for each of the following invoices:

   a. Dated June 7, terms 2/10, n/30, invoice amount $200, payment made on June 17
   b. Dated June 8, terms 1/10, n/30, invoice amount $200, payment made on June 20
   c. Dated July 14, terms 2/10, n/30 EOM, invoice amount $500, payment made on August 4
   d. Dated August 26, terms 2/10, n/30, invoice amount $60, payment made on September 10
   e. Dated September 5, terms 5/10, n/60, invoice amount $150, payment made on September 14
   f. Dated July 14, terms 3/10, n/30 Prox., invoice amount $400, payment made on August 4

Problem 7

For a given period, a hospitality operation has recorded the following amounts: food sales $50,000; food allowances $400; cost of sales $15,000; chef and kitchen labor $4,000; servers' payroll $3,200; and other operating expenses $18,000. Calculate the net food sales and the gross profit on food.

Problem 8

Assume a hospitality operation uses the gross method for recording invoices and treats discounts as revenue items. It uses the periodic inventory system. An invoice for storeroom food provisions totaling $700 is received. The credit terms are 2/10, n/30.

   a. Record the receipt of the invoice.
   b. Record the payment of the invoice if paid after the discount period.
   c. Record the payment of the invoice if paid within the discount period.

Problem 9

Assume a hospitality operation uses the gross method for recording invoices and treats discounts as nonrevenue items. It uses the periodic inventory system. An invoice for storeroom food provisions totaling $700 is received. The credit terms are 2/10, n/30.

a. Record the receipt of the invoice.

b. Record the payment of the invoice if paid after the discount period.

c. Record the payment of the invoice if paid within the discount period.

REVIEW QUIZ

When you feel you have covered all of the material in this chapter, answer these questions. Choose the *best* answer. Check your answers with the correct ones found on the Review Quiz Answer Key at the end of this book.

True (T) or False (F)

T   F   1. Financial reports issued by revenue centers in a hotel are called supporting schedules or departmental income statements.

T   F   2. Net revenue represents sales less allowances and reflects the billable activities of a hospitality business.

T   F   3. Qualifying for trade discounts depends upon a hospitality establishment paying vendors within a specified period of time.

T   F   4. Cashiers post charges to guest accounts for food, beverages, and other miscellaneous items.

Multiple Choice

5. Which of the following is *not* a revenue center in a hotel?

   a. Food and beverage department
   b. Rooms department
   c. Personnel department
   d. Recreation department

6. Which of the following is *not* an example of a revenue account for a hotel?

   a. Room Sales
   b. Payroll
   c. Room Allowances
   d. Telephone Sales

7. Contra-revenue accounts representing rebates and refunds allowed after sales were initially recorded are referred to as:

   a. allowances accounts.
   b. other income.
   c. deposits.
   d. accounts receivable.

8. A line item on financial statements representing net revenue less cost of sales is called:

   a. net sales.
   b. gross profit.
   c. net income.
   d. allowances.

9. Reductions to the prices indicated on a vendor's price list are called:

    a. allowances.
    b. cash discounts.
    c. trade discounts.
    d. unearned income.

10. Which of the following statements about guest checks is true?

    a. They initiate the food and beverage order taken from the guest.
    b. They eventually represent the invoice given to the guest.
    c. They are prenumbered.
    d. All of the above.

Chapter Outline

Business Segmentation
Financial Reporting Centers
Responsibility Accounting
    Expenses
    Departmental Expense Accounting
Examples of Hotel Expense Accounts
    Cost of Sales
    Payroll and Related Expenses
    Rooms Department Expenses
    F&B Department Expenses
    A&G Department Expenses
    Marketing Department Expenses
    POM Department Expenses
    Energy Costs
    Fixed Charges
    Income Taxes
Accounting for Employee Meals
Accounting for Credit Card Fees
    Credit Card Fees on Bankcards
    Non-Bank Credit Card Fees
Bad Debts
    Direct Write-Off Method
    Allowance Method

Learning Objectives

1. Define business segmentation, and describe its relevance to a hospitality corporation comprising multiple hotels. (p. 40)

2. Define the term "financial reporting center," and give examples of the major classifications of financial reporting centers. (pp. 40–47)

3. Explain responsibility accounting, identify four broad categories of expenses, and describe the difference between direct and indirect expenses. (pp. 47–49)

4. Describe the cost of sales category of expense accounts, and identify the kind of departments to which this category applies. (pp. 49–51)

5. Describe the payroll and related expenses category of expense accounts, and identify the departments to which this category applies. (p. 51)

6. Identify the typical bookkeeping accounts used to record expenses for the various departments in a hotel property. (pp. 51–59)

7. Describe the special considerations involved in accounting for credit card fees, and differentiate between recording fees for bankcards and non-bank credit cards. (pp. 59–61)

8. Describe two major methods of accounting for bad debts. (pp. 61–66)

2

Hotel Expense Accounting

THE ACCOUNTING PROCEDURES examined in *Understanding Hospitality Accounting I*[1] considered expenses at the level of the business enterprise as a whole. By simplifying expense accounting in this way, the text was able to complete an entire accounting cycle—from journalizing and posting business transactions through preparing financial statements and setting up next year's general ledger.

While accounting for **expenses** at this level may be suitable for restaurant accounting, it is not satisfactory for hotel accounting. Hotel accounting requires that expenses be accounted for on the basis of specific responsibility areas. Often, these responsibility areas are departments within the hotel. Management decides how a hotel's departments are to be organized into responsibility areas. A hotel's accounting system reflects the organization of responsibility areas in its chart of accounts, which identifies the categories of expenses charged to each department.

The proper identification and departmentalization of expenses allows hotels to segment operating statements into separate departmental reports and schedules. These reports enable management to measure the efficiency of each responsibility area. Managers and supervisors can then be held accountable for the operating results of their assigned areas.

This chapter considers expense accounting from a hotel's perspective and addresses such questions as:

1. How are hotel operations departmentalized for purposes of expense accounting?

2. What are the functions of a hotel's various departments and how are these departments staffed?

3. How does accounting for credit card fees differ depending on the type of credit card involved?

4. Why do hotels make estimates of potentially uncollectible accounts receivable?

5. What methods are used to record an uncollectible account receivable?

This chapter presents an in-depth analysis of hotel expense accounts.[2] It introduces the topic of responsibility accounting through discussion of business segmentation, direct and indirect expenses, and departmental functions and personnel.

Specialized topics include accounting procedures for credit card fees and uncollectible accounts. The chapter presents the allowance method for estimating bad debts as well as an alternative way of recording uncollectibles—the direct write-off method.

Exhibit 1   Segmentation of the Somnus Corporation

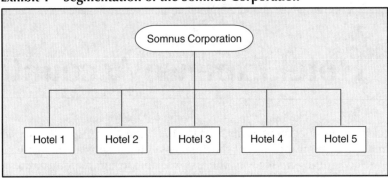

Business Segmentation

Business segmentation refers to the division of work into specialized areas of responsibility. Various accounting reports reflect the efficiency and/or profitability of each specific area of responsibility.

Business segmentation starts at the top echelons of a corporation and extends downward to the most detailed aspects of its operations. For example, assume that a hospitality company called the Somnus Corporation comprises five hotels (Exhibit 1). The first level of accounting reports for the Somnus Corporation combines the operating results of these five hotels. First-level accounting reports show the results of the corporation as a whole.

Accounting reports of this kind, however, are of very little use in measuring the performance of the individual hotels which compose the corporation. To achieve this second level of reporting, corporate operations must be segmented into individual hotels. For example, the top management of the Somnus Corporation assigns an executive or general manager to each of the five hotels shown in Exhibit 1. This individual is held responsible for the hotel's operation. Separate financial statements are produced to measure the performance of the general manager of each hotel.

In turn, the general manager of a hotel requires financial information to measure the efficiency of various areas of responsibility within the hotel. To achieve this third level of reporting, these areas of responsibility are identified as departments or other financial reporting centers. For our purposes, a financial reporting center is defined as an area of responsibility for which separate cost information must be collected and reported. Some of these financial reporting centers are considered departments, usually when top management assigns an individual as the manager of the area's operations.

Management determines the extent to which each hotel function is divided into various reporting centers. A large hotel may organize its business into the following financial reporting centers:

- Rooms
- Food and beverage

- Telephone
- Administrative and general
- Marketing
- Property operation and maintenance
- Data processing
- Human resources
- Guest transportation
- Energy costs
- Fixed charges

The following sections discuss these departments and other financial reporting centers typically found within a hotel. Positions within each of these areas of responsibility are identified.

Rooms. Many rooms department personnel come into direct contact with guests. Rooms personnel register guests, maintain and clean guestrooms, provide information, handle guest complaints, and perform other services throughout the guest's stay. The rooms department may include the following positions:

- Management positions—supervisory personnel responsible for the overall operation of the rooms department
- Front office positions—front office manager, room clerks, information clerks, and mail clerks
- Housekeeping positions—house attendants, janitors, housekeepers, linen keepers, and room attendants
- Service positions—concierge, door attendants, bell staff
- Security positions—security officers, patrollers, and guards

Exhibit 2 presents a sample organization chart for the rooms department of a large hotel. There are many other organizational possibilities, depending on an operation's size, the guest services it offers, and additional factors. In small lodging operations, the front office, telephone, guest information, and reservations functions may be performed by as few as one or two persons.

Food and Beverage. The food and beverage department is often referred to as **F&B**. Personnel in this department are associated with the preparation and service of food and beverages. This department may include the following positions:

- Management positions—supervisory personnel responsible for the overall operations of the food and beverage department
- Kitchen positions—chefs and assistants, preparation staff, runners, dishwashers, and utility persons
- Service positions—hosts/hostesses, captains, servers, dining room attendants, and personnel involved in room service, banquet service, and beverage service

Exhibit 2   Sample Organization Chart for the Rooms Department of a Large Hotel

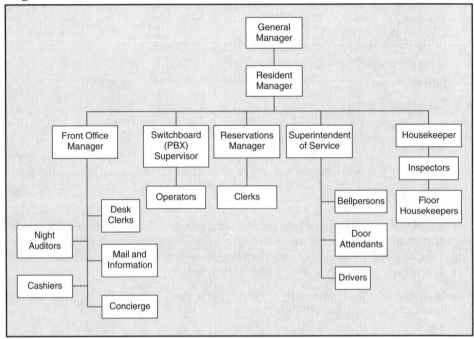

- Other positions—cashiers, checkers, food and beverage cost controllers, stewards, food and beverage purchasers, and entertainment managers

Exhibit 3 presents a sample organization chart for the food and beverage department of a medium-sized hotel, but a specific hotel's organization depends on its services and facilities. For instance, some large hotels separate the food and beverage department into several different revenue centers with separate managers or directors. Small hotels may not find this practical because of the joint costs (shared employees and common expenses) involved in various areas of operations.

Telephone. The telephone department handles in-house, local, and long-distance calls. The telephone department may consist of the following personnel:

- Chief operator
- Supervisors
- Operators
- Messengers

Exhibit 2 shows telephone personnel as part of the rooms department but, for financial reporting purposes, the telephone function may be established as a separate department.

Exhibit 3   Sample Organization Chart for the Food and Beverage Department of a Medium-Sized Hotel

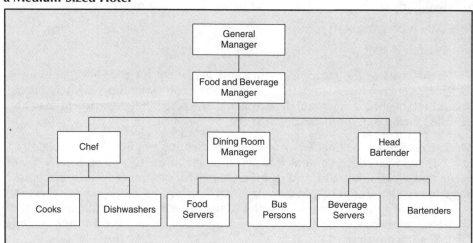

Technical advances in communications equipment have greatly influenced accounting for telephone services. A property using a state-of-the-art communications system can separate the costs of telephone calls incurred by guests from the costs incurred by the business. With this type of system, the business usage costs may be charged to the user departments.

For some properties, it may not be practical or possible to separate telephone costs incurred by the business from those incurred by guests. In that case, all telephone expenses are charged to the telephone department. Unless telephone costs are divided between guest usage and business usage, a loss may result from operations of the telephone department. This loss represents the hotel's net telephone cost.

Administrative and General. The administrative and general department is commonly referred to as **A&G.** It may be separated into several separate financial reporting centers in large hotels. Included as administrative and general personnel are executives of the hotel and other employees involved with executive and financial activities. This department may include the following positions:

- Manager's office positions—managing director, general manager, resident manager, executive or first assistant manager (not on floor duty), secretaries, clerks, and receptionists

- Accounting office positions—controller and assistants, general cashier, paymaster, accountants, income auditors, payroll clerks, file clerks, and secretaries

- Credit office positions—credit manager and assistants

- Front office bookkeeping positions—front office bookkeeper, accounts receivable clerks, cashiers, voucher clerks, and file clerks

- Night auditors
- Receiving clerks
- Data processing staff
- Personnel staff

If the costs of the data processing and personnel functions are significant, these areas are not included in the administrative and general department but are instead established as separate departments. The personnel department may also be called the human resources department.

Marketing. The marketing department is the sales and public relations center of a hotel. It conducts research aimed at developing sources of potential sales, plans group and convention sales, and maintains a network of travel agent contacts. The department also designs "package programs" to attract weekend or off-season business. It actively promotes the hotel's facilities for weddings, business meetings, and gatherings of professional organizations. This department may include the following positions:

- Director of marketing
- Sales manager
- Convention service manager
- Sales representatives

Exhibit 4 presents a sample organization chart for the marketing department of a large hotel. As is true with any other department, the specific levels of responsibility and authority depend upon the special needs of the hotel. Some hotels may include the guest entertainment function within this department. However, if guest entertainment expenses are substantial, it may be preferable to establish a separate financial reporting center to monitor these expenses.

Property Operation and Maintenance. This department, abbreviated **POM**, is concerned with the appearance and physical condition of the building, the repair and maintenance of equipment, and rubbish removal. Personnel in this department may include:

- Management positions—chief engineer and first assistant
- Engineer positions—watch engineers, boiler room engineers, oilers, elevator engineers, and air conditioning control personnel
- Grounds positions—gardeners, laborers, and other landscaping personnel
- Office and storeroom positions—engineer's storeroom clerk, secretaries and clerks in the engineer's office, cleaners, yard attendants, and incinerator attendants
- Other positions—electricians, mechanics, plumbers, painters, upholsterers, and various repair personnel

Exhibit 4   Sample Organization Chart for the Marketing Department of a Large Hotel

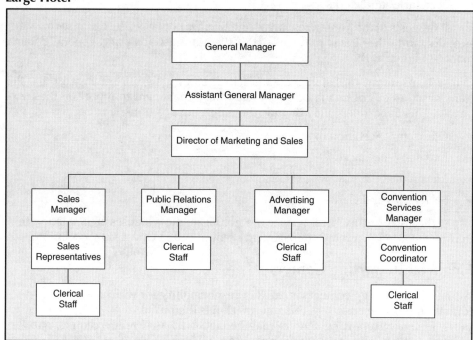

Data Processing. Establishments with a significant investment in computer equipment and staff may set up a separate department to report expenses. The data processing department may include the following positions:

- Data processing manager
- Supervisors and analysts
- Systems personnel and programmers
- Operators and data entry personnel

If the costs of the data processing facility are not large, the expenses for staff, supplies, and other items may be part of the administrative and general department, as shown earlier.

Human Resources. Establishments which incur a significant expense for employee housing, employee relations, recruiting, and training may set up a separate department to report on these expenses. The **human resources** (personnel) **department** may include the following positions:

- Director of human resources
- Personnel manager

- Training assistants
- Secretaries and clerks

If the costs of the human resources function are not large, the expenses for staff, supplies, and other items may be part of the administrative and general department, as shown earlier.

Guest Transportation. Establishments which incur a significant expense for the transportation of guests may set up a separate department to report on these expenses. This department may include the following positions:

- Guest transportation manager
- Drivers
- Mechanics
- Secretaries and clerks

If the costs of this guest service are not large, the expenses associated with it may be recorded in a rooms department account called Guest Transportation.

Financial Reporting Centers

A financial reporting center is an area of responsibility for which separate cost information must be collected; this information is then used to prepare financial reports. Financial reporting centers may be classified as revenue centers, support centers, and other financial reporting centers.

Revenue centers generate revenue through sales of products and/or services to guests. The number of revenue centers varies from property to property. Typical revenue centers within a relatively large hotel may include:

- Rooms
- Food and beverage
- Telephone
- Gift shop
- Garage and parking
- Other operated departments
- Rentals and other income

Some of these revenue centers may not be defined as departments within a hotel—but all of them are financial reporting centers.

Support centers are those departments that have minimal guest contact and do not produce sales. Support centers provide services to revenue centers which, in turn, provide services to guests. The following are typical support centers in the hotel industry:

- Administrative and general
- Marketing

- Property operation and maintenance
- Data processing
- Human resources

Certain departments may not be large enough to warrant a separate responsibility area and, regardless of their physical locations, may be combined with other departments. For example, the data processing and personnel functions may be combined with other hotel functions to form the financial reporting center called administrative and general.

Other financial reporting centers include energy costs and fixed charges. A separate center for energy costs may be created as a means of centralizing all energy costs in a single reporting center. A separate center for fixed charges may be used to consolidate expenses such as rent, property taxes, insurance, interest expense, and depreciation and amortization.

To collect financial information on the various responsibility areas, each financial reporting center is assigned an identification number. A hotel may choose any numbering configuration that it finds meaningful. For instance, the following numbering system could be assigned:

Financial Reporting Center	Identification No.
Rooms	11
Food and beverage	15
Telephone	17
Administrative and general	31
Marketing	36
Property operation and maintenance	38
Energy costs	41
Fixed charges	51

In this example, the high-order (left-most) digit indicates the type of financial reporting center. A high-order 1 represents a revenue center, a high-order 3 represents a support center, a high-order 4 represents energy costs, and a high-order 5 represents fixed charges.

Responsibility Accounting

The purpose of responsibility accounting is to provide financial information useful in evaluating the effectiveness of managers and department heads. Managers should be judged on the basis of revenues and expenses directly under their control. For this reason, only direct expenses are charged to specific departments. Any cost not associated with a specific department is charged to the hotel as a whole.

Expenses

Expenses include the day-to-day costs of operating a business, the expired costs of assets through depreciation and amortization, and the "write-off" of prepaid items. For purposes of financial reporting, expenses may be separated into four broad categories: cost of sales, operating expenses, fixed charges, and income taxes. Cost of sales and **operating expenses** can be classified as direct expenses. Fixed charges can be classified as indirect expenses. Income taxes are a separate class of expenses.

Direct Expenses. Direct expenses are costs incurred solely for the benefit of a particular department. A department is charged for only those expenses that can be identified as specifically associated with that department. Such expenses are within the responsibility area and control of the department head or manager.

Direct operating expenses include the following types of expenses:

- Cost of sales
- Payroll
- Payroll-related costs
- Operating supplies
- China, glassware, silver, and linen
- Laundry and dry cleaning

Indirect Expenses. Indirect expenses are incurred for the benefit of the hotel as a whole, and cannot be identified with any particular department. These expenses are not controllable by any single department head or manager and are the responsibility of top management.

Some indirect expenses are fixed charges (also called fixed costs or fixed expenses). A fixed charge is one which is incurred regardless of whether the hotel is open or closed and is independent of sales volume. Examples of fixed charges are:

- Property insurance
- Interest expense
- Property taxes
- Rent expense
- Depreciation and amortization

Depreciation is the allocation of the cost of a tangible long-lived asset over its useful life. Amortization is a procedure similar to depreciation except it involves leaseholds, leasehold improvements, and other long-lived intangible assets.

For purposes of financial reporting, fixed charges are considered a financial reporting center and are reported on a separate supporting schedule. Information from this schedule is brought forward to the hotel's summary income statement.

Income Taxes. Income taxes expense is neither a fixed charge nor an indirect expense. Income tax appears as a separate line item on a hotel's summary income statement.

Departmental Expense Accounting

The presentation of expenses on the hotel financial statements and supporting schedules should be in a prescribed sequence. For the present, the sequence of expense accounts is not considered.

The expense accounts appearing in a chart of accounts depend on the size of the hotel, the number of financial reporting centers, and the level of detail that management requires in the financial reports. To collect information useful for departmental reporting, management needs to establish separate departmental accounts for various types of revenue and expenses. For example, one account for payroll would not be sufficient in meeting the demands of departmental reporting, which requires a separate payroll account for each responsibility area.

Exhibit 5 lists some expenses that are typically found in a hotel. In studying this list, it important to realize that it is not a chart of accounts and therefore may not relate to the actual names of the bookkeeping accounts. Also, the indication of the departments charged for these expenses is a representation. Determining which departments to charge for various expenses will depend on a hotel's size, type of operation, and accounting system.

Some expenses are temporarily recorded as one lump-sum amount in a non-departmental expense account and later are allocated to specific departments. Types of allocated expenses include payroll taxes, workers' compensation insurance, and other employee benefits. Allocations to specific departments are made by distribution formulas derived from an analysis of various criteria. For example, payroll taxes are paid based on the total payroll of the hotel. A department's share of the payroll taxes expense may be determined by analyzing the relationship of its payroll to the hotel's total payroll.

Examples of Hotel Expense Accounts

The number and types of bookkeeping accounts used by any given department or financial reporting center depend on the size of a property and the design of its management information system. The accounts to be discussed are representative of those used by most hotel properties.[3]

Cost of Sales

A cost of sales account is required for each merchandising center of a hotel. The cost of sales accounts should have the same classifications as the accounts for revenue to permit a gross profit analysis of each merchandising facility.

Cost of Food Sales. This account represents the **food cost**: the cost of food served to guests in the revenue process. Cost of Food Sales is also called Cost of Food Sold. Employee meals are excluded from cost of food sold.

The food cost includes delivery charges. It is reduced by any trade discounts or any sales of grease and bones. Food cost is not reduced by cash discounts because, according to *USASH*, these discounts should be recorded to Cash Discounts Earned and should appear on the hotel's schedule of rentals and other income.

Cost of Beverage Sales. This account represents the cost of wines, liquors, and beer, as well as the cost of mineral water, syrups, sugar, bitters, and other ingredients used in the preparation of mixed drinks. Costs include invoice amounts (less any trade discounts) plus transportation, storage, and delivery charges.

Exhibit 5   Typical Expenses Classified by Responsibility Area

Account Name	Rooms	F&B	Tel.	A&G	Mktg.	POM	Energy	Fixed
Cost of Food Sales		X						
Cost of Beverage Sales		X						
Cost of Calls			X					
Salaries and Wages	X	X	X	X	X	X		
Payroll Taxes	X	X	X	X	X	X		
Employee Meals	X	X	X	X	X	X		
Workers' Compensation Insurance	X	X	X	X	X	X		
Employee Group Plans	X	X	X	X	X	X		
Commissions	X							
Reservation Expense	X							
Contract Cleaning	X	X						
Laundry and Dry Cleaning	X	X						
Guest Transportation	X							
Linen	X							
Guest Supplies	X	X						
Cleaning Supplies	X	X				X		
Printing and Stationery	X	X	X	X	X	X		
Uniforms	X	X				X		
China, Glassware, Silver, and Linen		X						
Kitchen Fuel		X						
Licenses		X						
Music and Entertainment		X						
Paper Supplies		X						
Bar Supplies		X						
Menus		X						
Utensils		X						
Credit Card Commissions				X				
Cash Short or Over				X				
Dues and Subscriptions				X	X			
Contributions				X				
Human Resources				X				
Insurance—General				X				
Postage and Telegrams				X	X			
Professional Fees				X				
Bad Debts				X				
Travel and Entertainment				X				
Direct Mail Advertising					X			
Outdoor Advertising					X			
Print Advertising					X			
Radio and Television Advertising					X			
In-House Graphics					X			
Point of Sale Material					X			
Selling Aids					X			
Advertising Agency Fees					X			
Franchise Fees					X			
Other Fees and Commissions					X			
Travel and Entertainment				X	X			
Repairs and Maintenance						X		
Removal of Waste Matter						X		
Electricity							X	
Fuel							X	
Steam							X	
Water							X	
Rent								X
Property Taxes								X
Property Insurance								X
Interest Expense								X
Depreciation Expense								X
Amortization Expense								X

According to the revenue treatment, cash discounts are not used to reduce beverage cost; rather, cash discounts are credited to the hotel's other income account called Cash Discounts Earned (or Purchase Discounts).

Cost of Calls. This telephone department account includes the total cost of local and long-distance calls. Separate accounts should be established for Cost of Calls—Local and Cost of Calls—Long-Distance.

Payroll and Related Expenses

Any department having one or more employees requires bookkeeping accounts to record expenditures for payroll and related expenses. Hotel-operated departments (such as rooms, food and beverage, administrative and general, marketing, and property operation and maintenance) must be assigned payroll and payroll-related accounts.

Payroll and related expenses do not appear on the schedule of rentals and other income or on the schedule of fixed charges. These financial reporting centers are merely sources of data and have no physical existence or personnel.

Salaries and Wages. This account may also be called Payroll Expense. It includes salaries, wages, overtime pay, and any employee bonuses and commissions. Separate accounts should be established to record vacation pay and holiday pay if they are treated as employee benefits.

Payroll Taxes. This account includes social security taxes (employer's portion), and federal and state unemployment taxes.

Employee Meals. This account includes the cost of food furnished to employees as a convenience to the employer.

Workers' Compensation Insurance. This account includes the expense of workers' compensation insurance.

Employee Group Plans. This account includes life and health insurance, and other forms of employee group-plan fringe benefits. Separate accounts may be established for Group Health, Group Life, Group Retirement, and other such benefits if the costs are to be separately identified.

Rooms Department Expenses

Housekeeping labor costs and wages for room clerks, mail clerks, concierge, door attendants, and other rooms operations personnel are significant expenses in the rooms department. The rooms department expenses also include housekeeping supplies and other expenses related to the rooms operations. There isn't a cost of rooms sold account because the rental of a room is not a merchandising transaction. In addition to payroll and related expenses, the rooms department has the following expense accounts.

Commissions. This account is used to record payments to authorized agents for rooms business secured for the hotel, including commissions to travel agents. Commissions also include amounts paid to rental agents for permanent rooms business which may involve leases. In the case of leases, the payment is expensed to this account over the term of the lease.

Reservation Expense. This account includes the cost of reservation services including telephone, teletype, and reservation computer.

Contract Cleaning. This account includes any costs of contracting outside companies to clean areas of the rooms department. This may include washing windows, exterminating pests, and disinfecting.

Laundry and Dry Cleaning. This account includes outside laundry and dry-cleaning costs applicable to the rooms department. For work done by the property's laundry, all costs are assigned to a separate financial reporting center (House Laundry) and allocated to the user departments.

Guest Transportation. This account includes the cost of transporting guests to and from the property. If these costs are significant, a separate financial reporting center may be established.

Linen. This account includes the allocated costs of linen owned or rented by the hotel (including towels, facecloths, blankets, sheets, and similar items).

Guest Supplies. This account includes the cost of guest supplies and amenities which the rooms department provides to a property's guests on a gratis basis. The following is a partial list of guest supplies and amenities:

Newspapers	Guest stationery	Shoe cloths
Coffee	Writing supplies	Toilet requisites
Flowers	Hangers	Matches
Ice	Candy	Other favors

Cleaning Supplies. This account includes the cost of cleaning supplies applicable to the rooms department. The following is a partial list of items charged to this account:

Brooms	Soaps and polishes	Cleaning cloths
Mops	Cleaning chemicals	Dusters
Brushes	Insecticides	Dustpans
Pails	Disinfectants	Cleaning accessories

Printing and Stationery. Expenses included in this account are for printed forms, office supplies, service manuals, and similar items used by employees of the rooms department. Examples include:

Binders	Floor plans	Pencils and pens
Vouchers	Rack cards	Reports
Desk pads	Envelopes	

Uniforms. This account includes the expense of repairing, renting, or cleaning uniforms for employees of the rooms department. If uniforms are purchased, the cost is usually recorded to an asset account and then periodically allocated to the uniforms account based on the estimated useful life of the uniforms or other criteria.

F&B Department Expenses

The food and beverage department is a merchandising center and, therefore, has accounts for the cost of food sales and the cost of beverage sales. In addition to the cost of sales accounts and departmental accounts for payroll expenses, the food and beverage department has the following expense accounts.

China, Glassware, Silver, and Linen. This expense account should not be confused with the asset account of a similar name. The asset account is used to record the original purchase of new stock. The expense account contains the allocated adjustments for breakage, disappearance, deterioration based on age and condition, or depreciation based on estimated useful life.

Contract Cleaning. This account includes any costs of contracting outside companies to clean areas of the food and beverage department. This may include washing windows, exterminating pests, and disinfecting.

Kitchen Fuel. Fuel used for cooking is charged to this account rather than to utilities expense. If electric cooking units are used, separate metering is recommended. Otherwise, an allocation is required to separate kitchen fuel expense from electric expense. When the use of electricity for cooking purposes is only incidental, it is more practical to forgo any attempts to monitor the electricity used for cooking.

Laundry and Dry Cleaning. This account includes outside laundry and dry-cleaning costs applicable to the food and beverage department. For work done by the property's laundry, all costs are assigned to a separate financial reporting center (House Laundry) and allocated to the user departments.

Licenses. All federal, state, and municipal licenses, special permits, and inspection fees are charged to this account.

Music and Entertainment. This account includes costs for orchestras, musicians, entertainers, music services, piano rental, films, records, sheet music, royalties, booking agent fees, and courtesy meals served to entertainers.

Guest Supplies. This account includes expenses for complimentary guest items provided by the food and beverage department. Examples include:

Boutonnieres	Souvenirs	Newspapers
Corsages	Matches	Other favors

Cleaning Supplies. This account includes the expense of items used to keep the food and beverage areas and equipment clean and sanitary. The same types of items listed under the cleaning supplies account for the rooms department are included in this account.

Paper Supplies. This account includes the expense of paper supplies used by the food and beverage department, such as the following:

Wax paper	Paper napkins	Wrapping paper
Pastry bags	Paper plates	Twine
Filter paper	Soufflé cups	Straws

Bar Supplies. This account includes the expense for items such as the following:

Corkscrews	Swizzle sticks	Knives
Mixers	Toothpicks	Spoons
Strainers	Drink decorations	

Menus. This account includes the expense for menu design and printing.

Utensils. Included in this account are expenses for replacing all tools needed in the process of food preparation. Utensils may include kitchen tools, pots, pans, kettles, mixing bowls, beaters, can openers, and other small utensils.

Printing and Stationery. Expenses included in this account are for printed forms, office supplies, service manuals, and similar items used by employees of the food and beverage department. The following are examples:

Servers' books	Vouchers	Desk pads
Adding machine tapes	Guest checks	Staplers and staples
Pencils and pens	Rubber bands	Other office supplies

Uniforms. This account includes the expense of repairing, renting, or cleaning uniforms. If uniforms are purchased, the cost is usually recorded to an asset account and then periodically allocated to this expense account based on the estimated useful life of the uniforms or other criteria.

A&G Department Expenses

Unlike the rooms or food and beverage departments, the administrative and general department is a support center. In addition to accounts for payroll and related expenses, this department has the following expense accounts.

Credit Card Commissions. All credit card fees are charged to this administrative and general departmental account.

Cash Short or Over. Cash shortages and overages of cashiers are charged to this account of the administrative and general department.

Dues and Subscriptions. This account includes the cost of representing the property in business organizations and the cost of subscribing to periodicals for use by employees. Dues and subscriptions related to marketing are charged to the marketing department's Dues and Subscriptions account.

Contributions. This account is charged for charitable donations and contributions.

Human Resources. This account includes the expense of recruiting, relocating, and training personnel. If human resources expenditures are significant, the related staffing and operating expenses should be removed from the administrative and general department. In this case, a separate human resources department would be established with individual expense accounts identifying various expenditures.

Insurance—General. This account includes expenses for liability insurance, theft insurance, and fidelity bonds. This account does not include workers' compensation insurance or fire insurance on buildings and contents. Examples of the types of insurance that are charged to this account are:

Burglary	Fraud	Parcel post
Business interruption	Holdup	Products liability
Elevator liability	Public liability	Fidelity bonds
Forgery	Lost/damaged goods	Robbery

Postage and Telegrams. This account includes postage and telegram costs, but excludes amounts which apply to the marketing department.

Professional Fees. This account includes the cost of attorneys, public accountants, and professional consultants.

Bad Debts Expense. This account represents the expense for accounts receivable that are judged uncollectible. Other names for this account are Uncollectible Accounts Expense and (as it is shown in *USASH*) Provision for Doubtful Accounts.

Travel and Entertainment. This account includes the cost of travel and reimbursable expenses of hotel employees (except marketing department employees) traveling on business.

Printing and Stationery. Expenses included in this account are for printed forms, office supplies, service manuals, and similar items used by employees of the administrative and general department.

Marketing Department Expenses

The marketing department is a support center. In addition to accounts for payroll and related expenses, this department has the following expense accounts.

Direct Mail Advertising. This account includes the cost of mailing lists, writing letters, addressing envelopes or cards, postage, and other work of this type performed by outside companies.

Outdoor Advertising. Included here are the expenses for posters, billboards, and other signs used to merchandise hotel facilities.

Print Advertising. This account includes expenses for newspaper, magazine, and directory advertising.

Radio and Television Advertising. This account includes the cost of advertising on radio and television, and associated production costs.

In-House Graphics. Included in this account are expenses for directories, signs, brochures, and similar items used to merchandise services within the hotel.

Point-of-Sale Material. This account includes expenses for special tent cards, menu fliers, and other displays to stimulate sales.

Selling Aids. This account includes the expense of selling aids such as salespersons' kits, maps, floor plans, and similar material used to describe products and services of the hotel.

Advertising Agency Fees. Included in this account are fees paid to advertising and/or public relations agencies.

Franchise Fees. Included in this account are all fees charged by the franchise company, including royalty fees and national advertising charges.

Other Fees and Commissions. This account includes additional marketing fees and commissions not provided for in other bookkeeping accounts.

Printing and Stationery. Expenses included in this account are for printed forms, office supplies, service manuals, and similar items used by employees of the marketing department.

Dues and Subscriptions. This account includes membership fees and the costs of subscriptions to papers, magazines, and books for use by members of the marketing department.

Postage and Telegrams. This account includes postage and telegram costs incurred by the marketing department.

Travel and Entertainment. This account includes the cost of travel and reimbursable expenses related to marketing functions.

POM Department Expenses

The property operation and maintenance department is a support center. With the exception of outside cleaning contracted by the rooms and food and beverage departments, this department is charged for the cost of services and contracts relating to all repairs and maintenance work. In addition to accounts for payroll and related expenses, this department has the following expense accounts.

Repairs and Maintenance. According to *USASH*, repairs and maintenance expenses should be assigned to the following accounts instead of to a single account for all repairs and maintenance.

Building Supplies is an account charged with the cost of materials and contracts associated with the repair and maintenance of the building, both interior and exterior.

Electrical and Mechanical Equipment is an account charged with the cost of materials and contracts associated with repairing equipment. The term "equipment" includes ventilating systems, air conditioning systems, kitchen equipment, plumbing and heating systems, elevators, refrigeration systems, and general electrical and mechanical equipment.

Engineering Supplies is an account charged with supplies used in maintaining the property, such as small tools, water treatment chemicals, greases and oils, solvents, fuses, and light bulbs.

Furniture, Fixtures, Equipment, and Decor is an account charged for the cost of materials and contracts associated with the repair of curtains, floor coverings, and furniture, as well as painting and redecorating.

Grounds and Landscaping is an account charged for materials and contracts associated with the maintenance of grounds.

Swimming Pool is an account charged for all maintenance costs associated with swimming pools.

Removal of Waste Matter. This account is charged for the expense of the hotel's rubbish removal and the expense of operating an incinerator.

Printing and Stationery. Expenses included in this account are for printed forms, office supplies, service manuals, and similar items used by employees of the property operation and maintenance department.

Uniforms. This account includes the expense of repairing, renting, or cleaning uniforms used by employees of the property operation and maintenance department. If uniforms are purchased, the cost is usually recorded to an asset account and then periodically allocated to this expense account based on the estimated useful life of the uniforms or other criteria.

Energy Costs

The financial reporting center termed "energy costs" has no physical existence or facility; it is simply a means of consolidating a property's energy costs for purposes of reporting on a separate statement. With the exception of energy used for cooking, all utility expenses are charged to this center.

Electricity. This account is charged for the hotel's total electricity cost. The cost should exclude any charges pertaining to electricity used for cooking unless such use is considered incidental. If electricity for cooking is a significant cost, it should be charged to the food and beverage department.

Fuel. This account is charged for the hotel's total heating fuel cost. The cost should exclude fuel used for cooking unless such use is considered incidental. If the cost of fuel used for cooking is significant, it should be charged to the food and beverage department.

Steam. The cost of steam purchased from outside producers is charged to this account.

Water. This account is charged with the cost of water and sewage services purchased from outside companies. This account should include water especially treated for circulating ice water systems or purchased for drinking purposes.

Fixed Charges

The financial reporting center termed **fixed charges** does not have a physical existence or facility. The purpose of this financial reporting center is to consolidate those expenses that are incurred regardless of whether the property is open or closed. These expenses are independent of sales volume. A department head cannot control these expenses; they are the responsibility of top management and are chargeable to the hotel as a whole. The following accounts are classified as fixed charges.

Rent—Land and Buildings. This account is charged for the expense associated with renting land or buildings.

Rent—Electronic Data Processing Equipment. This account is charged with the rental or operating lease expense of computer equipment. Any items on a capital lease should be recorded to an asset account.

Rent—Telephone Equipment. This account is charged with the rental or operating lease expense of telephone equipment. Any items on a capital lease should be recorded to an asset account.

Rent—Other Equipment. Other rentals would include the cost of renting any other major items which, had they not been rented, would be purchased as fixed assets.

Rental of miscellaneous equipment (copiers, projectors, and sound equipment) for a specific function, such as a banquet, should not be charged to this account; such expenses should be charged to the specific user department.

Any items on a capital lease should be recorded to an asset account.

Property Taxes. Under *USASH,* instead of only one account to record all property taxes, the following accounts may be used for taxes other than income and payroll taxes.

Real Estate Taxes is an account charged with taxes assessed on real property. Assessments for public improvements are not charged to this expense account; they are recorded as fixed assets.

Personal Property Taxes is an account charged for personal property taxes.

Utility Taxes is an account charged for sewer taxes and other utility taxes.

Business and Occupation Taxes is an account charged for business and occupation taxes imposed on the establishment. Such taxes are for gross receipts taxes on room sales or food and beverage sales and cannot be passed on to customers.

Property Insurance. This account is charged for the cost of insuring the building and its contents against financial loss due to destruction by fire, weather, and other casualties.

Interest Expense. This account includes all interest expense on mortgages, promissory notes, and other forms of indebtedness. If the interest expense is significant, separate accounts should be established which indicate the source of the principal indebtedness on which the interest is incurred. For example, the following accounts may be used:

- Interest Expense—Mortgages
- Interest Expense—Notes Payable
- Interest Expense—Capital Leases

Depreciation Expense. This account is charged with the periodic allocation of the cost of depreciable fixed assets. Separate accounts should be used to identify the principal source of the depreciation expense. For example, the following accounts may be used:

- Depreciation—Buildings and Improvements

- Depreciation—Furnishings and Equipment
- Depreciation—Capital Leases

Amortization Expense. This account is charged with the periodic allocation of the cost of leaseholds, leasehold improvements, and other purchased intangible assets. For example, the following accounts may be used:

- Amortization—Leaseholds and Improvements
- Amortization—Preopening Expenses
- Amortization—Goodwill

Income Taxes

The income taxes category includes the expenses charged for taxes imposed on the income of the business by federal, state, and, in some cases, municipal taxing authorities. Separate accounts should be maintained for each type of income tax.

Accounting for Employee Meals

A cost of sales account should reflect only that merchandise actually used to generate revenue. To meet this requirement, the cost of employee meals must be excluded from the net cost of food used (cost of sales). Otherwise, the cost of employee meals would inflate the cost of sales account.

Employee meals may be accounted for by keeping a log of meals served to employees. Employee meals should be charged to each employee's department. Some hotels charge the actual cost of a meal, but small properties may not have the information or staff readily available to maintain such detailed records. In such a case, the cost of a typical employee meal may be averaged to arrive at a standard cost for each type of meal: breakfast, lunch, and dinner.

In a perpetual inventory system, the approach used to remove the cost of employee meals from the cost of food sold is to debit (increase) the various departmental expense accounts for employee meals and to credit (decrease) the cost of food sales account. This approach is illustrated by the following journal entry:

Employee Meals Expense—(F&B Department)	60	
Employee Meals Expense—(Rooms Department)	80	
Employee Meals Expense—(A&G Department)	50	
Cost of Food Sales		190

Officers' checks should be deducted from the cost of sales figure and charged to employee meals or entertainment accounts as appropriate. Accounting for employee meals and officers' checks under the periodic inventory system requires an entirely different procedure.

Accounting for Credit Card Fees

Credit card companies generally impose a fee for their services. This fee is considered an expense of doing business and is charged to an expense account called Credit Card Commissions within the administrative and general department. Until the credit card fee is provided for in the financial records, it represents a hidden expense to the hotel.

Two generally accepted accounting principles may influence a company's decision about how to treat credit card fees. The matching principle states that all expenses must be recorded in the same accounting period as the revenue which they helped to generate. The materiality principle, however, provides that the recording of an event may depend on its magnitude, surrounding circumstances, and whether its omission on financial statements would make a difference in the decision process of a reasonable user of those statements.

From a practical viewpoint, the estimation of credit card fees as they occur may result in time-consuming and tedious bookkeeping procedures. Since credit cards fees are usually processed and reported within a short period of time, the unrecorded expense at the end of any month may be insignificant. Unless the volume of a hotel's credit card business is large, it is easier to simply record credit card fees upon receiving notice from the credit card company.

Whether a hotel records credit card fees at the time of billing from the credit card company or at the time of sale depends on the business's accounting policy. For purposes of this discussion, credit card fees will be recorded at the time of notification from the credit card company. This procedure is popular with small hotels as well as hotels whose outstanding credit card fees at the end of the accounting month are not considered to be significant.

The recording of credit card fees also depends on whether the fee relates to a bankcard or a non-bank credit card.

Credit Card Fees on Bankcards

At the end of each day, a hotel totals the bankcard drafts and deposits them with cash items into the hotel's checking account. Assuming that the hotel's credit card drafts total $1,000, the entry made at the time of deposit is:

Cash—Checking Account	1,000	
Sales		1,000

Banks usually deduct credit card fees directly from the checking account balance of the hotel and report them on the hotel's monthly bank statement. Many banks will mail a charge memo notifying the business of this action on the day the fee is charged. Assume that on this initial $1,000 deposit, the credit card company charges a 4% fee totaling $40 (4% × $1,000). Upon receipt of the bank's charge memo or bank statement, the entry made to record the credit card fee is:

Credit Card Commissions	40	
Cash—Checking Account		40

Once posted, this entry increases the expense account Credit Card Commissions and decreases the asset account for cash.

Non-Bank Credit Card Fees

When non-bank credit card drafts are received from customers at the point of sale, they are summarized and recorded as accounts receivable. Assume that the total of non-bank credit card drafts is $1,000; the entry is:

Accounts Receivable	1,000	
Sales		1,000

These drafts are then forwarded to the credit card company. The credit card company will not remit a check for the full amount of the drafts; it will deduct its credit card fee and remit a check for the net balance.

For example, assume that the credit card company in this case charges a fee of 4%. After processing, the credit card company will send the hotel a check for $960; upon receipt and deposit of the check, the entry is:

Cash—Checking Account	960	
Credit Card Commissions	40	
Accounts Receivable		1,000

Although only $960 in cash was received, the balance of Accounts Receivable is credited for $1,000. The receipt of $960 represents payment in full for the $1,000 credit card charges. The difference of $40 was deducted by the credit card company as a fee.

Bad Debts

A business that sells goods or services on credit to its customers will usually incur **bad debts** regardless of how effectively its credit department evaluates its guests and customers. Bad debts are also called "uncollectible accounts" or "uncollectible receivables." A bad debt affects the general ledger account Accounts Receivable and the subsidiary ledger (the city ledger or possibly the guest ledger).

Bad debts occur when an account receivable cannot be collected. An account receivable originates when a sale is made on open account to a customer. A sale would never be made to a specific customer whose ultimate payment of the receivable would be doubtful. However, it is probable that collection of 100% of a receivable will not be possible because of the following:

- Customer bankruptcy

- Customer death

- A disagreement with the customer

- A faulty credit check

- Customer fraud

There are two methods of accounting for bad debts:

- Direct write-off method

- Allowance method

Under the **direct write-off method,** bad debt losses are recorded when they occur. Under the **allowance method,** an estimate of potential bad debts is made before a specific customer's account is uncollectible.

Direct Write-Off Method

The direct write-off method can only be used by companies that have small amounts of accounts receivable; thus the potential for any bad debt losses is not significant. The direct write-off method, also called the direct charge-off method, is a simple procedure that records a loss on an uncollectible account immediately as it occurs. The entry upon realization of a bad debt is:

Bad Debts Expense	xxx	
Accounts Receivable		xxx

In this entry an expense account, Bad Debts Expense, is debited, and the general ledger account, Accounts Receivable, is credited. This entry will remove the uncollectible amount from the books. In addition, the uncollectible account is removed from the subsidiary ledger (city ledger or guest ledger).

Companies that have large amounts of accounts receivable are more likely to realize significant bad debt losses. Therefore, they cannot use the direct write-off method; they must use the allowance method.

Allowance Method

If a company has a large amount of sales on accounts receivable, generally accepted accounting principles mandate the company to estimate the expected bad debts that might occur because of the following requirements:

- The conservatism principle requires that assets must not be overstated.

- The matching principle requires that expenses are to be recorded in the period incurred.

While it is not known exactly who will not pay their open account balance when sales are made, a representative dollar amount of bad debt losses can be estimated based on the company's experience. A review of prior years will usually show a relationship of bad debts to sales volume or to the age of an open account.

Recording Estimated Bad Debts. The allowance method *forecasts* potential bad debts before they occur. At the time the forecast is made, the estimated bad debts are "expensed"; that is, they are charged to the expense account Bad Debts Expense.

The estimated amount of potential bad debts that may occur in the future is maintained in an account called **Allowance for Doubtful Accounts.**

When the original forecast is made, the journal entry is:

Bad Debts Expense	xxx	
Allowance for Doubtful Accounts		xxx

Keep in mind that the actual bad debts have not occurred. This is "a prediction of the future" that is contained in the Allowance for Doubtful Accounts. This allowance account is increased by a credit entry because it is a contra-asset account.

Recording Actual Bad Debts. When a bad debt does occur, an expense account cannot be charged because the bad debt loss was expensed during the forecast entry. Remember that Allowance for Doubtful Accounts contains the estimate; therefore, the actual bad debts will be charged off against this estimate.

When a bad debt actually does occur, the journal entry is:

Allowance for Doubtful Accounts   xxx
     Accounts Receivable   xxx

Accounts Receivable is credited to remove the account that cannot be collected. Allowance for Doubtful Accounts is debited, which reduces the amount of potential bad debts expected in the future.

Presentation on the Balance Sheet. The current assets section of the balance sheet shows the status of Accounts Receivable and the related amount of potential uncollectible accounts as follows:

Cash		$77,000
Accounts Receivable	$90,000	
Less Allowance for Doubtful Accounts	5,700	84,300

Procedures Used to Calculate the Estimate. Under the allowance method, two different procedures may be used to estimate bad debts:

- Percentage of sales
- Percentage of receivables

Percentage of Sales Procedure. The percentage of sales procedure is also called the income statement approach. It calculates the potential bad debts based on net sales volume, which is the total sales billed minus any allowances due to price adjustments. Net sales can be shown as:

$$\text{Sales} - \text{Allowances} = \text{Net Sales}$$

At this point, the use of the word "allowances" may be confusing. When "allowances" is used with sales, it refers to price adjustments. When "allowances" is used with Accounts Receivable, it refers to the Allowance for Doubtful Accounts.

A study of past sales and bad debt losses is performed to develop a percentage relationship of bad debts to sales volume. The resulting percentage is then consistently used. It is not changed unless it eventually proves to be unreliable.

The percentage of sales method can be explained by the following example.

1. A company has the following balance in its Allowance account:

Allowance for Doubtful Accounts	
Bal	2,200

2. Based on experience, the expected bad debts are forecasted at 1% of net sales.
3. The net sales for this period are $350,000.
4. The forecast is computed as follows:

$350,000 \text{ (net sales)} \times 1\% = \$3,500 \text{ (potential bad debts increase)}$

5. The journal entry is as follows:

Bad Debts Expense	3,500	
Allowance for Doubtful Accounts		3,500

IMPORTANT: *Under the percentage of sales procedure, the computed estimate is used to increase the existing balance in Allowance for Doubtful Accounts.*

6. The Allowance account now appears as follows:

Allowance for Doubtful Accounts

Bal	2,200
AJE	3,500
Bal	5,700

Percentage of Receivables Procedure. The percentage of receivables procedure is also called the balance sheet approach. This procedure also requires research into past sales and bad debt losses. However, the research is based upon the relationship of the age of an account to any bad debt losses.

The accounts receivable are "aged" and categorized as not yet due, 1 to 30 days past due, 31 to 60 days past due, etc. Aging an account requires an analysis of the invoice date and the billing terms. If the billing terms are net 10 days, an account 40 days old is 30 days past due; it does not belong in the 31- to 60-day aging.

Then the aging categories are analyzed to determine the percentage that actually became uncollectible. For example, assume research shows that over the last three years, $20,000 of accounts that were 31 to 60 days past due resulted in bad debt losses of $2,000.

The relationship of the uncollectible percentage to accounts receivable is calculated as follows:

$$\frac{\text{Actual Bad Debts}}{\text{Accounts Receivable}} = \frac{2,000}{20,000} = 10\%$$

The 10% would then be applied to the current amount of accounts aged 31 to 60 days to estimate the potential bad debts for that aging category. Other uncollectible percentages would be calculated and applied to their aging categories to arrive at the total estimated bad debts.

The percentage of receivables procedure can be explained by the following example.

1. A company has the following balance in its Allowance account:

Allowance for Doubtful Accounts

Bal	2,200

2. Based on experience, the expected bad debts based on an aging analysis showed the following:

Aging Category	Percentage Considered Uncollectible
Not yet due	1%
1 to 30 days past due	5%
31 to 60 days past due	10%
61 to 90 days past due	35%
Over 90 days past due	60%

3. The Accounts Receivable balance at the end of this period is $90,000.

4. Exhibit 6 shows the computation of the estimated bad debts. The $90,000 of accounts receivable at the end of this period are aged. Each amount in the various aging categories is multiplied by the percentage considered uncollectible. The result of the multiplication becomes the estimated bad debt for that aging category. All categories are added to arrive at the total of $3,500 in *estimated potential bad debts.*

5. The journal entry is as follows:

Bad Debts Expense	1,300	
Allowance for Doubtful Accounts		1,300

IMPORTANT: *Under the percentage of receivables procedure, the computed estimate becomes the new balance in Allowance for Doubtful Accounts.*

6. The Allowance account now appears as follows:

Allowance for Doubtful Accounts

	Bal	2,200
	AJE	1,300
	Bal	3,500

Recovery of a Bad Debt. Sometimes an account that has been written off to bad debts may later be paid by the customer. In these cases, the original entry that wrote off the account must be reversed to reinstate Accounts Receivable, and the collection is recorded in the usual way.

Exhibit 6   Estimating Bad Debts by an Aging of Accounts Receivable

Aging Category	Accounts Receivable	Percentage Considered Uncollectible	Estimated Uncollectible Accounts
Not yet due	$60,000	1%	$ 600
1 to 30 days past due	22,000	5%	1,100
31 to 60 days past due	5,000	10%	500
61 to 90 days past due	2,000	35%	700
Over 90 days past due	1,000	60%	600
Total	$90,000		$3,500

Remember that the entry to write off a bad debt using the Allowance Method is as follows:

Allowance for Doubtful Accounts	xxx	
Accounts Receivable		xxx

Later, if a customer remits an amount in part or in full, the recovery is recorded by the following entries:

(1)

Accounts Receivable	xxx	
Allowance for Doubtful Accounts		xxx

To reinstate an account receivable previously written off to bad debts.

(2)

Cash	xxx	
Accounts Receivable		xxx

To record the collection.

Endnotes

1. Raymond Cote, *Understanding Hospitality Accounting I*, 3d ed. (East Lansing, Mich.: Educational Institute of the American Hotel & Motel Association, 1995).
2. Defined in accordance with recommendations of the Committee on Financial Management of the American Hotel & Motel Association.
3. The accounts in this section generally follow the recommendations of the *Uniform System of Accounts and Expense Dictionary for Small Hotels, Motels, and Motor Hotels*, 4th ed. (commonly abbreviated *USASH*), published by the Educational Institute of the American Hotel & Motel Association.

Key Terms

A&G	F&B
Allowance for Doubtful Accounts	fixed charges
allowance method	food cost
bad debts	human resources department
direct expenses	indirect expenses
direct write-off method	operating expenses
expenses	POM

Review Questions

1. What is the concept of responsibility accounting?
2. What is business segmentation?
3. What is a support center? Give examples of support centers found in a hotel.
4. How are the terms "direct expense" and "indirect expense" defined?
5. How is the term "fixed charges" defined? Give examples of expenses that are classified as fixed charges.

6. What is included in the Cost of Food Sales account? Specify whether these items increase or decrease the cost of food sold.

7. What types of items are considered Payroll and Related Expenses?

8. What accounts are commonly used to record repairs and maintenance expenses?

9. What is the major difference between the allowance method and the direct write-off method in terms of when a bad debt is recorded?

10. What is the major difference between the percentage of sales procedure and the percentage of receivables procedure in the recording of the *estimated* bad debts calculation under the allowance method?

Problems

Problem 1

Specify whether each of the following statements is true (T) or false (F).

_____ 1. Dividing a corporation into reporting areas by hotel location is a form of business segmentation.

_____ 2. Dividing a particular hotel into reporting areas by department is a form of business segmentation.

_____ 3. The payroll expense for housekeepers is charged to the rooms department.

_____ 4. The salary of the general manager is charged to the A&G department.

_____ 5. The payroll expense for the night auditor and front office bookkeeper is charged to the A&G department.

_____ 6. Repairs to an oven located in the restaurant is charged to the F&B department.

_____ 7. The cost of food sold includes employee meals expenses.

_____ 8. Contracting with an outside maintenance company to clean the restaurant is charged to the F&B department.

_____ 9. The expense for water used by registered guests is charged to the rooms department.

_____ 10. The percentage of sales procedure and the percentage of receivables procedure are classified as allowance methods.

Problem 2

A hospitality business receives a bank memo regarding bankcard fees. The memo states that the bank has charged the business's checking account a fee of $175 for processing bankcard vouchers previously deposited in this account. Journalize the entry recorded upon receipt of the bank memo.

Problem 3

Non-bank credit card vouchers totaling $4,000 were remitted to a private credit card company. The entry at that time was a debit to Accounts Receivable for $4,000, and a credit to Sales for $4,000. A check is received from the credit card company for $3,800, representing payment in full for these vouchers less a $200 credit card fee. Journalize the entry recorded upon receipt of the check.

Problem 4

Assume that a hospitality company uses the direct write-off method. Show the journal entry used to record an uncollectible receivable of $210.

Problem 5

Assume that a hospitality company uses the allowance method. Show the journal entry used to record an uncollectible receivable of $210.

Problem 6

Assume that a hospitality company uses the allowance method. The contra-asset account Allowance for Doubtful Accounts has a credit balance of $1,200. Based on an aging of the accounts receivable subsidiary ledger, estimated uncollectible accounts total $1,800. Journalize the entry to adjust Allowance for Doubtful Accounts using the percentage of receivables procedure.

Problem 7

Assume that a hospitality operation uses the allowance method. The contra-asset account Allowance for Doubtful Accounts has a credit balance of $1,200. Based on an analysis of sales for the period, the estimate for uncollectible accounts equals $1,800. Journalize the entry to adjust Allowance for Doubtful Accounts using the percentage of sales procedure.

REVIEW QUIZ

When you feel you have covered all of the material in this chapter, answer these questions. Choose the *best* answer. Check your answers with the correct ones found on the Review Quiz Answer Key at the end of this book.

True (T) or False (F)

T   F   1. The division of a company's work into specialized areas of responsibility is called business segmentation.

T   F   2. An area of responsibility within a hospitality business for which separate cost information must be collected and reported is called a financial reporting center.

T   F   3. Direct expenses are incurred for the benefit of the hotel as a whole, and cannot be identified with any particular department.

T   F   4. When energy costs are collected into a separate financial reporting center, energy used for cooking should always be included in the reported costs.

Multiple Choice

5. Which of the following is *not* a financial reporting center in a hospitality business?

   a. Rooms department
   b. Food and beverage department
   c. Service bar
   d. Energy costs

6. Which of the following is *not* classified as a support center within a hospitality business?

   a. Administrative and general
   b. Telephone
   c. Human resources
   d. Data processing

7. Which of the following is *not* a direct expense properly allocated to a particular department within a hospitality business?

   a. Cost of sales
   b. Payroll
   c. Operating supplies
   d. Property insurance

8. Which of the following is *not* an expense account associated with the food and beverage department?

   a. China, glassware, silver, and linen
   b. Kitchen fuel
   c. Credit card commissions
   d. Menus

9. Which of the following statements about the financial reporting center called fixed charges is true?

    a. Department heads are directly responsible for controlling these expenses.
    b. These are expenses incurred whether a property is open or closed.
    c. These expenses depend on sales volume.
    d. b and c

10. When received from customers, non-bank credit card drafts are:

    a. treated the same as cash.
    b. recorded as accounts receivable.
    c. accounted for using the allowance method.
    d. classified as uncollectible accounts.

Chapter Outline

Food and Beverage Inventory Accounting
    Methods
        Perpetual Inventory Accounting
            Method
        Periodic Inventory Accounting Method
Cost of Food Sold
        Logic for Calculating Cost of Sales
        Cost of Sales Procedure Expressed in
            Accounting Terms
Adjusting Entries for Beginning and Ending
    Inventories
Inventories on the Worksheet

Learning Objectives

1. Differentiate between an inventory accounting method and an inventory system, and explain the need for separate food and beverage inventory accounts. (p. 74)

2. Describe the perpetual inventory accounting method, cite the advantages and disadvantages of using a perpetual inventory system, and explain the accounting entries used. (pp. 74–75)

3. Describe the periodic inventory accounting method, cite the advantages and disadvantages of using a periodic inventory system, and explain the accounting entries used. (pp. 76–78)

4. Explain the logic and procedure for calculating cost of sales. (pp. 78–80)

5. Identify the adjusting entries used to account for beginning and ending inventories at the end of the accounting year. (pp. 81–82)

6. Explain the treatment of inventory adjustments on the worksheet for a hospitality business using the periodic inventory accounting method. (p. 82)

3

The Periodic Inventory Accounting Method

F OOD AND BEVERAGE INVENTORIES represent products for resale to customers. Inventory must be sufficient to avoid stock-outs, which result in lost sales, and worse, dissatisfied customers. However, the need for adequate inventory levels must be balanced by cash flow considerations, inventory turnover, storage costs, and losses due to spoilage and waste.

To monitor inventory levels and demand, department managers might use a perpetual inventory system in which individual records are kept on each item in inventory. These perpetual inventory systems are costly and time-consuming. A small hospitality business might adopt a perpetual inventory system for only the expensive items and visually monitor the other items, or it might decide not to use a perpetual inventory system at all.

So far in this chapter, only the inventory concerns of the operations areas have been addressed. However, beginning and ending inventories are also important to the accounting department for the production of financial statements. The management of any hospitality business relies on financial statements to make business decisions, perform long-range planning, and measure current operating results and the financial well-being of the business.

There is a relationship between the operations areas and the accounting department for inventory reporting. If the operations area uses a perpetual inventory system, then the accounting department can use the perpetual inventory accounting method in its bookkeeping system. Without a perpetual inventory system in operations, the accounting department must use the periodic inventory accounting method in its bookkeeping system.

This chapter focuses on the periodic inventory accounting method. However, a review of the perpetual inventory accounting method is presented first so that the reader may understand the critical differences between these two accounting methods.[1]

Our focus on the periodic inventory accounting method will address such questions as:

1. What are the advantages and disadvantages of the periodic inventory accounting method?

2. What are the accounting entries for recording storeroom and direct purchases?

3. How is the problem of having no Cost of Sales bookkeeping account in the periodic inventory accounting method resolved?

4. What are the procedures for calculating monthly and year-to-date cost of sales?

5. How are beginning and ending inventories adjusted using the Income Summary account?

6. How are beginning and ending inventories treated on the worksheet?

Food and Beverage Inventory Accounting Methods

An **inventory accounting method** refers to the bookkeeping accounts and accounting procedures used; the recordkeeping is performed by the accounting department. An **inventory system** refers to the actual receipt and issue of products in the storeroom. The purpose of this chapter is to present the *accounting* methods that relate to inventories. The complete coverage of inventory *systems* is best left to food and beverage purchasing courses.

Food and beverage inventories are the products held for resale to customers. The ending inventory represents a current asset that is shown on the balance sheet. The usage of inventory to generate sales is a conversion of this asset into an expense called cost of sales.

An inventory accounting method must provide data regarding the ending inventories and cost of goods sold for a given period. This information is necessary for preparing financial statements.

Regardless of the inventory accounting method selected, the food inventory and beverage inventory accounts are recorded separately. The Cost of Food Sold and Cost of Beverages Sold are also separate bookkeeping accounts. This accounting treatment makes it possible to report the gross profit on the sale of food separately from the gross profit on the sale of beverages such as beer, wine, and liquor.

Even though the accounting records for food and beverage inventories are kept separately, the specific accounting procedures for food and beverage inventories are identical. Therefore, to simplify the following material, our discussion will be confined to inventory accounting for food items.

The two inventory accounting methods used in the hospitality industry are:

- Perpetual
- Periodic

Perpetual Inventory Accounting Method

If a hospitality business plans to adopt the perpetual inventory accounting method for financial purposes, the operations area must install a perpetual inventory *system* in the food operation. A **perpetual inventory system** requires that the receipts and issues for each item in inventory be recorded on a separate inventory record.

A manual inventory system is characterized by numerous forms and tedious clerical effort. Such an inventory system may easily be converted to a computerized system for instant and random access of any inventory record. A computer-based perpetual inventory system decreases the clerical labor required. The receipts and issues require keyboard entry, but the totals and balances are performed by the computer.

Advantages of a Perpetual Inventory System. From an operations standpoint, the storeroom records provide:

- Up-to-the-minute stock balance data

- Automatic reorder status reminders

- Internal control—Spot checks can be made at any time and compared to the stock balance in the inventory record files.

From an accounting standpoint, the bookkeeping system provides the following information:

- Inventory on hand at the end of the month

- Cost of food sold for the period

Merchandise Inventory	Cost of Food Sold

Disadvantages of a Perpetual Inventory System. Management must decide if the cost of maintaining a perpetual inventory system is justified when weighed against the benefits received. The following cost and operational factors must be evaluated:

- High labor cost—Staff is required to maintain inventory records.

- Diligence—The system will not produce desired results unless paperwork procedures are followed and performed daily.

- Hindered production flow—Storeroom food issues require that documents are properly authorized.

The perpetual inventory system, whether manual or automated, does not eliminate the need to perform physical counts for internal control purposes.

Accounting Entries. Many food items are purchased for delivery to the storeroom. These **storeroom purchases** are recorded as follows:

Food Inventory	xxx	
Cash (or Accounts Payable)		xxx

Food products may also be purchased for immediate use by the kitchen; these products bypass the storeroom. These **direct purchases** are recorded as follows:

Cost of Food Sold	xxx	
Cash (or Accounts Payable)		xxx

During the month, the operations area sends to the accounting department the food requisitions for food issued from the storeroom. At the end of the month, these issues are recorded as follows:

Cost of Food Sold	xxx	
Food Inventory		xxx

Periodic Inventory Accounting Method

This inventory accounting method is favored by small hospitality operations and those facilities that do not want to invest in a computer-based perpetual inventory system or incur the intensive labor and recordkeeping requirements characteristic of a manual perpetual inventory system.

Advantages of a Periodic Inventory System. The benefits of a **periodic inventory system** are the following:

- No perpetual recordkeeping cards are maintained.

- No recordkeeping function is necessary in the storeroom.

- Since no inventory records are maintained, there is no need to record receipts and issues.

- There are no associated recordkeeping costs.

Disadvantages of a Periodic Inventory System. The disadvantages of this type of inventory system are as follows:

- Internal control is very weak.

- Vigilance is required to reorder correct quantities.

- Unless constant monitoring is performed, or a partial manual perpetual inventory system is used on popular menu items, an unacceptable level of stock-outs is possible.

- The inventory must be counted and costed whenever financial statements are desired.

- The absence of the recording of issues means that the bookkeeping system does not provide the cost of food sold. Therefore, there is no bookkeeping account for this expense.

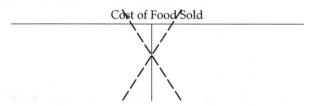

- The absence of the recording of receipts and issues means that the general ledger asset account Inventory only shows the beginning inventory on hand.

Merchandise Inventory	
Beginning Inventory	

- A physical inventory is required to determine the ending inventory at any time. Thus, a business that prepares monthly financial statements must perform monthly physical inventories or estimate the inventory on hand at the end of each month.

Accounting Entries. The entries for recording purchases and employee meals in the periodic inventory accounting method are incompatible with those in the perpetual inventory accounting method. The lack of an updated Inventory asset account and the absence of a Cost of Sales expense account require specialized procedures to calculate ending inventory and food cost.

Purchases. During the month, all purchases (storeroom and direct) are recorded to an **expense account** called Purchases. No entries are made to the Inventory asset account.

Purchases	
xxx	
xxx	

Employee meals. Employee meals are recorded at the restaurant's cost and not at the menu price. In actual practice, applying the cost of each actual serving might be impractical. Instead, a standard cost (average cost) is developed for breakfast, lunch, and dinner. Each standard cost is multiplied by the number of employees eating these meals to arrive at the employee meals expense for each department.

Because there is no Cost of Sales account, a journal entry cannot be made that would charge the various departments and credit Cost of Sales as is done under the perpetual inventory accounting method.

Under the periodic inventory accounting method, an account called Employee Meals Credit is required. This account is necessary to calculate the cost of sales amount required for the financial statements. The entry is recorded as follows:

Employee Meals Expense—Rooms Department	xxx	
Employee Meals Expense—F&B Department	xxx	
Employee Meals Expense—A&G Department	xxx	
(etc.)		
Employee Meals Credit		xxx

It is important to fully understand the purpose of these accounts. The account Employee Meals Expense—xxx Department will appear on each department's statement in the operating expenses section. The account Employee Meals Credit is a contra-expense account and will be used to eliminate the cost of employee meals from food used to arrive at cost of food sold. Another name for this account is Cost of Employee Meals.

In effect, the cost of all food consumed by employees is removed from the F&B department and allocated to each department whose employees consumed meals. The income statement for the F&B department will show the departmental expense account for meals consumed by its employees. The statement will also show the employee meals credit in the cost of sales area. *It is important to realize that the Employee Meals Credit account represents food consumed by all employees of the hotel.*

Officers' checks. Some hospitality businesses may desire to keep the meal expenses for staff separate from the meal expenses for management. In these cases, an account called Officers' Checks is charged for each department. The credit could be posted to the Employee Meals Credit account. Some hotels might credit an account called Officers' Checks Credit; this account would be treated exactly like the Employee Meals Credit account.

For our purposes, meals for staff and managers will be combined into one amount that will be recorded as a debit to the departmental Employee Meals Expense account and as a credit to the Cost of Sales contra account called Employee Meals Credit.

Accounting Problems. Financial statements cannot be produced without an ending inventory and an amount for cost of food sold. Under the periodic inventory accounting method, a physical inventory is required at the end of each month to provide information necessary for producing the financial statements.

Since there is no bookkeeping account to record cost of food sold, the **cost of sales** must be computed by an accounting procedure that will yield accurate information regarding the cost of goods sold.

Cost of Food Sold

Cost of food sold represents only the cost of food prepared for guest consumption. Employee meals are not part of cost of food sold. Cost of food sold can also be called *cost of food sales* or *net food cost*.

Food cost is an important figure because it is used to measure the efficiency of the food operation and for menu planning. Food cost is also used to determine the profit on sales of food before all other expenses; this profit is called the gross profit and is calculated as follows:

$$\text{Sales (net)} - \text{Cost of food sold} = \text{Gross profit}$$

Because the bookkeeping records used in the periodic inventory accounting method do not include a Cost of Sales account, it is necessary to compute the cost of food sold using a cost of sales procedure that is explained later in the chapter. Under the periodic inventory accounting method, cost of sales can easily be computed using readily available information. However, the ending inventory must be estimated or a physical inventory performed at the end of the period.

Logic for Calculating Cost of Sales

Before we discuss the actual procedure used to arrive at the amount for cost of food sold, it is beneficial to understand the logic or reasoning behind this procedure. The following terminology should be clearly understood.

- **Beginning inventory:** what we started the period with
- Purchases: increases to the beginning inventory
- Goods available: beginning inventory + purchases = everything that was available for use during the period
- Ending inventory: what was not used (what is on hand)

If we take everything that was available to use during the period and subtract what was not used, the result is what was used or consumed.

	Starting point	(beginning inventory)
+	Add-ons	(purchases)
	Everything available for use	(food available)
−	What was not used	(ending inventory)
	What was used	(cost of food sold)

The cost of food *used* does *not* represent cost of food *sold*. Remember that a hospitality business may provide meals to its employees. To arrive at cost of food sold, the adjustment for the cost of meals to employees and managers must be eliminated from the cost of food used. This is accomplished as follows:

	What was used	(cost of food used)
−	Employee meals credit	(all hotel employees)
	Cost of food sales	(food prepared for customers)

Cost of Sales Procedure Expressed in Accounting Terms

Now that the terms and logic for the calculation of cost of food sold have been explained, the procedure can be presented in accounting terms. This procedure will appear on the F&B income statement or on a supplemental schedule attached to the statement. The accounting procedure is as follows:

	Beginning inventory
+	Purchases
	Cost of food available
−	Ending inventory
	Cost of food used (consumed)
−	Employee meals credit
	Cost of food sales (cost of food sold)

Under the periodic inventory accounting method, the procedure for computing cost of beverages sold is identical to that for cost of food sold. However, the computations are performed independently of each other because the information for food and beverages is presented separately on the F&B departmental income statement.

Example. Calculating the cost of food sold is relatively simple if the time period is clearly understood. If the monthly cost of food sold is being calculated, only data pertaining to that particular month can be used. Last month's ending inventory becomes this month's beginning inventory. For example, calculating the cost of sales for the month of April means that the ending inventory of $13,000 on March 31 is brought forward as the beginning inventory of $13,000 for April 1.

In addition to reporting monthly results, the financial statements show year-to-date (YTD) information. If the cost of sales is being calculated for the four-month period ended April 30, then a different treatment is required. The beginning

Exhibit 1   Monthly Cost of Food Sold Solution

Beginning inventory, April 1	$13,000
Purchases	22,500
Cost of food available	$35,500
Ending inventory	(10,500)
Cost of food consumed	$25,000
Employee meals credit	(1,000)
Cost of food sold	$24,000

Exhibit 2   YTD Cost of Food Sold Solution

Beginning inventory, January 1	$12,500
Purchases	86,000
Cost of food available	$98,500
Ending inventory	(10,500)
Cost of food consumed	$88,000
Employee meals credit	(4,000)
Cost of food sold	$84,000

inventory for a four-month period could not logically be March 31; the only possible beginning inventory is four months back, which is January 1. To this inventory would be applied the YTD purchases and other related activities. Of course, the ending inventory on April 30 is the same for either a monthly or YTD cost of sales calculation.

To illustrate the calculation of monthly and YTD cost of sales, the following facts will be used:

Food Inventory Data

January 1:	$12,500
March 31:	$13,000
April 30:	$10,500

Food Transaction Data	Month of April	Four Months Ended April 30
Food Purchases	$22,500	$86,000
Employee Meals Credit	1,000	4,000

Monthly cost of food sold solution. Exhibit 1 shows the procedure used to solve for the monthly cost of food sold. The beginning inventory of April 1 is the carryover of the March 31 inventory. The monthly transactions are used to arrive at the cost of food sold for the period of April 1 to April 30.

YTD cost of food sold solution. Exhibit 2 shows the procedure used to arrive at the YTD cost of food sold. The beginning inventory is the inventory at the start of the fiscal year, in this case January 1. The YTD transactions are used to compute the cost of food sold for the four-month period of January 1 to April 30.

Adjusting Entries for Beginning and Ending Inventories ────

Under the periodic inventory accounting method, the general ledger asset account called Food Inventory contains only the beginning-of-period inventory amount. For purposes of this discussion, the inventory account contains the balance as at the start of the year on January 1.

Food Inventory	
1/1/X1 Bal 6,000	

At the end of the business year, it is necessary to remove the old inventory and record the ending inventory as of 12/31/X1. To accomplish this, a temporary account is required to record the adjustment. Since a temporary account called **Income Summary** will be used for the year-end closing process, it can also be used during the year-end adjustments process.

The result of using the Income Summary account is that *the beginning inventory becomes an expense* because it is *debited* in the Income Summary account and the *ending inventory is a credit*. This can be shown as follows:

Income Summary	
Beginning Inventory	Ending Inventory

Assume that the inventory on 12/31/X1 is $7,500. The inventory adjustment is accomplished by the following two journal entries:

```
                    (1)
        Income Summary                      6,000
             Food Inventory                         6,000
        To remove the beginning-of-year inventory


                    (2)
        Food Inventory                       7,500
             Income Summary                         7,500
        To remove the end-of-year inventory
```

Posting these adjusting entries would result in the following Food Inventory and Income Summary accounts:

Food Inventory				Income Summary			
1/1 Bal	6,000	12/31 AJE1	6,000	12/31 AJE1	6,000	12/31 AJE2	7,500
12/31 AJE2	7,500						

Now the beginning food inventory of $6,000 is eliminated from the Food Inventory account, and the year-end inventory of $7,500 is the new balance. The Income Summary account contains both the beginning and year-end inventories. During the year-end **closing entries** process, the temporary Income Summary account will be eliminated.

Exhibit 3   Inventory Adjustments on the Worksheet

	Trial Balance		Adjustments		Adjusted Trial Balance		Income Statement		Balance Sheet	
	dr	cr	dr	cr	dr	cr	dr	cr	dr	cr
Cash on Hand										
(other accounts)										
Food Inventory	6 000 00		7 500 00	6 000 00	7 500 00				7 500 00	
(other accounts)										
Income Summary			6 000 00	7 500 00	6 000 00	7 500 00	6 000 00	7 500 00		
(other accounts)										

Inventories on the Worksheet

The worksheet procedure for a hospitality business using the periodic inventory accounting method is almost identical to that for a business using the perpetual inventory accounting method.[2] The only significant difference pertains to the inventory adjustments. To accentuate the treatment of the Inventory and Income Summary accounts on the **worksheet,** Exhibit 3 presents only these two accounts.

The Food Inventory account is treated just like any other account on the worksheet; its **trial balance** amount is combined with the adjustments, and the new balance is entered in the **adjusted trial balance** column and carried over to the balance sheet column.

However, the treatment of the inventory adjustments shown in the Income Summary account differs from any process presented in this chapter. Notice that the adjustments are not combined; they maintain their separate debit and credit identity in the adjusted trial balance columns and in the income statement columns of the worksheet. This separation allows the accountant to find, with a glance at the income summary line, the following information for calculating cost of sales:

- The debit represents the beginning inventory.

- The credit represents the ending inventory.

Exhibit 4 illustrates a completed worksheet for Louie's Diner, Inc. The Income Summary account discloses that the beginning inventory is $500 and the ending inventory is $800. This is easily determined by following the rule that the debit in Income Summary represents the beginning inventory and the credit represents the ending inventory. Also, the current asset account Food Inventory shows the $800 ending inventory in the balance sheet section of the worksheet.

Endnotes

1. For further information on perpetual inventory systems and the perpetual inventory accounting method, see Raymond Cote, *Understanding Hospitality Accounting I,* 3d ed. (East Lansing, Mich.: Educational Institute of the American Hotel & Motel Association, 1995), pp. 143–148.

2. For further information on worksheet preparation by a business using the perpetual inventory accounting method, see Raymond Cote, *Understanding Hospitality Accounting I,* 3d ed. (East Lansing, Mich.: Educational Institute of the American Hotel & Motel Association, 1995).

Exhibit 4 Completed Worksheet—Louie's Diner

Louie's Diner, Inc.
Worksheet
December 31, 19X2

	1 Trial Balance Dr	2 Trial Balance Cr	3 Adjustments Dr	4 Adjustments Cr	5 Adj. Trial Balance Dr	6 Adj. Trial Balance Cr	7 Income Statement Dr	8 Income Statement Cr	9 Balance Sheet Dr	10 Balance Sheet Cr
Cash on Hand	300 00				300 00				300 00	
Cash—Checking	2 700 00				2 700 00				2 700 00	
Food Inventory	500 00		(b) 800 00	(a) 500 00	800 00				800 00	
Furniture	3 500 00				3 500 00				3 500 00	
Equipment	6 000 00				6 000 00				6 000 00	
Accum. Depreciation—Furniture		770 00		(c) 30 00		800 00				800 00
Accum. Depreciation—Equipment		1 530 00		(c) 70 00		1 600 00				1 600 00
Accounts Payable		1 900 00				1 900 00				1 900 00
Sales Tax Payable		600 00				600 00				600 00
Accrued Payroll				(d) 900 00		900 00				900 00
Accrued Income Taxes				(f) 600 00		600 00				600 00
Common Stock		3 100 00				3 100 00				3 100 00
Retained Earnings		800 00				800 00				800 00
Income Summary			(a) 500 00	(b) 800 00	500 00	800 00	500 00	800 00		
Food Sales		80 000 00				80 000 00		80 000 00		
Food Purchases	29 000 00				29 000 00		29 000 00			
Employee Meals Credit		150 00		(e) 20 00		170 00		170 00		
Payroll	27 300 00		(d) 900 00		28 200 00		28 200 00			
Payroll Taxes	2 700 00				2 700 00		2 700 00			
Employee Meals	150 00		(e) 20 00		170 00		170 00			
Utilities	2 700 00				2 700 00		2 700 00			
Operating Supplies	2 100 00				2 100 00		2 100 00			
Rent	9 600 00				9 600 00		9 600 00			
Depreciation	2 300 00		(c) 100 00		2 400 00		2 400 00			
Income Taxes			(f) 600 00		600 00		600 00			
TOTAL	88 850 00	88 850 00	2 920 00	2 920 00	91 270 00	91 270 00	77 970 00	80 970 00	13 300 00	10 300 00
Net Income							3 000 00			3 000 00
TOTAL							80 970 00	80 970 00	13 300 00	13 300 00

Key Terms

adjusted trial balance
beginning inventory
closing entries
cost of sales
direct purchases
expense accounts
Income Summary account

inventory accounting methods
inventory systems
periodic inventory system
perpetual inventory system
storeroom purchases
trial balance
worksheet

Review Questions

1. What are the disadvantages of a periodic inventory system?

2. Under the periodic inventory accounting method, what is the journal entry to record storeroom purchases of food products on open account?

3. Under the periodic inventory accounting method, what is the journal entry to record direct purchases of food products on open account?

4. What other terms can be used instead of "cost of food sales"?

5. How is gross profit calculated?

6. What is the accounting procedure for calculating cost of sales?

7. What is the beginning inventory date for the cost of sales computation for the following reporting periods?

        Month of December   _____

        Three-month period ended June 30   _____

        Year ended December 31   _____

        Month of May   _____

8. In an analysis of the Income Summary account after the inventory adjustments, how can the beginning and ending inventories be determined?

Problems

Problem 1

Specify whether each of the following statements is true (T) or false (F).

_____ 1. The accounting department cannot use the perpetual inventory accounting method unless the operations area is on a perpetual inventory system.

_____ 2. The accounting department cannot use the periodic inventory accounting method if the operations area is using a perpetual inventory system.

_____ 3. The accounting records for food and beverage inventories must be kept separately.

_____ 4. The inventory accounting methods used for food and beverage inventories are identical.

_____ 5. A cost of sales account is required in the periodic inventory accounting method.

_____ 6. Under the periodic inventory accounting method, the journal entries to record purchases do not differentiate between storeroom and direct purchases.

_____ 7. The employee meals amount that appears in the cost of food sales section represents only the food consumed by the food department employees.

_____ 8. Cost of food consumed represents food prepared for guests and employees.

_____ 9. Cost of food sold represents food prepared for guests.

_____ 10. The ending inventory amount is the same whether cost of sales is being calculated for the month of June or for the six months ended June 30.

Problem 2

Assume that a hospitality company uses the periodic inventory accounting method. Journalize the following activities:

a. Storeroom food provisions totaling $674 are purchased on open account.

b. Direct food provisions totaling $126 are purchased on open account.

c. Free employee meals for the month total:

Rooms Department	$95
F&B Department	$80
POM Department	$25

Problem 3

What is the gross profit based on the following information?

Sales	$90,000
Sales allowances	1,000
Cost of sales	24,000
All other expenses	60,000

Problem 4

A physical inventory shows that a total of $675 in food provisions are on hand as of March 31. Using the following information, compute the cost of food sold for the year-to-date period ending March 31:

Food Inventory		Food Sales		
1/1	860		1/31	6,000
			2/28	4,500
			Bal	10,500
			3/31	8,000
			Bal	18,500

Food Purchases		
1/31	2,100	
2/28	1,400	
Bal	3,500	
3/31	2,500	
Bal	6,000	

Employee Meals Credit		
	1/31	55
	2/28	30
	Bal	85
	3/31	65
	Bal	150

Problem 5

Using the information from Problem 4, compute the cost of food sold for the month of March. (Assume the ending food inventory on February 28 was $540.)

Problem 6

On December 31, a business using a calendar business year has an ending beverage inventory of $3,800 at cost. The general ledger account Beverage Inventory shows a January 1 balance of $2,900. Journalize the adjusting entries on December 31 for the beverage inventory.

REVIEW QUIZ

When you feel you have covered all of the material in this chapter, answer these questions. Choose the *best* answer. Check your answers with the correct ones found on the Review Quiz Answer Key at the end of this book.

True (T) or False (F)

T   F   1. Food and beverage inventories should be accounted for separately.

T   F   2. A periodic inventory system affords a higher level of internal control of inventory than does a perpetual inventory system.

T   F   3. Employee meals are *not* part of cost of food sold.

T   F   4. The Income Summary account is used to record the inventory adjustment at the end of the year.

Multiple Choice

5. Which of the following is characteristic of a perpetual inventory system?

   a. Storeroom records provide accurate information about stock balances.
   b. Storeroom records do *not* provide automatic reorder reminders.
   c. Recordkeeping cards are *not* maintained.
   d. Labor costs are low.

6. Direct purchases are food products that:

   a. require minimal amounts of paperwork and recordkeeping.
   b. are delivered directly to the kitchen.
   c. are delivered directly to the storeroom.
   d. have reached total stock-out status.

7. Which of the following accounts is *not* used in the calculation of cost of sales using a periodic inventory accounting method?

   a. Inventory
   b. Purchases
   c. Employee Meals Credit
   d. Cost of Sales

8. Under the periodic inventory accounting method:

   a. the procedure for computing cost of beverages sold is identical to that for cost of food sold.
   b. the procedure for computing cost of beverages sold differs from that for cost of food sold.
   c. the computations for cost of beverages sold and cost of food sold are performed independently.
   d. a and c

9. When the periodic inventory accounting method is used, part of the year-end procedure is to:

   a. total entries made to the Food Inventory account.
   b. remove the beginning inventory amount from the general ledger account Food Inventory.
   c. add the cost of employee meals to the cost of sales.
   d. adjust the Food Purchases account to record transportation costs.

10. The worksheet procedure for a business using the periodic inventory accounting method _____ that for a business using the perpetual inventory accounting method.

    a. is almost identical to
    b. is the opposite of
    c. requires more worksheet pages than
    d. requires fewer worksheet pages than

Chapter Outline

Computer Technology
    Software
    Hardware
Hotel Computer Systems
Accounting Systems
    Developing an Accounting System
Hotel Financial Information Systems
    Classification of Hotel Departments
The Uniform System of Accounts
Account Numbering Systems
Designing Financial Statements
    Captions

Learning Objectives

1. Define management, and explain its four functions. (p. 91)

2. Explain the functions of computer software, and describe the two major categories of software. (pp. 92–93)

3. Describe computer hardware components and their functions. (pp. 93–96)

4. Explain the role of computer systems in hotel property management, list front and back office applications, and describe four common front office applications. (pp. 96–98)

5. Define an accounting system, and explain the phases of its development. (pp. 98–100)

6. Describe how the departments of a hotel are commonly classified, and summarize management's need for financial information about each. (pp. 100–102)

7. Describe the purpose of a uniform system of accounts, and explain the purpose for having standardized formats for financial statements. (p. 103)

8. Explain the purpose of an account numbering system, and describe the formats used in five-digit and eight-digit account numbering systems. (pp. 103–106)

9. Cite important considerations in the design of financial statements. (pp. 106–108)

4

Computer, Accounting, and Financial Information Systems

MANAGEMENT IS THE PROCESS of using all of a company's resources—such as personnel, property, and equipment—to accomplish objectives. The managerial process is characterized by these four functions:

- Planning
- Organizing
- Leading (directing)
- Controlling

Planning includes determining objectives and developing a course of action to accomplish these objectives. **Organizing** involves allocating the resources and assigning the tasks required to accomplish the planned objectives. **Leading**, also known as directing, involves motivating, instructing, and supervising the personnel responsible for the accomplishment of objectives. **Controlling** includes measuring actual accomplishments against the original plan and determining any corrective action.

Hospitality managers rely on accounting information systems throughout the managerial process. Upper managers require reliable information to conduct the long-range planning necessary for growth and survival. The major roles of middle managers are to disseminate pertinent information to upper management and delegate responsibility to lower management. The responsibility of lower managers is to supervise the day-to-day activities that are necessary to accomplish company objectives. A business's accounting and financial information systems must be designed to accommodate the requirements of these different levels of management.

This chapter will discuss the basic components of computer, accounting, and financial information systems and their role in the financial reporting and operations areas of a hotel. The following questions will be addressed:

1. What are the typical components of computers?
2. What computer systems are available to integrate the needs of management, accounting, and the various operations areas of a hotel?
3. Why is a uniform system of accounts important?

Computer Technology

The hospitality industry operates in a competitive environment and complex society. Market survival depends upon having timely and reliable information. Today, computer systems are an integral part of the gathering and processing of financial information. Computers sort data and perform mathematical functions more quickly and accurately than any alternative. An important function of computers is their ability to store and retrieve data.

Even a small business can afford a computer system. Computers are inexpensive, and ready-to-use programs are available for many business applications at modest cost. Most computers require little space and can be operated by anyone who has fundamental computer skills.

A general knowledge of computers is expected of hospitality students entering the industry. The first step in learning about computers is to study the software and hardware environment.

Software

In order for the computer to perform its tasks, instructions are needed to command and direct the computer. These instructions are called **computer programs**. A set of programs is called computer **software**. This software instructs the computer step-by-step in:

- What to do
- How to do it
- When to do it

  The two major categories of software are:

- Operating systems software
- Applications software

Operating Systems Software. Operating systems are usually included with the purchase of a computer. An **operating system** is necessary for a computer to carry out the instructions found in any applications software. A major function of the *operating systems software* is to manage the routine functions of the computer, such as receiving input and producing output. It also controls the execution of the applications software and directs the flow of data to the various hardware units of the computer system.

Applications Software. *Applications software* performs a group of tasks related to a specific business activity. Because of the similarity of business tasks from one hospitality operation to another, prepackaged applications software is readily available and inexpensive. These programs have been developed by computer professionals for users who are not computer specialists. Most hospitality businesses can benefit from one or more of the following applications software packages:

- Payroll
- General ledger
- Inventory control
- Billing and accounts receivable

- Accounts payable
- Rooms management
- Reservations

Hardware

The physical computer equipment is called **hardware.** A computer system is made up of the following hardware components:

- Input/output units
- Central processing unit (CPU)
- External storage devices

Exhibit 1 illustrates various components of a microcomputer system.

Input/Output Units. An *input unit* allows the CPU to receive data, and an *output unit* permits the visual display of information or the storage of information. Disk drives can perform both input and output functions; they provide input of data and record updated data.

Typical input units are:

- Keyboards
- Touch-screen terminals
- Computer mouse
- Disk drives

Typical output units are:

- Printers
- Monitors
- Disk drives

Keyboards. A computer keyboard is similar to a typewriter keyboard. The keys allow the input of letters, numbers, and special characters. The keyboard also has keys which control the movement of data and the computer's operations.

Touch-screen terminals. A touch-screen terminal allows the input of data without the use of a keyboard. Touching a designated area of the screen automatically creates input to the computer. Touch-screen terminals are especially useful as order-entry devices in a food service operation.

Computer mouse. A computer mouse is a small device which a computer user rolls or moves on a flat surface. This action moves an on-screen arrow which allows the user to choose commands, move text, and perform other operations. A mouse can be used in place of or in conjunction with a keyboard.

Printers. A printer is necessary to produce documentation or reports. Printer speed is usually measured in characters per second (cps). Because laser printers are very fast, their speed is measured in pages per minute (ppm).

Monitors. A monitor displays text and graphics on a screen. Monitors look like television screens and are available in monochrome or color units.

Exhibit 1   Sample Microcomputer Illustration

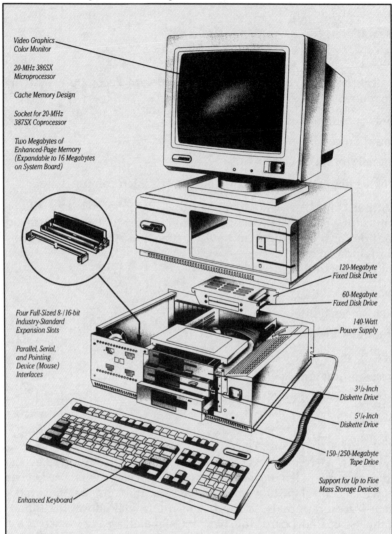

Video Graphics
Color Monitor

20-MHz 386SX
Microprocessor

Cache Memory Design

Socket for 20-MHz
387SX Coprocessor

Two Megabytes of
Enhanced-Page Memory
(Expandable to 16 Megabytes
on System Board)

Four Full-Sized 8-/16-bit
Industry-Standard
Expansion Slots

Parallel, Serial,
and Pointing
Device (Mouse)
Interfaces

Enhanced Keyboard

120-Megabyte
Fixed Disk Drive

60-Megabyte
Fixed Disk Drive

140-Watt
Power Supply

3½-Inch
Diskette Drive

5¼-Inch
Diskette Drive

150-/250-Megabyte
Tape Drive

Support for Up to Five
Mass Storage Devices

Central Processing Unit (CPU). The CPU is the "brain" of the computer system. It performs all the mathematical and logical operations and directs all the other components of the system. The microprocessor chip is the heart of the CPU. There are two types of internal storage (memory) found in the CPU:

- Read only memory
- Random access memory

Read only memory (ROM). The read only memory (ROM) is preset by the manufacturer of the computer. It is not accessible by the user. ROM contains programmed commands which direct the basic computer operations. For example, a manufacturer may have selected the command "START" to initiate the running of a program. If the computer user enters "GO," the user would get a "SYNTAX ERROR" message because the computer does not recognize the command. However, another computer manufacturer may have used "GO" as its command to start a program. Computers recognize only their own programmed commands as preset by the manufacturer; this is why one type of software may not work on all brands of computers.

Random access memory (RAM). The random access memory (RAM) is user accessible. It temporarily stores all the data being processed by the computer. This data can be accessed and altered by the user. Whenever electrical power is lost or the computer is turned off, all user data in RAM is "erased." If another program is started, all previous data in RAM is also no longer available. RAM is available only during the operation of a program. For this reason, any information that must be saved for future use is recorded on an external storage device.

External Storage Devices. External storage devices permit the recording of data and programs so they can be accessed and updated in the future. For example, employee payroll files contain each employee's name, pay rate, and other fixed information. In addition, year-to-date payroll data is updated every time a paycheck is issued. This information must be recorded on an external storage device because it is necessary each time payroll is processed.

Three common types of external storage devices are:

- Magnetic tapes
- Diskettes
- Hard disks

Magnetic tapes. Magnetic tapes are similar in construction to the cassette tapes used in tape recorders; their size varies depending on the type of computer used. Magnetic tape storage is not as popular as disk storage because of the way in which tape provides accessibility to the stored data. Magnetic tapes store data in a *sequential access* mode, which means the computer must wind and rewind the tape drive to find a particular record. For example, assume a hotel has 100 rooms numbered from 1 to 100. To access the records for Room 65, the records for Rooms 1 to 64 must be passed in the search. If the next transaction is for information on Room 25, it is necessary to rewind the tape until the record for Room 25 is found.

Diskettes. A diskette (or disk) is made of thin, flexible plastic coated with a magnetized oxide and protected by a covering. Diskettes permit *random access* of data because data can be recorded in any available space on the disk; therefore, sequential arrangement and access of records is not necessary. The surface of a diskette is divided into tracks and sectors, which are numbered by the computer and related to each record stored on the disk. However, the user need not be concerned with this indexing feature in order to access a record. For example, if a computer user needs the record for Room 65, the user need only key in the digits "65," and the operating system will access that record directly.

Diskettes come in different sizes—8-inch, 5 $1/4$-inch, and 3 $1/2$-inch; the latter two are the most popular. The size used depends on the type of computer system. Today, most microcomputers are sold with the 3 $1/2$-inch disk as the major disk system. Exhibit 2 illustrates the construction of 5 $1/4$-inch and 3 $1/2$-inch diskettes.

Hard disks. A hard disk is made of metal and is not easily removable from a computer by the user. A hard disk has far greater storage capacity than a standard diskette and is faster in operation; however, it is more expensive than a diskette system. Because the hard disk is an integral part of the computer hardware and its records may be accessible to anyone using the computer, the difficulty of maintaining the privacy of the information stored on it is a consideration. Most computer systems today are sold with both a hard disk and one or more diskette drives.

Hotel Computer Systems

Computer systems for hotel property management are as varied as the hotels they serve. They are available for both small and large hotels. Some systems are modular and can be expanded to fit the needs of the hotel and its management. A computer-based property management system offers the opportunity for improved guest services, increased employee productivity, and maximized efficiency of management.

Property management systems are designed to provide hotel personnel access to the hotel's electronic information system. Various types of computer terminals allow users to have direct access and communication with this information system, thus permitting users at remote locations of the hotel to instantaneously update information relevant to a hotel's accounts. Terminals are usually equipped with keyboards and display screens (and sometimes printers) and are located at vital areas of the hotel. Computer systems can be interfaced with telephone call accounting systems, point-of-sale systems, and in-house entertainment systems.

Property management system applications can be divided into two broad functional areas: front office applications and back office applications. Front office applications integrate such functions as reservations, rooms management, and guest accounting within a hotel's information network. Back office applications typically include such functions as accounts receivable, accounts payable, payroll accounting, check writing and bank reconciliations, fixed asset accounting, financial reporting, and the general ledger.

The rest of this section will concentrate on typical property management system front office applications.[1] These applications are grouped broadly into four common software **modules:**

- Reservations

- Rooms management

- Guest accounting

- General management

Reservations. A reservations module enables a hotel to rapidly process room requests and generate timely and accurate rooms, revenue, and forecasting reports.

Exhibit 2   Diagrams of 5 ¹/₄- and 3 ¹/₂-Inch Diskettes

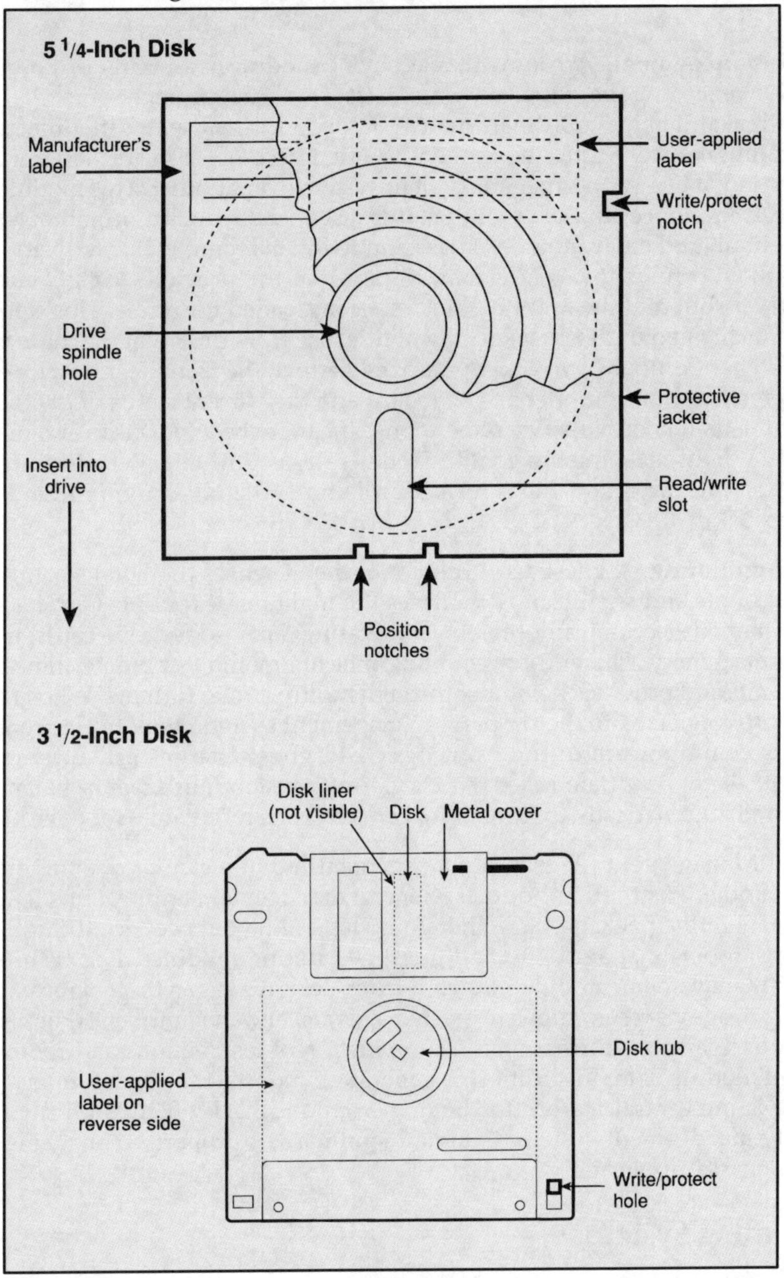

5 ¹/₄-Inch Disk

Manufacturer's label

User-applied label

Write/protect notch

Drive spindle hole

Protective jacket

Insert into drive

Read/write slot

Position notches

3 ¹/₂-Inch Disk

Disk liner (not visible)   Disk   Metal cover

Disk hub

User-applied label on reverse side

Write/protect hole

Reservations received at a central reservations site can be processed, confirmed, and instantly communicated to the destination property whose files are immediately updated. In addition, the reservations data which is received can be automatically reformatted into preregistration materials and an updated expected arrivals list can be generated.

Rooms Management. A rooms management module maintains up-to-date information regarding the status of rooms, assists in the assignment of rooms during registration, and helps coordinate many guest services. Since this module replaces most traditional front office equipment, it often becomes a major determinant in the selection of one property management system over another. This module alerts front desk employees to each room's status just as room and information racks do in non-automated environments. For example, with a room rack, an upside-down card without a folio covering it may signify that the previous night's guest has checked out, but that the room has not yet been cleaned for resale. This status will remain unchanged until housekeeping notifies the front desk that the room is clean and ready for occupancy. In a computerized system, the front desk employee simply enters the room's number at a keyboard and the current status of the room appears immediately on a display screen. Once the room becomes clean and ready for occupancy, housekeeping changes the room's status through a terminal in housekeeping's work area and the information is immediately communicated to the front desk.

Guest Accounting. A guest accounting module increases the hotel's control over guest accounts and significantly modifies the night audit routine. Guest accounts are maintained electronically, thereby eliminating the need for folio cards, trays, or posting machinery. The guest accounting module monitors predetermined guest credit limits and provides flexibility through multiple folio formats. When revenue centers are connected to the property management system, remote electronic cash registers communicate to the front desk and guest charges are automatically posted to the appropriate folios. At check-out, outstanding account balances are transferred automatically to the city ledger (accounts receivable) for collection.

General Management. A general management module cannot operate independently of other front office modules. General management applications tend to be report-generating packages and, therefore, depend on data collected through reservations, rooms management, and guest accounting modules. For example, the general management module allows a front desk manager to generate a report showing the day's reservations (expected arrivals) and the number of rooms ready for occupancy. This information is a combination of reservations and rooms management module data. In addition to generating reports, the general management module is the central feature for linking front and back office applications of a property management system. Exhibit 3 summarizes property management system front office applications.

Accounting Systems

An accounting system is a collection of forms, records, procedures, management policies, and computer systems that process data into useful information. Accounting systems can range from simple manual systems to sophisticated computerized systems. When a hospitality company's operations become too complex or its

Exhibit 3   Front Office Applications of a Property Management System

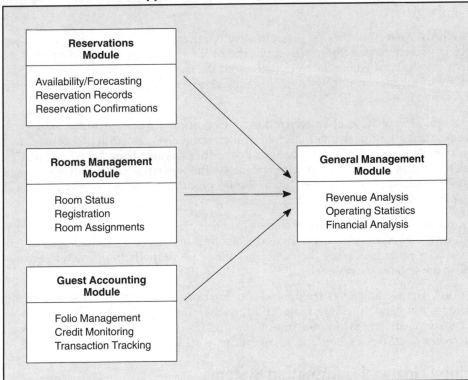

transactions too voluminous to be processed efficiently and quickly by a manual accounting system, the company should consider conversion to a computerized system.

Developing an Accounting System

Accounting systems should be designed to process data quickly and accurately at reasonable cost. Data is then converted to financial information. While the terms "data" and "information" may seem synonymous, there is an important difference. **Data** are facts or quantities; **information** is data that has been processed in a format that is useful and relevant.

A thorough understanding of the hospitality company's operations, policies, and objectives is necessary to develop a good accounting system. Many large hospitality firms have a systems department that is responsible for developing accounting and operations systems. Developing a meaningful and useful accounting system involves four major phases:

- Analysis
- Design

- Implementation
- Follow-up

Analysis. Analysis is the first phase in developing an accounting system. The major objective here is to gather facts about the needs of management and operations areas. A study of where data originates and the flow of information is also made. Many of the facts resulting from this analysis are used later to prepare or revise operating manuals.

Design. This phase is characterized by a team approach that includes managers, accountants, key personnel, and computer specialists. Documents, forms, and information reports are designed. Procedures are outlined and job duties identified and documented. Operationally, the system should optimize guest service. Administratively, the system should produce financial information useful in planning and decision making.

Implementation. This phase transforms the plan into action. The forms are printed, and equipment is purchased. Personnel are selected, trained, and supervised closely to make sure their responsibilities are properly performed to accomplish the organization's goals.

Follow-Up. Getting a system up and running does not complete its development. The accuracy and timeliness of its reporting, the efficiency of personnel, and the satisfaction of customers must be continuously reviewed, and the system must be evaluated for weaknesses, bottlenecks, or failure in achieving the original objectives.

Hotel Financial Information Systems

The foundation of a financial information system for a hotel consists of the financial reports issued to management. A hotel is a unique business institution. Unlike other retail operations, a hotel's operating environment is composed of several different revenue centers and numerous support centers. A hotel's management requires more than the typical **income statement** and **balance sheet** for the company as a whole. Hotel managers need financial statements for the major departments in order to measure the income and expenses of each responsibility area.

Classification of Hotel Departments

A hotel's departments can generally be classified as follows:

- Revenue centers
- Support centers
- Energy costs
- Fixed charges

Exhibit 4 illustrates this classification of the departments of a hotel. Small hotels may not have all of the listed departments, while large hotels may have more departments. For example, a large hotel may have several food and beverage

Exhibit 4   Hotel Financial Information System

```
                              ┌────────┐
                             ╱  HOTEL   ╲
                            ╱────────────╲
                                  │
        ┌──────────────┬──────────┴──────────┬──────────────┐
   ╭─────────╮    ╭─────────╮         ╭─────────╮      ╭─────────╮
   │ Revenue │    │ Support │         │ Energy  │      │  Fixed  │
   │ Centers │    │ Centers │         │  Costs  │      │ Charges │
   ╰─────────╯    ╰─────────╯         ╰─────────╯      ╰─────────╯
```

Revenue Centers	Support Centers	Energy Costs	Fixed Charges
Rooms	Administrative and General	Electricity	Rent
Food and Beverage	Marketing	Heating Fuel	Property Taxes
Telephone	Property Operation and Maintenance	Water	Property Insurance
Other Operated Departments			Interest
Rentals and Other Income			Depreciation
			Amortization

facilities, such as a main dining room, patio, and cafeteria. Each of these areas would be shown separately.

Revenue Centers. A revenue center serves guests and generates sales but does not necessarily earn profits. The generation of sales, no matter how small, qualifies a facility as a revenue center. A departmental income statement is produced for each facility classified as a revenue center.

Typical revenue centers are:

- Rooms

- Food and beverage (F&B): dining room, cafeteria, patio, coffee shop, and the banquet operation
- Telephone
- **Other operated departments:** gift shop, recreation, and any other department operated by the hotel and not by a concessionaire
- Schedule of rentals and other income: This is not an actual physical department. It is a schedule to report revenue that is not attributable to any other revenue center. The schedule lists revenue such as interest income, dividend income, rentals of store and office space, concessions income, commissions, vending machine profits (if owned), cash discounts earned, and salvage income.

Support Centers. A support center provides services essential to the operation of revenue centers. A support center does not directly generate sales. A departmental statement is produced for each support center to show its expenses. A support center's departmental statement cannot be called an income statement because an income statement shows sales and expenses.

Many hospitality students mistakenly believe that the housekeeping function is a support center. From an operations standpoint, housekeeping does serve a revenue center; however, housekeeping is a service dedicated to the rooms department and does not provide a service to other revenue centers. All housekeeping expenses and wages are combined in the rooms department income statement.

Typical support centers are:

- Administrative and general (A&G)
- Marketing
- Property operation and maintenance

Energy Costs. In most hotels, this department has no physical presence. Because energy costs are significant, management needs a report that lists the energy costs of the hotel for:

- Electricity
- Heat
- Water

Fixed Charges. This department has no physical presence. Fixed charges are important for management to track because fixed costs are incurred regardless of the volume of sales; in fact, they are incurred even when a hotel is closed.

The typical fixed charges are:

- Rent
- Property taxes
- Property insurance
- Interest
- Depreciation
- Amortization

The Uniform System of Accounts

A **uniform system of accounts** provides standardized formats for financial statements and a full range of account titles. Standardization permits readers of financial statements to compare the financial data on a particular property with that of similar properties in the hospitality industry.

In 1961, the American Hotel & Motel Association (AH&MA) asked the National Association of Accountants to develop a uniform system of accounts for small hotels and motels. The Committee on Financial Management of the AH&MA has periodically revised this uniform system of accounts to reflect the current needs and changing technology of the dynamic hospitality industry. This uniform system of accounts is the *Uniform System of Accounts and Expense Dictionary for Small Hotels, Motels, and Motor Hotels* (or *USASH*), published by the Educational Institute of AH&MA.

Due to variations in the activities and services of hotels, each property must adapt the uniform system of accounts to meet its particular needs. Changes can be made to the **chart of accounts** by selecting only those accounts that apply to the property. Changes can be made to the standardized financial statement formats by simply deleting or adding line items as appropriate. The uniform system of accounts is designed to provide optimum flexibility while remaining consistent with generally accepted accounting principles.

The appendix to this chapter contains a sample chart of accounts for a hotel from *USASH*.

Account Numbering Systems

An account numbering system should reflect the organization of accounts in the company's chart of accounts. Computerized systems require that account numbers be assigned to each account in the chart of accounts. A computer system uses account numbers to identify each account by department and the type of information stored in it. Computerized systems can sort the information stored in accounts according to department and type in order to produce financial statements in the format requested by management.

An account numbering system should be versatile. It should be broad enough to have a major number for each account used in standard reporting, and sufficiently detailed to provide sub-accounts for all areas of significance.

There is no universal account numbering system. An operation can create a numbering system that best fits its needs. The following discussion presents examples of a five-digit system and an eight-digit system.

A Five-Digit Account Numbering System. Small hotels and motels often use a five-digit account numbering system. For instance, an **account number** can be composed of a two-digit prefix representing the department (or the hotel itself), followed by a three-digit account number:

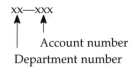

The two-digit department numbers may be assigned as follows:

Hotel, no specific department	00
Rooms	11
Food and beverage	15
Telephone	17
Administrative and general	31
Marketing	36
Property operation and maintenance	38
Energy costs	41
Fixed charges	51

The three-digit portion of the account numbers may be assigned according to account classification as follows:

Asset accounts	100 to 199
Liability accounts	200 to 299
Equity accounts	300 to 399
Revenue accounts	400 to 499
Expense accounts	500 to 799

For example, assume that the Salaries and Wages account number is 600. The Salaries and Wages account number for the food and beverage department would be 15-600.

Assuming the sales account for merchandise or services is 400, then sales for the rooms department, the food and beverage department, and the telephone department would be recorded in the following accounts:

11-400	Room Sales
15-400	Food Sales
17-400	Telephone Sales

Balance sheet accounts (i.e., those in the asset, liability, and equity classifications) are hotel accounts, not department accounts. In this case, the two-digit prefix is 00 for the hotel as a whole. For instance, the following account numbers may be used to represent cash accounts:

00-100	House Bank—Front Office
00-102	House Bank—Food and Beverage
00-103	Regular Checking Account
00-104	Payroll Checking Account

An Eight-Digit Account Numbering System. A five-digit system may not be flexible enough to meet the information needs of a large hotel. In this case, a more sophisticated eight-digit account numbering system may be necessary.

For instance, an eight-digit system can have three sets of numbers representing the department or major balance sheet classification, the major account, and the sub-account:

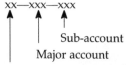

xx—xxx—xxx

Sub-account
Major account
Department number or major balance sheet classification

Exhibit 5　Account Numbers for Sales Accounts

Rooms Department Sales:	
Transient Guests	11-400-001
Permanent Guests	11-400-002
Food and Beverage Department Sales:	
Dining Room	15-400-001
Coffee Shop	15-400-002
Food Sales: Guestrooms	15-400-003
Food Sales: Bar	15-400-004
Telephone Department Sales:	
Local	17-400-001
Long Distance	17-400-002
Service Charges	17-400-003

The first two digits of an eight-digit account number may be based on the departmental assignments previously given for the five-digit account. Assuming that Salaries and Wages is assigned a major account number of 600, the payroll expense for the food and beverage department would have the account number 15-600-xxx. The last three digits of the eight-digit number (shown here as xxx) represent the sub-account number. The payroll expense may be further defined as either regular or vacation payroll by the use of this sub-account number. For example, the payroll account numbers for the food and beverage department may be:

Regular Payroll:	15-600-001
Vacation Payroll:	15-600-002

In this example, the account represented by the number 15-600-002 would be the food and beverage department account (15) for payroll (600); specifically, vacation payroll (002).

Assuming the rooms department is assigned a department number of 11, its payroll account numbers would parallel the payroll accounts for the food and beverage department:

Regular Payroll:	11-600-001
Vacation Payroll:	11-600-002

This numbering system would prevail throughout the revenue and expense classifications. For instance, the major account number 400 may represent sales accounts for various revenue centers. Using the eight-digit numbering system, Exhibit 5 lists possible sales accounts for the revenue centers of rooms, food and beverage, and telephone.

When balance sheet accounts are involved, the eight-digit account numbering system varies somewhat from the five-digit system previously presented. Rather than using 00 to represent a hotel account, the first two digits of an eight-digit number for a balance sheet account may be used to represent the major balance sheet classification, either asset, liability, or equity. It may be made even more detailed to represent a current asset, a fixed asset, a current liability, or any other financial classification management decides is useful for its financial information system.

For example, an account numbering system may assign 01 as the first two digits (major class) representing the current asset accounts. The account numbering system may further assign 010 as the next three digits (major account) representing cash accounts. Under this system, all cash accounts would have the basic format of 01-010-xxx, where xxx represents the specific cash account. For example, the cash accounts may be numbered as follows:

House Bank—Front Office	01-010-001
House Bank—Food and Beverage	01-010-002
Regular Checking Account	01-010-101
Payroll Checking Account	01-010-102

Along these same lines, if the major account number for accounts receivable is 013, then the following accounts may be used to indicate specific types of accounts receivable:

Guest Ledger	01-013-001
City Ledger	01-013-002

The orderly assignment of account numbers helps to ensure compatibility with computer systems. The sample chart of accounts from *USASH* in the chapter appendix presents an example of a detailed five-digit account numbering system.

Designing Financial Statements

The major objective of financial statements is to present management with timely financial information that will be reliable and useful in the decision-making process. To accomplish this objective, the statements should be designed to meet the following requirements:

- The contents are easy to read.

- The information serves the needs of the readers.

- The format is consistent.

- The statements comply with generally accepted accounting principles.

The rest of this chapter describes how to make statements easy to read.

Many bookkeeping **accounts** exist for internal control purposes and for preparing detailed schedules for operations supervisors. Upper and middle managers need statements that summarize the income and expenses of the various departments. Therefore, it is not necessary to present individually all accounts on the financial statements. Many minor accounts may be combined into a single line item by the use of captions.

Exhibit 6   Composition of Employee Benefits

> Payroll Taxes
>
> Employee Group Plans (medical, life, pension, etc.)
>
> Employee Meals
>
> Vacation and Holiday Pay (if separately accounted for)
>
> Workers' Compensation Insurance

Captions

Assume that a general ledger consists of the following cash accounts:

Cash in Bank—Checking Account	$40,000
Change Fund—Front Office	2,000
Change Fund—Restaurant	1,000
Petty Cash Fund—A&G	500
Total	$43,500

The balance sheet could show each of these accounts separately or else could show a single line item to condense the statement's presentation for better readability. For instance, *cash* could simply be shown as a single line item title on the balance sheet as follows:

Cash	$43,500

Captions are line item titles designed to consolidate several bookkeeping accounts, which by themselves are not pertinent to the intended reader. This consolidation of bookkeeping accounts for financial statement purposes is determined during the design phase of the accounting system.

USASH contains a set of suggested formats for financial statements. These statements include captions that represent a number of various accounts in one line item. For example, the captioned line item *Employee Benefits* appears on all departmental statements for areas that have employees. Because labor costs and associated expenses are substantial in the hospitality industry, hospitality professionals should be aware of this important line item. Exhibit 6 shows the different bookkeeping accounts that make up the Employee Benefits caption on a financial statement.

The charges included in the line item Operating Supplies depend on which department the financial statement is for. A department manager should understand the charges that are represented in Operating Supplies. Exhibit 7 shows the kinds of charges represented in this line item for several departments.

Regardless of how well any accounting system or financial statements are designed, there is always a group of miscellaneous bookkeeping accounts that represent small expenditures. Some accountants group these accounts into a single line item called Miscellaneous Expenses. Another name for these expenses is Other Operating Expenses.

Exhibit 7   Composition of Operating Supplies

Operating Supplies—Rooms Department:

Guest Supplies	Cleaning Supplies	Printing and Stationery

Operating Supplies—F&B Department:

Guest Supplies	Bar Supplies	Menus
Printing and Stationery	Cleaning Supplies	Paper Supplies
Utensils		

Operating Supplies—A&G Department:

Printing and Stationery	Office Supplies

Exhibit 8   Composition of Other Operating Expenses

Other Operating Expenses—Rooms Department:

Licenses and Permits	Books for Guest Library	Directories
Firewood for Lobby	Safe-Deposit Box Keys	Decorations

Other Operating Expenses—F&B Department:

Food Inspections	Garbage Cans	Signs

Other Operating Expenses—A&G Department:

Cash Short or Over	Help-Wanted Ads	Contributions
Travel and Entertainment	Safe-Deposit Box Rental	Mail Bags
Credit and Collection Costs	Equipment Storage	Uniforms

The accounts included in the line item Other Operating Expenses depend on which department the financial statement is for. A department manager should understand the charges that are represented in Other Operating Expenses. Exhibit 8 shows the kinds of charges represented in this captioned line item for several departments.

Endnotes

1. This discussion on front office modules is adapted from Michael L. Kasavana and John J. Cahill, *Managing Computers in the Hospitality Industry* (East Lansing, Mich.: Educational Institute of the American Hotel & Motel Association, 1987).

Key Terms

account	chart of accounts
account number	computer program
balance sheet	controlling
caption	data

hardware
income statement
information
leading
modules
operating system

organizing
other operated departments
planning
software
uniform system of accounts

Review Questions

1. What are the four functions in the managerial process? Explain each function.

2. What are the two major categories of software? Describe each category.

3. What is the difference between data and information?

4. What are the four major phases in developing an accounting system? Explain each phase.

5. What are the four classifications of hotel departments? Describe each classification.

6. What is the advantage of a uniform system of accounts?

7. What is the major objective of financial statements?

8. What are four requirements in designing financial statements?

9. What are captions on financial statements?

10. What bookkeeping accounts make up the line item Employee Benefits on any financial statement?

Problems

Problem 1

A small motel has assigned department numbers to its revenue centers as follows:

00	The motel as a whole
10	Rooms department
20	F&B department
49	Rentals and other income

The motel has assigned the following code numbers to its revenue bookkeeping accounts:

300	Rooms Revenue
321	Food Sales
322	Liquor, Wine, and Beer Sales
386	Cash Discounts
387	Interest Income

Complete the journal entries for the following transactions according to this hotel's chart of accounts and in compliance with recommendations of the *Uniform System of Accounts*. Show the account number and account name in the spaces provided.

a. Received interest income of $500.

00-107	Cash—Savings Account	500	
_____	_____		500

b. Billed guest $90 for daily room charge.

00-121	Guest Ledger (Receivable)	90	
_____	_____		90

c. An invoice in the amount of $300 was paid for food purchased for the F&B department. The invoice provided terms of a $6 cash discount. The invoice was timely paid and a check was issued for $294.

20-401	Food Purchases	300	
00-103	Cash—Checking Account		294
_____	_____		6

Problem 2

Design a hotel financial information system similar to that shown in Exhibit 4 in this chapter. Design the system for a small motel that has a rooms operation, housekeeping department, food and beverage operation, telephone service, gift shop operated by the hotel, beauty salon operated by a concessionaire, administrative office, marketing department, and maintenance operation. Like other motels, it incurs energy costs and fixed charges.

Problem 3

A small hotel is designing a five-digit account numbering system.

a. Department numbers will be two digits (xx), based on the following identification system:

Revenue centers will start with 1 (1x).

Support centers will start with 2 (2x).

Energy costs will start with 3 (3x).

Fixed charges will start with 4 (4x).

The first department in a group will use a 1 (x1). A successive department in that group will be incremented by 2. For example, the support center group consists of two departments: A&G and marketing. Support centers are to be represented by 2x; thus A&G will be numbered as 21 and marketing will be numbered as 23.

b. The departmental expenses will consist of three digits and be based on the following identification:

Payroll expenses will consist of 5xx.

Salaries and wages will consist of 51__.

Payroll taxes will consist of 55__.

The first item in an expense group will use a 1 (xx1). A successive expense in that group will be incremented by 1. For example, management salaries for A&G would be coded as 551 and employee wages would be coded as 552.

c. The completed departmental and account number should consist of five digits. For example:

A&G—Management Salaries	21-551
A&G—Employee Wages	21-552

Your Assignment: Design a departmental and account numbering system in a format of xx-xxx for the payroll expense accounts below that may be applicable to any of the following departments:

The revenue centers are:
   Rooms
   F&B
   Schedule of rentals and other income

The support centers are:
   A&G
   Marketing

The payroll expense accounts are:
   Management Salaries
   Employee Wages
   Payroll Tax—FICA
   Payroll Tax—FUTA
   Payroll Tax—SUTA
   Medical Insurance
   Life Insurance
   Employee Meals

Appendix

Sample Chart of Accounts

The following pages present a sample chart of accounts which is intended to be used only as a guide to establishing an accounting system for recording business transactions. No attempt has been made to meet the specific needs of every property. The chart of accounts presented here is sufficiently flexible to allow individual owners or managers to add or delete accounts to meet the individual needs and requirements of their properties.

The sample chart of accounts uses a five-digit numbering system. The first two digits represent a department or cost center, and the last three digits indicate the account number. Suggestions for assigning the first two digits follow:

00   The whole hotel or motel; no specific department

10   Rooms Department as an entity; possible subdivisions include:
12   Front Office
14   Reservations
16   Housekeeping
18   Uniform Service

20   Food and Beverage Department as an entity; possible subdivisions include:
21   Coffee Shop
22   Specialty/Fine Dining Room
23   Banquet
24   Room Service
25   Bar
27   Kitchen
29   Employee Cafeteria

30   Telephone Department

40   Gift Shop

45   Garage and Parking

47   Other Operated Departments

49   Rentals and Other Income

50   Administrative and General as an entity; possible subdivisions include:
51   Accounting
52   Data Processing
54   Human Resources
55   Purchasing
57   Security
59   Transportation

60   Marketing

70   Property Operation and Maintenance

75   Energy Costs

80   Management Fees

85   Fixed Charges

Suggestions for assigning the last three digits follow:

100–199   Assets
200–280   Liabilities
280–299   Equity
300–399   Revenue
400–499   Cost of Sales
500–599   Payroll and Related Expenses
600–699   Other Expenses
700–799   Fixed Charges

Assets

100 Cash
 101 House Funds
 103 Checking Account
 105 Payroll Account
 107 Savings Account
 109 Petty Cash

110 Marketable Securities/Short-Term Investments

120 Accounts Receivable
 121 Guest Ledger
 123 Credit Card Accounts
 125 Direct Bill
 127 Other Accounts Receivable
 128 Intercompany Receivables
 129 Allowance for Doubtful Accounts

130 Notes Receivable
 134 Receivable from Owner
 137 Due from Employees

140 Inventory
 141 Food
 142 Liquor
 143 Wine
 145 Operating Supplies
 146 Paper Supplies
 147 Cleaning Supplies
 149 Other

150 Prepaids
   151 Prepaid Insurance
   152 Prepaid Taxes
   153 Prepaid Workers' Compensation
   155 Prepaid Supplies
   157 Prepaid Contracts
   159 Other Prepaids

160 Noncurrent Receivables

165 Investments (not short-term)

170 Property and Equipment
   171 Land
   172 Buildings
   173 Accumulated Depreciation—Buildings
   174 Leaseholds and Leasehold Improvements
   175 Accumulated Depreciation—Leaseholds
   176 Furniture and Fixtures
   177 Accumulated Depreciation—Furniture and Fixtures
   178 Machinery and Equipment
   179 Accumulated Depreciation—Machinery and Equipment
   180 Data Processing Equipment
   181 Accumulated Depreciation—Data Processing Equipment
   182 Automobiles and Trucks
   183 Accumulated Depreciation—Automobiles and Trucks
   184 Construction in Progress
   185 China
   186 Glassware
   187 Silver
   188 Linen
   189 Uniforms

190 Other Assets
   191 Security Deposits
   192 Preopening Expenses
   194 Deferred Expenses
   196 Cash Surrender Value—Life Insurance
   199 Miscellaneous

Liabilities

200 Payables
   201 Accounts Payable
   205 Dividends Payable
   207 Notes Payable
   209 Intercompany Payables

210 Employee Withholdings
    211 FICA—Employee
    212 State Disability—Employee
    213 SUTA—Employee
    214 Medical Insurance—Employee
    215 Life Insurance—Employee
    216 Dental Insurance—Employee
    217 Credit Union
    218 United Way
    219 Miscellaneous Deductions

220 Employer Payroll Taxes
    221 FICA—Employer
    222 FUTA—Employer
    223 SUTA—Employer
    224 Medical Insurance—Employer
    225 Life Insurance—Employer
    226 Dental Insurance—Employer
    227 Disability—Employer
    228 Workers' Compensation—Employer
    229 Miscellaneous Contributions

230 Taxes
    231 Federal Withholding Tax
    232 State Withholding Tax
    233 County Withholding Tax
    234 City Withholding Tax
    236 Sales Tax
    238 Property Tax
    241 Federal Income Tax
    242 State Income Tax
    244 City Income Tax

255 Advance Deposits

260 Accruals
    261 Accrued Payables
    262 Accrued Utilities
    263 Accrued Vacation
    264 Accrued Taxes
    269 Accrued Expenses—Other
    270 Current Portion—Long-Term Debt
    274 Other Current Liabilities
    275 Long-Term Debt
    278 Capital Leases
    279 Other Long-Term Debt

Equity

For Proprietorships and Partnerships
- 280–287   Owner's or Partners' Capital Accounts
- 290–297   Owner's or Partners' Withdrawal Accounts
- 299   Income Summary

For Corporations
- 280–285   Capital Stock
- 286   Paid-in Capital
- 289   Retained Earnings
- 290–295   Treasury Stock
- 299   Income Summary

Revenue

300 Rooms Revenue
- 301 Transient—Regular
- 302 Transient—Corporate
- 303 Transient—Package
- 304 Transient—Preferred Customer
- 309 Day Use
- 311 Group—Convention
- 312 Group—Tour
- 317 Permanent
- 318 Meeting Room Rental
- 319 Other Room Revenue

320 Food and Beverage Revenue
- 321 Food Sales
- 322 Liquor Sales
- 323 Wine Sales
- 324 Cover Charges
- 325 Miscellaneous Banquet Income
- 326 Service Charges
- 328 Meeting Room Rental
- 329 Other Food and Beverage Revenue

330 Telephone Revenue
- 331 Local Call Revenue
- 332 Long-Distance Call Revenue
- 333 Service Charges
- 335 Commissions
- 336 Pay Station Revenue
- 339 Other Telephone Revenue

340 Gift Shop Revenue

350 Garage and Parking Revenue
   351 Parking and Storage
   352 Merchandise Sales
   359 Other Garage and Parking Revenue

370 Space Rentals
   371 Clubs
   372 Offices
   373 Stores
   379 Other Rental Income

380 Other Income
   381 Concessions
   382 Laundry/Valet Commissions
   383 Games and Vending Machines
   384 In-house Movies
   386 Cash Discounts
   387 Interest Income
   388 Salvage
   389 Other

390 Allowances
   391 Rooms Allowance
   392 Food and Beverage Allowance
   393 Telephone Allowance
   394 Gift Shop Allowance
   395 Garage and Parking Allowance
   399 Other Allowance

Cost of Sales

400 Cost of Food Sales
   401 Food Purchases
   408 Trade Discounts
   409 Transportation Charges

419 Other Cost of Food and Beverage Sales

420 Cost of Beverage Sales
   421 Liquor Purchases
   422 Wine Purchases
   423 Beer Purchases
   424 Other Beverage Purchases
   428 Trade Discounts
   429 Transportation Charges

430 Cost of Telephone Calls
   431 Local Calls
   432 Long-Distance Calls

440 Cost of Gift Shop Sales
    441 Gift Shop Purchases
    448 Trade Discounts
    449 Transportation Charges

450 Cost of Garage and Parking Sales
    451 Garage and Parking Purchases
    458 Trade Discounts
    459 Transportation Charges

490 Cost of Employee Meals

492 Bottle Deposit Refunds

495 Grease and Bone Sales Revenue

496 Empty Bottle/Barrel Sales Revenue

Payroll and Related Expenses

510 Salaries and Wages
    511–519 Departmental Management and Supervisory Staff
    521–539 Departmental Line Employees

550 Payroll Taxes
    551 Payroll Taxes—FICA
    552 Payroll Taxes—FUTA
    553 Payroll Taxes—SUTA
    558 Workers' Compensation

560 Employee Benefits
    561 Vacation, Holiday, and Sick Pay
    564 Medical Insurance
    565 Life Insurance
    566 Dental Insurance
    567 Disability
    569 Employee Meals

599 Payroll Tax and Benefit Allocation

Other Expenses

600 Operating Supplies
    601 Cleaning Supplies
    602 Guest Supplies
    603 Paper Supplies
    604 Postage and Telegrams
    605 Printing and Stationery
    606 Menus
    607 Utensils

610 Linen, China, Glassware, etc.
    611 China
    612 Glassware
    613 Silver
    614 Linen
    618 Uniforms

621 Contract Cleaning Expenses

623 Laundry and Dry Cleaning Expenses

624 Laundry Supplies

625 Licenses

627 Kitchen Fuel

628 Music and Entertainment Expenses

629 Reservations Expense

630 Data Processing Expenses
    631 Hardware Maintenance
    632 Software Maintenance
    635 Service Bureau Fees
    639 Other Data Processing Expenses

640 Human Resource Expenses
    641 Dues and Subscriptions
    642 Employee Housing
    643 Employee Relations
    644 Medical Expenses
    645 Recruitment
    646 Relocation
    647 Training
    648 Transportation

650 Administrative Expenses
    651 Credit Card Commissions
    652 Donations
    653 Insurance—General
    654 Credit and Collections Expense
    655 Professional Fees
    656 Losses and Damages
    657 Provision for Doubtful Accounts
    658 Cash Over/Short
    659 Travel and Entertainment

660 Marketing Expenses
    661 Commissions
    662 Direct Mail Expenses
    663 In-house Graphics

664 Outdoor Advertising
665 Point-of-Sale Materials
666 Print Materials
667 Radio and Television Expenses
668 Selling Aids
669 Franchise Fees

670 Property Operation Expenses
671 Building Supplies
672 Electrical and Mechanical Equipment
673 Elevators
674 Engineering Supplies
675 Furniture, Fixtures, Equipment, and Decor
676 Grounds and Landscaping
677 Painting and Decorating
678 Removal of Waste Matter
679 Swimming Pool Expense

680 Energy Costs
681 Electrical Cost
682 Fuel Cost
686 Steam Cost
687 Water Cost
689 Other Energy Costs

690 Guest Transportation
691 Fuel and Oil
693 Insurance
695 Repairs and Maintenance
699 Other Expense

Fixed Charges

700 Management Fees

710 Rent or Lease Expenses
711 Land
712 Buildings
713 Equipment
714 Telephone Equipment
715 Data Processing Equipment
716 Software (includes any license fees)
717 Vehicles

720 Tax Expense
721 Real Estate Tax
722 Personal Property Taxes
723 Utility Taxes
724 Business and Occupation Taxes

730 Building and Contents Insurance

740 Interest Expense
     741 Mortgage Interest
     742 Notes Payable Interest
     743 Interest on Capital Leases
     744 Amortization of Deferred Financing Costs

750 Depreciation and Amortization
     751 Building and Improvements
     752 Leaseholds and Leasehold Improvements
     753 Furniture and Fixtures
     754 Machinery and Equipment
     755 Data Processing Equipment
     756 Automobiles and Trucks
     757 Capital Leases
     758 Preopening Expenses

770 Gain or Loss on Sale of Property

790 Income Taxes
     791 Current Federal Income Tax
     792 Deferred Federal Income Tax
     795 Current State Income Tax
     796 Deferred State Income Tax

Source: *Uniform System of Accounts and Expense Dictionary for Small Hotels, Motels, and Motor Hotels,* 4th ed. (East Lansing, Mich.: Educational Institute of the American Hotel & Motel Association, 1987), pp. 103–110.

REVIEW QUIZ

When you feel you have covered all of the material in this chapter, answer these questions. Choose the *best* answer. Check your answers with the correct ones found on the Review Quiz Answer Key at the end of this book.

True (T) or False (F)

T   F   1. The management function called directing includes measuring accomplishments against original plans and determining corrective action.

T   F   2. An operating system is necessary for a computer to carry out instructions found in applications software.

T   F   3. The monitor is considered to be the "brain" of a computer system.

T   F   4. In accounting terms, "data" and "information" are synonymous.

Multiple Choice

5. Back office computer applications in a hotel may include all of the following *except:*

   a. accounts receivable.
   b. payroll accounting.
   c. reservations.
   d. check writing.

6. Which phase in the development of an accounting system includes a review of the accuracy and timeliness of the system's reporting?

   a. analysis
   b. design
   c. implementation
   d. follow-up

7. The departmental income statement for rentals and other income includes:

   a. cost of sales information.
   b. payroll expenses.
   c. other direct expenses.
   d. cash discounts earned.

8. Fixed charges may include all of the following *except:*

   a. rent.
   b. electricity.
   c. depreciation.
   d. interest.

9. The first two digits of a five-digit account number may represent:

   a. a captioned account.
   b. a hotel department.
   c. a hotel as a whole.
   d. b and c

10. In an eight-digit account numbering system, the last three digits specify:

    a. a particular department within the hotel.
    b. whether the account is classified as an asset, liability, equity, revenue, or expense account.
    c. a sub-account within a major account.
    d. whether the department is a revenue or support center.

Chapter Outline

Learning Objectives

1. Summarize the purposes and users of a hotel's departmental statements. (p. 125)

2. Differentiate between the general formats for financial statements for revenue and support centers. (pp. 125–126)

3. List the information included in the standard reporting of departmental payroll expenses. (p. 126)

4. Recognize the ways in which financial statements are identified and referenced in relation to other statements. (p. 127)

5. Describe the general formats used for a hotel's departmental financial statements. (pp. 127–131)

6. Explain how information from departmental statements is used to prepare a hotel's income statement. (pp. 131–132)

5

Hotel Departmental Statements

In HOTELS, departmental statements (also called internal financial statements) are an important part of any financial information system. Top managers require statements regarding the property as a whole, and middle and lower managers need detailed information about the departments for which they are responsible.

The purposes of these internal financial statements are to present information for management to monitor the profitability of operations and to be useful for long-range planning. Internal financial statements include numerous **supporting schedules** that provide significant detail about each department's operations and the financial affairs of the company. The appendix to this chapter contains samples of common supporting schedules.

Departmental statements are issued only to internal users, such as top management, department heads, and supervisors. Departmental statements are not issued to external users, such as stockholders, creditors, and potential investors.

The financial statements presented in this chapter follow the *Uniform System of Accounts and Expense Dictionary for Small Hotels, Motels, and Motor Hotels*, 4th ed. The ultimate design and distribution of the internal financial statements used by a company are determined by the implementation of its financial information system and the assignment of responsibility areas.

In discussing hotel departmental statements, this chapter will address such questions as:

1. What is the basic format for a revenue center statement?

2. What is the basic format for a support center statement?

3. Why is the presentation of payroll information standardized for all departmental statements?

4. Which financial statements compose the set of internal financial statements used by management?

5. How is information from the departmental statements used to prepare the hotel's income statement?

Basic Format of Revenue Center Statements

A revenue center generates sales. Revenue centers that sell merchandise have a Cost of Sales account. After all expenses are deducted, the operating result for any revenue center is either departmental income or loss.

125

The basic format of a financial statement for revenue-producing departments is:

$$
\begin{array}{l}
\text{Revenue} \\
-\ \underline{\text{Allowances}} \\
\text{Net revenue} \\
-\ \underline{\text{Cost of sales}} \\
\text{Gross profit} \\
-\ \underline{\text{Expenses}} \\
\text{Departmental income (or loss)}
\end{array}
$$

Basic Format of Support Center Statements

A support center does not generate sales; thus it cannot have a gross profit resulting in departmental income or loss. Therefore, the departmental statement for a support center is a list of the expenses incurred for the period.

Presentation of Payroll Expenses

Because salaries and wages are a significant part of any department's expenses, management requires pertinent information on this important expense. Whether a department is a revenue or support center, the reporting of its payroll expense is standardized as follows:

- Salaries and wages
- Employee benefits
- Total payroll and related expenses

These three lines are included on each departmental statement. Supporting schedules that explain salaries, wages, and benefits are shown in the appendix to this chapter.

Example of Hotel Departmental Statements

A set of departmental statements for the fictitious Hotel DORO is presented in this chapter to serve as an example. These departmental statements are:

- Exhibit 1—Rooms Department Income Statement
- Exhibit 2—Food and Beverage Department Income Statement
- Exhibit 3—Telephone Department Income Statement
- Exhibit 4—Other Operated Departments Income Statement
- Exhibit 5—Schedule of Rentals and Other Income
- Exhibit 6—Administrative and General Department Statement
- Exhibit 7—Marketing Department Statement
- Exhibit 8—Property Operation and Maintenance Department Statement

- Exhibit 9—Schedule of Energy Costs

- Exhibit 10—Schedule of Fixed Charges

Identification and Referencing of Departmental Statements

Each departmental statement contains an identifier in the upper right corner. For example, the identifier for the rooms department income statement (Exhibit 1) is A1. These identifiers are used as references on the hotel's income statement, shown in Exhibit 11. In the operated departments section of this statement, the reference to A1 in the schedule column indicates that the corresponding information came from Schedule A1.

Observe that the Hotel DORO's income statement is identified as Schedule A. This indicates that it is a summary or master statement. The identifier for each supporting statement for Schedule A is preceded by A and followed by the supporting statement's sequential number. Because the statement for the rooms department is the first departmental statement that supports the summary hotel statement, it is assigned the identifier of A1.

Rooms Department Income Statement

Exhibit 1 presents the Hotel DORO's rooms department income statement, which is referenced as Schedule A1. Notice that the rooms department does not have a Cost of Sales account because it does not sell merchandise. (Sales from the honor bar in a guestroom are credited to the food and beverage department.) Since there is no Cost of Sales account, it is not necessary to show a gross profit line.

Some hotel managers prefer to have the rooms department income statement itemize the rooms revenue derived from transient guests, permanent guests, or other designations. The management of the Hotel DORO does not need this itemized information because all the hotel guests are transient.

The net revenue of $897,500 is the result of subtracting the allowances of $2,500 from the total billings of $900,000. The total payroll and related expenses of $143,140 represent the salaries and wages of $120,000 plus the employee benefits of $23,140. The total other expenses of $62,099 are arrived at by adding all the items listed under other expenses; from commissions down to other operating expenses in this case. The total expenses of $205,239 are arrived at by adding the total payroll and related expenses of $143,140 to the total other expenses of $62,099. *(Because the procedures explained above are similar for all departments, they will not be repeated in the analyses of the rest of the financial statements for the Hotel DORO in this chapter.)*

The departmental income (loss) of $692,261 is arrived at by subtracting the total expenses of $205,239 from the net revenue of $897,500. The amount of $692,261 is interpreted as departmental income because the amount is not enclosed in parentheses. *The departmental income (loss) line demonstrates an "accounting shorthand" labeling technique. The number on this line will be shown without any mathematical sign if the result is income; the number on this line will be shown in parentheses if the result is a loss.*

Food and Beverage Department Income Statement

Exhibit 2 presents the Hotel DORO's food and beverage department income statement, identified as Schedule A2. Notice that sales are shown for food, beverage, and "other." The other sales represent sales of souvenirs, postcards, candy, popcorn, and other nonvending-machine sales in the restaurant and lounge.

The Hotel DORO uses the periodic inventory accounting method to compute cost of sales. A supporting schedule detailing the food and beverage inventory activities would be attached to the department income statement. For example, the cost of food sales supporting schedule could appear as follows:

Hotel Doro, Inc.
Cost of Food Sales Supporting Schedule
For the year ended December 31, 19X2   Schedule A2.1

	Beginning inventory	$ 5,800
+	Purchases	145,600
	Cost of food available	$151,400
−	Ending inventory	7,000
	Cost of food consumed	$144,400
−	Employee meals credit	9,200
	Cost of food sales	$135,200

Observe that the food and beverage department income statement repeats the last three lines from the cost of food sales supporting schedule A2.1: the cost of goods consumed of $144,400 and the cost of all employee meals of $9,200 subtracted from the cost of goods consumed to arrive at the $135,200 cost of sales.

Net other income of $3,800 is the result of other revenue of $6,400 less its respective cost of sales of $2,600.

The gross profit of $346,260 is arrived at by subtracting the $175,710 food and beverage cost of sales from the food and beverage net revenue of $518,170 and adding net other income of $3,800. The total expenses of $258,883 are subtracted from the gross profit of $346,260 to arrive at the **departmental income** of $87,377.

Telephone Department Income Statement

Exhibit 3 presents the Hotel DORO's telephone department income statement, identified as Schedule A3. There are several methods of accounting for the revenue and expenses of a hotel's telephone service.

With today's sophisticated computerized accounting systems, the telephone service for guests and for various hotel departments can be reported separately. Each department can be charged for its telephone usage, which would appear on each department's statement. The revenue and expenses pertaining to guests would be the only items appearing on the telephone department statement. An advantage of this accounting method is that it provides a means to evaluate the telephone department as a profit-making center.

The Hotel DORO has selected a different alternative. While the telephone department is a revenue center because it generates sales, management prefers to show all the expenses for telephone usage by guests and by all departments of the hotel on this departmental statement. Therefore, this statement shows 100% of the costs of the telephone system and costs for the hotel as a whole.

Management's philosophy is that the revenue from guests helps to defray the costs of the hotel's total telephone service. While Schedule A3 may appear to show a loss, management would instead interpret the results as follows: *The net cost of the total telephone service for the hotel was $27,623 for the year.*

In the body of the statement, the line item gross profit (loss) shows a loss of $8,904, indicated by the parentheses. This gross loss occurred because the cost of calls expense of $60,044 exceeded the net revenue of $51,140. Remember that this is not unusual for the Hotel DORO because the cost of calls includes the telephone usage of the guests and all departments of the hotel.

Because the $8,904 is a loss, it has the same effect as an expense; additional expenses of $18,719 increase the final loss to $27,623 for the year. This final loss is shown in parentheses on the departmental income (loss) line.

Other Operated Departments Income Statement

Exhibit 4 presents the Hotel DORO's **other operated departments** income statement, identified as Schedule A4. The format and line items on this schedule may vary according to the different kinds of goods and services sold to guests, such as items from the gift shop, apparel shop, or package store, recreation, and garage and parking (if guests are charged). Each operated department may be shown separately on its dedicated departmental statement so that each can be evaluated independently.

The Hotel DORO is a small hotel with minor sales from each of its other operated departments. Instead of having a report for each area, management has decided to combine all these reports into one statement until one or more individual departments have significant sales volume.

Schedule of Rentals and Other Income

Exhibit 5 presents the Hotel DORO's schedule of rentals and other income, identified as Schedule A5. This schedule reports revenue that is not attributable to any other revenue center. The schedule lists revenue from such sources as:

- Interest income

- Dividend income

- Rentals of store and office space

- Concessions income

- Commissions

- Vending machine profits (if owned)

- Cash discounts earned

- Salvage income

Minor gains or losses from the sale of fixed assets could also appear on this schedule. The Hotel DORO's management prefers that such gains or losses appear as a separate line item on the hotel's income statement.

Administrative and General Department Statement

Exhibit 6 presents the Hotel DORO's administrative and general (A&G) department statement, identified as Schedule A6. The statement for any support center does not include sections for sales or cost of sales because support centers do not generate revenue by the sales of services or merchandise.

The management of the Hotel DORO includes the following support services in the A&G department:

- General manager and staff
- Accounting
- Human resources
- Data processing

Some hotels prefer to have separate reports for each of these areas, especially human resources and data processing services.

Marketing Department Statement

Exhibit 7 presents the Hotel DORO's marketing department statement, identified as Schedule A7. Costs associated with advertising, public relations, and research are shown on this statement.

Property Operation and Maintenance Department Statement

Exhibit 8 presents the Hotel DORO's property operation and maintenance department statement, identified as Schedule A8. This statement shows all maintenance and repair expenses for the equipment for all departments, grounds, and buildings of the hotel.

Schedule of Energy Costs

Exhibit 9 presents the Hotel DORO's schedule of energy costs, identified as Schedule A9. This statement reports the expenses for electricity, fuel, and water used by all departments of the hotel. However, energy costs associated with the cooking of food are shown on the food and beverage departmental income statement.

Schedule of Fixed Charges

Exhibit 10 presents the Hotel DORO's schedule of fixed charges, identified as Schedule A10. These expenses are important because they are incurred regardless of sales volume, even if the hotel is closed. Another characteristic of these fixed charges is that they benefit the hotel as a whole, not any specific department. Notice that the fixed charges are classified into six major areas:

- Rent
- Property taxes

- Property insurance
- Interest expense
- Depreciation
- Amortization

Income Statement

All the results of the revenue centers, support centers, energy costs, and fixed charges are consolidated into one statement called the income statement. Information from each departmental statement is brought forward to prepare this statement. Departmental managers do not receive this statement; it is issued to top management and the board of directors.

Exhibit 11 presents the income statement for the Hotel DORO, identified as Schedule A, which indicates that it is a master schedule. The format illustrated is the long-form income statement.

The operated departments section includes information from the statements of each revenue center as indicated by the references shown in the schedule column. The information brought forward from the departmental statements is as follows:

- Net revenue
- Cost of sales
- Payroll and related expenses
- Total other expenses
- Departmental income (loss)

Refer to each departmental statement in Exhibits 1 through 10, and trace the amounts that were brought forward to this master statement. Keep in mind the following points:

- The total expenses should not be brought forward to the other expenses column. Rather, this column is the total of expenses exclusive of payroll and related expenses.
- The net revenue for the food and beverage department is computed from Schedule A2 as follows:

Food net revenue	$358,300
Beverage net revenue	+ 159,870
Other revenue	+ 6,400
Total net revenue	$524,570

- The cost of sales for the food and beverage department is computed from Schedule A2 as follows:

Food cost of sales	$135,200
Beverage cost of sales	+ 40,510
Other cost of sales	+ 2,600
Total cost of sales	$178,310

The undistributed expenses represent the expenses of the support centers and energy costs. The total expenses of these areas are entered under the income (loss) column for presentation purposes. These numbers are not to be interpreted as losses; they are expenses that will be deducted from income.

The income before fixed charges of $485,029 is arrived at by subtracting the total undistributed expenses of $340,915 from the total operating income of the revenue centers of $825,944.

The information for the fixed charges section comes from the schedule of fixed charges. The expenses for depreciation and amortization have been combined because both of these expenses are "noncash" expenses; that is, while they are a deduction from income, they did not and will not require any payment of cash.

The income before income taxes of $66,138 is the result of subtracting the total fixed charges of $418,891 from the income before fixed charges of $485,029.

Exhibit 11 is not a fully completed income statement for the Hotel DORO. Income taxes that are a hotel expense have not yet been entered. Also, there may be gains or losses from the sale of assets. The emphasis in this chapter has been on individual departments and not the hotel as a whole.

Exhibit 1   Rooms Department Income Statement—Hotel DORO

Hotel DORO, Inc.
Rooms Department Income Statement
For the year ended December 31, 19X2   Schedule A1

Revenue			
Lodging		$900,000	
Allowances		2,500	
Net Revenue			$897,500
Expenses			
Salaries and Wages	$120,000		
Employee Benefits	23,140		
Total Payroll and Related Expenses		143,140	
Other Expenses			
Commissions	2,500		
Contract Cleaning	5,285		
Guest Transportation	10,100		
Laundry and Dry Cleaning	7,000		
Linen	11,000		
Operating Supplies	11,125		
Reservation Expense	9,950		
Uniforms	2,167		
Other Operating Expenses	2,972		
Total Other Expenses		62,099	
Total Expenses			205,239
Departmental Income (Loss)			$692,261

Exhibit 2   Food and Beverage Department Income Statement—Hotel DORO

Hotel DORO, Inc.
Food and Beverage Department Income Statement
For the year ended December 31, 19X2   **Schedule A2**

	Food	Beverage	Total
Revenue	$360,000	$160,000	$520,000
Allowances	1,700	130	1,830
Net Revenue	358,300	159,870	518,170
Cost of Food and Beverage Sales			
Cost of Food and Beverage Consumed	144,400	40,510	184,910
Less Cost of Employees' Meals	9,200		9,200
Net Cost of Food and Beverage Sales	135,200	40,510	175,710
Other Income			
Other Revenue			6,400
Other Cost of Sales			2,600
Net Other Income			3,800
Gross Profit			
Expenses			
Salaries and Wages	177,214		
Employee Benefits	26,966		
Total Payroll and Related Expenses		204,180	
Other Expenses			
China, Glassware, and Silver	7,779		
Contract Cleaning	3,630		
Kitchen Fuel	2,074		
Laundry and Dry Cleaning	5,182		
Licenses	800		
Music and Entertainment	16,594		
Operating Supplies	11,409		
Uniforms	2,568		
Other Operating Expenses	4,667		
Total Other Expenses		54,703	
Total Expenses			258,883
Departmental Income (Loss)			$ 87,377

Exhibit 3   Telephone Department Income Statement—Hotel DORO

<table>
<tr><td colspan="3" align="center">Hotel DORO, Inc.
Telephone Department Income Statement
For the year ended December 31, 19X2</td><td>Schedule A3</td></tr>
<tr><td colspan="4"> </td></tr>
<tr><td colspan="4">**Revenue**</td></tr>
<tr><td>Local</td><td></td><td>$ 9,470</td><td></td></tr>
<tr><td>Long Distance</td><td></td><td>41,011</td><td></td></tr>
<tr><td>Service Charges</td><td></td><td>514</td><td></td></tr>
<tr><td>Total Revenue</td><td></td><td>51,265</td><td></td></tr>
<tr><td>Allowances</td><td></td><td>125</td><td></td></tr>
<tr><td>Net Revenue</td><td></td><td></td><td>$ 51,140</td></tr>
<tr><td colspan="4">**Cost of Calls**</td></tr>
<tr><td>Local</td><td></td><td>8,660</td><td></td></tr>
<tr><td>Long Distance</td><td></td><td>51,384</td><td></td></tr>
<tr><td>Total Cost of Calls</td><td></td><td></td><td>$ 60,044</td></tr>
<tr><td>**Gross Profit (Loss)**</td><td></td><td></td><td>(8,904)</td></tr>
<tr><td colspan="4">**Expenses**</td></tr>
<tr><td>Salaries and Wages</td><td></td><td>14,831</td><td></td></tr>
<tr><td>Employee Benefits</td><td></td><td>2,301</td><td></td></tr>
<tr><td>Total Payroll and Related Expenses</td><td></td><td>17,132</td><td></td></tr>
<tr><td>Other Operating Expenses</td><td></td><td>1,587</td><td></td></tr>
<tr><td>**Total Expenses**</td><td></td><td></td><td>18,719</td></tr>
<tr><td>**Departmental Income (Loss)**</td><td></td><td></td><td>$(27,623)</td></tr>
</table>

Exhibit 4   Other Operated Departments Income Statement—Hotel DORO

<table>
<tr><td colspan="3" align="center">Hotel DORO, Inc.
Other Operated Departments Income Statement
For the year ended December 31, 19X2</td><td>Schedule A4</td></tr>
<tr><td colspan="4"> </td></tr>
<tr><td colspan="4">**Revenue**</td></tr>
<tr><td>Services</td><td></td><td>$40,005</td><td></td></tr>
<tr><td>Sales of Merchandise</td><td></td><td>22,995</td><td></td></tr>
<tr><td>Net Revenue</td><td></td><td></td><td>$63,000</td></tr>
<tr><td>**Cost of Merchandise Sold**</td><td></td><td></td><td>10,347</td></tr>
<tr><td>**Gross Profit**</td><td></td><td></td><td>52,653</td></tr>
<tr><td colspan="4">**Expenses**</td></tr>
<tr><td>Salaries and Wages</td><td></td><td>30,164</td><td></td></tr>
<tr><td>Employee Benefits</td><td></td><td>3,112</td><td></td></tr>
<tr><td>Total Payroll and Related Expenses</td><td></td><td>33,276</td><td></td></tr>
<tr><td>Other Operating Expenses</td><td></td><td>6,731</td><td></td></tr>
<tr><td>**Total Expenses**</td><td></td><td></td><td>40,007</td></tr>
<tr><td>**Departmental Income (Loss)**</td><td></td><td></td><td>$12,646</td></tr>
</table>

Exhibit 5   Schedule of Rentals and Other Income—Hotel DORO

Hotel DORO, Inc.		
Schedule of Rentals and Other Income		
For the year ended December 31, 19X2		**Schedule A5**
Space Rentals		
Stores	$25,474	
Offices	16,723	
Total Rental Income		$42,197
Concessions Income		9,862
Commissions		
Laundry	1,814	
Valet	1,017	
Vending Machines	1,265	
Total Commissions Income		4,096
Cash Discounts Earned		3,200
Interest Income		1,928
Total Rentals and Other Income		$61,283

Exhibit 6   Administrative and General Department Statement—Hotel DORO

Hotel DORO, Inc.		
Administrative and General Department Statement		
For the year ended December 31, 19X2		**Schedule A6**
Salaries and Wages	$85,718	
Employee Benefits	11,914	
Total Payroll and Related Expenses		$ 97,632
Other Expenses		
Credit Card Commissions	14,389	
Data Processing Expense	7,638	
Dues and Subscriptions	3,265	
Human Resources Expense	3,743	
Insurance—General	6,614	
Operating Supplies	9,784	
Postage and Telegrams	4,416	
Professional Fees	4,136	
Uncollectible Accounts	1,291	
Traveling and Entertainment	4,250	
Other Operating Expenses	7,023	
Total Other Expenses		66,549
Total Administrative and General Expenses		$164,181

Exhibit 7   Marketing Department Statement—Hotel DORO

Hotel DORO, Inc.
Marketing Department Statement
For the year ended December 31, 19X2   **Schedule A7**

Salaries and Wages	$31,418	
Employee Benefits	4,407	
Total Payroll and Related Expenses		$35,825
Advertising		
Outdoor	600	
Print	11,560	
Radio and Television	2,800	
Other	700	
Total Advertising		15,660
Fees and Commissions		
Agency Fees	1,500	
Franchise Fees	11,250	
Total Fees and Commissions		12,750
Other Operating Expenses		3,633
Total Marketing Expense		$67,868

Exhibit 8   Property Operation and Maintenance Department Statement—Hotel DORO

Hotel DORO, Inc.
Property Operation and Maintenance Department Statement
For the year ended December 31, 19X2   **Schedule A8**

Salaries and Wages	$32,412	
Employee Benefits	4,505	
Total Payroll and Related Expenses		$36,917
Other Expenses		
Building Supplies	2,816	
Electrical and Mechanical Equipment	5,013	
Engineering Supplies	1,612	
Furniture, Fixtures, Equipment, and Decor	4,811	
Grounds and Landscaping	3,914	
Operating Supplies	1,018	
Removal of Waste Matter	2,416	
Swimming Pool	1,800	
Uniforms	137	
Other Operating Expenses	1,100	
Total Other Expenses		24,637
Total Property Operation and Maintenance		$61,554

Exhibit 9   Schedule of Energy Costs—Hotel DORO

Hotel DORO, Inc.
Schedule of Energy Costs
For the year ended December 31, 19X2   **Schedule A9**

Electric	$32,172
Fuel	10,509
Water	4,631
Total Energy Costs	**$47,312**

Exhibit 10   Schedule of Fixed Charges—Hotel DORO

Hotel DORO, Inc.
Schedule of Fixed Charges
For the year ended December 31, 19X2   **Schedule A10**

Rent		
Real Estate	$12,000	
Furnishings, Fixtures, and Equipment	7,500	
Data Processing Equipment	9,000	
Total Rent Expense		$ 28,500
Property Taxes and Other Municipal Charges		
Real Estate Taxes	35,762	
Personal Property Taxes	7,312	
Utility Taxes	750	
Business and Occupation Taxes	1,500	
Total Property Taxes and Other Municipal Charges		45,324
Insurance on Building and Contents		6,914
Interest Expense		194,153
Depreciation		
Buildings and Improvements	87,500	
Furnishings, Fixtures, and Equipment	56,000	
Total Depreciation Expense		143,500
Amortization		
Leasehold Improvements	1,000	
Preopening Expenses	1,500	
Total Amortization Expense		2,500
Total Fixed Charges		**$418,891**

Exhibit 11   Long-Form Income Statement—Hotel DORO

Hotel DORO, Inc.
Statement of Income
For the year ended December 31, 19X2   Schedule A

	Schedule	Net Revenue	Cost of Sales	Payroll and Related Expenses	Other Expenses	Income (Loss)
Operated Departments						
Rooms	A1	$ 897,500		$143,140	$ 62,099	$692,261
Food and Beverage	A2	524,570	$178,310	204,180	54,703	87,377
Telephone	A3	51,140	60,044	17,132	1,587	(27,623)
Other Operated Departments	A4	63,000	10,347	33,276	6,731	12,646
Rentals and Other Income	A5	61,283				61,283
Total Operated Departments		1,597,493	248,701	397,728	125,120	825,944
Undistributed Expenses						
Administrative and General	A6			97,632	66,549	164,181
Marketing	A7			35,825	32,043	67,868
Property Operation and Maintenance	A8			36,917	24,637	61,554
Energy Costs	A9				47,312	47,312
Total Undistributed Expenses				170,374	170,541	340,915
Income Before Fixed Charges		$1,597,493	$248,701	$568,102	$295,661	$485,029
Fixed Charges						
Rent	A10					28,500
Property Taxes	A10					45,324
Insurance	A10					6,914
Interest	A10					192,153
Depreciation and Amortization	A10					146,000
Total Fixed Charges						418,891
Income Before Income Taxes						66,138

Key Terms

departmental income
other operated departments
supporting schedules

Review Questions

1. Specify whether the following items are presented on the hotel income statement as Operated Departments, Undistributed Expenses, or Fixed Charges.

    a. Real Estate Rent Expense

    b. Administrative and General Department

    c. Depreciation

    d. Rentals and Other Income

    e. Food and Beverage Department

  f. Mortgage Interest Expense

  g. Telephone Department

2. How is net revenue computed on a departmental income statement?

3. How is gross profit computed on a departmental income statement?

4. What items are included as Total Payroll and Related Expenses on a departmental statement?

5. Which statement reports the revenue for vending machine sales of cigarettes in a public lobby?

6. What is the purpose of supporting schedules? Name some of these.

Problems

Problem 1

All of the problems in this section are based on the fictional Village Hotel, Inc. The following information summarizes various general ledger accounts of the Village Hotel for the year ended December 31, 19X9. Prepare the departmental statements for this hotel, and save these results for the preparation of the hotel income statement in several formats.

Prepare all the statements in accordance with the formats shown for the Hotel DORO's financial statements. *Any account information relating to employee benefits is to be consolidated and shown under the caption called Employee Benefits.*

1. Rooms Department:

	debit	credit
Room Sales		1,043,900
Allowances	2,700	
Salaries and Wages	159,304	
Payroll Taxes	18,716	
Employee Meals	3,450	
Other Employee Benefits	3,864	
Commissions	4,124	
Contract Cleaning	13,200	
Guest Transportation	12,494	
Laundry and Dry Cleaning	11,706	
Linen	7,742	
Operating Supplies	12,619	
Reservation Expense	7,288	
Uniforms	3,032	
Other Operating Expenses	6,875	

2. Food and Beverage Department:

	debit	credit
Food Sales		442,471
Beverage Sales		183,929

	debit	credit
Allowances—Food	600	
Allowances—Beverage	63	
Other Sales		1,070
Cost of Food Consumed	177,873	
Employee Meals Credit		12,832
Cost of Beverage Sales	43,407	
Other Cost of Sales	642	
Salaries and Wages	182,214	
Payroll Taxes	21,866	
Employee Meals	6,890	
Other Employee Benefits	7,562	
China, Glassware, and Silver	8,766	
Contract Cleaning	4,000	
Kitchen Fuel	2,505	
Laundry and Dry Cleaning	6,199	
Licenses	3,130	
Music and Entertainment	31,308	
Operating Supplies	12,523	
Uniforms	3,757	
Other Operating Expenses	7,271	

3. Telephone Department:

	debit	credit
Local		4,783
Long Distance		47,228
Service Charges		389
Allowances	372	
Local	4,587	
Long Distance	41,918	
Salaries and Wages	12,307	
Payroll Taxes	1,580	
Employee Meals	130	
Other Employee Benefits	300	
Other Operating Expenses	6,816	

4. Rentals and Other Income:

	debit	credit
Commissions: Vending Machines		1,500
Cash Discounts Earned		2,700
Interest Income		800

5. Administrative and General Department:

	debit	credit
Salaries and Wages	96,997	

	debit	credit
Payroll Taxes	8,719	
Employee Meals	1,259	
Other Employee Benefits	3,500	
Credit Card Commissions	11,330	
Data Processing Expense	6,400	
Dues and Subscriptions	1,200	
Human Resources Expense	1,000	
Insurance—General	6,817	
Operating Supplies	7,805	
Postage and Telegrams	3,203	
Professional Fees	4,000	
Uncollectible Accounts	1,432	
Traveling and Entertainment	2,000	
Other Operating Expenses	3,022	

6. Marketing Department:

	debit	credit
Salaries and Wages	22,420	
Payroll Taxes	2,690	
Employee Meals	769	
Other Employee Benefits	1,121	
Outdoor Advertising	500	
Print Advertising	3,500	
Radio and Television Advertising	1,800	
Other Advertising	288	
Agency Fees	1,200	
Franchise Fees	10,500	
Other Operating Expenses	3,421	

7. Property Operation and Maintenance Department:

	debit	credit
Salaries and Wages	27,790	
Payroll Taxes	3,335	
Employee Meals	334	
Other Employee Benefits	193	
Building Supplies	9,251	
Electrical and Mechanical Equipment	16,243	
Engineering Supplies	2,311	
Furniture, Fixtures, Equipment, and Decor	14,177	
Grounds and Landscaping	4,414	
Operating Supplies	2,749	
Removal of Waste Matter	2,499	
Swimming Pool	2,500	

	debit	credit
Uniforms	500	
Other Operating Expenses	2,000	

8. Energy Costs:

	debit	credit
Electric	29,012	
Fuel	44,638	
Water	7,770	

9. Fixed Charges:

	debit	credit
Rental Expense Accounts:		
Real Estate	100,225	
Furnishings, Fixtures, and Equipment	17,000	
Data Processing Equipment	18,000	
Real Estate Taxes	44,950	
Personal Property Taxes	8,650	
Utility Taxes	850	
Business and Occupation Taxes	1,200	
Insurance on Building and Contents	9,986	
Interest Expense (Notes Payable)	52,148	
Depreciation Accounts:		
Furnishings, Fixtures, and Equipment	85,272	
Amortization Accounts:		
Leasehold Improvements	30,588	

Problem 2

Using the departmental statements from Problem 1, prepare the preliminary statement of income for the Village Hotel. For your convenience, the following checkpoint amount is provided: The income before income taxes for the hotel is $140,424.

Problem 3

Management has requested an analysis of the employee meals expense for the Village Hotel. Prepare a supporting schedule showing the cost of employee meals for each department. For your convenience, the following checkpoint amount is provided: The total on this schedule must agree with the employee meals credit of $12,832 that appears on the food and beverage department income statement prepared in Problem 1.

Problem 4

Management has requested an analysis of the cost of food sold for the Village Hotel. Prepare a supporting schedule showing the cost of food sold. For your convenience, the following checkpoint amount is provided: The total on this schedule must agree with the $165,041 cost of food sales amount that appears on the food and beverage department income statement prepared in Problem 1.

Information from the following partial section of a worksheet is necessary for you to complete the supporting schedule in this problem:

| | Income Statement | | Balance Sheet | |
	debit	credit	debit	credit
Food Inventory			6,825	
Income Summary	5,570	6,825		
Food Purchases	179,128			
Employee Meals Credit		12,832		

Chapter Appendix ────────────────────────────────

This appendix contains samples of supporting schedules that accompany departmental statements. The purpose of these supporting schedules is to provide detailed information about certain line items on the statements. Supporting schedules help keep the departmental statements compact and easy to read. A company's executives and managers refer to the supporting schedules when they are interested in more detail than is found on the financial statements.

The samples shown in this appendix may be modified depending on the needs and requirements of individual properties. These schedules are not connected with the statements of the Hotel DORO presented in this chapter.

Salaries and Wages—Schedule 16

	Current Period	
	Number of Employees	Amount
Rooms		
Management		$
Front Office		
Housekeeping		
Service		
Security		
Total (Schedule 1)		$
Food and Beverage		
Management		$
Kitchen		
Service		
Other		
Total (Schedule 2)		$
Telephone (Schedule 3)		$
Gift Shop (Schedule 4)		$
Garage and Parking (Schedule 5)		$
Other Operated Departments (Schedule _)		$
Administrative and General		
Manager's Office		$
Accounting Office		
Credit Office		
Front Office Bookkeeping		
Night Auditors		
Receiving Clerks		
Timekeepers		
Total (Schedule 7)		$
Data Processing (Schedule 8)		$
Human Resources (Schedule 9)		$
Transportation (Schedule 10)		$
Marketing (Schedule 11)		$
Property Operation and Maintenance		
Management		$
Engineers		
Grounds		
Office and Storeroom		
Other		
Total (Schedule 12)		$
House Laundry		
Managers and Assistants		$
Finishing		
Washing		
Other		
Total (Schedule 18)		$
Total Salaries and Wages		$

Source: *Uniform System of Accounts and Expense Dictionary for Small Hotels, Motels, and Motor Hotels,* 4th ed. (East Lansing, Mich.: Educational Institute of the American Hotel & Motel Association, 1987), p. 74.

Payroll Taxes and Employee Benefits—Schedule 17

	Current Period
Payroll Taxes	
Federal Retirement	$
Federal Unemployment	
State Unemployment	
Total Payroll Taxes	———
Employee Benefits	
Nonunion Insurance	
Nonunion Pension	
Profit Sharing	
Union Insurance	
Union Pension	
Workers' Compensation Insurance	
Other	
Total Employee Benefits	———
Total Payroll Taxes and Employee Benefits	$———
Charged to Departments	
Rooms	Schedule 1	$
Food and Beverage	Schedule 2
Telephone	Schedule 3
Gift Shop	Schedule 4
Garage and Parking	Schedule 5
Other Operated Departments	Schedule _
Administrative and General	Schedule 7
Data Processing	Schedule 8
Human Resources	Schedule 9
Transportation	Schedule 10
Marketing	Schedule 11
Property Operation and Maintenance	Schedule 12
House Laundry	Schedule 18
Total Payroll Taxes and Employee Benefits		$———

Source: *Uniform System of Accounts and Expense Dictionary for Small Hotels, Motels, and Motor Hotels,* 4th ed. (East Lansing, Mich.: Educational Institute of the American Hotel & Motel Association, 1987), p. 79.

Income Taxes—Schedule 15

	Current Period
Federal	
Current	$
Deferred	
Total	———
State	
Current	
Deferred	
Total	———
Other	
Current	
Deferred	
Total	———
Total Federal and State Income Taxes	$———

Source: *Uniform System of Accounts and Expense Dictionary for Small Hotels, Motels, and Motor Hotels,* 4th ed. (East Lansing, Mich.: Educational Institute of the American Hotel & Motel Association, 1987), p. 73.

REVIEW QUIZ

When you feel you have covered all of the material in this chapter, answer these questions. Choose the *best* answer. Check your answers with the correct ones found on the Review Quiz Answer Key at the end of this book.

True (T) or False (F)

T   F   1.   A hotel's departmental financial statements are issued to internal and external users.

T   F   2.   The departmental statement for a hotel support center is a list of the expenses incurred for the period.

T   F   3.   The reporting of payroll expenses on a revenue center statement differs from that on a support center statement.

T   F   4.   The overall income statement for a hotel is issued to department managers, top managers, and the board of directors.

Multiple Choice

5.   A support center:

   a.   generates sales.
   b.   does *not* generate sales.
   c.   always shows a gross profit.
   d.   a and c

6.   The standardized reporting of a department's payroll expenses includes all of the following *except:*

   a.   salaries.
   b.   wages.
   c.   employee meals.
   d.   employee benefits.

7.   A hotel's schedule of rentals and other income includes revenue from which of the following?

   a.   interest income
   b.   data processing
   c.   guest telephone calls
   d.   b and c

8.   Costs associated with advertising, public relations, and research are shown on which statement?

   a.   administrative and general department
   b.   marketing department
   c.   profit-making evaluation
   d.   data processing department

9.   Energy costs associated with the cooking of food are shown on the:

   a.   schedule of energy costs.
   b.   schedule of fixed charges.
   c.   cost of sales report.
   d.   food and beverage department income statement.

10.   Which of the following is true of fixed charges?

   a.   They are incurred regardless of sales volume.
   b.   They are incurred even if a hotel is closed.
   c.   They benefit a hotel as a whole.
   d.   All of the above

Chapter Outline

The Fair Labor Standards Act (FLSA)
    Computing Time Worked
    Recording Time Worked
The Employer/Employee Relationship
Wages and Salaries
    Gross Pay and Net Pay
    Regular Pay and Overtime Pay
    Calculating Overtime Pay
Payroll Deductions
    Governmental Deductions
    Voluntary Deductions
    Federal Insurance Contributions Act
      (FICA)
    FICA Tax
    Federal Income Tax (FIT)
    State and City Income Tax
    State Temporary Disability Benefit
      Laws
Employer's Payroll Taxes
    Social Security Taxes
    IRS Form 941
    Unemployment Taxes
    IRS Form 940
    Depositing Payroll Taxes
The Payroll System
    Employee's Earnings Record
    Payroll Register
    Payroll Journal Entries
    Payroll Bank Account
    Computerized Payroll Applications
Payroll Accounting for Tipped Employees
    Service Charges
    Employee Tip Reporting
    FLSA Minimum Wage Rate
    Training Wage
    FLSA Tip Credit
    Net Pay of Tipped Employees
    State Wage and Tip Credit Provisions
    Overtime Pay of Tipped Employees
The 8% Tip Regulation
    Operations Affected by the 8% Tip
      Regulation
Tip Shortfall Allocation Methods
    Gross Receipts Method
    Hours Worked Method

Learning Objectives

1. Describe areas covered under the Fair Labor Standards Act (FLSA) including how time worked is computed and recorded. (pp. 152–154)

2. Define the terms "employer" and "employee." (pp. 154–155)

3. Differentiate the following sets of terms: wages and salaries; gross pay and net pay; and regular pay and overtime pay. (pp. 155–158)

4. Describe two methods of calculating overtime pay. (pp. 158–159)

5. Explain the major types of deductions affecting employee payroll. (pp. 159–163)

6. Describe the payroll taxes imposed on employers and the related forms and procedures. (pp. 163–165)

7. Explain the primary function of a payroll system and some of the forms, records, and procedures required to perform this function. (pp. 165–168)

8. Describe payroll accounting for tipped employees with respect to employee tip reporting, minimum wage, tip credit, net pay, and overtime pay. (pp. 168–174)

9. Explain the purpose of the 8% tip regulation and its relationship to employee tip reporting. (pp. 174–179)

10. Recognize methods of allocating tip shortfall among directly tipped employees. (pp. 179–182)

Hospitality Payroll Accounting

PAYROLL IS A SIGNIFICANT EXPENSE in a hotel's budget. However, salaries and wages are not the only costs of labor. When measuring the impact of labor costs, there are the additional expenses of payroll taxes and employee benefits. Because total labor costs are the largest single cost in hotel operations, they are a major concern of management and a first choice for cost cutting. However, cutting labor costs may prove self-defeating since a hotel is highly service-intensive. For example, a reduction in staff may produce poor service, which may lead to guest dissatisfaction, lost business, and a bad reputation.

Anyone responsible for personnel functions and/or payroll preparation should be knowledgeable about the most current employment and payroll laws and regulations—federal, state, and, in some cases, local. It is possible for federal and state payroll regulations to differ on the same issue. In this event, as a general rule, the employer must apply those standards, federal or state, that are the most beneficial to the employee. The issue is further complicated by contract law, such as union-negotiated rights. Contract rights prevail over federal and state laws if their provisions are more beneficial to the employee.

Maintaining a current knowledge of these laws is a never-ending effort. Significant changes may occur regarding minimum wages, income tax rates, Social Security taxes, and employment rights. These changes are regulated by both federal and state governments. In addition, certain cities have income tax withholding laws. Violations of payroll laws or labor regulations may bring civil and/or criminal penalties.

This chapter will discuss payroll accounting by addressing such questions as:

1. What are the major federal and state payroll laws?

2. How are weekly wages and annual salaries converted to an hourly rate?

3. How are governmental and voluntary deductions computed?

4. How is net pay for tipped and non-tipped employees computed?

5. What is the 8% tip allocation regulation?

6. How are tips allocated for a payroll period using either the gross receipts method or the hours worked method?

After discussing the Fair Labor Standards Act (FLSA), the chapter addresses important payroll accounting concepts. Next, typical procedures for calculating time worked and gross pay are presented, followed by a discussion of federal and state payroll laws. The chapter closes with a detailed examination of payroll accounting for tipped employees. Operations and employees affected by the 8% tip regulation are identified, and examples of tip shortfall allocation are discussed.

The Fair Labor Standards Act (FLSA)

The **Fair Labor Standards Act (FLSA),** commonly known as the federal wage and hour law, covers such areas as equal pay for equal work, child labor, recordkeeping requirements, minimum wage rate, and conditions defining **overtime pay.** The FLSA applies to most hospitality enterprises. However, certain small businesses with exceptionally low sales volumes may be exempt.

In addition to establishing a minimum wage rate, the FLSA requires that all hotel and motel employees covered by this act be paid at the rate of at least one and one-half times their regular hourly rate for all hours worked in excess of 40 hours per week. The FLSA makes no provisions for rest periods or coffee breaks. It also makes no provisions for vacation, holiday, severance, or sick pay. In addition, the FLSA does not require extra pay for work on Saturdays or Sundays.

For example, an employer is not required to pay employees one and one-half times their regular pay for any weekend or holiday hours worked during a week if the total hours worked do not exceed 40. Also, if an employee works 40 hours in a three-day workweek, the employee is not entitled to overtime pay according to FLSA provisions. However, custom, union contracts, and many states have established overtime provisions that are more generous to the employee. In these situations, the FLSA provisions are superseded.

States may have legislation which contradicts standards established by the FLSA. In cases where state and federal laws differ, the law offering the greater benefit to the employee prevails. For example, state laws may set a minimum wage rate that is greater than that set by federal law, and this higher minimum wage rate would prevail. State laws may also contain provisions to regulate overtime pay, employee meals and lodging, tips, uniforms, and more.

Computing Time Worked

An employee must be paid for any work that is for the benefit of the employer, including productive work or any activity controlled or required by the employer for the employer's benefit. An employee's personal travel time to and from the job is generally not considered time worked. Exceptions apply to travel performed during the workday for the benefit of the employer.

The FLSA does not cover payment for time spent on coffee breaks or rest periods; however, custom, union contracts, or state laws may consider these periods time worked. Meal periods are not considered time worked unless an employee is required to perform some duty during the meal, whether active or inactive, for the benefit of the employer. Changing clothes or washing-up for the employee's own convenience is not considered time worked unless such activities are directly related to the nature of the employee's duties. Training sessions are considered time worked.

The FLSA requires that employees be paid for all time worked, including fractions of an hour. It is not necessary to compute time worked to the nearest minute if an employer adopts a consistent, equitable method of computation. For example, employers may adopt a practice of computing time worked to the nearest 5 minutes, to the nearest tenth of an hour, or to the nearest quarter of an hour.

The nearest tenth of an hour is based on the decimal system. Each hour is divided into 10 units of 6 minutes each. Six minutes would be recorded as .1, 12 minutes as .2, and 60 minutes as 1.0 or 1 hour. In using the decimal system, rounding techniques must be applied. Some companies use conventional rounding techniques and others always round up to the next highest time unit. For example, depending on company policy, 7 minutes may be recorded as .1 (conventional rounding) or as .2 (rounding up). For our purposes, the conventional rounding method is used. The following example illustrates how the decimal system is used to compute time worked.

Assume that an employee worked 5 hours and 20 minutes and that time worked is recorded to the nearest tenth of an hour. The employee's time worked is computed by converting the 5 hours and 20 minutes into decimals. The 5 hours converts to 5.0; the 20 minutes converts to .3 (20 minutes divided by 60 minutes equals .3333 hours, or .3 rounded). The employee's total time worked would be recorded as 5.3 hours by conventional rounding.

Recording Time Worked

The FLSA requires that an employer maintain records of the time worked by hourly-paid employees. Time sheets or time cards are used to satisfy this timekeeping requirement. The form of records used depends on the size of a company and the type of payroll periods. Other factors determining the selection of a recordkeeping format are the use of time clocks and computerized systems.

Many businesses use a time card form (Exhibit 1). Entries to this form may be made either manually by designated personnel or mechanically by an electronic time-clock system. When time clocks are used, early arrival or wait time may create a problem. Some time clocks flag any "In" or "Out" times that vary from assigned shift hours. These few seconds or minutes are usually ignored when computing time worked because this time does not match the employees' assigned work hours.

We usually divide the day into two 12-hour periods. For example, 1 o'clock in the morning is 1 A.M. and 1 o'clock in the afternoon is 1 P.M. Another time system considers a day to be one period of 24 consecutive hours, beginning and ending at midnight. This time system may be called the 24-hour time system, the continental system, or military time. Four digits are used to state time under this system, the first two representing the hour and the next two representing the minutes past the hour.

A simple technique by which to express time in the 24-hour time system is to convert the conventional time by placing a zero in front of any single digit A.M. hour and adding 1200 to any P.M. hour. The minutes are expressed in units of 00 to 59. Examples of converting conventional time to military time are as follows:

1 A.M.	=	0100 hours	1 P.M.	=	1300 hours
2 A.M.	=	0200 hours	2 P.M.	=	1400 hours
5:30 A.M.	=	0530 hours	5:30 P.M.	=	1730 hours
noon	=	1200 hours	midnight	=	2400 hours

Exhibit 1   Sample Employee Time Card

| WEEK ENDING _____ 19 _____ |
| Form No. 1212 |

No.

NAME

DAY	MORNING IN	NOON OUT	NOON IN	NIGHT OUT	EXTRA IN	EXTRA OUT	TOTAL

TOTAL TIME _____ HRS.

RATE_____

TOTAL WAGES FOR WEEK $ _____

The Employer/Employee Relationship

The Internal Revenue Service has issued technical regulations preventing employers from defining workers as independent contractors in order to evade payroll laws and related employer taxes. "Circular E, Employer's Tax Guide,"[1] a publication issued by the Internal Revenue Service, defines an employer/employee relationship that makes an employer subject to existing payroll laws and related employer taxes. An employer is defined as:

Generally ... a person or organization for whom a worker performs a service as an employee. The employer usually gives the worker the tools and place to work and has the right to fire the worker. A person or organization paying wages to a former employee after the work ends is also considered an employer.

An employee is defined as:

> *Anyone who performs services … if you, the employer, can control what will be done and how it will be done. This is so even when you give the employee freedom of action. What matters is that you have the legal right to control the method and result of the services.*

Circular E goes on to state that if an employer/employee relationship exists, it does not matter what the employee is called. That is, it does not matter if the employer chooses to call workers by names other than employees. If an employer/employee relationship exists, workers who are called partners, agents, or independent contractors are *employees*—and the employer is subject to existing payroll laws and related employer taxes.

In addition, Circular E stresses that there are no class distinctions among employees:

> *An employee can be a superintendent, manager, or supervisor. Generally, an officer of a corporation is an employee, but a director is not. An officer who performs no services or only minor ones, and who neither receives nor is entitled to receive pay of any kind, is not considered an employee.*

Any person or organization considered to be an employer must file Form SS-4 with the Internal Revenue Service requesting an Employer Identification Number (EIN).

Similarly, any employee who is working in an employment covered by Social Security is supposed to have a Social Security card bearing the employee's Social Security account number. If an employer takes on an employee who does not have a Social Security card and number, then, according to the Federal Insurance Contributions Act (FICA), the employee is required to apply for an account number by filing Form SS-5 with the nearest District Office of the Social Security Administration.

Wages and Salaries

The terms "wages" and "salaries" are often used interchangeably. The term **wages** usually applies to payrolls computed on an hourly, weekly, or piecework basis. However, a fixed weekly pay may be called a **salary.** The term "salaries" usually applies to payrolls which are paid monthly, bimonthly, biweekly, or annually. Generally, qualified supervisors and executives who receive a fixed amount each pay period (regardless of the number of hours worked) are considered salaried employees.

An employee who is paid a salary may or may not be paid for overtime hours worked. However, an employer cannot arbitrarily designate a salaried employee as exempt from overtime pay. Federal and state regulations must be satisfied in order to classify an employee as exempt from provisions regarding overtime pay. Under federal law, there are four types of exemptions from the overtime provisions of the Fair Labor Standards Act: executive, administrative, professional, and outside sales. In the hospitality industry, the most often used exemption is the executive exemption (although the administrative exemption sometimes applies to

Exhibit 2   Computation of Net Pay

Gross Pay		$500.00
Less:		
FICA	$38.25	
FIT	89.00	
SIT	22.75	
TDI	7.90	
Union Dues	10.00	
Health Insurance	15.00	
TOTAL DEDUCTIONS		182.90
Net Pay (amount of check)		$317.10

certain positions). Under the executive exemption, the employee's duties and salary must satisfy the following conditions:

1. The employee's primary duty must be that of managing.

2. The employee must customarily and regularly direct the work of a specified number of employees.

3. The employee can hire, fire, and suggest changes in the status of other employees.

4. The employee may exercise discretionary powers.

5. The employee's salary must be over an amount specified by law.

Gross Pay and Net Pay

Gross pay includes all of an employee's regular pay, overtime pay, commissions, and bonuses—before any payroll deductions. Gross pay may be calculated weekly, biweekly, bimonthly, monthly, daily, or over some other time period.

Salaried employees exempt from overtime do not require any special computation for gross pay because they are paid a fixed amount regardless of the actual number of hours worked. Tipped employees, on the other hand, require a special payroll computation, which is addressed in detail later in this chapter.

Net pay is the actual amount of an employee's paycheck. Net pay is the result of subtracting governmental and voluntary deductions from gross pay. Exhibit 2 illustrates a typical computation of net pay.

Regular Pay and Overtime Pay

The definition of regular pay varies because of different state laws, company policies, and contracts. However, under the FLSA, regular pay is based on a 40-hour workweek. The term "regular hourly rate" refers to the rate per hour that is used to compute regular pay.

The definition of overtime pay also varies because of different state laws, company policies, and contracts. According to the FLSA, overtime pay is required for any hours worked in excess of 40 hours in a week. The term "overtime hourly rate" refers to the rate per hour used to compute overtime pay. According to FLSA provisions, overtime is paid at the rate of 1.5 times the employee's regular hourly rate. The FLSA prescribes this rate regardless of the number of overtime hours worked and regardless of whether the overtime hours were worked on a weekend or on a legal holiday.

In order to calculate the overtime pay for some employees, it may first be necessary to convert either a weekly wage or a monthly salary to an hourly rate.

Converting a Weekly Wage to an Hourly Rate. Some employees are hired at a stated weekly wage. This wage is generally fixed except for overtime pay and adjustments for absences. For these employees, it is often necessary to convert the weekly wage to a regular hourly rate. These calculations may require rounding. Actual practice varies as to the number of decimal places used in calculating a regular hourly rate. For our purposes, all hourly rates are rounded to the nearest cent.

The regular hourly rate is computed by dividing the weekly wage by the number of hours in a regular 40-hour workweek. For example, assume that an employee is hired at $262 per week for a regular workweek. The regular hourly rate for this employee is calculated as follows:

$$\text{Regular Hourly Rate} \ = \ \frac{\text{Weekly Wage}}{\text{No. of Hours in Regular Workweek}}$$

$$\text{Regular Hourly Rate} \ = \ \frac{\$262}{40 \text{ hours}} \ = \ \$6.55$$

Once an employee's regular hourly rate is known, an overtime hourly rate can be determined. Following FLSA provisions, overtime is paid at the rate of one and one-half times the employee's regular hourly rate. Therefore, the overtime hourly rate is simply 1.5 times the regular hourly rate:

Overtime Hourly Rate   =   Regular Hourly Rate   ×   1.5

Overtime Hourly Rate   = $6.55 × 1.5   = $9.825 or $9.83

Converting a Monthly Salary to an Hourly Rate. As stated previously, some salaried employees may not be exempt from overtime pay. Therefore, it may be necessary to calculate an overtime hourly rate for some salaried employees. Since the number of pay weeks (and, therefore, the number of hours worked) varies from month to month, it is first necessary to annualize the monthly salary and then convert it to a weekly amount. Once the weekly amount is determined, the regular hourly rate and the overtime hourly rate can be computed by following the same procedure as in converting a weekly wage to an hourly rate.

For example, assume that an employee is hired at a monthly salary of $900 and that the employee is not exempt from overtime pay provisions. First, the monthly salary is annualized by multiplying the monthly salary by 12 months. Then, the weekly regular pay of the employee is calculated by dividing the annual salary figure by 52 weeks. These computations are summarized as follows:

$$\text{Annualized Salary} \ = \ \$900 \times 12 \ = \ \$10{,}800$$

$$\text{Weekly Rate} \ = \ \frac{\$10{,}800}{52} \ = \ \$207.69$$

The regular and overtime hourly rates of the salaried employee can now be determined by following the same procedure as in converting a weekly wage to a regular hourly rate.

$$\text{Regular Hourly Rate} \ = \ \frac{\$207.69}{40 \text{ hours}} \ = \ \$5.19$$

$$\text{Overtime Hourly Rate} \ = \ \$5.19 \times 1.5 \ = \ \$7.79$$

Calculating Overtime Pay

Two methods by which to compute an employee's overtime pay are the overtime pay method and the overtime premium method. These methods produce identical results with respect to gross pay. The major difference is in the classification of regular pay and overtime pay. According to the overtime pay method, all overtime hours are classified as overtime pay. According to the overtime premium method, overtime hours are separated into regular pay and overtime premium pay.

Overtime Pay Method. The **overtime pay method** computes overtime pay by multiplying the number of overtime hours by the employee's overtime hourly rate. In a state where FLSA provisions prevail, overtime hours are those hours worked in excess of 40 hours in a week. Using the overtime pay method, hours worked up to this 40-hour limit are the basis for computing regular pay. Any hours worked over the 40-hour limit are the basis for computing overtime pay.

Using the overtime pay method and assuming that FLSA provisions prevail, the gross pay for an employee is calculated by: (1) computing the employee's regular pay, (2) computing the employee's overtime pay, and (3) totaling the employee's regular and overtime pay. For example, assume that an employee receives a regular hourly rate of $8 and reports time worked of 46 hours. Using the overtime pay method, regular pay is computed on a basis *not to exceed 40 hours*. Multiplying 40 hours by the hourly rate of $8 results in $320 regular pay.

The employee's overtime pay is computed by first determining the employee's overtime hourly rate and then multiplying the overtime hourly rate by the number of overtime hours. Under the FLSA provisions used in this example, the employee's overtime hourly rate is $12 (1.5 times the regular hourly rate of $8). Since the employee worked 6 hours in excess of the 40-hour limit for regular pay, the employee's overtime pay is $72 (6 overtime hours multiplied by the $12 overtime hourly rate). The employee's gross pay can now be determined as follows:

Regular Pay (40 hours × $8)	$320.00
Overtime Pay (6 hours × $12)	72.00
Gross Pay	$392.00

Overtime Premium Method. The **overtime premium method** differs from the overtime pay method in two respects. First, the overtime premium method computes regular pay by multiplying the total hours worked (regular *and* overtime hours) by the employee's regular hourly rate. Second, the overtime premium method multiplies overtime hours by an overtime premium rate, which is half of the employee's regular hourly rate.

For example, using the overtime premium method and assuming that FLSA provisions prevail, the gross pay for an employee who receives a regular hourly rate of $8 and works 46 hours in one week is calculated by: (1) computing the employee's regular pay, (2) computing the employee's overtime premium, and (3) totaling the employee's regular pay and overtime premium. The employee's regular pay is computed by multiplying the 46 hours worked by the hourly rate of $8. The employee's overtime premium is computed by multiplying the 6 overtime hours by half the employee's regular hourly rate, or $4 (.5 times the regular hourly rate of $8). The employee's gross pay can now be determined as follows:

Regular Pay (46 hours × $8)	$368.00
Overtime Pay (6 hours × $4)	24.00
Gross Pay	$392.00

Payroll Deductions

An employee's gross pay is reduced by payroll deductions. Payroll deductions are classified as either governmental or voluntary deductions.

Governmental Deductions

Governmental deductions are mandatory deductions over which an employee has little control. These deductions consist of federal income taxes, FICA taxes, state income taxes, and other state taxes on employee earnings. These deductions are not an expense of the business because the employer merely acts as a collection agent for the government.

Voluntary Deductions

Voluntary deductions include premiums for health insurance group plans, life insurance group plans, retirement plans, savings plans, stock purchase plans, union dues, and contributions to charities. All voluntary deductions must be approved by the employee. Employees usually indicate approval by signing authorization forms. When the payroll check is processed, governmental deductions are subtracted before any voluntary deductions are made.

Federal Insurance Contributions Act (FICA)

The **Federal Insurance Contributions Act**, commonly known as **FICA**, was enacted to provide workers with retirement and medical benefits. It is also referred to as Social Security and Medicare. The law requires (1) a tax upon the employer, and (2) a tax upon the employee that is deducted from the employee's paycheck. The FICA tax imposed on the employer will be discussed later in this chapter.

The retirement and medical benefits of this act also extend to self-employed persons under provisions of the Self-Employment Contributions Act. The self-employed person pays the FICA tax, which is computed from the profits of the business. This computation is performed on a special form that is part of the individual's personal income tax return.

FICA Tax

Current Social Security and Medicare tax rates and ceilings are described in "Circular E, Employer's Tax Guide."

The FICA tax consists of two computations—one for the Social Security tax and one for the Medicare tax. Each tax has its own rate and its own "ceiling"; a ceiling is the maximum amount of earnings subject to taxation for a calendar year. Many companies combine these two taxes and show them as one deduction on the paycheck, usually labeled as FICA tax or Social Security tax.

Effective January 1, 1996, the FICA tax rates and ceilings are:

	Tax Rate	Ceiling
Social Security	6.2%	$62,700
Medicare	1.45%	none

If the Social Security rate is 6.2% and the wage ceiling is $62,700, then the Social Security deduction for any individual cannot exceed $3,887.40 ($62,700 × 6.2%) in 1996. However, the Medicare portion of the FICA tax is unlimited because there is no wage ceiling for this portion.

> Example: An employee earns $500.00 gross pay this week. The employee's year-to-date (YTD) Social Security deductions total $3,000.00 prior to this week's earnings.

> The current week's FICA deduction is calculated as follows:

> | | | |
> |---|---|---|
> | Social Security portion: $500.00 × 6.2% | = | $31.00 |
> | Medicare portion: $500.00 × 1.45% | = | 7.25 |
> | FICA deduction: | | $38.25 |

> Note: The employee's new YTD Social Security deduction totals $3,031.00, which is less than the maximum deduction of $3,887.40.

The previous example did not involve a situation where the current week's computed Social Security deduction exceeded the maximum legal amount. When this happens, the Social Security percentage computation is ignored and the actual deduction is "squeezed."

> Example: An employee earns $500.00 gross pay this week. The employee's previous YTD Social Security deductions total $3,860.00.

> 1. The first step is to test the Social Security percentage computation:

> $500.00 × 6.2% = $31.00
> $31.00 + $3,860.00 = $3,891.00 (exceeds maximum of $3,887.40)

> 2. The second step is to compute an amount for the current week's Social Security deduction that will bring the YTD deduction to $3,887.40.

> | | |
> |---|---|
> | Maximum allowable Social Security deduction: | $3,887.40 |
> | Previous YTD Social Security taxes deducted: | 3,860.00 |
> | Allowable Social Security deduction: | $ 27.40 |

The current week's FICA deduction can then be calculated as follows:

Allowable Social Security deduction	=	$27.40
Medicare portion: $500.00 × 1.45%	=	7.25
FICA deduction:		$34.65

Federal Income Tax (FIT)

The federal government requires an employer to withhold income taxes from the wages and salaries of employees and pay these taxes directly to the federal government. This constitutes part of the system under which most persons pay their income tax during the year in which income is received or earned. For many employees whose entire income is wages, the amount withheld approximates the total tax due so that the employee will pay little or no additional tax at the end of the year. Circular E outlines the requirements for withholding income tax and includes tables showing the amounts to be withheld.

Before a newly hired employee starts to work, he or she should complete and sign an IRS Form W-4 (Exhibit 3). This form provides the employer with the employee's marital status (for tax withholding purposes), withholding allowances, and other pertinent data. The employer retains this form and the information is transferred to the employee's payroll record for future use in preparing the employee's paycheck.

An employee may submit a new Form W-4 whenever there is a change in his or her marital status or withholding allowances. For tax withholding purposes, marital status is designated as either single or married. A married employee may claim a single status in order to have larger amounts withheld from his or her paycheck. However, an unmarried employee may not claim a married status in order to have smaller amounts withheld.

Withholding allowances may be claimed by an employee in accordance with the rules provided with Form W-4. Generally, an employee may claim (1) an

Exhibit 3 IRS Form W-4

Form **W-4**	**Employee's Withholding Allowance Certificate**	OMB No. 1545-0010
Department of the Treasury Internal Revenue Service	▶ For Privacy Act and Paperwork Reduction Act Notice, see reverse.	19**96**

1 Type or print your first name and middle initial	Last name		2 Your social security number

Home address (number and street or rural route)	3 ☐ Single ☐ Married ☐ Married, but withhold at higher Single rate. **Note:** *If married, but legally separated, or spouse is a nonresident alien, check the Single box.*
City or town, state, and ZIP code	4 If your last name differs from that on your social security card, check here and call 1-800-772-1213 for a new card . . . . . ▶ ☐

5	Total number of allowances you are claiming (from line G above or from the worksheets on page 2 if they apply) .	**5**	
6	Additional amount, if any, you want withheld from each paycheck	**6**	$
7	I claim exemption from withholding for 1996 and I certify that I meet **BOTH** of the following conditions for exemption: • Last year I had a right to a refund of **ALL** Federal income tax withheld because I had **NO** tax liability; **AND** • This year I expect a refund of **ALL** Federal income tax withheld because I expect to have **NO** tax liability. If you meet both conditions, enter "EXEMPT" here . . . . ▶	**7**	

Under penalties of perjury, I certify that I am entitled to the number of withholding allowances claimed on this certificate or entitled to claim exempt status.

Employee's signature ▶		Date ▶	, 19
8 Employer's name and address (Employer: Complete 8 and 10 only if sending to the IRS)	9 Office code (optional)	10 Employer identification number	

allowance, called a personal allowance, (2) an allowance for each dependent the employee is entitled to claim on his or her federal income tax return, and (3) other special withholding allowances and tax credit allowances as described on Form W-4. An employee does not have to claim all the allowances to which he or she is entitled, but an employee may only claim valid allowances.

The amount to be withheld from an employee's gross pay for federal income taxes is computed by using income tax withholding tables or by using the income tax withholding percentage method. Both of these methods are explained in Circular E. Computerized payroll procedures usually involve the income tax withholding percentage method, while employees using manual payroll systems commonly find it more convenient to use the tax withholding tables. Circular E contains a full set of these tables.

Tax withholding tables are labeled in terms of an employee's marital status and the type of payroll period. A payroll period is generally determined by how frequently payroll checks are issued by the employer. Payroll periods may be weekly, biweekly, bimonthly, monthly, daily, or some other designation.

Tax withholding tables are used by selecting the proper table and then locating the intersection of the number of withholding allowances claimed and the employee's wages. The following example demonstrates how to use tax withholding tables to calculate the FIT withholding for an employee who has claimed a single marital status and is paid on a weekly basis. Refer to the tax withholding tables in the appendix at the end of this chapter. Assuming an employee has claimed zero withholding allowances and receives wages of $245, the FIT withholding is calculated by following a four-step procedure:

Step 1   Select the appropriate tax table. Since the employee has claimed a single marital status and is paid on a weekly basis, the Single Persons—Weekly Payroll Period table is used.

Step 2   Locate the column which identifies the number of allowances claimed. In terms of our example the appropriate column is the one labeled 0.

Step 3   Locate the row which identifies the amount of the employee's wages. Since in our example the employee's wages are $245, the correct row is "at least $240 but less than $250."

Step 4   Locate the figure at the intersection of the allowances claimed column and the wages row. The figure is $29. This means that $29 will be withheld as FIT from the employee's paycheck.

The same steps can be used to calculate the FIT withholding for an employee who has claimed a married status and is paid on a weekly basis. Assuming an employee has claimed two withholding allowances and receives wages of $270, the FIT withholding is calculated as follows:

Step 1   Select the appropriate tax table. Since the employee has claimed a married status and is paid on a weekly basis, the Married Persons—Weekly Payroll Period table is used.

Step 2   Locate the column which identifies the number of allowances claimed. In terms of our example the appropriate column is the one labeled 2.

Step 3   Locate the row which identifies the amount of the employee's wages. Since in our example the employee's wages are $270, the correct row is "at least $270 but less than $280."

Step 4   Locate the figure at the intersection of the allowances claimed column and the wages row. The figure is $8. This means that $8 will be withheld as FIT from the employee's paycheck.

State and City Income Tax

Most states have a state income tax. The employer is responsible for withholding these taxes from the employee's gross pay and remitting them to the state as prescribed by law.

Computing the amount to be withheld from an employee's wages for state income taxes is generally similar to the methods used to compute the withholding of federal income taxes. The state's division of taxation provides employers with the proper tax tables or withholding percentages. In some states, state income taxes are a "piggyback tax" on the federal income tax. For example, a state may impose its income tax at the rate of 25% of the federal income tax. Therefore, once the federal income tax is determined, the state income tax may be computed at 25% of the federal income tax.

The methods for computing withholdings for city income taxes are similar to the methods discussed previously for computing federal and state income tax withholdings.

State Temporary Disability Benefit Laws

A few states have passed tax laws to provide benefits for employees who are absent from employment because of illness or injury not connected with their jobs. This tax is sometimes referred to as a temporary disability insurance (TDI) tax. It is withheld from the employee's gross pay. In addition, certain states may require employers to contribute to this fund.

Generally, TDI is computed by multiplying an employee's gross pay by a percentage figure specified by the state. Amounts may be withheld from the employee's paycheck until a year-to-date ceiling is reached.

Employer's Payroll Taxes ──────────────────────────────

The previous section discussed payroll taxes imposed on the employee. In these cases, the employer deducts governmental taxes from the employee's gross pay and remits them to the appropriate federal or state agency. Since these payroll taxes are levied on the employee, they are not an expense of the business.

In addition to payroll taxes imposed on employees, there are also payroll taxes imposed on the employer. Such taxes are a business expense. The employer's payroll taxes discussed in this section are as follows:

- Social Security taxes (FICA)
- Federal unemployment taxes
- State unemployment taxes

Social Security Taxes

The Federal Insurance Contributions Act (FICA) imposes a separate tax on the taxable payroll of a business. Generally, the FICA rate and the FICA taxable ceiling are similar to those specified for employees.

The Social Security tax deducted from an employee's payroll check is not a business expense because the tax is collected from the employee (withheld from his or her wages to arrive at net pay). In addition to an employee Social Security tax, there is also an employer Social Security tax which is imposed directly on the employer. A business is responsible for an employer Social Security tax on each employee's wages and tips until the wages (including tips) reach the maximum amount subject to Social Security taxes. This employer's Social Security tax is a business expense.

IRS Form 941

Form 941 is filed quarterly by an employer. The purpose of this form is to report the amount of employees' FICA and federal income taxes withheld, the FICA tax imposed on the employer, and the remittance of these taxes made by the employer as required by law. The appendix to this chapter contains a sample of IRS Form 941 and the instructions to complete the form. The appendix also contains a reprint from Circular E explaining the rules for making 941 tax deposits and general information for filing Form 941.

Unemployment Taxes

The **Federal Unemployment Tax Act (FUTA)** imposes a tax on the taxable payroll of a business. Only the employer pays FUTA tax, which is based on the wages of each employee. Like FICA tax, FUTA tax is assessed at a given rate and subject to a ceiling. The federal government passes these collected taxes on to the state agency which administers the state's unemployment program.

Similarly, a state may have an unemployment insurance act (commonly referred to as SUTA). Generally, the SUTA tax is imposed on the employer based on the SUTA taxable portion of each employee's gross pay. However, some states impose this tax on both the employer and the employee.

IRS Form 940

Form 940 is filed annually by an employer. The purpose of this form is to report on the employer's liability for FUTA taxes. The appendix to this chapter contains a sample of IRS Form 940 and the instructions to complete the form. The appendix also contains a reprint from Circular E explaining the rules for making 940 tax deposits and general information for filing Form 940.

Exhibit 4 Sample Employee's Earnings Record

Employee's Earnings Record

NAME:
ADDRESS:
SOCIAL SECURITY NUMBER:

Pay Period Ending	EARNINGS				Wages for WH	Meals & Lodging	Wages for F.I.C.A.	F.I.C.A.	DEDUCTIONS				NET PAY
	Regular	Overtime	Gross	Tips					Fed. Income WH	St. Income WH	Ret. Cont.	Health Ins.	

Depositing Payroll Taxes

The rules for depositing payroll taxes depend upon whether the taxes are 941 or 940 payroll taxes. The 941 taxes are employee withheld income taxes, employee withheld Social Security/Medicare taxes, and the Social Security/Medicare taxes imposed on the employer. The 940 taxes are referred to as FUTA taxes.

Form 8109, the federal tax deposit (FTD) coupon, is used to make deposits. Deposits are made at federal reserve banks or authorized depositaries. A sample of the FTD coupon and deposit rules for 941 and FUTA taxes are included in the appendix to this chapter.

The Payroll System

A primary function of a payroll system is to provide information necessary to compute employee payroll. An employee's earnings record is the basis for preparing his or her payroll check. Once the payroll checks have been prepared, they are recorded on a payroll register. From data in the payroll register, journal entries are prepared to record the payroll expense as well as the liability for payroll taxes. The net pay shown on the payroll register represents the cash demand that will be placed on the company's checking account. A payroll system comprises the forms, records, and procedures required to carry out these and other tasks.

Employee's Earnings Record

For each employee, an individual earnings record must be kept by calendar year. Exhibit 4 presents a sample employee's earnings record. The earnings record indicates gross wages earned and amounts withheld and deducted. Properties generally design the format of the earnings record to make it easy to conform with government reporting requirements. Also, for tax reporting purposes, it is important that earnings be entered in the proper payroll quarter; the determining date is the date of the payroll check, not the date of the workweek.

At the end of the year, an employee's earnings record is used to prepare IRS Form W-2, which is sent to federal and state agencies and to the employee. A sample IRS Form W-2 is shown in Exhibit 5. A new employee earnings record is started each calendar year.

Payroll Register

Another payroll accounting requirement is the preparation of reports for internal purposes. Management needs payroll cost information by department or area of responsibility. The accounting department supplies this information by maintaining a payroll register (Exhibit 6). The payroll register can also be used to reconcile the payroll checking account.

Payroll Journal Entries

A payroll journal is used to record payroll expense, employee withholdings, and the employer's payroll tax liabilities. The journal entry to record the payroll register in Exhibit 6 is as follows:

Payroll Expense	1,520.35	
FICA Tax Payable		116.31
Federal Income Tax Withheld Liability		175.00
State Income Tax Withheld Liability		45.50
Group Insurance Withheld Liability		51.50
Cash—Checking Account		1,132.04

The credit to the cash account assumes that the payroll checks are issued at the same time the payroll register is prepared. If the checks are to be issued at a later date, the credit would be to Accrued Payroll; when the checks are issued, the payment is recorded by a debit to Accrued Payroll and a credit to the checking account.

The previous journal entry recorded the payroll expense and the employer's liability for taxes withheld from employees' wages. Another journal entry is required to record the employer's liability for those taxes imposed on the employer. Assume that the employer is liable for the following payroll taxes:

Employer's FICA tax	$116.31
Federal unemployment tax (FUTA)	68.42
State unemployment tax (SUTA)	12.16
Total payroll taxes imposed on employer	$196.89

The journal entry to record these taxes is as follows:

Payroll Taxes Expense	196.89	
Accrued Payroll Taxes		196.89

Instead of one credit to Accrued Payroll Taxes, some accountants prefer to use separate liability accounts for each type of tax due.

Payroll Bank Account

Most hospitality businesses that pay their payroll by check establish a separate bank account for payroll. After the paychecks are prepared and the total disbursement is

Exhibit 5   IRS Form W-2

a Control number	22222	Void ☐	For Official Use Only ► OMB No. 1545-0008		
b Employer's identification number				1 Wages, tips, other compensation	2 Federal income tax withheld
c Employer's name, address, and ZIP code				3 Social security wages	4 Social security tax withheld
				5 Medicare wages and tips	6 Medicare tax withheld
				7 Social security tips	8 Allocated tips
d Employee's social security number				9 Advance EIC payment	10 Dependent care benefits
e Employee's name (first, middle initial, last)				11 Nonqualified plans	12 Benefits included in box 1
				13 See Instrs. for box 13	14 Other

	15 Statutory employee ☐	Deceased ☐	Pension plan ☐	Legal rep. ☐	Hshld. emp. ☐	Subtotal ☐	Deferred compensation ☐
f Employee's address and ZIP code							

16 State	Employer's state I.D. No.	17 State wages, tips, etc.	18 State income tax	19 Locality name	20 Local wages, tips, etc.	21 Local income tax

Cat. No. 10134D   Department of the Treasury—Internal Revenue Service

Form **W-2** Wage and Tax Statement **1995**

For Paperwork Reduction Act Notice, see separate instructions.

Copy A For Social Security Administration

Exhibit 6   Sample Payroll Register

		PAYROLL REGISTER								
		For period ending: 3/10/XX								

Time Card No.	Name	Earnings			Deductions				Net Pay	
		Regular	Overtime	Gross	FICA Tax	Federal Income Tax	State Income Tax	Group Insurance	Check No.	Amount
101	Deborah Stephens	320 00		320 00	24 48	34 00	9 00	10 00	386	242 52
103	Roland Kenwood	208 00	32 40	231 40	17 70	30 00	7 75	15 75	387	160 20
104	Thomas Lawton	222 30		222 30	17 01	28 00	7 25	10 00	388	160 04
105	Robert Paul	188 00	21 15	209 15	16 00	21 00	5 50		389	166 65
106	Steve Brentwood	537 50		537 50	41 12	62 00	16 00	15 75	390	402 63
	Total	1 475 80	44 55	1 520 35	116 31	175 00	45 50	51 50		1 132 04

known, funds are transferred from the regular bank account to the payroll account. The separate account for payroll offers better control, since only sufficient funds to cover the current payroll are deposited. Furthermore, a separate bank statement is obtained that can be reconciled item by item with the payroll expenditures recorded in the payroll journal.

When an electronic funds transfer system (EFT) is used, employees do not receive payroll checks. Instead, they are given a statement of their gross pay, deductions, and net pay. The employer's bank receives a register of employees from the employer. This register indicates each employee's net pay, bank, and bank account number. The employer's bank then processes this information and deposits each employee's net pay into his or her bank account. (For those employees who do not maintain an account at the employer's bank, the employer's bank remits the pertinent information to an automated clearinghouse that transmits the information to each employee's bank shown on the register.)

Computerized Payroll Applications

Advances in computer technology have made computers affordable, practical, and cost-efficient for most hospitality operations. An operation lacking a sophisticated guest accounting system may still use a computer to prepare payroll checks, perform general ledger accounting, and carry out other tasks involving numerical computation and accumulation of data.

However, a small property may not be able to justify an in-house computer system. In this case, banks and computer service companies offer a low-cost alternative. They sell computer services such as payroll preparation and general ledger accounting for modest fees.

The employee earnings record takes a different form in a computerized payroll application than in a manual accounting system. Information such as employee number, pay rate, deductions, and earnings is not recorded on paper, but stored on a computer file. Computer files are usually maintained on magnetic disks, which allow random access of information. In computer terminology, the earnings records for all employees are called the payroll master file or database.

The payroll process begins when hours worked are entered into the payroll master file. The computer then processes each employee's hours worked in accordance with information on that employee's file record and instructions in the computer program. This process emulates the manual procedures previously discussed.

The output of a computerized payroll application is similar to that of a manual system, namely, the payroll register and the payroll checks. Each employee's record in the master file is updated during the payroll process to maintain current and year-to-date earnings information.

Payroll Accounting for Tipped Employees

Preparing the payroll for tipped employees is complex because tipped employees earn wages from two sources: the employer they work for and the guests they serve. A tip is considered payment by a guest to a hospitality employee for services rendered and must be included as part of the gross income reported by the employee on his or her personal income tax return. For purposes of determining tip income, tips include cash tips, charge tips, and tips on credit cards. If an employee splits tips among other employees, only the portion which the employee retains is included in

Exhibit 7   IRS Form 4070

Form **4070** (Rev. July 1996) Department of the Treasury Internal Revenue Service	**Employee's Report of Tips to Employer** ▶ **For Paperwork Reduction Act Notice, see back of form.**		OMB No. 1545-0065
Employee's name and address		**Social security number**	
Employer's name and address (include establishment name, if different)		**1** Cash tips received	
		2 Credit card tips received	
		3 Tips paid out	
Month or shorter period in which tips were received from , 19 , to , 19		**4** Net tips (lines **1** + **2** − **3**)	
Signature		Date	

his or her gross income. All income earned by an employee, whether received as wages or as tips, is taxable and subject to both federal and state income tax withholding provisions.

Service Charges

Some hospitality operations, especially in resort areas, may add service charges to guests' billings. These service charges are distributed to servers and other customarily tipped employees. A service charge is not considered a tip. Such charges are defined as wages by the IRS and are treated the same as other wages for purposes of tax withholding requirements.

Employee Tip Reporting

IRS Publication 531 provides information on tip income reporting and employers' responsibilities. It also includes sample tip reporting forms. This publication is reproduced in the appendix to this chapter.

Employees must report cash tips received from customers as well as charge or credit card tips the employer passed on to them. An employee may use IRS Form 4070 (Exhibit 7) or a similar statement in reporting tips to the employer. A daily report or card showing the employee's name, cash tips received, and charge tips received is sufficient. Many employers require tipped employees to record their tips daily on the backs of their time cards.

FLSA Minimum Wage Rate

The FLSA minimum hourly wage rate recently changed. The new law sets the minimum hourly wage rate at two effective dates as follows:

October 1, 1996   — $4.75 an hour

September 1, 1997   — $5.15 an hour

This chapter will use the $5.15 minimum hourly wage rate in the examples and discussions that follow.

Training Wage

The FLSA permits employers to pay a training wage of $4.25 an hour for newly hired employees under the age of 20 for the first 90 days of employment. No specific training is required during this period. Hospitality employers should consult their particular state laws to determine if this federal training wage is permissible in their states.

FLSA Tip Credit

Provisions of the FLSA allow employers to apply a tip credit toward the minimum wage of tipped employees. This tip credit effectively lowers the gross wages payable by the employer because tips may be treated as supplemental wages.

The FLSA maximum allowable tip credit is $2.13 per hour. This means that an employer may apply a credit of $2.13 toward the hourly rate of tipped employees *as long as the actual tips received by the employee are not less than the FLSA maximum allowable tip credit.*

Effective September 1, 1997, an employer is in compliance with the FLSA minimum wage and hour standards by paying a tipped employee as follows:

Minimum hourly rate	$5.15
Allowable tip credit	2.13
Effective hourly payment rate	$3.02

If an employee's tips are less than the FLSA maximum allowable tip credit, the employer may not use the FLSA formula to compute a tip credit. Instead, the actual tips received by the employee are used as the tip credit. This ensures that the employee does not earn less than the minimum hourly wage from the combined payments of the employer (in the form of a wage) and guests (in the form of tips).

Using the FLSA Formula to Compute the Tip Credit. The following example illustrates how the gross wages payable by the employer are calculated when the actual tips received by an employee are greater than the maximum FLSA tip credit. Assume that Employee #1 has worked 40 hours and the employer has elected to use the allowable tip credit against the minimum wage. The employee reports tips from all sources amounting to $98. The maximum FLSA tip credit is $85.20 (40 hours × $2.13 per hour). The gross wages payable by the employer are calculated as follows:

Gross wages (minimum wage: 40 hours × $5.15 per hour)		$206.00
Less the lower of:		
Maximum FLSA tip credit (40 hours × $2.13)	$85.20	
Actual tips received	98.00	
Allowable tip credit		85.20
Gross wages payable by the employer		$120.80

Using Actual Tips Received as the Tip Credit. Another example illustrates how the gross wages payable by the employer are calculated when the actual tips received by an employee are less than the maximum FLSA tip credit. Assume that

Exhibit 8   Computing Net Pay for Employee #1—Hourly Rate at Minimum Wage

Gross Wages Payable by Employer

Gross wages (40 hours × $5.15 per hour)		$ 206.00
Less the lower of:		
Maximum FLSA tip credit (40 hours × $2.13)	$85.20	
Actual tips received	98.00	
Allowable tip credit		85.20
Gross wages payable by the employer		$ 120.80

Gross Taxable Earnings

Gross wages payable by employer	$120.80	
Actual tips received	98.00	
Gross taxable earnings	$218.80	

Less Governmental and Voluntary Deductions

FICA ($218.80 × 7.65%)	16.74
Income tax withholding ($218.80 × 12%)	26.26
Voluntary deduction (group health plan)	10.00
Net pay (amount of payroll check)	$ 67.80

Employee #2 has worked 40 hours and the employer has elected to use the allowable tip credit against the minimum wage. The employee reports tips from all sources amounting to $70. The maximum FLSA tip credit is again $85.20. The gross wages payable by the employer are calculated as follows:

Gross wages (minimum wage: 40 hours × $5.15 per hour)		$206.00
Less the lower of:		
Maximum FLSA tip credit (40 hours × $2.13)	$85.20	
Actual tips received	70.00	
Allowable tip credit		70.00
Gross wages payable by the employer		$136.00

Net Pay of Tipped Employees

A tipped employee's gross taxable earnings include the gross wages payable by the employer *and* the actual tips the employee receives from guests. Exhibits 8 and 9 illustrate how net pay is computed for the previous example's Employee #1 and Employee #2. To simplify the illustration, state and local taxes are not considered, a 12% federal income tax rate is used, and a $10 voluntary deduction for a group health plan is assumed.

It is possible for the governmental and voluntary deductions of a tipped employee to exceed the gross wages payable by the employer for a payroll period. In this case, available amounts are first applied to FICA taxes, then to federal and state income taxes, and finally to voluntary deductions. However, an employee's

Exhibit 9   Computing Net Pay for Employee #2—Hourly Rate at Minimum Wage

Gross Wages Payable by Employer

Gross wages (40 hours × $5.15 per hour)		$ 206.00
Less the lower of:		
Maximum FLSA tip credit (40 hours × $2.13)	$85.20	
Actual tips received	70.00	
Allowable tip credit		70.00
Gross wages payable by the employer		$ 136.00

Gross Taxable Earnings

Gross wages payable by employer	$136.00
Actual tips received	70.00
Gross taxable earnings	$206.00

Less Governmental and Voluntary Deductions

FICA ($206.00 × 7.65%)	15.76
Income tax withholding ($206.00 × 12%)	24.72
Voluntary deduction (group health plan)	10.00
Net pay (amount of payroll check)	$ 85.52

paycheck may never be less than zero; if the gross wages payable by the employer are insufficient to cover an employee's governmental and voluntary deductions, the employee may pay over the deficiency to the employer. If the employer is unable to withhold FICA taxes, this fact is reported on the employee's W-2 form and is reported as taxes due on the employee's personal income tax return. It is not necessary to report any deficiency on withheld income taxes because any deficiency will be made up when the employee's total income tax liability is computed on his or her personal income tax return.

State Wage and Tip Credit Provisions

Many states have passed minimum wage legislation which is more generous to the employee than the federal minimum wage. In these cases, the state law takes precedence over the federal law. In addition, some employers voluntarily pay tipped employees at rates above federal and state minimum hourly wages. Exhibits 10 and 11 illustrate how the allowable tip credit is applied and how the net pay is calculated for Employee #1 and Employee #2 when their hourly rates are above the applicable minimum wage.

Some states also limit the maximum tip credit that may be used against the minimum wage. For example, assume a state's minimum wage provision is identical to the federal provision. However, the employer's maximum tip credit allowable by the state is $1.75. In this case, the employer must use the state's $1.75 as the maximum allowable tip credit and not the $2.13 allowed under federal provisions.

Exhibit 10   Computing Net Pay for Employee #1—Hourly Rate Above Minimum Wage

Gross Wages Payable by Employer		
Gross wages (40 hours × $6.00 per hour)		$ 240.00
Less the lower of:		
Maximum FLSA tip credit (40 hours × $2.13)	$85.20	
Actual tips received	98.00	
Allowable tip credit		85.20
Gross wages payable by the employer		$ 154.80
Gross Taxable Earnings		
Gross wages payable by employer	$154.80	
Actual tips received	98.00	
Gross taxable earnings	$252.80	
Less Governmental and Voluntary Deductions		
FICA ($252.80 × 7.65%)		19.34
Income tax withholding ($252.80 × 12%)		30.34
Voluntary deduction (group health plan)		10.00
Net pay (amount of payroll check)		$ 95.12

Exhibit 11   Computing Net Pay for Employee #2—Hourly Rate Above Minimum Wage

Gross Wages Payable by Employer		
Gross wages (40 hours × $6.00 per hour)		$ 240.00
Less the lower of:		
Maximum FLSA tip credit (40 hours × $2.13)	$85.20	
Actual tips received	70.00	
Allowable tip credit		70.00
Gross wages payable by the employer		$ 170.00
Gross Taxable Earnings		
Gross wages payable by employer	$170.00	
Actual tips received	70.00	
Gross taxable earnings	$240.00	
Less Governmental and Voluntary Deductions		
FICA ($240.00 × 7.65%)		18.36
Income tax withholding ($240.00 × 12%)		28.80
Voluntary deduction (group health plan)		10.00
Net pay (amount of payroll check)		$ 112.84

Overtime Pay of Tipped Employees

Overtime pay for tipped employees is calculated in exactly the same manner as for non-tipped employees. However, in computing the gross wages payable by the employer, the federal or state tip credit is multiplied by the total hours worked (regular hours plus overtime hours) by the employee.

For example, assume that Employee #1 and Employee #2 each work 45 hours and report actual tips received of $98 and $70, respectively. Assume further that the employer pays tipped employees $6.00 per hour and that the state's overtime provisions are identical to FLSA provisions. Exhibits 12 and 13 illustrate how to calculate the net pay for these employees.

As stressed earlier, the definition of overtime pay varies because of different state laws, company policies, and contracts. Federal law requires that overtime be paid for any hours worked in excess of 40 in a payroll week. Thus, an employee who works ten-hour shifts for four days within a payroll week is not entitled to overtime under the FLSA. Some states require that employees receive overtime pay for any hours worked in excess of eight hours in a payroll day.

The 8% Tip Regulation

The Tax Equity and Fiscal Responsibility Act of 1982 (TEFRA) established regulations affecting food and beverage operations with respect to tip reporting requirements. The intent of the regulation is for all tipped employees to report tips of at least 8% of the gross receipts of the hospitality establishment. If tips reported by employees fail to meet this 8% requirement for a particular period, the deficiency is called a tip shortfall. This shortfall will require allocation to those employees classified as directly tipped employees.

The 8% tip regulation distinguishes between directly tipped employees and indirectly tipped employees. Directly tipped employees are those who receive tips directly from customers. Examples of directly tipped employees are servers, bartenders, and other employees, such as maitre d's. Indirectly tipped employees are employees who do not normally receive tips directly from customers. These employees include buspersons, service bartenders, and cooks.

When a shortfall is allocated, the employer is required to provide each directly tipped employee with an informational statement showing the tips reported by the employee and the tips that should have been reported. An employer does not have to provide employees with tip allocation statements when the total tips reported for a period are greater than 8% of the gross receipts for that period. For example, assume that a large food and beverage establishment records gross receipts of $100,000 for a particular period. If the actual tips reported by employees total more than $8,000 ($100,000 × 8%), the employer does not have to provide employees with tip allocation statements.

An employee's tip allocation for a calendar year is stated separately from any wages and reported tips appearing on the employee's W-2 form. Employees should maintain adequate records to substantiate the total amount of tips included in income. If possible, the employee should keep a daily record of his or her sales, cash tips, charge tips, and hours worked. To facilitate recordkeeping, a business

Exhibit 12   Computing Net Pay for Employee #1—Overtime Pay Calculation

Gross Wages Payable by Employer		
Regular Pay (40 hours × $6.00 per hour)		$240.00
Overtime Pay (5 hours × $6.00 × 1.5)		45.00
Gross Wages		$285.00
Less the lower of:		
Maximum FLSA tip credit (45 hours × $2.13)	$95.85	
Actual tips received	98.00	
Allowable tip credit		95.85
Gross wages payable by the employer		$189.15

Gross Taxable Earnings	
Gross wages payable by employer	$189.15
Actual tips received	98.00
Gross taxable earnings	$287.15

Less Governmental and Voluntary Deductions	
FICA ($287.15 × 7.65%)	21.97
Income tax withholding ($287.15 × 12%)	34.46
Voluntary deduction (group health plan)	10.00
Net pay (amount of payroll check)	$122.72

Exhibit 13   Computing Net Pay for Employee #2—Overtime Pay Calculation

Gross Wages Payable by Employer		
Regular Pay (40 hours × $6.00 per hour)		$240.00
Overtime Pay (5 hours × $6.00 × 1.5)		45.00
Gross Wages		$285.00
Less the lower of:		
Maximum FLSA tip credit (45 hours × $2.13)	$95.85	
Actual tips received	70.00	
Allowable tip credit		70.00
Gross wages payable by the employer		$215.00

Gross Taxable Earnings	
Gross wages payable by employer	$215.00
Actual tips received	70.00
Gross taxable earnings	$285.00

Less Governmental and Voluntary Deductions	
FICA ($285.00 × 7.65%)	21.80
Income tax withholding ($285.00 × 12%)	34.20
Voluntary deduction (group health plan)	10.00
Net pay (amount of payroll check)	$149.00

Exhibit 14   Sample Employee Report of Daily Sales and Tips

Employee Report of Daily Sales and Tips

Business _____   Week Ending _____/_____/_____

(Month/Day/Year)

Employee _____

	Date	Date	Date	Date	Date	Date	Date	
Enter day of the month								
	Mon.	Tues.	Wed.	Thurs.	Fri.	Sat.	Sun.	Grand Total
SALES 1. Total sales to patrons 2. Charge sales in								
TIPS 1. Total cash and charge tips 2. Total charge tips in								
Total hours worked								

Check shift worked: ☐ Days   ☐ Evenings   ☐ Split

may provide the employee with a multi-purpose form similar to the one shown in Exhibit 14.

Operations Affected by the 8% Tip Regulation

The 8% tip regulation does not apply to every food and beverage establishment. For example, cafeteria and fast-food operations are exempt from the 8% tip regulation. Cafeteria operations are defined as food and beverage establishments which are primarily self-service and in which the total cost of food and/or beverages selected by a customer is paid to a cashier (or is stated on a guest check) before the customer is seated. Fast-food operations are defined as food and beverage establishments where customers order, pick up, and pay for their orders at a counter or window and then consume the items at another location, either on or off the premises. In addition to cafeteria and fast-food operations, food and beverage establishments are exempt from the 8% tip regulation when at least 95% of their gross receipts include a service charge of 10% or more. As pointed out previously, service charges are not considered tips. Service charges are defined as wages by the IRS and are treated the same as other wages for purposes of tax withholding requirements.

The 8% tip regulation defines gross receipts as all receipts (both cash and charge sales) received for providing food and/or beverages. However, according to the 8% tip regulation, the following are typically *not* considered part of an operation's gross receipts because tipping is not customary for these services:

- Complimentary hors d'oeuvres served at a bar
- Complimentary dessert served to a regular patron
- Complimentary fruit baskets placed in guestrooms
- Carry-out sales
- State or local taxes
- Services to which a 10% (or more) service charge is added

An exception applies to gambling casinos. In casinos, the retail value of complimentary food and/or beverages served to customers is considered to be part of gross receipts because tipping is customary for this service.

Given these exemptions and exceptions, the 8% tip regulation applies to food and beverage establishments that normally employ the equivalent of more than ten employees on a typical business day and are thus classified as *large*. The phrase "the equivalent of more than ten employees" means any combination of full- or part-time employees whose hours worked on a typical business day total more than 80 hours.

Employers can determine whether the 8% tip regulation applies to their establishments by averaging the number of hours worked by employees during the best and worst months of the previous calendar year. For example, assume that an employer compiles the following statistics:

	Gross Receipts	Days Open	Employee Hours	Hours Worked per Day
Best month: July	$125,578	31	2,883	93
Worst month: February	$ 89,162	28	2,184	78

The number of hours worked by employees on a typical day for that calendar year can be determined by averaging the average hours worked per day in July and February:

$$\text{Typical Business Day} = \frac{\text{Hrs. Worked (July)} + \text{Hrs. Worked (February)}}{2}$$

$$\text{Typical Business Day} = \frac{93 + 78}{2} = \frac{171}{2} = 85.5 \text{ hrs. per day}$$

Since the result exceeds 80 hours per day, the employer's business is considered to have more than ten employees and is therefore subject to the 8% tip regulation. For a new food and beverage business (one which did not operate in the previous year), the time periods used in the calculations may be any two consecutive months.

If an employer conducts business at more than one location, each location is considered to be a separate food and beverage establishment. This also applies to separate activities within a single building if records of receipts are kept separately. If employees work at multiple locations for an employer, the employer may make a good faith estimate of the number of hours these employees worked for each location.

If a food and beverage establishment is subject to the 8% tip regulation, IRS Form 8027 (Exhibit 15) must be completed, whether or not a tip shortfall allocation

Exhibit 15   IRS Form 8027

Form **8027**	**Employer's Annual Information Return of Tip Income and Allocated Tips**	OMB No. 1545-0714
Department of the Treasury Internal Revenue Service		**19 95**

Use IRS label. Make any necessary changes. Otherwise, please type or print.

Name of establishment

Number and street (See instructions.)   Employer identification number

City or town, state, and ZIP code

Type of establishment (check only one box)

☐ 1 Evening meals only
☐ 2 Evening and other meals
☐ 3 Meals other than evening meals
☐ 4 Alcoholic beverages

Employer's name

Establishment number (See instructions.)

Number and street (P.O. box, if applicable.)   Apt. or suite no.

City, town or post office, state, and ZIP code (If a foreign address, enter city, province or state, postal code, and country.)

Check the box if applicable: Final Return ☐   Amended Return ☐

1	Total charged tips for 1995	**1**
2	Total charged receipts (other than nonallocable receipts) showing charged tips	**2**
3	Total amount of service charges of less than 10% paid as wages to employees	**3**
4a	Total tips reported by indirectly tipped employees	**4a**
b	Total tips reported by directly tipped employees	**4b**
c	Total tips reported (Add lines 4a and 4b.)	**4c**
5	Gross receipts from food or beverage operations (other than nonallocable receipts) . .	**5**
6	Multiply line 5 by 8% (.08) or the lower rate shown here ▶ _____ granted by the district director. Attach a copy of the district director's determination letter to this return .	**6**

Note: *If you have allocated tips using other than the calendar year (semimonthly, biweekly, quarterly, etc.), put an X on line 6 and enter the amount of allocated tips from your records on line 7.*

7	Allocation of tips. If line 6 is more than line 4c, enter the excess here	**7**

This amount must be allocated as tips to tipped employees working in this establishment. Check the box below that shows the method used for the allocation. (Show the portion, if any, attributable to each employee in box 8 of the employee's Form W-2.)

a Allocation based on hours-worked method (See instructions for restriction.) . . . ☐
Note: *If you checked line 7a, enter the average number of employee hours worked per business day during the payroll period. (See instructions.)* _____
b Allocation based on gross receipts method . . . . ☐
c Allocation based on good-faith agreement (Attach copy of agreement.) . . . . . ☐

8   Enter the total number of directly tipped employees at this establishment during 1995 ▶

Under penalties of perjury, I declare that I have examined this return, including accompanying schedules and statements, and to the best of my knowledge and belief, it is true, correct, and complete.

Signature ▶   Title ▶   Date ▶

For Paperwork Reduction Act Notice, see the separate instructions.   Cat. No. 49989U   Form **8027** (1995)

is made. IRS Form 8027 is called Employer's Annual Information Return of Tip Income and Allocated Tips.

Tip Shortfall Allocation Methods

If, during a particular period, the total tips reported by directly and indirectly tipped employees fall short of 8% of the gross receipts of the establishment for that same period, the employer must: (1) determine the shortfall (the amount by which the total reported tips falls short of 8% of the gross receipts), and (2) allocate the shortfall among *directly tipped employees*. After these computations have been completed, the tip shortfall allocations must be reported to each affected employee.

There are several acceptable methods by which to compute tip shortfall allocations for directly tipped employees. One method is through a good faith agreement. A good faith agreement is a written agreement between the employer and employees, consented to by two-thirds of the tipped employees at the time of the agreement. This agreement becomes the basis of allocating tip amounts to employees when the actual tips reported are short of the expected 8% of gross receipts.

In the absence of a good faith agreement, the 8% tip regulation provides tip allocation methods. For purposes of allocating the tip shortfall to directly tipped employees, these regulations permit the use of the gross receipts method or, under certain conditions, the hours worked method. The following examples explain and illustrate both methods.

Gross Receipts Method

The gross receipts method requires that gross receipts (food and beverage sales) and tip records be maintained for each directly tipped employee. Gross receipts are used as a basis for allocating each directly tipped employee's share of the tip shortfall. The tip shortfall allocation may be performed weekly, monthly, quarterly, annually, or at some other designated time period during the year. The following hypothetical example demonstrates the computations involved when the gross receipts method is used to allocate a tip shortfall among the directly tipped employees of Bruno's Restaurant.

Bruno's Restaurant is a food and beverage establishment with an equivalent of more than ten employees and, therefore, is subject to the government's 8% tip regulation. Bruno's Restaurant had food and beverage sales of $100,000 for a particular period. According to the government's 8% tip regulation, directly and indirectly tipped employees should have reported a minimum of $8,000 in tips for that period ($100,000 $\times$ 8% = $8,000); this amount will be referred to as "8% gross receipts." The tip records show that all employees reported total tips of only $6,200 for the period. Therefore, a tip shortfall of $1,800 ($8,000 − $6,200) has occurred.

Exhibit 16 presents information compiled by Bruno's management for this particular period, including the gross receipts (food and beverage sales) and tips reported by each directly tipped employee. It also shows that the total shortfall to be allocated is $1,800. This information will be used later in Exhibits 17 and 18 to compute tip shortfall allocations for directly tipped employees.

Exhibit 16   Sales and Tips Analysis—Bruno's Restaurant

Directly Tipped Employee	Gross Receipts for Period	Tips Reported by Employees
1	$ 18,000	$1,080
2	16,000	880
3	23,000	1,810
4	17,000	800
5	12,000	450
6	14,000	680
Total	$100,000	5,700
Indirectly tipped employees		500
Total		$6,200

Tips that should have been reported ($100,000 × 8%)	=	$8,000
Actual tips reported	=	6,200
Shortfall to be allocated		1,800
Tips that should have been reported	=	8,000
Tips reported by indirectly tipped employees	=	500
Directly tipped employees' portion of 8% gross receipts	=	$7,500

Exhibit 17   Determining Shortfall Ratios—Bruno's Restaurant

Directly Tipped Employee	Total Portion of 8% Gross Receipts		Gross Receipts Ratio		Employee's Share of 8% Gross Receipts		Actual Tips Reported		Employee's Shortfall Numerator
1	7,500	×	18,000/100,000	=	$1,350	−	$1,080	=	$ 270
2	7,500	×	16,000/100,000	=	1,200	−	880	=	320
3	7,500	×	23,000/100,000	=	1,725	−	1,810	=	0
4	7,500	×	17,000/100,000	=	1,275	−	800	=	475
5	7,500	×	12,000/100,000	=	900	−	450	=	450
6	7,500	×	14,000/100,000	=	1,050	−	680	=	370
Total					$7,500		$5,700		$1,885
									Shortfall Denominator

Exhibit 18   Allocation of the Tip Shortfall—Bruno's Restaurant

Directly Tipped Employee	Shortfall Ratio		Shortfall to be Allocated		Tip Allocation
1	270/1,885	×	$1,800	=	$ 258
2	320/1,885	×	1,800	=	306
4	475/1,885	×	1,800	=	453
5	450/1,885	×	1,800	=	430
6	370/1,885	×	1,800	=	353
Total					$1,800

While directly tipped employees are required to account for the tip shortfall, the tips of indirectly tipped employees may be counted toward the "8% gross receipts" estimate of total tips that should have been reported. For Bruno's Restaurant, total tips that should have been reported by all employees are $8,000; the tips reported by indirectly tipped employees total $500. Therefore, the directly tipped employees' portion of 8% gross receipts is $7,500.

Exhibit 17 uses the directly tipped employees' portion of 8% gross receipts as the basis for calculating shortfall allocation ratios. The shortfall allocation ratios will be used to allocate the $1,800 tip shortfall among directly tipped employees. However, before tip shortfall allocation ratios can be computed, a method must be used to determine each employee's share of the $7,500 portion of tips that should have been reported by directly tipped employees. Each employee's share will be compared to the tips actually reported by the employee in order to determine if the employee reported tips above or below his or her share of the $7,500 portion of 8% gross receipts.

Under the gross receipts method, a gross receipts ratio is used to determine each employee's share of the $7,500. A gross receipts ratio is the proportion of gross receipts attributable to each employee in relation to the total gross receipts for the period. This ratio is multiplied by $7,500 (directly tipped employees' portion of 8% gross receipts) to determine each directly tipped employee's share of this amount. Exhibit 17 illustrates these calculations for Bruno's Restaurant.

The actual tips reported by each employee are then subtracted from the employee's share of 8% gross receipts. The resulting figure is the employee shortfall numerator. For Bruno's Restaurant, this subtraction process is possible for all employees except Employee #3. This employee reported tips greater than his or her share of the tips that should have been reported. Therefore, Employee #3 does not have a tip shortfall. The total shortfall ($1,800) must be allocated on a proportional basis among the remaining directly tipped employees.

Exhibit 18 shows how the $1,800 tip shortfall is allocated among directly tipped employees whose reported tips did not equal or exceed their share of the 8% tip estimate. This proportional allocation is accomplished by the use of a shortfall ratio. The total of the employees' shortfall numerators, or 1,885, is used as the denominator of the shortfall ratio. Each employee's shortfall numerator, together with the shortfall denominator, form the shortfall ratio used to allocate his or her share of the tip shortfall.

Hours Worked Method

The use of the hours worked method is limited to those establishments with fewer than the equivalent of 25 full-time employees during the payroll period. The mathematical procedures in this method are identical to those explained for the gross receipts method. The only difference between the hours worked method and the gross receipts method is that employee hours worked are substituted wherever employee gross receipts were used in the previous method.

For example, Dot's Diner, a hypothetical food establishment employing fewer than the equivalent of 25 employees, elects to allocate the tip shortfall on the basis of hours worked. Exhibit 19 shows the hours worked and tips reported for the employees of this restaurant. Exhibit 20 shows the computation of the shortfall

Exhibit 19   Sales and Tips Analysis—Dot's Diner

Directly Tipped Employee	Employee Hours for Period	Tips Reported by Employees
1	40	$1,080
2	35	880
3	45	1,810
4	40	800
5	15	450
6	25	680
Total	200	$5,700
Indirectly tipped employees		500
Total		$6,200
Tips that should have been reported ($100,000 × 8%)	=	$8,000
Actual tips reported	=	6,200
Shortfall to be allocated		1,800
Tips that should have been reported	=	8,000
Tips reported by indirectly tipped employees	=	500
Directly tipped employees' portion of 8% gross receipts	=	$7,500

Exhibit 20   Determining Shortfall Ratios—Dot's Diner

Directly Tipped Employee	Total Portion of 8% Gross Receipts		Employee Hours Ratio		Employee's Share of 8% Gross Receipts		Actual Tips Reported		Employee's Shortfall Numerator
1	$7,500	×	40/200	=	$1,500	−	$1,080	=	$ 420
2	7,500	×	35/200	=	1,312	−	880	=	432
3	7,500	×	45/200	=	1,687	−	1,810	=	0
4	7,500	×	40/200	=	1,500	−	800	=	700
5	7,500	×	15/200	=	563	−	450	=	113
6	7,500	×	25/200	=	938	−	680	=	258
Total					$7,500		$5,700		$ 1,923
									Shortfall Denominator

Exhibit 21   Allocation of the Tip Shortfall—Dot's Diner

Directly Tipped Employee	Shortfall Ratio		Shortfall to be Allocated		Tip Allocation
1	420/1,923	×	$1,800	=	$ 393
2	432/1,923	×	1,800	=	404
4	700/1,923	×	1,800	=	656
5	113/1,923	×	1,800	=	106
6	258/1,923	×	1,800	=	241
Total					$1,800

allocation ratios based on the hours worked. Exhibit 21 shows the allocation of the tip shortfall using the ratios developed in Exhibit 20.

Endnotes

1. U.S. Department of Treasury, Internal Revenue Service, Publication 15, *Circular E, Employer's Tax Guide*. This publication can be obtained at an Internal Revenue Service office.

Key Terms

Fair Labor Standards Act (FLSA)

Federal Insurance Contributions
  Act (FICA)

Federal Unemployment Tax Act (FUTA)

gross pay

net pay

overtime pay

overtime pay method

overtime premium method

salary

wages

Review Questions

1. What wage and salary areas are not covered by the Fair Labor Standards Act?

2. What are the major provisions of the following federal acts or laws?

    a. Fair Labor Standards Act
    b. Federal Insurance Contributions Act
    c. Federal Income Tax Withholding Law
    d. Federal Unemployment Tax Act

3. An employer is interviewing job candidates for a server's position. The employer states that the person hired will be considered self-employed by mutual agreement. Is this arrangement in accordance with federal payroll provisions? Justify your answer.

4. In each of the following situations, which federal form is required?

    a. A new business is formed and employees will be hired.
    b. A new employee is hired.
    c. An employee requests a change in withholding status.
    d. An employer reports annual wages and taxes withheld to employees.

5. What are two methods of computing overtime pay? Describe how each method calculates overtime pay.

6. A restaurant where tipping is customary has 15 employees who collectively work 70 hours per business day. Are the employees of the establishment subject to the minimum 8% tip regulation? Explain your answer.

Problems

Problem 1

Convert the following time worked to the nearest tenth of an hour:

    a. 7 hours, 16 minutes

    b. 4 hours, 37 minutes

    c. 9 hours, 57 minutes

    d. 7 hours, 50 minutes

Problem 2

Convert the following conventional times to military time:

    a. 3 P.M.

    b. 3 A.M.

    c. 6:45 A.M.

    d. 6:45 P.M.

Problem 3

Convert the following weekly wages to an hourly rate (to three decimal places). The work-week is 37.5 hours.

    a. $416

    b. $295

    c. $325

Problem 4

Convert the following monthly salaries to an hourly rate (to three decimal places). The workweek is 37.5 hours.

    a. $1,500

    b. $1,200

    c. $2,150

Problem 5

Compute the regular pay, overtime pay, and gross pay for an employee who worked 49 hours this week. The employee's hourly rate is $5.15. The state overtime provisions apply to any hours worked in excess of 40 in a week.

    a. Use the overtime pay method.

    b. Use the overtime premium method.

Problem 6

Use the overtime premium method to compute the regular pay, overtime pay, and gross pay for an employee who worked 45 hours this week. The employee's hourly rate is $5.85. The following is the employee's time report.

Sunday	5
Monday	8
Tuesday	12
Wednesday	12
Thursday	8
Friday	0
Saturday	0
Total	45

a. Assume that state law requires overtime to be paid for any hours worked in excess of 8 hours in a day.

b. Assume that state overtime provisions apply to any hours worked in excess of 40 in a week.

Problem 7

Compute the net pay for a newly hired tipped employee who has worked 36 hours and has not qualified for overtime pay. The employee's pay rate is at the minimum hourly wage rate, which is $5.25 in this particular state. The state allows the employer a maximum tip credit of $1.75 an hour; the maximum is taken by this employer. Assume the FICA rate is 7.65% and federal withholding is computed at 12%.

a. Assume that the employee reports actual tips of $67.

b. Assume that the employee reports actual tips of $40.

Appendix

Sample IRS Tax Withholding Tables

SINGLE Persons—**WEEKLY** Payroll Period

(For Wages Paid in 1996)

If the wages are—		And the number of withholding allowances claimed is—										
At least	But less than	0	1	2	3	4	5	6	7	8	9	10
		The amount of income tax to be withheld is—										
$0	$55	0	0	0	0	0	0	0	0	0	0	0
55	60	1	0	0	0	0	0	0	0	0	0	0
60	65	2	0	0	0	0	0	0	0	0	0	0
65	70	3	0	0	0	0	0	0	0	0	0	0
70	75	3	0	0	0	0	0	0	0	0	0	0
75	80	4	0	0	0	0	0	0	0	0	0	0
80	85	5	0	0	0	0	0	0	0	0	0	0
85	90	6	0	0	0	0	0	0	0	0	0	0
90	95	6	0	0	0	0	0	0	0	0	0	0
95	100	7	0	0	0	0	0	0	0	0	0	0
100	105	8	0	0	0	0	0	0	0	0	0	0
105	110	9	1	0	0	0	0	0	0	0	0	0
110	115	9	2	0	0	0	0	0	0	0	0	0
115	120	10	3	0	0	0	0	0	0	0	0	0
120	125	11	3	0	0	0	0	0	0	0	0	0
125	130	12	4	0	0	0	0	0	0	0	0	0
130	135	12	5	0	0	0	0	0	0	0	0	0
135	140	13	6	0	0	0	0	0	0	0	0	0
140	145	14	6	0	0	0	0	0	0	0	0	0
145	150	15	7	0	0	0	0	0	0	0	0	0
150	155	15	8	1	0	0	0	0	0	0	0	0
155	160	16	9	1	0	0	0	0	0	0	0	0
160	165	17	9	2	0	0	0	0	0	0	0	0
165	170	18	10	3	0	0	0	0	0	0	0	0
170	175	18	11	4	0	0	0	0	0	0	0	0
175	180	19	12	4	0	0	0	0	0	0	0	0
180	185	20	12	5	0	0	0	0	0	0	0	0
185	190	21	13	6	0	0	0	0	0	0	0	0
190	195	21	14	7	0	0	0	0	0	0	0	0
195	200	22	15	7	0	0	0	0	0	0	0	0
200	210	23	16	8	1	0	0	0	0	0	0	0
210	220	25	17	10	3	0	0	0	0	0	0	0
220	230	26	19	11	4	0	0	0	0	0	0	0
230	240	28	20	13	6	0	0	0	0	0	0	0
240	250	29	22	14	7	0	0	0	0	0	0	0
250	260	31	23	16	9	1	0	0	0	0	0	0
260	270	32	25	17	10	3	0	0	0	0	0	0
270	280	34	26	19	12	4	0	0	0	0	0	0
280	290	35	28	20	13	6	0	0	0	0	0	0
290	300	37	29	22	15	7	0	0	0	0	0	0
300	310	38	31	23	16	9	1	0	0	0	0	0
310	320	40	32	25	18	10	3	0	0	0	0	0
320	330	41	34	26	19	12	4	0	0	0	0	0
330	340	43	35	28	21	13	6	0	0	0	0	0
340	350	44	37	29	22	15	7	0	0	0	0	0
350	360	46	38	31	24	16	9	2	0	0	0	0
360	370	47	40	32	25	18	10	3	0	0	0	0
370	380	49	41	34	27	19	12	5	0	0	0	0
380	390	50	43	35	28	21	13	6	0	0	0	0
390	400	52	44	37	30	22	15	8	0	0	0	0
400	410	53	46	38	31	24	16	9	2	0	0	0
410	420	55	47	40	33	25	18	11	3	0	0	0
420	430	56	49	41	34	27	19	12	5	0	0	0
430	440	58	50	43	36	28	21	14	6	0	0	0
440	450	59	52	44	37	30	22	15	8	0	0	0
450	460	61	53	46	39	31	24	17	9	2	0	0
460	470	62	55	47	40	33	25	18	11	3	0	0
470	480	64	56	49	42	34	27	20	12	5	0	0
480	490	65	58	50	43	36	28	21	14	6	0	0
490	500	67	59	52	45	37	30	23	15	8	0	0
500	510	70	61	53	46	39	31	24	17	9	2	0
510	520	73	62	55	48	40	33	26	18	11	3	0
520	530	76	64	56	49	42	34	27	20	12	5	0
530	540	79	65	58	51	43	36	29	21	14	6	0
540	550	81	68	59	52	45	37	30	23	15	8	1
550	560	84	70	61	54	46	39	32	24	17	9	2
560	570	87	73	62	55	48	40	33	26	18	11	4
570	580	90	76	64	57	49	42	35	27	20	12	5
580	590	93	79	65	58	51	43	36	29	21	14	7
590	600	95	82	68	60	52	45	38	30	23	15	8

SINGLE Persons—WEEKLY Payroll Period
(For Wages Paid in 1996)

If the wages are—		And the number of withholding allowances claimed is—										
At least	But less than	0	1	2	3	4	5	6	7	8	9	10
		The amount of income tax to be withheld is—										
$600	$610	98	84	71	61	54	46	39	32	24	17	10
610	620	101	87	74	63	55	48	41	33	26	18	11
620	630	104	90	76	64	57	49	42	35	27	20	13
630	640	107	93	79	66	58	51	44	36	29	21	14
640	650	109	96	82	68	60	52	45	38	30	23	16
650	660	112	98	85	71	61	54	47	39	32	24	17
660	670	115	101	88	74	63	55	48	41	33	26	19
670	680	118	104	90	77	64	57	50	42	35	27	20
680	690	121	107	93	79	66	58	51	44	36	29	22
690	700	123	110	96	82	68	60	53	45	38	30	23
700	710	126	112	99	85	71	61	54	47	39	32	25
710	720	129	115	102	88	74	63	56	48	41	33	26
720	730	132	118	104	91	77	64	57	50	42	35	28
730	740	135	121	107	93	80	66	59	51	44	36	29
740	750	137	124	110	96	82	69	60	53	45	38	31
750	760	140	126	113	99	85	72	62	54	47	39	32
760	770	143	129	116	102	88	74	63	56	48	41	34
770	780	146	132	118	105	91	77	65	57	50	42	35
780	790	149	135	121	107	94	80	66	59	51	44	37
790	800	151	138	124	110	96	83	69	60	53	45	38
800	810	154	140	127	113	99	86	72	62	54	47	40
810	820	157	143	130	116	102	88	75	63	56	48	41
820	830	160	146	132	119	105	91	77	65	57	50	43
830	840	163	149	135	121	108	94	80	66	59	51	44
840	850	165	152	138	124	110	97	83	69	60	53	46
850	860	168	154	141	127	113	100	86	72	62	54	47
860	870	171	157	144	130	116	102	89	75	63	56	49
870	880	174	160	146	133	119	105	91	78	65	57	50
880	890	177	163	149	135	122	108	94	80	67	59	52
890	900	179	166	152	138	124	111	97	83	70	60	53
900	910	182	168	155	141	127	114	100	86	72	62	55
910	920	185	171	158	144	130	116	103	89	75	63	56
920	930	188	174	160	147	133	119	105	92	78	65	58
930	940	191	177	163	149	136	122	108	94	81	67	59
940	950	193	180	166	152	138	125	111	97	84	70	61
950	960	196	182	169	155	141	128	114	100	86	73	62
960	970	199	185	172	158	144	130	117	103	89	75	64
970	980	202	188	174	161	147	133	119	106	92	78	65
980	990	205	191	177	163	150	136	122	108	95	81	67
990	1,000	207	194	180	166	152	139	125	111	98	84	70
1,000	1,010	210	196	183	169	155	142	128	114	100	87	73
1,010	1,020	213	199	186	172	158	144	131	117	103	89	76
1,020	1,030	216	202	188	175	161	147	133	120	106	92	78
1,030	1,040	219	205	191	177	164	150	136	122	109	95	81
1,040	1,050	222	208	194	180	166	153	139	125	112	98	84
1,050	1,060	225	210	197	183	169	156	142	128	114	101	87
1,060	1,070	228	213	200	186	172	158	145	131	117	103	90
1,070	1,080	231	216	202	189	175	161	147	134	120	106	92
1,080	1,090	234	219	205	191	178	164	150	136	123	109	95
1,090	1,100	237	222	208	194	180	167	153	139	126	112	98
1,100	1,110	240	225	211	197	183	170	156	142	128	115	101
1,110	1,120	243	228	214	200	186	172	159	145	131	117	104
1,120	1,130	247	231	216	203	189	175	161	148	134	120	106
1,130	1,140	250	234	219	205	192	178	164	150	137	123	109
1,140	1,150	253	238	222	208	194	181	167	153	140	126	112
1,150	1,160	256	241	225	211	197	184	170	156	142	129	115
1,160	1,170	259	244	229	214	200	186	173	159	145	131	118
1,170	1,180	262	247	232	217	203	189	175	162	148	134	120
1,180	1,190	265	250	235	220	206	192	178	164	151	137	123
1,190	1,200	268	253	238	223	208	195	181	167	154	140	126
1,200	1,210	271	256	241	226	211	198	184	170	156	143	129
1,210	1,220	274	259	244	229	214	200	187	173	159	145	132
1,220	1,230	278	262	247	232	217	203	189	176	162	148	134
1,230	1,240	281	265	250	235	220	206	192	178	165	151	137
1,240	1,250	284	269	253	238	223	209	195	181	168	154	140

$1,250 and over   Use Table 1(a) for a **SINGLE** person on page 34. Also see the instructions on page 32.

MARRIED Persons—WEEKLY Payroll Period
(For Wages Paid in 1996)

At least	But less than	0	1	2	3	4	5	6	7	8	9	10
							The amount of income tax to be withheld is—					
$0	$125	0	0	0	0	0	0	0	0	0	0	0
125	130	1	0	0	0	0	0	0	0	0	0	0
130	135	1	0	0	0	0	0	0	0	0	0	0
135	140	2	0	0	0	0	0	0	0	0	0	0
140	145	3	0	0	0	0	0	0	0	0	0	0
145	150	4	0	0	0	0	0	0	0	0	0	0
150	155	4	0	0	0	0	0	0	0	0	0	0
155	160	5	0	0	0	0	0	0	0	0	0	0
160	165	6	0	0	0	0	0	0	0	0	0	0
165	170	7	0	0	0	0	0	0	0	0	0	0
170	175	7	0	0	0	0	0	0	0	0	0	0
175	180	8	1	0	0	0	0	0	0	0	0	0
180	185	9	1	0	0	0	0	0	0	0	0	0
185	190	10	2	0	0	0	0	0	0	0	0	0
190	195	10	3	0	0	0	0	0	0	0	0	0
195	200	11	4	0	0	0	0	0	0	0	0	0
200	210	12	5	0	0	0	0	0	0	0	0	0
210	220	14	6	0	0	0	0	0	0	0	0	0
220	230	15	8	1	0	0	0	0	0	0	0	0
230	240	17	9	2	0	0	0	0	0	0	0	0
240	250	18	11	4	0	0	0	0	0	0	0	0
250	260	20	12	5	0	0	0	0	0	0	0	0
260	270	21	14	7	0	0	0	0	0	0	0	0
270	280	23	15	8	1	0	0	0	0	0	0	0
280	290	24	17	10	2	0	0	0	0	0	0	0
290	300	26	18	11	4	0	0	0	0	0	0	0
300	310	27	20	13	5	0	0	0	0	0	0	0
310	320	29	21	14	7	0	0	0	0	0	0	0
320	330	30	23	16	8	1	0	0	0	0	0	0
330	340	32	24	17	10	2	0	0	0	0	0	0
340	350	33	26	19	11	4	0	0	0	0	0	0
350	360	35	27	20	13	5	0	0	0	0	0	0
360	370	36	29	22	14	7	0	0	0	0	0	0
370	380	38	30	23	16	8	1	0	0	0	0	0
380	390	39	32	25	17	10	2	0	0	0	0	0
390	400	41	33	26	19	11	4	0	0	0	0	0
400	410	42	35	28	20	13	5	0	0	0	0	0
410	420	44	36	29	22	14	7	0	0	0	0	0
420	430	45	38	31	23	16	8	1	0	0	0	0
430	440	47	39	32	25	17	10	3	0	0	0	0
440	450	48	41	34	26	19	11	4	0	0	0	0
450	460	50	42	35	28	20	13	6	0	0	0	0
460	470	51	44	37	29	22	14	7	0	0	0	0
470	480	53	45	38	31	23	16	9	1	0	0	0
480	490	54	47	40	32	25	17	10	3	0	0	0
490	500	56	48	41	34	26	19	12	4	0	0	0
500	510	57	50	43	35	28	20	13	6	0	0	0
510	520	59	51	44	37	29	22	15	7	0	0	0
520	530	60	53	46	38	31	23	16	9	1	0	0
530	540	62	54	47	40	32	25	18	10	3	0	0
540	550	63	56	49	41	34	26	19	12	4	0	0
550	560	65	57	50	43	35	28	21	13	6	0	0
560	570	66	59	52	44	37	29	22	15	7	0	0
570	580	68	60	53	46	38	31	24	16	9	2	0
580	590	69	62	55	47	40	32	25	18	10	3	0
590	600	71	63	56	49	41	34	27	19	12	5	0
600	610	72	65	58	50	43	35	28	21	13	6	0
610	620	74	66	59	52	44	37	30	22	15	8	0
620	630	75	68	61	53	46	38	31	24	16	9	2
630	640	77	69	62	55	47	40	33	25	18	11	3
640	650	78	71	64	56	49	41	34	27	19	12	5
650	660	80	72	65	58	50	43	36	28	21	14	6
660	670	81	74	67	59	52	44	37	30	22	15	8
670	680	83	75	68	61	53	46	39	31	24	17	9
680	690	84	77	70	62	55	47	40	33	25	18	11
690	700	86	78	71	64	56	49	42	34	27	20	12
700	710	87	80	73	65	58	50	43	36	28	21	14
710	720	89	81	74	67	59	52	45	37	30	23	15
720	730	90	83	76	68	61	53	46	39	31	24	17
730	740	92	84	77	70	62	55	48	40	33	26	18

MARRIED Persons—WEEKLY Payroll Period
(For Wages Paid in 1996)

If the wages are—		And the number of withholding allowances claimed is—										
At least	But less than	0	1	2	3	4	5	6	7	8	9	10
		The amount of income tax to be withheld is—										
$740	$750	93	86	79	71	64	56	49	42	34	27	20
750	760	95	87	80	73	65	58	51	43	36	29	21
760	770	96	89	82	74	67	59	52	45	37	30	23
770	780	98	90	83	76	68	61	54	46	39	32	24
780	790	99	92	85	77	70	62	55	48	40	33	26
790	800	101	93	86	79	71	64	57	49	42	35	27
800	810	102	95	88	80	73	65	58	51	43	36	29
810	820	104	96	89	82	74	67	60	52	45	38	30
820	830	105	98	91	83	76	68	61	54	46	39	32
830	840	107	99	92	85	77	70	63	55	48	41	33
840	850	108	101	94	86	79	71	64	57	49	42	35
850	860	110	102	95	88	80	73	66	58	51	44	36
860	870	113	104	97	89	82	74	67	60	52	45	38
870	880	116	105	98	91	83	76	69	61	54	47	39
880	890	119	107	100	92	85	77	70	63	55	48	41
890	900	121	108	101	94	86	79	72	64	57	50	42
900	910	124	111	103	95	88	80	73	66	58	51	44
910	920	127	113	104	97	89	82	75	67	60	53	45
920	930	130	116	106	98	91	83	76	69	61	54	47
930	940	133	119	107	100	92	85	78	70	63	56	48
940	950	135	122	109	101	94	86	79	72	64	57	50
950	960	138	125	111	103	95	88	81	73	66	59	51
960	970	141	127	114	104	97	89	82	75	67	60	53
970	980	144	130	116	106	98	91	84	76	69	62	54
980	990	147	133	119	107	100	92	85	78	70	63	56
990	1,000	149	136	122	109	101	94	87	79	72	65	57
1,000	1,010	152	139	125	111	103	95	88	81	73	66	59
1,010	1,020	155	141	128	114	104	97	90	82	75	68	60
1,020	1,030	158	144	130	117	106	98	91	84	76	69	62
1,030	1,040	161	147	133	119	107	100	93	85	78	71	63
1,040	1,050	163	150	136	122	109	101	94	87	79	72	65
1,050	1,060	166	153	139	125	111	103	96	88	81	74	66
1,060	1,070	169	155	142	128	114	104	97	90	82	75	68
1,070	1,080	172	158	144	131	117	106	99	91	84	77	69
1,080	1,090	175	161	147	133	120	107	100	93	85	78	71
1,090	1,100	177	164	150	136	123	109	102	94	87	80	72
1,100	1,110	180	167	153	139	125	112	103	96	88	81	74
1,110	1,120	183	169	156	142	128	114	105	97	90	83	75
1,120	1,130	186	172	158	145	131	117	106	99	91	84	77
1,130	1,140	189	175	161	147	134	120	108	100	93	86	78
1,140	1,150	191	178	164	150	137	123	109	102	94	87	80
1,150	1,160	194	181	167	153	139	126	112	103	96	89	81
1,160	1,170	197	183	170	156	142	128	115	105	97	90	83
1,170	1,180	200	186	172	159	145	131	117	106	99	92	84
1,180	1,190	203	189	175	161	148	134	120	108	100	93	86
1,190	1,200	205	192	178	164	151	137	123	109	102	95	87
1,200	1,210	208	195	181	167	153	140	126	112	103	96	89
1,210	1,220	211	197	184	170	156	142	129	115	105	98	90
1,220	1,230	214	200	186	173	159	145	131	118	106	99	92
1,230	1,240	217	203	189	175	162	148	134	121	108	101	93
1,240	1,250	219	206	192	178	165	151	137	123	110	102	95
1,250	1,260	222	209	195	181	167	154	140	126	112	104	96
1,260	1,270	225	211	198	184	170	156	143	129	115	105	98
1,270	1,280	228	214	200	187	173	159	145	132	118	107	99
1,280	1,290	231	217	203	189	176	162	148	135	121	108	101
1,290	1,300	233	220	206	192	179	165	151	137	124	110	102
1,300	1,310	236	223	209	195	181	168	154	140	126	113	104
1,310	1,320	239	225	212	198	184	170	157	143	129	115	105
1,320	1,330	242	228	214	201	187	173	159	146	132	118	107
1,330	1,340	245	231	217	203	190	176	162	149	135	121	108
1,340	1,350	247	234	220	206	193	179	165	151	138	124	110
1,350	1,360	250	237	223	209	195	182	168	154	140	127	113
1,360	1,370	253	239	226	212	198	184	171	157	143	129	116
1,370	1,380	256	242	228	215	201	187	173	160	146	132	119
1,380	1,390	259	245	231	217	204	190	176	163	149	135	121

$1,390 and over   Use Table 1(b) for a **MARRIED person** on page 34. Also see the instructions on page 32.

Form **941**
(Rev. January 1995)
Department of the Treasury
Internal Revenue Service   (O)

4141

Employer's Quarterly Federal Tax Return
▶ See separate instructions for information on completing this return.
Please type or print.

OMB No. 1545-0029

Enter state code for state in which deposits made. ▶ ☐
(see page 3 of instructions).

Name (as distinguished from trade name)	Date quarter ended	
Trade name, if any	Employer identification number	T / FF
Address (number and street)	City, state, and ZIP code	FD / FP / I / T

If address is different from prior return, check here ▶ ☐

IRS Use

```
1  1  1  1  1  1  1  1  1  1     2     3  3  3  3  3  3     4  4  4
☐  ☐  ☐  ☐  ☐  ☐  ☐  ☐  ☐  ☐   ☐   ☐  ☐  ☐  ☐  ☐  ☐   ☐  ☐  ☐  ☐  ☐  ☐  ☐  ☐  ☐  ☐  ☐  ☐
5  5  5     6     7     8  8  8  8  8  8     9  9  9   10 10 10 10 10 10 10 10 10 10
```

If you do not have to file returns in the future, check here ▶ ☐   and enter date final wages paid ▶ _____

If you are a seasonal employer, see **Seasonal employers** on page 1 of the instructions and check here ▶ ☐

1	Number of employees (except household) employed in the pay period that includes March 12th ▶		
2	Total wages and tips, plus other compensation	**2**	
3	Total income tax withheld from wages, tips, and sick pay	**3**	
4	Adjustment of withheld income tax for preceding quarters of calendar year	**4**	
5	Adjusted total of income tax withheld (line 3 as adjusted by line 4—see instructions) . . .	**5**	
6a	Taxable social security wages . . . . $ _____ × 12.4% (.124) =	**6a**	
b	Taxable social security tips . . . . $ _____ × 12.4% (.124) =	**6b**	
7	Taxable Medicare wages and tips . . . . . $ _____ × 2.9% (.029) =	**7**	
8	Total social security and Medicare taxes (add lines 6a, 6b, and 7). Check here if wages are not subject to social security and/or Medicare tax . . . . ▶ ☐	**8**	
9	Adjustment of social security and Medicare taxes (see instructions for required explanation) Sick Pay $ _____ ± Fractions of Cents $ _____ ± Other $ _____ =	**9**	
10	Adjusted total of social security and Medicare taxes (line 8 as adjusted by line 9—see instructions)	**10**	
11	**Total taxes** (add lines 5 and 10)	**11**	
12	Advance earned income credit (EIC) payments made to employees, if any	**12**	
13	Net taxes (subtract line 12 from line 11). **This should equal line 17, column (d) below** (or line D of Schedule B (Form 941))	**13**	
14	Total deposits for quarter, including overpayment applied from a prior quarter	**14**	
15	**Balance due** (subtract line 14 from line 13). Pay to Internal Revenue Service	**15**	

16 Overpayment, if line 14 is more than line 13, enter excess here ▶ $ _____
and check if to be: ☐ Applied to next return   **OR**   ☐ Refunded.

• **All filers:** If line 13 is less than $500, you need not complete line 17 or Schedule B.
• **Semiweekly depositors:** Complete Schedule B and check here . . . . ▶ ☐
• **Monthly depositors:** Complete line 17, columns (a) through (d), and check here . . . . ▶ ☐

17	**Monthly Summary of Federal Tax Liability.**		
(a) First month liability	**(b)** Second month liability	**(c)** Third month liability	**(d)** Total liability for quarter

Sign Here

Under penalties of perjury, I declare that I have examined this return, including accompanying schedules and statements, and to the best of my knowledge and belief, it is true, correct, and complete.

Signature ▶ _____   Print Your Name and Title ▶ _____   Date ▶ _____

For Paperwork Reduction Act Notice, see page 1 of separate instructions.   Cat. No. 17001Z   Form **941** (Rev. 1-95)

Department of the Treasury
Internal Revenue Service

Instructions for Form 941

(Revised January 1995)
Employer's Quarterly Federal Tax Return

(Section references are to the Internal Revenue Code unless otherwise noted.)

Paperwork Reduction Act Notice.—We ask for the information on this form to carry out the Internal Revenue laws of the United States. You are required to give us the information. We need it to ensure that you are complying with these laws and to allow us to figure and collect the right amount of tax.

The time needed to complete and file this form will vary depending on individual circumstances. The estimated average time is:

Recordkeeping	11 hr., 43 min.
Learning about the law or the form	28 min.
Preparing the form	1 hr., 37 min.
Copying, assembling, and sending the form to the IRS	.16 min.

If you have comments concerning the accuracy of these time estimates or suggestions for making this form simpler, we would be happy to hear from you. You can write to the **Internal Revenue Service**, Attention: Tax Forms Committee, PC:FP, Washington, DC 20224. **DO NOT** send the tax form to this address. Instead, see **Where To File** on page 2.

Important Changes for 1995

Federal Tax Deposits by Electronic Funds Transfer (EFT)

Generally, taxpayers whose total deposits of withheld income, social security, and Medicare taxes during calendar year 1993 exceeded $78 million are required to deposit all depositary taxes due after 1994 by electronic funds transfer (EFT). TAXLINK, an electronic remittance processing system, must be used to make deposits by EFT. Taxpayers who are not required to make deposits by EFT may voluntarily participate in TAXLINK. For more details on TAXLINK, call the toll-free TAXLINK HELPLINE at 1-800-829-5469.

Social Security Wage Base for 1995

Stop withholding social security tax after an employee reaches **$61,200** in taxable wages.

Form 945

Income tax withholding on nonpayroll payments made during 1994 must be reported on the new **Form 945**, Annual Return of Withheld Federal Income Tax. The return for 1994 is due January 31, 1995. Nonpayroll items include backup withholding and withholding on pensions, annuities, IRAs, and gambling winnings. Get the separate **Instructions for Form 945** for more information.

All income tax withholding reported on Forms 1099 or W-2G must be reported on Form 945. All income tax withholding reported on Form W-2 must be reported on Form 941 (or 943). For example, because distributions from nonqualified pension plans and nonqualified deferred compensation plans are treated as wages and are reported on Form W-2, they must be reported on Form 941, not Form 945.

Household Employees

1994 Social Security and Medicare Taxes for Household Employees.—The tax liability threshold for cash wages paid to household employees increased from $50 per quarter to $1,000

per year for 1994. If you withheld and paid social security and Medicare taxes for a household employee to whom you paid less than $1,000 in cash wages, you can get a refund. See **Circular E,** Employer's Tax Guide, for details.

Household Employees Under Age 18.—Beginning in 1995, payments for household services are exempt from social security and Medicare taxes if performed by an individual who is under age 18 during any portion of the calendar year, unless this is the principal occupation of the employee.

New Reporting Requirements.—For wages paid after 1994, report social security and Medicare taxes and income tax withholding for household employees on your individual income tax return. These taxes will no longer be reported quarterly. However, if you are a sole proprietor and file Form 941 for business employees, you must include taxes for household employees on your Form 941. See Circular E for more information.

Expired Provision

Educational Assistance Programs.—The provision exempting educational assistance payments from income tax withholding and employment taxes was scheduled to expire on December 31, 1994, unless extended by law.

General Instructions

Purpose of Form.—To report—
- Income tax you withheld from wages, tips, supplemental unemployment compensation benefits, and third-party payments of sick pay.
- Social security and Medicare taxes.

Who Must File.—Employers who withhold income tax on wages, social security tax, or Medicare tax, must file Form 941 quarterly.

Seasonal employers are not required to file for quarters when they regularly have no tax liability because they have paid no wages. To alert the IRS that you will not have to file a return for one or more quarters during the year, check the **Seasonal employer** box above line 1 on page 1. The IRS will mail two Forms 941 to you once a year after March 1. The preprinted label will not include the date the quarter ended. You must enter the date the quarter ended when you file the return. The IRS will generally not inquire about unfiled returns if at least one taxable return is filed each year. However, you must check the **Seasonal employer** box on each quarterly return you file. Otherwise, the IRS will expect a return to be filed for each quarter.

Employers who report wages on household employees, see Circular E and **Pub. 926,** Employment Taxes for Household Employers.

Employers who report wages on farmworkers, see **Form 943,** Employer's Annual Tax Return for Agricultural Employees, and Circular A.

Business Reorganization or Termination.—If you sell or transfer your business, both you and the new owner must file a return for the quarter in which the change took place. Neither should report wages paid by the other. (An example of a transfer is when a sole proprietor forms a partnership or corporation. The partnership or corporation is considered a new business and must apply for a new employer identification number (EIN). See section 2 of Circular E.) If a change occurs, please attach to

Cat. No. 14625L

your return a statement that shows: new owner's name (or new name of the business); whether the business is now a sole proprietorship, partnership, or corporation; kind of change that took place (sale, transfer, etc.); and date of the change.

When a business is merged or consolidated with another, the continuing firm must file the return for the quarter in which the change took place. The return should show all wages paid for that quarter. The other firm should file a final return.

If you go out of business or stop paying wages, you should file a final return. Be sure to mark the final return checkbox and enter the date final wages were paid above line 1. You may also file Forms W-2 with the Social Security Administration now, but not later than February 29, 1996.

Form Preparation Suggestions.—The red color of Form 941 permits machine scanning, which results in faster and more accurate processing. Below are suggestions that will allow the IRS to process Form 941 by machine scanning:

- Make dollar entries without the dollar sign and comma (0000.00).
- Use the "red" Form 941 provided by the IRS.
- Entries should not be handwritten; type or machine print data entries using black ink.
- Do not staple, tape, or clip anything to the form.
- Do not tear.

When To File.—File starting with the first quarter in which you are required to withhold income tax or pay wages subject to social security and Medicare taxes.

Quarter	Ending	Due Date
Jan.-Feb.-Mar.	March 31	April 30
Apr.-May-June	June 30	July 31
July-Aug.-Sept.	Sept. 30	Oct. 31
Oct.-Nov.-Dec.	Dec. 31	Jan. 31

If you deposited all taxes when due for a quarter, you have 10 more days after the above due date to file. If the due date for filing a return falls on a Saturday, Sunday, or legal holiday, you may file the return on the next business day.

After you file your first return, we will send you a form every 3 months. Please use this form. If you don't have a form, get one from an IRS office in time to file the return when due.

Where To File.—In the list below, find the state where your legal residence, principal place of business, office, or agency is located. Send your return to the **Internal Revenue Service** at the address listed for your location. No street address is needed.

Note: *Where you file depends on whether or not you are including a payment.*

Florida, Georgia, South Carolina

Return without payment:	**Return with payment:**
Atlanta, GA 39901-0049	P.O. Box 105703
	Atlanta, GA 30348-5703

New Jersey, New York (New York City and counties of Nassau, Rockland, Suffolk, and Westchester)

Return without payment:	**Return with payment:**
Holtsville, NY 00501-0049	P.O. Box 416
	Newark, NJ 07101-0416

New York (all other counties), Connecticut, Maine, Massachusetts, New Hampshire, Rhode Island, Vermont

Return without payment:	**Return with payment:**
Andover, MA 05501-0049	P.O. Box 371493
	Pittsburgh, PA 15250-7493

Illinois, Iowa, Minnesota, Missouri, Wisconsin

Return without payment:	**Return with payment:**
Kansas City, MO 64999-0049	P.O. Box 970007
	St. Louis, MO 63197-0007

Delaware, District of Columbia, Maryland, Pennsylvania, Virginia

Return without payment:	**Return with payment:**
Philadelphia, PA 19255-0049	P.O. Box 8786
	Philadelphia, PA 19162-8786

Indiana, Kentucky, Michigan, Ohio, West Virginia

Return without payment:	**Return with payment:**
Cincinnati, OH 45999-0049	P.O. Box 7329
	Chicago, IL 60680-7329

Kansas, New Mexico, Oklahoma, Texas

Return without payment:	**Return with payment:**
Austin, TX 73301-0049	P.O. Box 970013
	St. Louis, MO 63197-0013

Alaska, Arizona, California (counties of Alpine, Amador, Butte, Calaveras, Colusa, Contra Costa, Del Norte, El Dorado, Glenn, Humboldt, Lake, Lassen, Marin, Mendocino, Modoc, Napa, Nevada, Placer, Plumas, Sacramento, San Joaquin, Shasta, Sierra, Siskiyou, Solano, Sonoma, Sutter, Tehama, Trinity, Yolo, and Yuba), Colorado, Idaho, Montana, Nebraska, Nevada, North Dakota, Oregon, South Dakota, Utah, Washington, Wyoming

Return without payment:	**Return with payment:**
Ogden, UT 84201-0049	P.O. Box 7922
	San Francisco, CA 94120-7922

California (all other counties), Hawaii

Return without payment:	**Return with payment:**
Fresno, CA 93888-0049	P.O. Box 60407
	Los Angeles, CA 90060-0407

Alabama, Arkansas, Louisiana, Mississippi, North Carolina, Tennessee

Return without payment:	**Return with payment:**
Memphis, TN 37501-0049	P.O. Box 70503
	Charlotte, NC 28272-0503

If you have no legal residence or principal place of business in any state

	All returns:
	Philadelphia, PA 19255-0005

Forms W-4.—Each quarter, send with Form 941 copies of any Forms W-4 received during the quarter from employees claiming (1) more than 10 withholding allowances or (2) exemption from income tax withholding if their wages will normally be more than $200 a week. For details, see section 9 of Circular E.

Form W-5.—Each eligible employee wishing to receive any advance earned income credit (EIC) payments must give you a completed Form W-5. The employer's requirement to notify certain employees about the EIC can be met by giving each eligible employee **Notice 797,** Possible Federal Tax Refund Due to the Earned Income Credit (EIC). See Circular E and **Pub. 596,** Earned Income Credit, for more information.

Employer Identification Number (EIN).—If you do not have an EIN, apply for one on **Form SS-4,** Application for Employer Identification Number. Get this form from the IRS or the Social Security Administration (SSA). If you do not have an EIN by the time a return is due, write "Applied for" and the date you applied in the space shown for the number. You can receive your EIN over the telephone and use it immediately to file a return or make a payment (get Form SS-4 instructions for details).

Note: *Always be sure the EIN on the form you file matches the EIN assigned to your business by the IRS. Do not show your personal social security number on forms calling for an EIN. Filing a Form 941 with an incorrect EIN or using another business' EIN may result in penalties and delays in processing your return.*

Penalties and Interest.—There are penalties for filing a return late and paying or depositing taxes late, unless there is a reasonable cause. If you are late, please attach an explanation to your return. There are also penalties for willful failure to file returns and pay taxes when due, furnish Forms W-2 to employees and file copies with the SSA, keep records, deposit taxes when required, and for filing false returns or submitting bad checks. Interest is charged on taxes paid late at the rate set by law. See Circular E for additional information.

Caution: *A trust fund recovery penalty may apply where income, social security, and Medicare taxes that should be withheld are not withheld or are not paid to the IRS. Under this penalty, certain officers or employees of a corporation, employees of a sole proprietorship, or partners or employees of a partnership become personally liable for payment of the taxes and are penalized an amount equal to the unpaid taxes. This penalty may be applicable when these unpaid taxes cannot be immediately collected from the employer or business. The trust fund recovery penalty may be imposed on all persons who are determined by the IRS to be responsible for collecting, accounting for, and paying over these taxes, and who acted willfully in not doing so. Willfully in this case means voluntarily, consciously, and intentionally. Please see Circular E for more information concerning who may be liable for the trust fund recovery penalty.*

Depositing Taxes.—Use **Form 8109,** Federal Tax Deposit Coupon, to deposit your taxes. See section 11 of Circular E for information and rules concerning Federal tax deposits.

Do not use the deposit coupons to pay delinquent taxes for which you have received a notice from the IRS. These payments should be sent directly to your Internal Revenue Service Center with a copy of any related notice the IRS sent you.

State Code.—If you made your deposits in a state other than that shown in your address on Form 941, enter the state code for that state in the box provided in the upper left corner of the form. Use the Postal Service two-letter state abbreviation as the state code. Enter the code "MU" in the state code box if you deposit in more than one state. If you deposit in the same state as shown in your address, do not make an entry in this box.

Related Publications.—Circular E explains the rules for withholding, paying, depositing, and reporting Federal income tax, social security and Medicare taxes, and Federal unemployment (FUTA) tax on wages and fringe benefits. See **Pub. 952,** Sick Pay Reporting, for information on sick pay paid by third-party payers. **Circular A,** Agricultural Employer's Tax Guide, explains rules for employers who have farm workers. These publications are available free at IRS offices.

Specific Instructions

Reconciliation of Forms 941 and W-3.— Certain amounts reported on the four quarterly Forms 941 for 1995 should agree with the **Form W-2,** Wage and Tax Statement, totals reported on **Form W-3,** Transmittal of Wage and Tax Statements, or with information filed on equivalent magnetic media reports with the SSA. The amounts that should agree are social security wages, social security tips, Medicare wages and tips, and the advance earned income credit. If the totals do not agree, the IRS will require you to explain any differences and correct any errors. You can avoid this by making sure correct amounts (including adjustments) are reported on Forms 941 and W-3. See section 12 of Circular E for more details.

Line 1—Number of employees.—Enter the number of employees on your payroll during the pay period including March 12 (on the January–March calendar quarter return only). Do not include household employees, persons who received no pay during the pay period, pensioners, or members of the Armed Forces. An entry of 250 or more on line 1 indicates a need to file wage reports on magnetic media. You should immediately request Publication TIB-4 from the SSA if not already a magnetic media filer. Call 1-800-772-1213 for more information.

Line 2.—Enter the total of all wages paid, tips reported, taxable fringe benefits provided, and other compensation paid to your employees, **even if you do not have to withhold income or social security and Medicare taxes on it.** Do not include supplemental unemployment compensation benefits, even if you withheld income tax on them. Do not include contributions to employee plans that are excluded from the employee's wages (e.g., section 401(k) and 125 plans).

If you get timely notice from your insurance carrier concerning the amount of third-party sick pay it paid your employees, include the sick pay on line 2. If you are an insurance company, do not include sick pay you paid policyholders' employees here if you gave the policyholders timely notice of the payments. See Pub. 952 for more details.

Line 3.—Enter the income tax you withheld on wages, tips, taxable fringe benefits, and supplemental unemployment compensation benefits. An insurance company should enter the income tax it withheld on third-party sick pay here.

Line 4—Adjustment of withheld income tax.—Use line 4 to correct errors in income tax withheld from wages paid in earlier quarters of the same calendar year. Because any amount shown on line 4 increases or decreases your tax liability, the adjustment must be taken into account on line 17, Monthly Summary of Federal Tax Liability, or on **Schedule B (Form 941),** Employer's Record of Federal Tax Liability. Your deposit requirements determine which liability report is used. For details on how to report adjustments on the record of Federal tax liability, see the instructions for line 17 (on page 4) or the instructions for Schedule B (Form 941).

Explain any amount on **Form 941c,** Supporting Statement To Correct Information, or attach a statement that shows (a) what the error was, (b) quarter in which the error was made, (c) the amount of the error for each quarter, (d) date on which you found the error, and (e) how you and your payees have settled any overcollection or undercollection.

Do not adjust income tax withholding for quarters in earlier years unless it is to correct an administrative error. An administrative error is any error that does not change the amount of income tax that was actually withheld or deducted from an employee. For example, if the total income tax actually withheld was incorrectly reported due to a mathematical error, this is an administrative error. You may not adjust or claim a refund or credit for any overpayment of income tax that you withheld or deducted from an employee in a prior year. This is because the employee uses the amount shown on Form W-2 as a credit when filing his or her income tax return (Form 1040, etc.).

Line 5—Adjusted total of income tax withheld.—Add line 4 to line 3 if you are reporting additional income tax withheld for an earlier quarter. Subtract line 4 from line 3 if you are reducing the amount of income tax withheld. If there is no entry on line 4, the entry will be the same as line 3.

Line 6a—Taxable social security wages.—Enter the total wages subject to social security taxes that you paid your employees during the quarter. Also include any sick pay and taxable fringe benefits subject to social security taxes. See section 5 of Circular E for information on types of wages subject to social security taxes. Enter the amount before deductions. Do not include tips on this line. Stop reporting an employee's wages (including tips) when they reach $61,200 for 1995. However, continue to withhold income tax for the whole year on wages and tips even when the social security wage base of $61,200 is reached. See the line 7 instructions for Medicare tax. **If none of the payments are subject to social security tax, mark the checkbox in line 8.**

Line 6b—Taxable social security tips.—Enter all tips your employees reported during the quarter, until tips and wages for each employee reach $61,200 in 1995. Do this even if you were not able to withhold the employee tax (6.2%). However, see the line 9 instructions.

An employee must report to you cash tips, including tips you paid the employee for charge customers, totaling $20 or more in a month by the 10th of the next month. The employee may use **Form 4070,** Employee's Report of Tips to Employer, or a written statement.

Do not include allocated tips on this line. Instead, report them on **Form 8027,** Employer's Annual Information Return of Tip Income and Allocated Tips. Allocated tips are not reportable on Form 941 and are not subject to withholding of income, social security, or Medicare taxes.

Line 7—Taxable Medicare wages and tips.—Use this line to report all wages and tips subject to the Medicare portion of social security. Also include any sick pay and taxable fringe benefits subject to Medicare taxes. See section 5 of Circular E for information on types of wages subject to Medicare taxes. There is no limit on the amount of wages subject to Medicare tax. **If none of the payments are subject to Medicare tax, mark the checkbox in line 8.**

Page 3

Include all tips your employees reported during the quarter, even if you were not able to withhold the employee tax (1.45%). However, see the line 9 instructions below.

Line 9—Adjustment of social security and Medicare taxes.—

Current Period Adjustments.—In certain cases, amounts reported as social security and Medicare taxes on lines 6a, 6b, and 7 must be adjusted to arrive at your correct tax liability. See section 13 of Circular E for information on the following adjustments:

- Adjustment for the uncollected employee share of social security and Medicare taxes on tips.
- Adjustment for the employee share of social security and Medicare taxes on group-term life insurance premiums paid for former employees.
- Adjustment for the employee share of social security and Medicare taxes for sick pay withheld by a third-party payer.
- Fractions of cents adjustment.

Enter the adjustments for sick pay and fractions-of-cents in the appropriate line 9 entry spaces, Enter the amount of all other adjustments in the "Other" entry space and enter the total of the three types of adjustments in the line 9 entry space to the right. Provide a supporting statement explaining any adjustments reported in the "Other" entry space.

Prior Period Adjustments.—Use line 9 to correct errors in social security and Medicare taxes reported on an earlier return. If you report both an underpayment and an overpayment, show only the difference.

Because any prior period adjustments shown on line 9 increase or decrease your tax liability, the adjustments must be taken into account on line 17, Monthly Summary of Federal Tax Liability, or on **Schedule B (Form 941),** Employer's Record of Federal Tax Liability. Your deposit requirements determine which liability report is used. For details on how to report adjustments on the record of Federal tax liability, see the instructions for line 17 below or the instructions for Schedule B (Form 941).

Explain any prior period adjustments on Form 941c. DO NOT file Form 941c separately from Form 941. Form 941c is not an amended return, but is a statement providing necessary background information and certifications supporting the adjustments on lines 4 and/or 9 on Form 941. You can get Form 941c from the IRS or by calling 1-800-TAX-FORM (1-800-829-3676).

If you do not have a Form 941c, attach a statement that shows (a) what the error was; (b) ending date of each quarter in which the error was made and the amount of the error; (c) date on which you found the error; (d) that you repaid the employee tax or got each affected employee's written consent to this refund or credit, if the entry corrects an overcollection; and (e) if the entry corrects social security and Medicare taxes overcollected in an earlier year, that you got from the employee a written statement that he or she has not claimed and will not claim a refund or credit for the amount.

If you are adjusting an employee's social security wages or tips, Medicare wages or tips, or tax withheld for a prior year, you must file **Form W-2c,** Statement of Corrected Income and Tax Amounts. Send Copy A of the Form W-2c, together with **Form W-3c,** Transmittal of Corrected Income and Tax Statements, to the Social Security Administration, Data Operations Center, Wilkes-Barre, PA 18769, regardless of where the original Forms W-2 were filed.

Line 10—Adjusted total of social security and Medicare taxes.—Add line 9 to line 8 if the net adjustment on line 9 is positive (e.g., you are reporting additional taxes for a prior period). Subtract line 9 from line 8 if the net adjustment on line 9 is negative.

Line 12—Advance earned income credit (EIC) payments made to employees.—Enter advance EIC payments made to employees, if any. Your eligible employees may elect to receive part of the EIC as an advance payment. Eligible employees who have a qualifying child must give you a completed Form W-5 stating that they qualify for the EIC. Once the employee gives you a signed and completed Form W-5, you must make the advance EIC payments. The advance EIC payments made to eligible employees are generally made from withheld income tax and employee and employer social security and Medicare taxes. See **Pub. 937,** Employment Taxes; section 16 of Circular E; and Pub. 596 for more information on advance EIC payments and eligibility requirements.

If the amount of your advance EIC payments exceeds your total taxes (line 11) for the quarter, you may claim a refund of the overpayment or elect to have the credit applied to your return for the following quarter. Provide a statement with your return identifying the amount of excess payment(s) and the pay period(s) in which it was paid. See section 16 of Circular E for more details.

Line 15—Balance due.—You should have a balance due only if your net tax liability for the quarter (line 13) is less than $500. (However, see section 11 of Circular E regarding payments made under the Accuracy of Deposits rule.) If line 13 is $500 or more and you have deposited all taxes when due, the amount shown on line 15 (balance due) should be zero. **Caution:** *If you fail to make required deposits at a qualified depositary and instead pay these amounts with your return, you may be subject to a penalty.* Enter your EIN, "Form 941," and the tax period to which the payment applies on your check or money order.

Line 16—Overpayment.—If you deposited more than the correct amount for a quarter, you can have the overpayment refunded or applied to your next return by checking the appropriate box. If you do not check either box, your overpayment will be applied to your next return. The IRS may apply your overpayment to any past-due tax account that we have under your EIN.

Line 17—Monthly Summary of Federal Tax Liability.— Note: *This is a summary of your monthly tax liability, NOT a summary of deposits made. If line 13 is less than $500, you need not complete line 17 or Schedule B (Form 941).*

Complete line 17 if you are qualified to deposit on a monthly basis (see section 11 of Circular E for more details on the deposit rules). You are a monthly depositor for the calendar year if the amount of employment and withholding tax liability accumulated during the lookback period is not more than $50,000. The lookback period is defined as the four consecutive quarters ending on June 30 of the prior year. For 1995, the lookback period begins 07/01/93 and ends 06/30/94. If you accumulated more than $50,000 during the lookback period or accumulated $100,000 or more on any day during a month, do not complete columns (a) through (d) of line 17. Instead, complete and attach Schedule B (Form 941).

Reporting adjustments on line 17.—If the net adjustment during a month is negative (e.g., correcting an overreported liability in a prior period) and it exceeds the total liability for the month, do not enter a negative amount for the month. Instead, enter -0- for the month and carry over the unused portion of the adjustment to the next month. For example, Employer A discovered on 2/10/95 that it overreported social security tax on a prior quarter return by $2,500. Its employment tax liabilities for the 1st quarter of 1995 were: January $2,000, February $2,000, March $2,000. Employer A should enter $2,000 in column (a), -0- in column (b), $1,500 in column (c), and $3,500 in column (d). The prior period adjustment ($2,500) offsets the $2,000 liability for February and the excess $500 must be used to offset March liabilities. Since the error was not discovered until February, it does not affect January liabilities reported in column (a).

If excess negative adjustments are carried forward to the next quarter, do not show these excess adjustments on lines 4 or 9. Line 17, column (d), must equal line 13.

Page 4   Printed on recycled paper   *U.S. Government Printing Office: 1995 - 405-493/20199

Form **940**	**Employer's Annual Federal Unemployment (FUTA) Tax Return**	OMB No. 1545-0028
Department of the Treasury Internal Revenue Service (O)	▶ For Paperwork Reduction Act Notice, see separate instructions.	19**95**

		T	
⌐ Name (as distinguished from trade name)	Calendar year ⌐	FF	
		FD	
Trade name, if any		FP	
		I	
Address and ZIP code	Employer identification number	T	
⌐	⌐		

A Are you required to pay unemployment contributions to only one state? (If no, skip questions B and C.) . .   ☐ Yes   ☐ No

B Did you pay all state unemployment contributions by January 31, 1996? (If a 0% experience rate is granted, check "Yes.") (If no, skip question C.) . . . .   ☐ Yes   ☐ No

C Were all wages that were taxable for FUTA tax also taxable for your state's unemployment tax? . . . . .   ☐ Yes   ☐ No

If you answered "No" to any of these questions, you must file Form 940. If you answered "Yes" to all the questions, you may file Form 940-EZ, which is a simplified version of Form 940. You can get Form 940-EZ by calling 1-800-TAX-FORM (1-800-829-3676).

If you will not have to file returns in the future, check here, complete, and sign the return . . . . . . ▶ ☐

If this is an Amended Return, check here . . . . ▶ ☐

Part I	**Computation of Taxable Wages**

1 Total payments (including exempt payments) during the calendar year for services of employees .   **1**

2 Exempt payments. (Explain each exemption shown, attach additional sheets if necessary.) ▶ -------------------------------   Amount paid

---   **2**

3 Payments of more than $7,000 for services. Enter only amounts over the first $7,000 paid to each employee. Do not include payments from line 2. The $7,000 amount is the Federal wage base. Your state wage base may be different. **Do not use the state wage limitation**   **3**

4 Total exempt payments (add lines 2 and 3) **4**

5 **Total taxable wages** (subtract line 4 from line 1) . . . . ▶   **5**

Be sure to complete both sides of this return and sign in the space provided on the back.   Cat. No. 11234O   Form **940** (1995)

DETACH HERE

Form **940-V**	**Form 940 Payment Voucher**	OMB No. 1545-0028
Department of the Treasury Internal Revenue Service	For Paperwork Reduction Act Notice, see Form 940 instructions.	19**95**

Complete boxes 1,2,3, and 4. Make your check or money order payable to the **Internal Revenue Service**. Include your employer identification number on your check or money order. Do not send cash.

1 Enter the amount of the payment you are making	**2** Enter the first four characters of your business name	**3** Enter your employer identification number
▶ $		
	4 Enter your name	
Do not staple your check or money order to the voucher or the return.	Enter your address	
	Enter your city, state, and ZIP code	

Form 940 (1995)   Page **2**

| **Part II** | **Tax Due or Refund** |

1	Gross FUTA tax. Multiply the wages in Part I, line 5, by .062	1	
2	Maximum credit. Multiply the wages in Part I, line 5, by .054 . . .	2			
3	**Computation of tentative credit** (Note: *All taxpayers must complete the applicable columns.*)

(a) Name of state	(b) State reporting number(s) as shown on employer's state contribution returns	(c) Taxable payroll (as defined in state act)	(d) State experience rate period		(e) State experience rate	(f) Contributions if rate had been 5.4% (col. (c) x .054)	(g) Contributions payable at experience rate (col. (c) x col. (e))	(h) Additional credit (col. (f) minus col.(g)). If 0 or less, enter -0-.	(i) Contributions actually paid to state
			From	To					

3a	Totals . . . ▶						
3b	**Total tentative credit** (add line 3a, columns (h) and (i) only—see instructions for limitations on late payments) ▶		
4			
5			
6	**Credit:** Enter the smaller of the amount in Part II, line 2, or line 3b	6	
7	**Total FUTA tax** (subtract line 6 from line 1)	7	
8	Total FUTA tax deposited for the year, including any overpayment applied from a prior year . .	8	
9	**Balance due** (subtract line 8 from line 7). This should be $100 or less. Pay to the Internal Revenue Service. See page 3 of the Instructions for Form 940 for details . . . . ▶	9	
10	**Overpayment** (subtract line 7 from line 8). Check if it is to be: ☐ **Applied to next return,** or ☐ **Refunded** . . . . ▶	10	

| **Part III** | **Record of Quarterly Federal Unemployment Tax Liability** *(Do not include state liability)* |

Quarter	First	Second	Third	Fourth	Total for year
Liability for quarter					

Under penalties of perjury, I declare that I have examined this return, including accompanying schedules and statements, and to the best of my knowledge and belief, it is true, correct, and complete, and that no part of any payment made to a state unemployment fund claimed as a credit was or is to be deducted from the payments to employees.

Signature ▶   Title (Owner, etc.) ▶   Date ▶

95

 Department of the Treasury
Internal Revenue Service

Instructions for Form 940

Employer's Annual Federal Unemployment (FUTA) Tax Return

Section references are to the Internal Revenue Code unless otherwise noted.

Paperwork Reduction Act Notice

We ask for the information on this form to carry out the Internal Revenue laws of the United States. You are required to give us the information. We need it to ensure that you are complying with these laws and to allow us to figure and collect the right amount of tax.

The time needed to complete and file this form will vary depending on individual circumstances. The estimated average time is:

Recordkeeping	11 hr., 43 min.
Learning about the law or the form	18 min.
Preparing and sending the form to the IRS	30 min.

If you have comments concerning the accuracy of these time estimates or suggestions for making this form simpler, we would be happy to hear from you. You can write to the Tax Forms Committee, Western Area Distribution Center, Rancho Cordova, CA 95743-0001. Do not send the tax form to this office. Instead, see **Where To File** on page 2.

Items To Note

FUTA Tax Rate and Wage Base.—The FUTA tax rate is 6.2% through 1998, and the Federal wage base is $7,000. Your state wage base may be different.

Household Employers.—Starting in 1995, if you have only household employees, you are not required to make deposits of FUTA tax. Instead, report and pay FUTA tax on **Schedule H (Form 1040),** Household Employment Taxes, with your individual income tax return (e.g., Form 1040 or 1040A), or estate or trust tax return (Form 1041).

State Unemployment Information.—Employers must contact their state unemployment insurance offices to receive their state reporting number, state experience rate, and details about their state unemployment tax obligations.

General Information

Purpose of Form.—File Form 940 to report your annual Federal unemployment (FUTA) tax. You, as the employer, must pay this tax. Do not collect or deduct it from your employee's wages.

Use Form 940-EZ, a less complicated version of Form 940, to report your annual FUTA tax if—

1. You paid unemployment taxes ("contributions") to only one state.

2. You paid these taxes by January 31.

3. All wages that were taxable for FUTA tax were also taxable for your state's unemployment tax. If, for example, you paid wages to corporate officers (these wages are taxable for FUTA tax) in a state that exempts these wages from its unemployment taxes, you cannot use Form 940-EZ.

For more details, get Form 940-EZ. Do not file Form 940 if you have already filed Form 940-EZ for 1995.

Use the current year form to avoid delays in processing.

Who Must File.—In general, you must file Form 940 if you were not a household or agricultural employer during 1994 or 1995, and you pass either of the following tests:

1. You paid wages of $1,500 or more in any calendar quarter.

2. You had one or more employees for some part of a day in any 20 different weeks. Count all regular, temporary, and part-time employees. A partnership should not count its partners.

Note: *If there is a change in ownership or other transfer of business during the year, each employer who meets test* **1** *or* **2** *must file. Organizations described in section 501(c)(3) do not have to file.*

The filing tests are different for household and agricultural employers, as explained below.

Household Employers.—File a FUTA tax return **ONLY** if you paid cash wages of $1,000 or more in any calendar quarter in 1994 or 1995 for household work in a private home, local college club, or a local chapter of a college fraternity or sorority. Individuals, estates, and trusts that owe FUTA tax for domestic service in a private home, in most cases must file Schedule H (Form 1040) instead of Form 940 or 940-EZ. See the Instructions for Schedule H. In some cases, such as when you employ both household employees and other employees, you may have the option to report social security, Medicare and withheld Federal income taxes for your household employee(s) on Form 941 or Form 943 instead of on Schedule H. If you reported your household employee's wages on Form 941 or 943, you must use Form 940 or 940-EZ to report FUTA taxes.

Agricultural Employers.—File Form 940 if either test below applies to you:

1. You paid cash wages of $20,000 or more to farmworkers during any calendar quarter in 1994 or 1995.

2. You employed 10 or more farmworkers during some part of a day (whether or not at the same time) for at least 1 day during any 20 different weeks in 1994 or 1995.

Count aliens admitted on a temporary basis to the United States to perform farmwork, also known as workers with H-2(a) visas, to determine if you meet either test. Wages paid to these aliens are subject to FUTA tax after 1994.

Magnetic Media Reporting.—You may file Form 940 using magnetic media. **Pub. 1314,** Magnetic Tape Reporting of Form 940, Employer's Annual Federal Unemployment Tax Return (FUTA), explains the requirements. You can get this publication by calling 1-800-TAX-FORM (1-800-829-3676).

Penalties and Interest.—Avoid penalties and interest by making tax deposits when due, filing a correct return, and paying the proper amount of tax when due. The law provides penalties for late deposits and late filing unless you show reasonable cause for the delay. If you file late, attach an explanation to the return. Get **Circular E,** Employer's Tax Guide, for information on penalties.

There are also penalties for willful failure to pay tax, keep records, make returns, and filing false or fraudulent returns.

Cat. No. 13660I

Not Liable for FUTA Tax.—If you receive Form 940 and are not liable for FUTA tax for 1995, write "Not Liable" across the front, sign the return, and return it to the IRS.

Credit for Contributions Paid Into State Funds.—You can claim credit for amounts you pay into a certified state (including Puerto Rico and the U.S. Virgin Islands) unemployment fund by the due date of Form 940. Your FUTA tax will be higher if you do not pay the state contributions timely.

"Contributions" are payments that state law requires you to make to an unemployment fund because you are an employer. These payments are contributions only to the extent that they are not deducted or deductible from the employees' pay.

Do not take credit for penalties, interest, or special administrative taxes that are not included in the contribution rate the state assigned to you. Do not take credit for voluntary contributions paid to get a lower assigned rate.

You may receive an additional credit if you have an experience rate lower than 5.4% (.054). This applies even if your rate is different during the year. This **additional** credit is equal to the difference between actual payments and the amount you would have been required to pay at 5.4%.

The total credit allowable may not be more than 5.4% of the total taxable FUTA wages.

Special Credit for Successor Employers.—A successor employer is an employer who received a unit of an employer's trade or business or all or most of the property used in the trade or business of another employer. The successor employer must employ one or more individuals who were employed by the previous owner immediately after the acquisition.

You may be eligible for a credit based on the state unemployment contributions paid by the previous employer. You may claim these credits if you are a successor employer and acquired a business in 1995 from a previous employer who was not an employer for FUTA purposes during 1995. The previous employer must not (1) have paid wages of $1,500 or more in any calendar quarter in 1995, or (2) have employed any employee(s) for any 20 or more weeks during 1995. See section 3302(e) and Regulations 31.3302(e)-1. Enter in Part II, line 3, columns (a) through (i) the information of the predecessor employer as if you paid the amounts.

Successor employers may be able to count the wages that the previous employer paid to their employees when reporting the payments for services that exceed $7,000 on line 3. See the instructions for line 3 on page 3.

General Instructions

When To File.—The due date of the 1995 Form 940 is January 31, 1996. However, if you deposited all tax when due, you have 10 additional days to file your return. Your form is filed on time if it is properly addressed and postmarked no later than the due date.

Where To File.—In the list below, find the state where your legal residence, principal place of business, office, or agency is located. Send your return to the **Internal Revenue Service** at the address listed for your location. No street address is needed.

Note: *Where you file depends on whether or not you are including a payment.*

Florida, Georgia, South Carolina

Return without payment:	Return with payment:
	P.O. Box 105887
Atlanta, GA 39901-0006	Atlanta, GA 30348-5887

New Jersey, New York (New York City and counties of Nassau, Rockland, Suffolk, and Westchester)

Return without payment:	Return with payment:
	P.O. Box 1365
Holtsville, NY 00501-0006	Newark, NJ 07101-1365

New York (all other counties), Connecticut, Maine, Massachusetts, New Hampshire, Rhode Island, Vermont

Return without payment:	Return with payment:
	P.O. Box 371307
Andover, MA 05501-0006	Pittsburgh, PA 15250-7307

Illinois, Iowa, Minnesota, Missouri, Wisconsin

Return without payment:	Return with payment:
	P.O. Box 970010
Kansas City, MO 64999-0006	St. Louis, MO 63197-0010

Delaware, District of Columbia, Maryland, Pennsylvania, Puerto Rico, Virginia, U.S. Virgin Islands

Return without payment:	Return with payment:
	P.O. Box 8726
Philadelphia, PA 19255-0006	Philadelphia, PA 19162-8726

Indiana, Kentucky, Michigan, Ohio, West Virginia

Return without payment:	Return with payment:
	P.O. Box 6977
Cincinnati, OH 45999-0006	Chicago, IL 60680-6977

Kansas, New Mexico, Oklahoma, Texas

Return without payment:	Return with payment:
	P.O. Box 970017
Austin, TX 73301-0006	St. Louis, MO 63197-0017

Alaska, Arizona, California (counties of Alpine, Amador, Butte, Calaveras, Colusa, Contra Costa, Del Norte, El Dorado, Glenn, Humboldt, Lake, Lassen, Marin, Mendocino, Modoc, Napa, Nevada, Placer, Plumas, Sacramento, San Joaquin, Shasta, Sierra, Siskiyou, Solano, Sonoma, Sutter, Tehama, Trinity, Yolo, and Yuba), Colorado, Idaho, Montana, Nebraska, Nevada, North Dakota, Oregon, South Dakota, Utah, Washington, Wyoming

Return without payment:	Return with payment:
	P.O. Box 7024
Ogden, UT 84201-0006	San Francisco, CA 94120-7024

California (all other counties), Hawaii

Return without payment:	Return with payment:
	P.O. Box 60378
Fresno, CA 93888-0006	Los Angeles, CA 90060-0378

Alabama, Arkansas, Louisiana, Mississippi, North Carolina, Tennessee

Return without payment:	Return with payment:
	P.O. Box 1210
Memphis, TN 37501-0006	Charlotte, NC 28201-1210

FUTA Tax Amount To Deposit.—Although Form 940 covers a calendar year, you may have to make deposits of the tax before filing the return. Determine your FUTA tax for each of the first three quarters by multiplying by .008 that part of the first $7,000 of each employee's annual wages that you paid during the quarter. If any part of the amounts paid are exempt from state unemployment taxes, you may deposit an amount more than the .008 rate. For example, in certain states, wages paid to corporate officers, certain payments of sick pay by unions, and certain fringe benefits, are exempt from state unemployment tax.

If the tax is $100 or less at the end of a quarter, you do not have to deposit it, but you must add it to the tax for the next quarter. Then, in the next quarter, if the total undeposited tax is more than $100, you must deposit it. For the fourth quarter, follow the instructions in Part III on page 4 to figure your tax liability. If your liability for the fourth quarter (plus any undeposited amount from any earlier quarter) is over $100, deposit the entire amount by the due date of Form 940 (January 31). If the tax is $100 or less, you can either make a deposit or pay it by sending your payment and the payment voucher (Form 940-V) along with your Form 940 by its due date.

The deposit due dates are shown in the following chart:

If underdeposited FUTA taxes are over $100 on—	Deposit them by—
March 31	April 30
June 30	July 31
September 30	October 31
December 31	January 31

How To Deposit.—Use **Form 8109**, Federal Tax Deposit Coupon, when you make each tax deposit. The IRS will send you a book of deposit coupons when you apply for an employer identification number (EIN). Follow the instructions in the coupon book. If you do not have coupons, see "Depositing Taxes" in Circular E.

Make your deposits with an authorized financial institution (e.g., a commercial bank that is qualified to accept Federal tax deposits) or the Federal Reserve bank for your area. To avoid a possible penalty, do not mail deposits directly to the IRS. Records of your deposits will be sent to the IRS for crediting to your business accounts.

Identifying Your Payments.—Write your EIN, "Form 940," and the tax period to which the payment applies on your check or money order. This will help ensure proper crediting of your account. On balance due payments of $100 or less (Part II, line 9), make your check or money order payable to the "Internal Revenue Service." Enter the amount of payment on the payment voucher at the bottom of Form 940. If the employer information is not preprinted on the payment voucher, enter the requested information. On payments over $100, make your check or money order payable to the depositary or Federal Reserve bank where you make your deposit.

Federal Tax Deposits By Electronic Funds Transfer (EFT).—Taxpayers whose total deposits of withheld income, social security, and Medicare taxes during calendar year 1993 or 1994 exceeded $47 million are required to deposit all depository taxes due after 1995 by electronic funds transfer (EFT). TAXLINK, an electronic remittance processing system, must be used to make deposits by EFT. Taxpayers who are not required to make deposits by EFT may voluntarily participate in TAXLINK. For more details on TAXLINK, call the toll-free TAXLINK HELPLINE at 1-800-829-5469 (for TAXLINK information only).

Specific Instructions

Employer's Name, Address, and Identification Number.—Use the preaddressed Form 940 mailed to you. If you must use a form that is not preaddressed, type or print your name, trade name, address, and EIN on it. If you do not receive your EIN by the time a return is due, write "Applied for" and the date you applied for the number.

Questions A through C.—Answer the applicable questions. The answers will direct you to the correct form to file. If you answered "Yes" to all the questions, you may file Form 940-EZ, a simplified version of Form 940. If you answer "No" to any of the questions, complete and file Form 940.

Final Return.—If you will not have to file returns in the future, check the box on the line below question C. Then complete and sign the return. If you start paying FUTA wages again, file Form 940 or 940-EZ.

Amended Return.—Be sure to use a Form 940 for the year you are amending. Check the amended return box above Part I. File the amended return with the Internal Revenue Service Center where you filed the original return. Complete and sign a new Form 940 with the correct amounts for the tax year you are correcting. Attach a statement explaining why you are filing an amended return. For example, you are filing to claim the 90% credit for contributions paid to your state unemployment fund after the due date of Form 940.

If you are filing an amended return after June 30 to claim contributions to your state's unemployment fund that you paid after January 31, attach a copy of the certification from the state. This will expedite the processing of the amended return.

Part I—Computation of Taxable Wages

Line 1—Total payments.—Enter the total payments you made to employees during the calendar year. Include payments even if they are not taxable for Federal unemployment. Report salaries, wages, commissions, fees, bonuses, vacation allowances, amounts paid to temporary or part-time employees, the value of goods, lodging, food, clothing, noncash fringe benefits, benefits made from a section 125 (cafeteria) plan and sick pay (including third party if liability transferred to employer). For details on sick pay, see **Pub. 15-A**, Employer's Supplemental Tax Guide. Include the amount of tips reported to you in writing by your employees. Also, include contributions to a 401(k) pension plan. Enter the amount before any deductions.

How the payments are made is not important in determining if they are wages. Thus, you may pay wages for piecework or as a percentage of profits, and you may pay wages hourly, daily, weekly, monthly, or yearly. You may pay wages in cash or some other way, such as goods, lodging, food, or clothing. For items other than cash, use the fair market value at the time of payment.

Line 2—Exempt payments.—For FUTA purposes, "wages" and "employment" do not include every payment and every kind of service an employee may perform. In general, payments excluded from wages and payments for services excepted from employment are not subject to tax. The amounts reported on line 2 are exempt from FUTA tax. You may deduct these exempt payments from total payments only if you explain them on line 2. Amounts that may be exempt from your state's unemployment tax, for example, corporate officer's wages, may not be exempt from Federal unemployment tax.

Enter payments for the following items:

1. Agricultural labor, if you did not meet either of the tests in **Agricultural Employers** on page 1.

2. Benefit payments for sickness or injury under a worker's compensation law.

3. Household service if you did not pay cash wages of $1,000 or more in any calendar quarter in 1994 or 1995, and you included the amount on line 1.

4. Certain family employment.

5. Certain fishing activities.

6. Noncash payments for farmwork or household services in a private home that are included on line 1. Only cash wages to these workers are taxable.

7. Value of certain meals and lodging.

8. Cost of group-term life insurance.

9. Payments attributable to the employee's contributions to a sick pay plan.

10. Benefits that are excludable under a section 125 (cafeteria) plan.

11. Any other exempt service or pay.

Page 3

For more information, see **Special Rules for Various Types of Services and Payments** in Circular E.

Line 3.—Enter the total amounts over $7,000 you paid each employee. For example, if you have 10 employees to whom you paid $8,000 each during the year, enter $80,000 on line 1 and $10,000 on line 3. **Only the first $7,000 paid to your employee is subject to FUTA tax. DO NOT use the state wage limitation for this entry. Generally, the state wage base is a different amount than the Federal wage base of $7,000.**

If you are a successor employer and have acquired a business from a previous owner who was an employer liable for FUTA tax, you may be able to count the wages that employer paid to the employees who continue to work for you when you figure the $7,000 wage limit. Enter on line 3 the payments that exceed the $7,000 wage base, including the payments by the previous employer. See code section 3306(b) and Regulations 31.3306(b)(1)-1(b).

Line 5—Total taxable wages.—This is the total Federal taxable wage amount. Use this amount in Part II to compute the maximum FUTA tax and the maximum credit.

Part II—Tax Due or Refund

Line 1.—Multiply the total taxable wages in Part I, line 5, by .062. This is the maximum amount of FUTA tax.

Line 2.—Multiply the total taxable wages in Part I, line 5, by .054. This is the maximum credit that is used to offset FUTA tax.

Line 3.—You must complete all applicable columns to receive any amount of credit. Your state will provide an experience rate. If you have been assigned an experience rate of 0% or more, but less than 5.4% for all or part of the year, use columns (a) through (i). If you have not been assigned any experience rate, use columns (a), (b), (c), and (i) only. If you have been assigned a rate of 5.4% or higher, use columns (a), (b), (c), (d), (e), and (i) only. If you were assigned an experience rate for only part of the year or the rate was changed during the year, complete a separate line for each rate period.

If you need additional lines, attach a separate statement with a similar format. Also, if you are a successor employer, see **Special Credit for Successor Employers** on page 2.

Column (a).—Enter the two-letter abbreviation of the name of the state(s) that you were required to pay contributions to (including Puerto Rico and the U.S. Virgin Islands).

Column (b).—Enter the state reporting number that was assigned to you when you registered as an employer with each state. **Be sure to enter the correct number.** Failure to enter the correct number may result in unnecessary correspondence.

Column (c).—Enter the state taxable payroll on which you must pay taxes to the unemployment fund of each state shown in column (a). If your experience rate is 0%, enter the amount of wages that you would have had to pay on if the rate had not been granted.

Column (d).—Enter the beginning and ending dates of the experience rate shown in column (e).

Column (e).—Your "state experience rate" is the rate the state taxes your payroll for state unemployment purposes.

This rate may change from time to time based on your "experience" with the state tax fund. For example, unemployment compensation paid to your former employees. If you do not know your rate, contact your state unemployment insurance service. The state experience rate can be stated as a percent or a decimal.

Column (f).—Multiply the amount in column (c), Taxable payroll, by 5.4% (.054).

Column (h).—Subtract column (g) from column (f). If zero or less, enter zero. This additional credit is the difference between the 5.4% and the state experience rate.

Column (i).—Enter the contributions actually paid to the state unemployment fund by January 31, 1996. Do not include amounts you are required to pay but have not paid by the January 31 due date. See **Amended Return** on page 3. If you are filing after the due date, see the instructions for line 3b. If you are claiming excess credits as payments of state unemployment contributions, attach a copy of the letter from your state. Do not include any penalties, interest, or special administrative taxes (such as surcharges, employment and training taxes, excise tax, and assessments which are generally listed as a separate item on the state's quarterly wage report) not included in the contribution rate assigned to you.

Line 3a.—Enter the totals of columns (c), (h), and (i) on this line.

Line 3b.—Add line 3a, columns (h) and (i) only. If you **file Form 940 after its due date** and any contributions in column (i) were made after January 31, 1996, your credit for late contributions is limited to **90%** of the amount which would have been allowable as a credit on account of such contributions had they been paid on or before January 31, 1996. For example, if $1,500 of state contributions was paid on time, and $1,000 was paid after January 31, 1996, the total tentative credit on line 3b would be $2,400 ($1,500 + $900 (90% of $1,000)). This is assuming there is no additional credit in column (h). If this situation occurs, enter the total payments to the state in column (i) and explain below the signature line how you arrived at the amount on line 3b.

Note: *If you are receiving additional credit (column (h)) because your state experience rate is less than 5.4%, the additional credit is not subject to the 90% limitation.*

Line 6.—Enter the smaller of Part II, line 2, or line 3b. This is the credit allowable for your payments to state unemployment funds. If you do not have to make payments to the state, enter zero on this line.

Part III—Record of Quarterly Federal Unemployment Tax Liability

Complete this part if your total tax (Part II, line 1, or line 7) is over $100. To figure your FUTA tax liability **for each of the first three quarters of 1995,** see **FUTA Tax Amount To Deposit** on page 2. Enter this amount in the column for that quarter. This is your liability, not your deposit.

Your liability for the fourth quarter is the total tax (Part II, line 7) minus your liability for the first three quarters of the year. The total liability must equal your total tax. Otherwise, you may be charged a failure to deposit penalty figured on your average liability.

Printed on recycled paper

*U.S.GPO:1995-389-137

Depositing Federal Payroll Taxes

The following are excerpts from Publication 15, *Circular E, Employer's Tax Guide.*

1. Employer Identification Number (EIN)

If you are required to report employment taxes or give tax statements to employees or annuitants, you need an EIN.

The EIN is a nine-digit number the IRS issues. The digits are arranged as follows: 00-0000000. It is used to identify the tax accounts of employers and certain others that have no employees. **Use your EIN on all the items you send to the IRS and SSA.** For more information, get **Pub. 1635,** Understanding Your EIN.

If you have not asked for an EIN, request one on **Form SS-4,** Application for Employer Identification Number. You can get this form at IRS or SSA offices. You can ask for an EIN immediately by calling the tele-TIN phone number for your state's IRS Service Center listed in the instructions for Form SS-4.

You should have only one EIN. If you have more than one and are not sure which one to use, please check with the Internal Revenue Service Center where you file your return. Give the numbers you have, the name and address to which each was assigned, and the address of your main place of business. The IRS will tell you which number to use.

If you took over another employer's business, do not use that employer's EIN. If you don't have your own EIN by the time a return is due, write "Applied for" and the date you applied in the space shown for the number.

See **Depositing without an EIN** on page 17 if you must make a deposit and you don't have an EIN.

11. Depositing Taxes

In general, you must deposit income tax withheld and both the employer and employee social security and Medicare taxes (minus any advance EIC payments) by mailing or delivering a check, money order, or cash to an authorized financial institution or Federal Reserve bank. However, some taxpayers are required to deposit by electronic funds transfer (EFT) as discussed below. The requirement to deposit electronically is being phased in over a period of years and an increasing number of taxpayers will be required to use this method each year.

Federal tax deposits by electronic funds transfer (EFT).— Taxpayers whose total deposits of withheld income, social security, and Medicare taxes during calendar year 1993 or 1994 exceeded $47 million are required

Page 16

to deposit all depository taxes due after 1995 by EFT. TAXLINK, an electronic remittance processing system, must be used to make deposits by EFT. If you are required to make deposits by EFT and fail to do so, you may be subject to a penalty. Taxpayers who are not required to make deposits by EFT may voluntarily participate in TAXLINK. For more details on TAXLINK, call the toll-free TAXLINK HELPLINE at 1–800–829–5469 (for TAXLINK information only), or write to:

Internal Revenue Service
Cash Management Site Office
P.O. Box 47669, Stop 295
Doraville, GA 30362

Payments with returns.— You may make payments with your return instead of depositing if:

• Your net tax liability for the return period (line 13 on Form 941) is less than $500, or

• You are making a payment in accordance with the **Accuracy of Deposits Rule** discussed on page 21. This amount may exceed $500. *Caution: Only monthly schedule depositors are allowed to make this underpayment with the return.*

Separate deposit requirements for nonpayroll (Form 945) tax liabilities.— Separate deposits are required for nonpayroll income tax withholding. **Do not** combine deposits for Form 941 and Form 945 tax liabilities. Generally, the deposit rules for nonpayroll liabilities are the same as discussed below. See the separate **Instructions for Form 945** for more information.

Federal tax deposit (FTD) coupon.— Use **Form 8109,** Federal Tax Deposit Coupon, to make the deposits. **Do not** use the deposit coupons to pay delinquent taxes assessed by the IRS. Send those payments directly to your Internal Revenue Service Center with a copy of any related notice the IRS sent you.

For new employers, the IRS will send you an FTD coupon book 5 to 6 weeks after you receive an employer identification number (EIN). (Apply for an EIN on Form SS–4.) The IRS will keep track of the number of FTD coupons you use and **automatically** will send you additional coupons when you need them. If you do not receive your resupply of FTD coupons, call 1–800–829–1040. You can have the FTD coupon books sent to a branch office, tax preparer, or service bureau that is making your deposits by showing that address on **Form 8109C,** FTD Address Change, which is in the FTD coupon book. (Filing Form 8109C will not change your address of record; it will change only the address where the FTD coupons are mailed.) The FTD coupons will be preprinted with your name, address, and EIN. They have entry boxes for indicating the type of tax and the tax period for which the deposit is made.

It is very important to clearly mark the correct type of tax and tax period on each FTD coupon. This information is used by the IRS to credit your account.

If you have branch offices depositing taxes, give them FTD coupons and complete instructions so they can deposit the taxes when due.

Please use only your FTD coupons. If you use anyone else's FTD coupon, you may be subject to the failure to deposit penalty. This is because your account will be underpaid by the amount of the deposit credited to the other person's account. See **Penalties** below for details.

How to make deposits.— Mail or deliver each FTD coupon and a single payment covering the taxes to be deposited to an authorized depositary or to the Federal Reserve bank or branch (FRB) serving your area. An authorized depositary is a financial institution (e.g., a commercial bank) that is authorized to accept Federal tax deposits. Follow the instructions in the FTD coupon book. Make the check or money order payable to the depositary or FRB where you make your deposit. To help ensure proper crediting of your account, include your EIN, the type of tax (e.g., Form 941), and tax period to which the payment applies on your check or money order. Reporting agents who make deposits for their clients should see Revenue Procedure 89-48, in Internal Revenue Cumulative Bulletin 1989-2, page 599.

Deposits at depositaries.— Authorized depositaries must accept cash, a postal money order drawn to the order of the depositary, or a check or draft drawn on and to the order of the depositary. You can deposit taxes with a check drawn on another financial institution only if the depositary is willing to accept that form of payment.

Note: Be sure that the financial institution where you make deposits is an authorized depositary. Deposits made at an unauthorized institution may be subject to the failure to deposit penalty.

Deposits at FRBs.— If you want to make a deposit at an FRB, make the deposit with the FRB serving your area. Deposits may be subject to the failure to deposit penalty if the payment is not considered an immediate credit item on the day it is received by the FRB. A personal check, including one drawn on a business account, is not an immediate credit item. To avoid a penalty, deposits made by personal checks drawn on other financial institutions must be made in advance of the deposit due date to allow time for check clearance. To be considered timely, the funds must be available to the FRB on the deposit due date before the FRB's daily cutoff deadline. Contact your local FRB to obtain information concerning check clearance and cutoff schedules.

Depositing on time.— The IRS determines if deposits are on time by the date they are received by an authorized depositary or FRB. However, a deposit received by

the authorized depositary or FRB after the due date will be considered timely if the taxpayer establishes that it was mailed in the United States at least 2 days before the due date.

Note: If you are required to deposit any taxes more than once a month, any deposit of $20,000 or more must be made by its due date to be timely.

Depositing without an EIN.— If you have applied for an EIN but **have not** received it, and you must make a deposit, make the deposit with your Internal Revenue Service Center. **Do not** make the deposit at an authorized depositary or FRB. Make it payable to the Internal Revenue Service and show on it your name (as shown on Form SS–4), address, kind of tax, period covered, and date you applied for an EIN. Send an explanation with the deposit. **Do not** use Form 8109–B in this situation.

Depositing without Form 8109.— If you do not have the preprinted Form 8109, you may use Form 8109–B to make deposits. Form 8109–B is an over-the-counter FTD coupon that is not preprinted with your identifying information. You may get this form by calling 1–800–829–1040. Be sure to have your EIN ready when you call. You will not be able to obtain this form by calling the general 1–800–TAX–FORM number.

Use Form 8109–B to make deposits only if—

• You are a new employer and you have been assigned an EIN, but you have not received your initial supply of Forms 8109.

• You have not received your resupply of preprinted Forms 8109.

Deposit record.— For your records, a stub is provided with each FTD coupon in the coupon book. The FTD coupon itself will not be returned. It is used to credit your account. Your check, bank receipt, or money order is your receipt.

How to claim credit for overpayments.— If you deposited more than the right amount of taxes for a quarter, you can request on Form 941 for that quarter to have the overpayment refunded or applied as a credit to your next return. Do not ask the depositary or FRB to request a refund from the IRS for you.

Penalties.— Penalties may apply if you do not make required deposits on time. The penalties do not apply if any failure to make a proper and timely deposit was due to reasonable cause and not to willful neglect. For amounts not timely deposited, the penalty rates are:

2% - Deposits made 1 to 5 days late.
5% - Deposits made 6 to 15 days late.
10% - Deposits made 16 or more days late. Also applies to amounts paid to the IRS within 10 days of the date of the first notice the IRS sent asking for the tax due.
15% - Amounts still unpaid more than 10 days after the date of the first notice the IRS sent asking for the tax due or the day on which you receive notice and demand for immediate payment, whichever is earlier.

Caution: You may be subject to a penalty if you make deposits at an unauthorized financial institution, you pay directly to the IRS, or you pay with your tax return (but see Depositing without an EIN and Payments with returns earlier for exceptions).

Order in which deposits are applied.— Tax deposits are applied first to satisfy any past due underdeposits for the quarter, with the oldest underdeposit satisfied first.

Example: Cedar Inc. is required to make a deposit of $1,000 on February 15 and $1,500 on March 15. It does not make the deposit on February 15. On March 15, Cedar Inc. deposits $1,700 assuming that it has paid its March deposit in full and applied $200 to the late February deposit. However, because deposits are applied first to past due underdeposits in due date order, $1,000 of the March 15 deposit is applied to the late February deposit. The remaining $700 is applied to the March 15 deposit. Therefore, in addition to an underdeposit of $1,000 for February 15, Cedar Inc. has an underdeposit for March 15 of $800. Penalties will be applied to both underdeposits as explained above.

Trust fund recovery penalty.— If income, social security, and Medicare taxes that must be withheld are not withheld or are not paid to the IRS, the trust fund recovery penalty may apply. The penalty is the full amount of the unpaid trust fund tax. This penalty may apply to you if these unpaid taxes cannot be immediately collected from the employer or business.

The trust fund recovery penalty may be imposed on all persons who are determined by the IRS to be *responsible* for collecting, accounting for, and paying over these taxes, and who acted *willfully* in not doing so.

A *responsible person* can be an officer or employee of a corporation, a partner or employee of a partnership, an accountant, a volunteer director/trustee, or an employee of a sole proprietorship. A responsible person also may include one who signs checks for the business or otherwise has authority to cause the spending of business funds.

Willfully means voluntarily, consciously, and intentionally. A responsible person acts willfully if the person knows the required actions are not taking place.

Page 18

Separate accounting when deposits are not made or withheld taxes are not paid.— Separate accounting may be required if you do not pay over withheld employee social security, Medicare, or income taxes; deposit required taxes; make required payments; or file tax returns. In this case, you would receive written notice from the district director requiring you to deposit taxes in a special trust account for the U.S. Government. You would also have to file monthly tax returns on **Form 941–M,** Employer's Monthly Federal Tax Return.

When To Deposit

There are two deposit schedules—monthly or semiweekly—for determining when you deposit Federal employment and withholding taxes (other than FUTA taxes). The IRS will notify you each November whether you are a monthly or semiweekly schedule depositor for the coming calendar year. If you do not receive the notification, you must determine your deposit schedule using the following rules. The rules apply to social security and Medicare tax and Federal income tax withheld on wages, tips, and sick pay. Similar rules apply for Federal income tax withholding for nonpayroll items such as backup withholding and withholding on pensions, annuities, and gambling winnings. These rules do not apply to Federal unemployment (FUTA) tax. See section 14 for information on depositing FUTA tax.

Lookback period.— Your deposit schedule for a calendar year is determined from the total employment taxes reported on your Forms 941 (line 13) in a four-quarter lookback period—July 1 through June 30—as shown in the chart below. If you reported $50,000 or less of employment taxes for the lookback period, you are a monthly schedule depositor; if you reported more than $50,000, you are a semiweekly schedule depositor. There are two exception rules—the $500 rule and the $100,000 rule. The deposit rules and exceptions are discussed below.

Table 1. **Lookback Period for Calendar Year 1996**

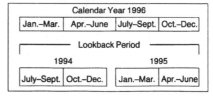

Calendar Year 1996			
Jan.–Mar.	Apr.–June	July–Sept.	Oct.–Dec.

Lookback Period			
1994		1995	
July–Sept.	Oct.–Dec.	Jan.–Mar.	Apr.–June

Monthly Deposit Schedule

You are a monthly schedule depositor for a calendar year if the total employment taxes for the four quarters in your lookback period were $50,000 or less. Under the monthly deposit schedule, employment taxes with-held on payments made during a calendar month must be deposited by the 15th day of the following month.

Monthly schedule depositors should **not** file Form 941 on a monthly basis. Do not file **Form 941–M,** Employer's Monthly Federal Tax Return, unless you are instructed to do so by an IRS representative.

New Employers.— During the first calendar year of your business, your tax liability for each quarter in the lookback period is considered to be zero. Therefore, you are a monthly schedule depositor for the first calendar year of your business (but see the **$100,000 One-Day Rule** on page 20).

Semiweekly Deposit Schedule

You are a semiweekly schedule depositor for a calendar year if the total employment taxes during your lookback period were more than $50,000. Under the semiweekly deposit schedule, employment taxes withheld on payments made on Wednesday, Thursday, and/or Friday must be deposited by the following Wednesday. Amounts accumulated on payments made on Saturday, Sunday, Monday, and/or Tuesday must be deposited by the following Friday.

Table 2. **Semiweekly Deposit Schedule**

Payment Days/ Deposit Periods	Deposit By:
Wednesday, Thursday, and/or Friday	Following Wednesday
Saturday, Sunday, Monday, and/or Tuesday	Following Friday

If a quarterly return period ends on a day other than Tuesday or Friday, employment taxes accumulated on the days covered by the return period just ending are subject to one deposit obligation, and employment taxes accumulated on the days covered by the new return period are subject to a separate deposit obligation. For example, if one quarterly return period ends on Thursday and a new quarter begins on Friday, employment taxes accumulated on Wednesday and Thursday are subject to one deposit obligation and taxes accumulated on Friday are subject to a separate obligation. Separate Forms 8109 are required for each deposit because two different quarters are affected. Be sure to mark the quarter for which the deposit is made on each Form 8109.

Example of Monthly and Semiweekly Schedules

Rose Co. reported employment tax liability on Form 941 as follows:

1995 Lookback Period			**1996 Lookback Period**		
3rd Quarter	1993 –	$12,000	3rd Quarter	1994 –	$12,000
4th Quarter	1993 –	$12,000	4th Quarter	1994 –	$12,000
1st Quarter	1994 –	$12,000	1st Quarter	1995 –	$12,000
2nd Quarter	1994 –	$12,000	2nd Quarter	1995 –	$15,000
		$48,000			$51,000

Rose Co. is a monthly schedule depositor for 1995 because its tax liability for the four quarters in its lookback period (third quarter 1993 through second quarter 1994) was not more than $50,000. However, for 1996, Rose Co. must follow the semiweekly deposit schedule because its liability exceeded $50,000 for the four quarters in its lookback period (third quarter 1994 through second quarter 1995).

Application of Monthly and Semiweekly Schedules

The terms "monthly schedule depositor" and "semiweekly schedule depositor" do not refer to how often your business pays its employees, or even how often you are required to make deposits. The terms identify which set of rules you must follow when a tax liability arises (e.g., when you have a payday). The deposit rules are based on the dates wages are paid; **not** on when payroll liabilities are accrued.

Monthly schedule example: Spruce Co. is a monthly schedule depositor with seasonal employees. It paid wages each of the four Fridays during January but did not pay any wages during February. Under the monthly schedule, Spruce Co. must deposit the combined tax liabilities for the four January paydays by February 15. Spruce Co. does not have a deposit requirement for February (due by March 15) because no wages were paid and, therefore, it did not have a tax liability for the month.

Semiweekly schedule example: Green Inc., which has a semiweekly deposit schedule, pays wages once each month on the last day of the month. Although Green Inc. has a semiweekly deposit schedule, it will deposit just once a month because it pays wages only once a month. The deposit, however, will be made under the semiweekly deposit schedule as follows: Green Inc.'s tax liability for the January 31, 1996 (Wednesday) payday must be deposited by February 7, 1996 (Wednesday). Under the semiweekly deposit schedule, liabilities for wages paid on Wednesday through Friday must be deposited by the following Wednesday.

Deposits on Banking Days Only

If a deposit is required to be made on a day that is not a banking day, the deposit is considered timely if it is made by the close of the next banking day. In addition to Federal and state bank holidays, Saturdays and Sundays are treated as nonbanking days. For example, if a deposit is required to be made on a Friday and Friday is not a banking day, the deposit will be considered timely if it is made by the following Monday.

A special rule is provided for **semiweekly schedule depositors** that allows these depositors at least 3 banking days to make a deposit. That is, if any of the 3 weekdays after the end of a semiweekly period is a banking holiday, they will have one additional banking day to deposit. For example, if a semiweekly schedule depositor accumulated taxes for payments made on Friday and the following Monday is not a banking day, the deposit normally due on Wednesday may be made on Thursday (allowing 3 banking days to make the deposit).

$500 Rule

If an employer accumulates less than a $500 tax liability during a return period (e.g., during a quarter for Form 941), no deposits are required and this liability may be paid with the tax return for the period. However, if you are unsure that you will accumulate less than $500, deposit under the appropriate rules so that you will not be subject to failure to deposit penalties.

$100,000 One-Day Rule

If you accumulate an undeposited income, social security, and Medicare tax liability of $100,000 or more on any day during a deposit period, you must deposit the tax by the next banking day, whether you are a monthly or semiweekly schedule depositor. For monthly schedule depositors, the deposit period is a calendar month. The deposit periods for a semiweekly schedule depositor are Wednesday through Friday and Saturday through Tuesday.

For purposes of the $100,000 rule, do not continue accumulating employment tax liability after the end of a deposit period. For example, if a semiweekly schedule depositor has accumulated a liability of $95,000 on a Tuesday (of a Saturday-through-Tuesday deposit period) and accumulated a $10,000 liability on Wednesday, the $100,000 one-day rule does not apply. Thus, $95,000 must be deposited by Friday and $10,000 must be deposited by the following Wednesday.

In addition, once you accumulate at least $100,000 in a deposit period, stop accumulating at the end of that day and begin to accumulate anew on the next day. For example, Fir Co. is a semiweekly schedule depositor. On Monday, Fir Co. accumulates taxes of $110,000 and must deposit this amount on Tuesday, the next banking day. On Tuesday, Fir Co. accumulates additional taxes of $30,000. Because the $30,000 is not added to the previous $110,000 and is less than $100,000, Fir Co. must deposit the $30,000 by Friday following the semiweekly deposit schedule.

If you are a monthly schedule depositor and accumulate a $100,000 employment tax liability on any day during a month, you become a semiweekly schedule depositor on the next day and remain so for at least the rest of the calendar year and for the following calendar year.

Example: Elm Inc. started its business on February 1, 1996. On February 7, it paid wages for the first time and accumulated an employment tax liability of $40,000. On February 14, Elm Inc. paid wages and accumulated a liability of $60,000, bringing its accumulated (undeposited) employment tax liability to $100,000. Because this was the first year of its business, the tax liability for its lookback period is considered to be zero, and it would be a monthly schedule depositor based on the lookback rules. However, since Elm Inc. accumulated a $100,000 liability on February 14, it became a semiweekly schedule depositor on February 15. It will be a semiweekly schedule depositor for the remainder of 1996 and for 1997. Elm Inc. is required to deposit the $100,000 by February 15 (Thursday), the next banking day.

When to Deposit Employment Taxes

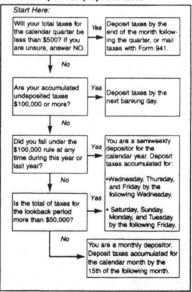

Page 20

14. Federal Unemployment (FUTA) Tax

The Federal Unemployment Tax Act (FUTA), with state unemployment systems, provides for payments of unemployment compensation to workers who have lost their jobs. Most employers pay both a Federal and a state unemployment tax. Only the employer pays FUTA tax; it is not deducted from the employee's wages.

Use the following three tests to determine whether you must pay FUTA tax. Each test applies to a different category of employee, and each is independent of the others. If a test describes your situation, you are subject to FUTA tax on the wages you pay to employees in that category during the current calendar year.

Test 1. In general. You are subject to FUTA tax on the wages you pay employees who are not farmworkers or household workers if in the current or preceding calendar year:

a) The wages you paid to employees in this category totaled $1,500 or more in any calendar quarter, or

b) In each of 20 different calendar weeks, there was at least a part of a day in which you had an employee in this category. The 20 weeks do not have to be consecutive. Nor does it have to be the same employee each week. Individuals on sick leave or vacation are counted as employees.

Test 2. Household workers. You are subject to FUTA tax on the cash wages you pay to household workers if the wages totaled $1,000 or more in any calendar quarter of the current or preceding year. A household worker is an employee who performs domestic services in a private home, local college club, or local fraternity or sorority chapter.

Test 3. Farmworkers. You are subject to FUTA tax on the wages you pay to farmworkers if in the current or preceding calendar year:

a) Total cash wages you paid for the farm labor were $20,000 or more in any calendar quarter, or

b) In each of 20 different calendar weeks in the current or preceding calendar year, there was at least 1 day in which you had 10 or more farmworker employees. The 20 weeks do not have to be consecutive. Nor does it have to be the same 10 employees each week. Nor do all 10 employees have to work a full day or the same part of the day. Individuals on sick leave or vacation are counted as employees.

Computing FUTA tax.— For 1995 and 1996, the FUTA tax is 6.2% of wages paid during the year. The tax applies to the first $7,000 you pay each employee as wages during the calendar year. The $7,000 amount is the Federal wage base. Your state wage base may be different. Generally, you can take a credit against your FUTA tax for amounts you paid into state unemployment funds. This credit cannot be more than 5.4% of taxable wages. The FUTA tax rate after the credit is .8%. (See **Instructions for Form 940** for details.)

Successor employer.— If you acquired a business from an employer who was liable for FUTA tax, you may count the wages that employer paid to the employees who continue to work for you when you figure the FUTA wage limit. If the prior owner was not subject to FUTA tax, you may be eligible for a credit based on the state unemployment contributions paid by that owner. See **Instructions for Form 940.**

Depositing FUTA tax.— For deposit purposes, figure FUTA tax quarterly. Determine your FUTA tax liability by multiplying the amount of wages paid during the quarter by .008. Stop depositing FUTA tax on an employee's wages when he or she reaches $7,000 in wages for the calendar year. If any part of the amount paid is exempt from state unemployment taxes, you may deposit an amount more than the .008 rate. For example, in certain states, wages paid to corporate officers, certain payments of sick pay by unions, and certain fringe benefits, are exempt from state unemployment tax.

If your FUTA tax liability is $100 or less, you do not have to deposit the tax. Instead, you may carry it forward and add it to the liability figured in the next quarter to see if you must make a deposit. If your FUTA tax liability for any calendar quarter in 1996 is over $100 (including any FUTA tax carried forward from an earlier quarter), you must deposit the tax in an authorized financial institution using **Form 8109,** Federal Tax Deposit Coupon.

If your liability for the fourth quarter (plus any undeposited amount from any earlier quarter) is over $100, deposit the entire amount by the due date of Form 940 or Form 940-EZ (January 31). If it is $100 or less, you can either make a deposit or pay the tax with your Form 940 or Form 940-EZ by its due date.

Note: *You are not required to deposit FUTA taxes for household employees unless you report their wages on Form 941 or 943. See Pub. 926, Household Employer's Tax Guide, for more information.*

When to deposit.— Deposit the FUTA tax by the last day of the first month after the quarter ends.

Table 4. **When To Deposit FUTA Taxes**

Quarter	Ending	Due Date
Jan.–Feb.–Mar.	Mar. 31	Apr. 30
Apr.–May–June	June 30	July 31
July–Aug.–Sept.	Sept. 30	Oct. 31
Oct.–Nov.–Dec.	Dec. 31	Jan. 31

AMOUNT OF DEPOSIT (Do NOT type, please print.)

DOLLARS | CENTS

| | Darken only one
TYPE OF TAX | a
n
d | Darken only one
TAX PERIOD |

TAX YEAR MONTH →

EMPLOYER IDENTIFICATION NUMBER →

BANK NAME/
DATE STAMP

Name _____

Address _____

City _____

State _____ ZIP _____

Telephone number ( )

Darken only one TYPE OF TAX				Darken only one TAX PERIOD
941	945		1st Quarter	
990C	1120		2nd Quarter	
943	990-T		3rd Quarter	
720	990PF		4th Quarter	
CT-1	1042			
940			**35**	

IRS USE ONLY

FOR BANK USE IN MICR ENCODING

Federal Tax Deposit Coupon
Form 8109-B (Rev. 1-94)

- -

↑ SEPARATE ALONG THIS LINE AND SUBMIT TO DEPOSITARY WITH PAYMENT ↑

IMPORTANT   OMB NO. 1545-0257

Read instructions carefully before completing Form 8109-B, Federal Tax Deposit Coupon.

Note: *Except for the name, address, and telephone number, entries are processed by optical scanning equipment and must be made in pencil. Please* **use a soft lead** *(for example, a #2 pencil) so that the entries can be read more accurately by the optical scanning equipment. The name, address, and telephone number may be completed other than by hand. You* **CANNOT** *use photocopies of the coupons to make your deposits.* **DO NOT** *staple, tape or fold the coupons.*

Schedule A, Form 941 Filers (4th quarter 1993 ONLY).—If you are making a deposit for the 4th quarter 1993 during January 1994, darken the **945** box under TYPE OF TAX and the **4th quarter** box under TAX PERIOD.

Paperwork Reduction Act Notice.—We ask for the information on this form to carry out the Internal Revenue laws of the United States. You are required to give us the information. We need it to ensure that you are complying with these laws and to allow us to figure and collect the right amount of tax.

The time needed to complete and file this form will vary depending on individual circumstances. The estimated average time is 3 min. If you have comments concerning the accuracy of this time estimate or suggestions for making this form more simple, we would be happy to hear from you. You can write to both the **Internal Revenue Service,** Attention: Reports Clearance Officer, PC:FP, Washington, DC 20224; and the **Office of Management and Budget,** Paperwork Reduction Project (1545-0257), Washington, DC 20503. **DO NOT** send this form to either of these offices. Instead, see the instructions on the back of this page.

Purpose of Form.—Use Form 8109-B deposit coupons to make tax deposits **only** in the following two situations:

1. You have not yet received your resupply of preprinted deposit coupons (Form 8109); or

2. You are a new entity and have already been assigned an employer identification number (EIN), but have not yet received your initial supply of preprinted deposit coupons (Form 8109).

Note: *If you do not receive your resupply of deposit coupons and a deposit is due or you do not receive your initial supply within 5–6 weeks of receipt of your EIN, please contact your local IRS office.*

If you have applied for an EIN, have not received it, and a deposit must be made, send your payment to your Internal Revenue Service Center. Make your check or money order payable to the Internal Revenue Service and show on it your name (as shown on **Form SS-4,** Application for Employer Identification Number), address, kind of tax, period covered, and date you applied for an EIN. Also attach an explanation to the deposit. Do **NOT** use Form 8109-B in this situation. Do **NOT** use Form 8109-B to deposit delinquent taxes assessed by the IRS. Pay those taxes directly to the IRS.

How To Complete the Form.—Enter your name exactly as shown on your return or other IRS correspondence, address, and EIN in the spaces provided. If you are required to file a Form 1120, 990-C, 990-PF (with net investment income), 990-T, or 2438, enter the month in which your tax year ends in the **TAX YEAR MONTH** boxes. For example, if your tax years ends in January, enter 01; if it ends in June, enter 06; if it ends in December, enter 12. Please make your entries for EIN and tax year month (if applicable) in the manner specified in *Amount of Deposit* below. Darken one box each in the *Type of Tax* and *Tax Period* columns as explained below.

Amount of Deposit.—Enter the amount of the deposit in the space provided. Enter the amount legibly, forming the characters as shown below:

$$1234567890$$

Hand-print money amounts without using dollar signs, commas, a decimal point, or leading zeros. The commas and the decimal point are already shown in the entry area. For example, a deposit of $7,635.22 would be entered like this:

DOLLARS | CENTS

$$763522$$

If the deposit is for whole dollars only, enter "00" in the **CENTS** boxes.

Types of Tax.—

Form 941	—Withheld Income From Wages and Other Compensation, Social Security, and Medicare Taxes (includes Form 941 series of returns)
Form 945	—Withheld Income Tax From Pension, Annuities, Gambling, and Backup Withholding.
Form 990-C	—Farmers' Cooperative Association Income Tax.
Form 943	—Agricultural Withheld Income, Social Security, and Medicare Taxes (includes Form 943PR).
Form 720	—Excise Tax.
Form CT-1	—Railroad Retirement and Railroad Unemployment Repayment Taxes.
Form 940	—Federal Unemployment (FUTA) Tax (includes Form 940-EZ and Form 940PR).
Form 1120	—Corporate Income Tax (includes Form 1120 series of returns and Form 2438).
Form 990-T	—Exempt Organization Business Income Tax.

Form 990-PF —Excise Tax on Private Foundation Net Investment Income.
Form 1042 —Withholding On Foreign Persons.

How To Determine the Proper Tax Period.—

Payroll Taxes and Withholding (Forms 941, 940, 943, 945, CT-1, and 1042. (See the separate Instructions for Form 1042. **Schedule A (Form 941)** filers see information above.)).

If your liability was incurred during:

- January 1 through March 31, darken the 1st quarter box
- April 1 through June 30, darken the 2nd quarter box
- July 1 through September 30, darken the 3rd quarter box
- October 1 through December 31, darken the 4th quarter box

Note: *If the liability was incurred during one quarter and deposited in another, darken the box for the quarter in which the tax liability was incurred. For example, if the liability was incurred in March and deposited in April, darken the 1st quarter box.*

(Continued on back of page.)

Department of the Treasury
Internal Revenue Service

Cat. No. 61042S

Form **8109-B** (Rev. 1-94)

Excise Taxes For Form 720, follow the instructions on the front page for Forms 941, 940, etc., **but** for exceptions see separate instructions for Form 720. For Form 990-PF, with net investment income, follow the instructions below for Form 1120, 990-C, etc.

Income Taxes (Form 1120, 990-C, 990-T, and 2438).—

To make a deposit for the current tax year for any quarter, darken **only** the 1st quarter box. Such deposits apply to estimated income tax payments.

Example 1: If your tax year ends on December 31, 1994, and a deposit for 1994 is being made between January 1 and December 31, 1994, darken the 1st quarter box.

Example 2: If your tax year ends on June 30, 1994, and a deposit for that fiscal year is being made between July 1, 1993 and June 30, 1994, darken the 1st quarter box.

To make a deposit for the prior tax year, darken **only** the 4th quarter box. Such deposits include the following:

● Deposits of balance due shown on the return (Forms 1120, 990-C, and 990-T (corporate filers), and Forms 990-PF and 990-T (trust filers)).

● Deposits of balance due shown on **Form 7004,** Application for Automatic Extension of Time To File Corporation Income Tax Return (be sure to darken the 1120, 990-C, or 990-T box as appropriate).

● Deposits of balance due (from Forms 990-T (trust filers) and 990-PF filers) shown on **Form 2758,** Application for Extension of Time To File Certain Excise, Income, Information, and Other Returns (be sure to darken the 990-PF or 990-T box as appropriate).

● Deposits of tax due shown on Form 2438 (darken the 1120 box).

Example 1: If your tax year ends on December 31, 1994, and a deposit for 1994 is being made after that date, darken the 4th quarter box.

Example 2: If your tax year ends on June 30, 1994, and a deposit for that fiscal year is being made after that date, darken the 4th quarter box.

How To Ensure Your Deposit is Credited to the Correct Account.—

1. Make sure your name and EIN are correct;

2. Prepare only one coupon for each type of tax deposit;

3. Darken only one box for the type of tax you are depositing; and

4. Darken only one box for the tax period for which you are making a deposit.

Telephone number.—A space is provided on the deposit coupon for you to enter your daytime telephone number. Our purpose for requesting it is to allow us to contact you if we have difficulty processing your deposit coupon.

Miscellaneous.—The IRS USE ONLY box is used during our processing to ensure proper crediting to your account. Do **not** darken this box when making a deposit.

Note: *DO NOT deposit delinquent taxes assessed by IRS. Pay those taxes directly to the IRS.*

How To Make Deposits.—Mail or deliver the completed coupon with the appropriate payment for the amount of the deposit to a qualified depositary for Federal taxes or to the Federal Reserve bank (FRB) servicing your geographic area. Make checks or money orders payable to that depositary or FRB. Federal agencies deposit at FRBs only. To help ensure proper crediting of your account, include your EIN, the type of tax (e.g., Form 940), and the tax period to which the payment applies on your check or money order.

Deposits at Depositaries.—Authorized depositaries are required to accept cash, postal money orders drawn to the order of the depositary, or checks or drafts drawn on and to the order of the depositary. If you want to make a tax deposit with a depositary by a check drawn on another financial institution, you may do so only if the depositary is willing to accept that payment as a deposit of Federal taxes.

Deposits at FRBs.—If you want to make a deposit at an FRB, you must make that deposit with the FRB servicing your area with a check or payment for which immediate credit is given according to the funds availability schedule of the receiving FRB. A personal check is not an immediate credit item. The FRB servicing your area can provide information regarding what are considered immediate credit items.

Timeliness of Deposits.—The IRS determines whether deposits are on time by the date they are received by an authorized depositary or collected by an FRB. However, a deposit received by the authorized depositary or FRB after the deposit due date will be considered timely if the taxpayer establishes that it was mailed in the United States on or before the second day before the due date.

Note: *If you are required to deposit any taxes more than once a month, any deposit of $20,000 or more must be made by its due date to be timely.*

When To Make Deposits.—Instructions are provided in IRS publications and tax returns. Copies of these documents and other information concerning tax procedures can be obtained from most IRS offices.

Penalties.—You may be charged a penalty for not making deposits when due or in sufficient amounts, unless you have reasonable cause. This penalty may also apply if you mail or deliver Federal tax deposits to IRS offices, rather than to authorized depositaries or FRBs. Additionally, a **trust fund recovery penalty may apply to any responsible person who willfully fails to collect, account for, and pay over trust fund taxes. For more information on penalties, see Circular E, Employer's Tax Guide.**

Publication 531
Cat. No. 15059V

Department
of the
Treasury

Internal
Revenue
Service

Reporting Tip Income

For use in preparing

1995 Returns

Introduction

This publication will help you understand how your tip income is taxed and how to report it on your federal income tax return. Employees of food and beverage establishments who receive tips are the focus of this publication. The recordkeeping rules and other information may also apply to other workers who receive tips, such as hairdressers, cab drivers, and casino dealers.

All tips you receive are taxable income and are subject to federal income tax. You must include in gross income all tips you receive directly from customers, tips from charge customers that are paid to you by your employer, and your share of any tips you receive under a tip-splitting arrangement.

In addition, cash tips of $20 or more that you receive in a month while working for any one employer are subject to withholding of income tax, social security or railroad retirement tax, and Medicare tax. Report the tips you receive to your employer so that the correct amount of these taxes can be determined.

Social security or railroad retirement benefits. Your tips and other pay are used to determine the amount of social security or railroad retirement benefits you or your family may receive if you retire, become disabled, or die. Also, your tip income will be considered in determining your eligibility for Medicare benefits at age 65 or if you become disabled. You can get information about these benefits from Social Security offices or Railroad Retirement Board offices. Noncash tips are not counted as wages for social security purposes.

Your future benefits can be figured correctly only if the Social Security Administration (SSA) has your correct information. To make sure that you have received credit for all your earnings, you should request a statement of your earnings from SSA at least every other year. You can get information on how to receive a statement of your earnings by calling 1–800–SSA–1213, or for the hearing impaired with access to TDD equipment, 1–800–325–0778. When you get the statement from SSA, you should check it to be sure it includes all of your earnings.

Tip allocation. Every large food or beverage establishment must report to the Internal Revenue Service (IRS) any tips allocated to its employees. Generally, tips must be allocated to employees when the total tips reported to an employer by employees are less than 8% of the establishment's food and beverage sales. For more information, see *Tip Allocation,* later.

Importance of good records. You and your employer must keep accurate records of your tip income. *Table 1,* shown later in this publication, shows how tips are reported to you by your employer and how to report tips on your return. It may be helpful to refer to this table when you are preparing your return.

Useful Items

You may want to see:

Publication

☐ **505** Tax Withholding and Estimated Tax

☐ **1244** Employee's Daily Record of Tips and Report to Employer

Form (and Instructions)

☐ **4137** Social Security and Medicare Tax on Unreported Tip Income

Ordering publications and forms. To order free publications and forms, call our toll-free telephone number 1–800–TAX–FORM (1–800–829–3676). If you have access to TDD equipment, you can call 1–800–829–4059. See your tax package for the hours of operation. You can also write to the IRS Forms Distribution Center nearest you. Check your income tax package for the address.

If you have access to a personal computer and a modem, you can also get many forms and publications electronically. See *How To Get Forms and Publications* in your income tax package for details.

Asking tax questions. You can call the IRS with your tax question Monday through Friday during regular business hours. Check your telephone book or your tax package for the local number or you can call toll-free 1–800–829–1040 (1–800–829–4059 for TDD users).

Reporting Tips

You must report all tips as wages on Form 1040, Form 1040A, or Form 1040EZ. This includes the value of tips not paid in cash, such as passes, tickets, goods, or services. If you received tips of $20 or more in a month and did not report all of them to your employer, you must file Form 1040 and Form 4137. You cannot file Form 1040A or Form 1040EZ. If you are a railroad employee and you did not report tips of $20 or more, contact your employer.

Service charges. A club, hotel, or restaurant may require customers who use its dining or banquet rooms to pay a service charge, which is given to the waiters or waitresses and other employees. Your share of this service charge is not a tip, but is part of your wages paid by the employer. You should not include your share of the service charge in your report of tips to your employer. Your employer should not include your share of the service charge as tips paid to you, but should include it in your wages.

Tip splitting. If you split tips with fellow employees, include only your share of the tips in your report to your employer. An example of tip splitting is a waiter giving part of his tips to busboys. "Tip splitting" may be referred to also as "tip sharing" or "tip pooling."

Daily Record of Tips

You must keep a *daily record* or *other documentation* to prove the amount of tip income you report on your return.

Daily record. Your daily record must show the following.

1) Your name and address,
2) Your employer's name, and
3) The establishment's name.

Also show for each workday:

1) The amount of cash tips you receive directly from customers or from other employees,
2) Tips from credit card charge customers when paid to you by your employer,
3) The amount of tips you paid out to other employees through tip splitting, etc., and
4) The names of the other employees to whom you paid tips.

Make the entries in your daily record on or near the date you receive the tip income. Your records should also show the date each entry is made.

Other documentation. If you do not keep a daily record of tips, you must maintain other documentation of the tip income you receive. This other documentation must be as credible and reliable as a daily record. The records must show:

1) Tips added to checks by customers and paid over to you, or
2) Amounts paid for food or beverages on which you generally would receive a tip.

Examples of other documentary records are copies of:

1) Restaurant bills,
2) Credit card charges, or
3) Charges under any other arrangement containing amounts added by customers as tips.

Which form to use. You can use *Form 4070A, Employee's Daily Record of Tips,* to record your tips.

Form 4070A can be found only in Publication 1244, *Employee's Daily Record of Tips and Report to Employer.* You can get Publication 1244 from the IRS or your employer. A filled-in Form 4070–A is shown at the end of this publication.

Your personal records. You should keep your daily tip record and a copy of the written reports you give your employer with your personal records.

When to Report Tips to Employer

You must give your employer a written report of your tips for each month by **the 10th day** of the next month. This report is required for

each month that you receive tips of $20 or more while working for that employer.

Saturday, Sunday, holiday rule. If the 10th day of the month falls on a Saturday, Sunday, or legal holiday, you can give your employer the report on the next day that is not a Saturday, Sunday, or legal holiday.

Example. You must report tips of $20 or more you receive during January 1996 to your employer by Monday, February 12, 1996.

How to Report Tips to Employer

The following discussions refer only to tips paid by cash, charge, and check.

Less than $20 in tips in one month. If you receive less than $20 in tips while working for one employer during a month, you do not have to report them to that employer. But you must include the tips in gross income on your income tax return. You do not have to pay social security tax, Medicare tax, or railroad retirement tax on these tips.

$20 or more of tips in one month. If you receive tips of $20 or more in a month while working for any one employer, you must report the total amount of your tips to that employer.

Example 1. You work for Watson's Restaurant during the month and receive $75 in tips. Because your tips are more than $20 for the month, you must report the $75 to your employer.

Example 2. You work for Watson's Restaurant during the month and receive $17 in tips. In that same month you work for Parkview Restaurant and get $14 in tips. Even though your tips total $31, you do not have to report tips to either employer because you did not receive $20 or more in tips from either job. However, you should keep a record of the $31 because you must report it as income on your tax return.

Example 3. You work for Watson's Restaurant and receive $25 in tips. In that same month you work for Parkview Restaurant and get $12 in tips. Because your tips for Watson's Restaurant are $20 or more for the month, you must report the $25 to that employer. You do not have to report the $12 in tips you received while working for Parkview Restaurant to either employer. However, you should keep a record of the $12 because you must report it as income on your tax return with your other tips.

Termination of employment. When you stop working for your employer, you should report your tips of $20 or more to your employer at that time. If you do not report the tips when you stop working, you must give a statement to your employer either before your final payday or by the 10th day following the month you receive the tips, whichever is earlier.

Example. You stop working as a waiter in April after receiving $85 in tips for the month. You will receive your final pay in May. You must report your tips for April to your employer before the earlier of May 10 or the day before you receive your final pay.

Date tips are treated as paid. Tips are treated as paid to you when you make the written report to your employer. However, if you make no report to your employer, tips are treated as paid to you when you receive them.

Example 1. During December 1995, you received $300 in tips. On January 10, 1996, you reported the tips to your employer. Your December 1995 tips will be treated as paid to you in January 1996, the time you made the report to your employer. You must report the $300 on your 1996 income tax return.

Example 2. If during December 1995 your tips were only $18, you would not have to make a report to your employer. In this case, your tips are treated as paid in December 1995, the time you actually received them. You must report the $18 on your 1995 income tax return.

Information you must report. To report tips to your employer, you can use **Form 4070,** *Employee's Report of Tips to Employer.* This form, available only in Publication 1244, tells you what information you must report. If you do not use Form 4070, your report should include the following.

• The amount of tips,

• Your employer's name and address,

• Your name, social security number, and address,

• The month (or shorter period) covered,

• Your signature, and

• The date of the report.

A filled-in Form 4070 is shown at the end of this publication.

Withholding on Tips by Employer

Your employer must withhold income tax, social security or railroad retirement tax, and Medicare tax on the tips you report. Your employer usually deducts the withholding due on tips from your regular wages. However, you do not have to have income tax withheld if you can claim exemption from withholding.

Exemption from withholding. Income tax will not be taken out of your pay if you give your employer a filled-in **Form W-4,** *Employee's Withholding Allowance Certificate,* claiming exemption from withholding. You can claim exemption only if you had no income tax liability last year and expect none this year. Your exemption from withholding is only good for 1 year. To continue your exemption, you must file a new Form W-4 by February 15 next year certifying that you meet the conditions for claiming exemption.

Employer's recordkeeping. Your employer may withhold an amount from your wages based on an estimate of your tips. Your employer also may require your written tip reports more than once a month and deduct the taxes due on your reported tips even though they do

not yet total $20. If this is done, your employer must adjust the amount of taxes withheld from time to time, based on the actual amount of tips you report.

Form W-2. The Form W-2, *Wage and Tax Statement,* which you get from your employer, includes your reported tips.

• Box 1 includes your total wages, other compensation, and the tips you reported.

• Box 3 is your social security wages not including tips.

• Box 7 is your social security tips, the tips you reported to your employer.

• Box 5 is your Medicare wages and tips, which for most persons will be the sum of boxes 3 and 7. Your Medicare wages and tips total will be higher if your wages and tips are more than $61,200.

Any tips that are allocated to you (discussed later) are shown in box 8. Allocated tips are not included in boxes 1, 5, and 7. Any errors you find in these amounts should be brought to your employer's attention as soon as possible so you can obtain a corrected form.

Giving your employer money for taxes. Your regular pay may not be enough for your employer to withhold all the tax due on your regular pay plus reported tips. You can give your employer money to pay this withholding tax up to the close of the calendar year.

If your wages and any money you provide are not enough to pay all of your withholding taxes, the amounts will be applied in the following order. Your employer will first withhold from your wages all taxes due on your regular wages. This includes withholding for state and local income tax. Next, your employer will withhold, from the balance of your wages, taxes due on your reported tips. Social security and Medicare tax on reported tips will be withheld before any income tax will be withheld. Any taxes that remain unpaid should be collected by the employer out of your next paycheck.

You may pay estimated tax instead of giving your employer extra money. Use **Form 1040–ES,** *Estimated Tax for Individuals.* See Publication 505, *Tax Withholding and Estimated Tax,* for more information.

Uncollected employee social security and Medicare tax on tips. Box 13 (code A) on your Form W-2 will show the amount of social security tax on tips that your employer was unable to withhold and for which you did not give your employer extra money to pay the tax.

Box 13 (code B) will show the amount of Medicare tax on tips that your employer was unable to withhold and for which you did not give your employer extra money to pay the tax.

You must file Form 1040 to report the amount of uncollected tax on tips from box 13 (codes A and B), Form W-2, and pay it with your return, even if you do not otherwise have to file a return. Include the amount of uncollected tax in the total on line 54 of Form 1040. On the dotted line next to line 54, write "UT" and show the amount.

Limit on social security tax. The pay you received and the tips you reported to a nonrailroad employer in 1995 were subject to the withholding of social security tax at the rate of 6.2% on the first $61,200 of compensation. Your pay and tips are also subject to withholding of Medicare tax at the rate of 1.45% on all compensation. No more than $3,794.40 for social security tax should have been withheld from your pay by any one employer.

Limit on railroad retirement tax. If your pay and the tips you reported to your railroad employer in 1995 were subject to the withholding of tier 1 and/or tier 2 railroad retirement tax, see the following discussions.

Tier 1. Your employer withheld tier 1 railroad retirement tax at the rate of 6.2% on the first $61,200 of compensation and Medicare tax at the rate of 1.45% on your total compensation. No more than $3,794.40 for railroad retirement tax should have been withheld from your pay by any one employer during 1995.

Tier 2. Your employer withheld tier 2 railroad retirement tax at the rate of 4.90% on the first $45,300 of your pay and tips. No more than $2,219.70 should have been withheld from your pay during 1995.

Two or more employers. If you worked for two or more employers in 1995, who together withheld more than $3,794.40 of social security tax or tier 1 railroad retirement tax, or $2,219.70 of tier 2 railroad retirement tax, you may claim the extra amount as a credit to reduce your income tax when you file your return. See *Excess Social Security or Railroad Retirement Tax Withholding* in Publication 505 for more information.

Overwithholding by one employer. If any one employer withheld too much social security, Medicare, or railroad retirement tax, you may not claim the extra amount as a credit to reduce your income tax. Your employer must adjust this for you.

No limit for withholding of income tax. Unlike the social security and railroad retirement taxes, there is no dollar limit on the income tax withheld on wages and tips. The income tax withheld by your employer will either decrease what you owe at the end of the year or increase your refund when you file your return.

Penalties. To ensure that all taxpayers pay their fair share of taxes, the law provides penalties for failure to file returns or pay taxes as required. Some other penalties that may be charged include those for:

1) Not supplying a correct social security number to an employer or other person required to file a report with IRS about the taxpayer,

2) Filing a frivolous income tax return,

3) Filing a fraudulent return, or

4) Failing to report tips, discussed later.

Some penalties may not be charged if failure to follow the tax laws and regulations was due to reasonable cause and not willful neglect.

Penalty for false information on Form W–4. If you make statements or claim withholding allowances on your Form W–4 that decrease the amount of tax withheld and there is no reasonable basis for such statements or allowances at the time you prepare your Form W–4, you may have to pay a penalty of $500.

There is also a criminal penalty for willfully supplying false or fraudulent information on your Form W–4 or for willfully failing to supply information that would increase the amount withheld. The penalty, upon conviction, is a fine of not more than $1,000, or imprisonment for not more than 1 year, or both.

Tips Not Reported to Employer

If you received tips of $20 or more in any month while working for one employer, but did not report all of them to your employer, you must figure your social security and Medicare tax on the tips not reported. You should use **Form 4137,** *Social Security and Medicare Tax on Unreported Tip Income,* and attach it to Form 1040. See *Social Security and Medicare Tax on Unreported Tip Income (Form 4137),* later.

Employees subject to the Railroad Retirement Act. If you receive tips while working for a railroad employer, you should report all of your tips to your employer. You cannot get railroad retirement credit for your tips unless you report these tips to your employer. A railroad employee cannot file Form 4137 for unreported tips. You should report these tips each pay period. Your tips will be subject to withholding from your regular pay. Any balance of tax due on your tips will be shown in box 13 of Form W–2.

If you do not report your tips throughout the year, contact your employer. Your employer will collect the tax. You must include all of the tips you received, including unreported tips, in your gross income.

Penalty for failure to report tips. If you do not report tips to your employer as required, you may be subject to a penalty equal to 50% of the employee social security or railroad retirement tax and Medicare tax, in addition to the tax that you owe.

Reasonable cause. You can avoid this penalty if you can show reasonable cause for not reporting these tips to your employer. To do so, attach a statement to your return explaining why you did not report them.

Tip Allocation

Large food or beverage establishments are required to report certain additional information about tips to the IRS.

To make sure that employees are correctly reporting tips, employers must keep records to verify amounts reported by employees. Certain employers must allocate tips if the percentage of tips reported by employees falls below a required minimum percentage of gross sales. To "allocate tips" means to assign an additional amount as tips to each employee whose reported tips are below the required percentage.

Who must follow the tip allocation rules. The rules apply to operations in which:

1) Food or beverages are provided for consumption on the premises,

2) Tipping is customary, and

3) The employer normally employed more than 10 people on a typical business day during the preceding calendar year.

To whom tip allocation rules do not apply. Food or beverage operations where tipping is not customary do not come under the rules. For example:

1) A cafeteria or "fast food" operation,

2) An operation that adds a service charge of 10% or more to 95% or more of its food or beverage sales, or

3) Food or beverage operations located outside the United States.

How the rules work. The rules apply only if the total amount of tips reported by all tipped employees to your employer is less than 8% (or some lower acceptable percentage) of the establishment's total food or beverage sales (with some adjustments).

If reported tips total less than 8% of total sales, your employer must allocate the difference between 8% of total sales (or some lower acceptable percentage) and the amount of reported tips among all tipped employees. Your employer will exclude carryout sales, state and local taxes, and sales with a service charge of 10% or more when figuring total sales.

Allocation to individual employees. Generally, your employer will allocate to all affected employees their share of allocated tips every payroll period. However, your employer may do this less frequently. Your employer *should not withhold* any taxes from the allocated amount.

No allocation will be made to you if you report tips at least equal to your share of 8% of the establishment's total food or beverage sales.

Allocation formula. The allocation can be done either under a formula agreed to by both the employer and the employees or, if they cannot reach an agreement in good faith, under a formula prescribed by IRS regulations.

The allocation formula in the regulations provides that tip allocations are made only to directly-tipped employees. If you receive tips directly from customers, you are a directly-tipped employee, even if the tips are turned over to a tip pool. For example, waiters, waitresses, and bartenders are usually considered directly-tipped employees.

If you do not normally receive tips directly from customers, you are an indirectly-tipped employee. Examples of indirectly-tipped employees are busboys, service bartenders, and cooks. If you receive tips both directly and indirectly through tip splitting or tip pooling, you are treated as a directly-tipped employee.

Lowering the tip allocation percentage. If customers of the establishment tip less than 8% on the average, either your employer or a majority of the directly-tipped employees (including those who turn their tips over to a tip pool) may petition to have the allocation percentage reduced from 8%. This petition is made to the district director for the Internal Revenue Service district in which the establishment is located. However, the percentage cannot be reduced below 2%. Also, a user fee must be paid with the petition.

User fee. A user fee is required to have the IRS consider a petition to lower the tip allocation percentage. The fee must be paid by check or money order made out to the Internal Revenue Service. The user fee amount for 1995 was $275. To check if this amount has changed, contact the district director for your area.

Employees' petition. The petition to lower the allocation percentage must be in writing and must contain enough information to allow the district director to estimate with reasonable accuracy the establishment's actual tip rate. This information might include the charged tip rate, type of establishment, menu prices, location, hours of operation, amount of self-service required, and whether the customer receives the check from the server or pays the server for the meal.

If the employer possesses any relevant information, the employer must provide it to the district director upon request of the employees or the district director.

An employee petition must be consented to by more than one-half of the directly-tipped employees working for the establishment at the time the petition is filed. If the petition covers more than one establishment, it must be consented to by more than one-half of the total number of directly-tipped employees of the covered establishments. The petition must state the total number of directly-tipped employees of the establishment (or establishments) and the number of directly-tipped employees consenting to the petition.

The petition may cover two or more establishments if the employees have made a good faith determination that the tip rates are essentially the same and if the establishments are:

1) Owned by the same employer,

2) Essentially the same type of business, and

3) In the same Internal Revenue Service region.

A petition that covers two or more establishments must include the names and locations of the establishments and must be sent to the district director for the district in which the greatest number of covered establishments are located. If there is an equal number of covered establishments in two or more districts, the employees can choose which district to petition.

Employees who file a petition must promptly notify their employer of the petition. The employer must then promptly furnish the district director with copies of any **Forms 8027**, *Employer's Annual Information Return of Tip Income and Allocated Tips*, filed for the establishment for the 3 immediately preceding calendar years.

Allocated tips on Form W–2. Your employer will report the amount of tips allocated to you on your Form W–2 (in box 8) separately from your wages and reported tips. Your employer bases withholding only on wages and reported tips. Your employer *should not withhold* income, social security, railroad retirement, or Medicare taxes from the allocated amount. Any incorrectly withheld taxes should be refunded to you by your employer.

If you leave your job before the end of the calendar year and request an early Form W–2, your employer does not have to include a tip allocation on the Form W–2. However, your employer may show the actual allocated amount if it is known, or show an estimated allocation. In January of the next year, your employer must provide Form W–2c, *Statement of Corrected Income and Tax Amounts*, if the early Form W–2 showed no allocation and your employer later determined that an allocation was required, or if the estimated allocation shown was wrong by more than 5% of the actual allocation.

Allocated tips you must report as income. If you do not have adequate records for your actual tips, you must include the allocated tips shown on your Forms W–2 as additional tip income on your tax return. If you have records,

do not include allocated tips on your return. Include additional tip income only if those records show you actually received more tips than the amount you reported to your employer. For recordkeeping requirements, see *Daily Record of Tips,* earlier, under *Reporting Tips.*

Allocated tips have not been included in the amount of wages and reported tips shown in box 1 of your Forms W–2, and no taxes have been withheld from these tips.

Example. Judy reported $4,000 tip income to her employer in 1995. Box 8 of her 1995 Form W–2 showed allocated tips of $1,000. Her daily record of tips made on or near the date she received her tip income totaled $6,000.

Judy must report an additional $2,000 of tip income ($6,000 total tips minus $4,000 tips reported to employer) on her 1995 income tax return.

Social security and Medicare tax. For allocated tips that you include in gross income on line 7 of Form 1040, use **Form 4137** to figure your social security and Medicare tax on the tips not reported to your employer.

Social Security and Medicare Tax on Unreported Tip Income (Form 4137)

Report on line 1 of Form 4137 *all* of the tips you received. This includes tips you reported

to your employer, unreported tips, and allocated tips that you must report as income. Report on line 2 the amount of tips you reported to your employer and on line 4 the amount of tips you did not report because the total was less than $20 in a calendar month. These amounts are subtracted from the amount on line 1. The balances on lines 9 and 5 are the unreported tips subject to social security and Medicare tax figured on Form 4137.

Note: Only include cash, check, and charge tips when completing Form 4137. The value of tips not paid in cash or by check or charge card are not counted as wages for social security and Medicare tax purposes.

Be sure to complete Schedule U on the bottom of Form 4137. Schedule U is used by the Social Security Administration to credit your social security and Medicare accounts.

Attach Form 4137 to Form 1040. Enter the tax on line 50 of Form 1040. You may not use Form 1040EZ or Form 1040A.

Note: Do not include on line 50, Form 1040, any amount of uncollected social security tax and Medicare tax on tips you **did** report to your employer. This amount, if any, is shown in box 13 on your Form W–2. Instead, see *Uncollected employee social security and Medicare tax on tips* under *Withholding on Tips by Employer* for the method of paying these taxes.

Table 1. **Understanding Tip Income Reporting**

	Will these tips be reported to you on Form W-2?	Does your employer withhold social security and Medicare tax on these tips?[1]	Should you file Form 4137 to figure your social security and Medicare tax on these tips?	Do you have to report these tips as income on your income tax return?
Tips you reported to your employer during the year	Yes (Box 1 of your W-2)	Yes	No	Yes
Allocated tips	Yes (Box 8 of your W-2)	No	Yes[2,3]	You must report **ALL** tip income
Tips of $20 or more in a month that you did not report to your employer	No	No	Yes[2,3]	Yes
Tips of less than $20 in a month that you did not report to your employer	No	No	No	Yes

[1] If you are a railroad employee the question would be, ''Does your employer withhold railroad retirement and Medicare tax?''
[2] You may be subject to a penalty equal to 50% of the employee social security or railroad retirement tax and Medicare tax in addition to the tax that you owe.
[3] Railroad employees should not file Form 4137 and should contact their employer who will collect the employment taxes.

Sample Filled-in Form 4070 from Publication 1244

Form **4070** (Rev. April 1994) Department of the Treasury Internal Revenue Service	**Employee's Report of Tips to Employer** ► For Paperwork Reduction Act Notice, see back of this form.	OMB No. 1545-0065
Employee's name and address JOHN W. ALLEN 1117 MAPLE AVE. ANYTOWN, NY 14202		Social security number 987 00 4321

Employer's name and address (include establishment name, if different.)
DIAMOND RESTAURANT
834 MAIN STREET
ANYTOWN, NY 14203

Month or shorter period in which tips were received	Tips
from OCTOBER 1 , 1995 . to OCTOBER 31 , 1995	$ 1,269.60
Signature *John W. Allen*	Date NOV. 6, 1995

Sample Filled-in Form 4070A from Publication 1244

Form **4070A** (Rev. April 1994) Department of the Treasury Internal Revenue Service	**Employee's Daily Record of Tips** (This is a voluntary form provided for your convenience. See instructions for records you must keep.)	OMB No. 1545-0065
Employee's name and address JOHN W. ALLEN 1117 MAPLE AVE. ANYTOWN, NY 14202	Employer's name DIAMOND RESTAURANT Establishment name (if different)	Month and year OCT. 1995

	Date tips rec'd	Date of entry	a. Tips received directly from customers and other employees	b. Credit card tips received	c. Tips paid out to other employees	d. Names of employees to whom you paid tips
1	10/3		- OFF -			
2	10/3		48.80	26.40	15.20	Judy Brown
3	10/3		28.00	21.60	8.00	Carl Jones
4	10/5		42.00	24.00	10.00	Judy Brown
5	10/7		40.80	28.00	12.00	Judy Brown + Brian Smith
Subtotals			159.60	100.00	45.20	

For Paperwork Reduction Act Notice, see Instructions for Form 4070.   Page 1

	Date tips rec'd	Date of entry	a. Tips received directly from customers and other employees	b. Credit card tips received	c. Tips paid out to other employees	d. Names of employees to whom you paid tips
6	10/7		- OFF -			
7	10/8		37.20	22.40	8.00	Carl Jones
8	10/9		50.80	17.20	10.00	Judy Brown + Carl Jones
9	10/9		33.60	16.40	8.00	Judy Brown
10	10/11		30.40	22.00	9.20	Judy Brown
11	10/11		42.00	11.60	8.80	Carl Jones
12	10/14		35.60	16.00	7.60	Judy Brown
13	10/14		- OFF -			
14	10/14		48.40	14.40	12.40	Judy Brown + Brian Smith
15	10/16		45.20	32.00	17.20	Brian Smith
Subtotals			323.20	152.00	81.20	

Page 2

	Date tips rec'd	Date of entry	a. Tips received directly from customers and other employees	b. Credit card tips received	c. Tips paid out to other employees	d. Names of employees to whom you paid tips
16	10/16		41.20	18.40	8.80	Judy Brown
17	10/18		39.20	21.20	9.60	Judy Brown
18	10/14		46.80	12.80	8.40	Carl Jones
19	10/21		34.00	19.20	10.00	Judy Brown
20	10/21		- OFF -			
21	10/22		34.80	26.00	12.80	Judy Brown + Brian Smith
22	10/24		42.40	22.80	12.40	Carl Jones
23	10/24		48.30	17.20	13.60	Judy Brown
24	10/25		33.60	19.20	10.80	Brian Smith
25	10/26		37.20	14.80	9.20	Judy Brown
Subtotals			358.00	171.60	95.60	

Page 3

	Date tips rec'd	Date of entry	a. Tips received directly from customers and other employees	b. Credit card tips received	c. Tips paid out to other employees	d. Names of employees to whom you paid tips
26	10/26		31.60	11.60	12.40	Judy Brown
27	10/26		- OFF -			
28	10/27		43.20	14.00	12.80	Carl Jones
29	10/30		34.80	22.40	7.20	Carl Jones
30	10/31		46.00	27.20	12.80	Judy Brown + Brian Smith
31	11/2		27.60	20.40	6.40	Judy Brown
Subtotals from pages 1, 2, and 3			159.60 323.20 358.00	100.00 152.00 171.60	45.20 81.20 95.60	
Totals			1,024.00	519.20	273.60	

Tips (col. a plus col. b minus col. c). Report this amount on Form 4070 ▶   1,269.60

Page 4

Page 7

REVIEW QUIZ

When you feel you have covered all of the material in this chapter, answer these questions. Choose the *best* answer. Check your answers with the correct ones found on the Review Quiz Answer Key at the end of this book.

True (T) or False (F)

T   F   1. According to FLSA provisions, if an employee works 40 hours in a three-day workweek, the employee is entitled to overtime pay.

T   F   2. Time worked should always be computed to the nearest minute.

T   F   3. Salaried employees who are exempt from overtime require a special computation for gross pay based on hours worked.

T   F   4. The information on an employee's W-4 form is used in preparing the employee's paycheck.

Multiple Choice

5. Under the 24-hour time system, which of the following represents 5 p.m.?

   a. 5.0 hours
   b. 0500 hours
   c. 1200 hours
   d. 1700 hours

6. The actual amount of an employee's paycheck is called the:

   a. gross pay.
   b. net pay.
   c. regular pay.
   d. salary.

7. According to FSLA provisions, under the overtime pay method, an employee's overtime hours are multiplied by:

   a. the employees' regular hourly rate.
   b. 1.5 times the employee's regular hourly rate.
   c. .5 times the employee's regular hourly rate.
   d. the employee's overtime premium rate.

8. The proper tax withholding table to use is determined by:

   a. the employee's marital status and the type of payroll period.
   b. the number of withholding allowances the employee claims.
   c. the employee's gross pay.
   d. none of the above.

9. A tip credit:

   a. lowers the amount of gross wages payable by the employer.
   b. is also known as a service charge.
   c. may result in an employee being paid less than minimum wage.
   d. is the result of a tip shortfall allocation.

10. If tips reported by all employees are less than 8% of gross receipts for a particular period, the tip shortfall must be:

    a. split evenly between the employer and tipped employees.
    b. allocated among all tipped employees.
    c. allocated among directly tipped employees.
    d. charged to indirectly tipped employees.

Chapter Outline

Acquisition Costs of Property and
  Equipment
    Land with Building to Be Demolished
    Land and Building for a Lump Sum
    Equipment Requiring Special
      Installation
    Land Improvements
    Building Repairs and Improvements
    China, Glassware, Silver, Uniforms,
      and Linen
Operating Leases and Capital Leases
Depreciation of Property and Equipment
    Straight-Line Method
    Declining Balance Method
    Sum-of-the-Years-Digits Method
    Comparison of Time-Factor Methods
    Depreciation for Partial Periods
    Productive-Output Method
Depreciation of China, Glassware, and
  Silver
Amortization of Leaseholds and Leasehold
  Improvements
    Leaseholds
    Leasehold Improvements
Sale or Disposal of Property and Equipment
Trade-In of Property and Equipment
    Exchange of Like-Kind Assets
    Exchange of Dissimilar Assets
    Tax Accounting for Exchange of Assets
Depreciation and Income Taxes
    Modified Accelerated Cost Recovery
      System

Learning Objectives

1. Explain the items typically classified as property and equipment. (p. 219)

2. Describe the determination of acquisition costs recorded for various types of property and equipment. (pp. 220–223)

3. Summarize the difference between accounting for building repairs and accounting for building improvements. (p. 222)

4. Describe the difference between operating leases and capital leases, and explain the four criteria for distinguishing capital leases from operating leases. (pp. 223–224)

5. Explain the purpose of depreciation, the affected accounts, and the different types of values of assets. (pp. 219, 224–226)

6. Explain the difference between time-factor and use-factor methods of depreciation. (p. 226)

7. Describe the straight-line method of depreciation. (pp. 226–227)

8. Describe the declining balance method of depreciation. (pp. 227–228)

9. Describe the sum-of-the-years-digits method of depreciation. (pp. 228–230)

10. Identify accelerated depreciation methods. (pp. 230–231)

11. Explain the options for computing depreciation for partial time periods. (pp. 231–233)

12. Describe the productive-output method of depreciation. (p. 233)

13. Explain what special considerations apply to the depreciation of china, glassware, and silver. (pp. 233–234)

14. Explain amortization and the amortization of leaseholds and leasehold improvements. (pp. 234–235)

15. Explain the accounting considerations involved in the sale, disposal, or trade-in of property and equipment. (pp. 235–241)

7

Property and Equipment Accounting

THE TERM **property and equipment** refers to long-lived assets which are acquired for use in the operation of a business and are not intended for resale to customers in the normal course of business. Land, buildings, furniture and fixtures, vehicles, office equipment, and kitchen equipment are examples of items typically classified as property and equipment. These items are also referred to as **tangible assets** because they have physical substance. Intangible assets include such items as copyrights, trademarks, franchises, and purchased goodwill.

This chapter focuses on accounting methods applicable to the acquisition, depreciation, and disposal of tangible long-lived assets. Questions answered within the chapter include:

1. How is the acquisition cost of a fixed asset determined?

2. What is the difference between a capital lease and an operating lease?

3. What is depreciation and what methods are used to compute it?

4. What is amortization and how is it computed?

5. What accounting methods are used to record the disposal or exchange of assets?

The chapter begins by illustrating how the acquisition cost of various property and equipment items is determined. Computing the acquisition cost of a tangible asset is important because this amount is used as the basis for capitalizing the item to an asset account and for computing depreciation.

Depreciation spreads the cost of an asset over the term of its estimated useful life. Estimated **useful life** refers to the estimated economic service life of an asset. The chapter illustrates and compares several depreciation methods which are used for financial accounting purposes. Special accounting procedures for depreciating china, glassware, and silver are also examined.

In addition, the chapter addresses the amortization of leaseholds and leasehold improvements. Like depreciation, amortization involves the write-off of the cost of an asset over its estimated useful life.

The final sections of the chapter examine accounting methods used to record the disposal of tangible assets. Accounting for exchanges involving either like-kind assets or dissimilar assets is addressed in relation to both financial and tax accounting rules.

Exhibit 1   Computing the Cost of a Land Purchase

Purchase price	$200,000
Brokerage fee	12,000
Legal, title, and recording fees	2,000
Razing of existing building to prepare for the construction of a new building	20,000
Less salvage proceeds of razed building	(8,000)
Site grading	5,000
Total acquisition cost	$231,000

Acquisition Costs of Property and Equipment

When a property or equipment item is purchased, it is generally recorded at its acquisition cost. Acquisition cost includes all expenditures necessary to acquire, install, and prepare an item for use. For example, in addition to the purchase price (including any sales tax), acquisition cost may consist of freight costs, the expense of insurance while the item is in transit, legal or brokerage fees, installation charges, and any costs required to make the asset ready for use.

If a property and equipment item is purchased with an installment note or mortgage, the interest is not part of the acquisition cost. An exception to this rule occurs when a company is constructing an asset for its own use. In this case, Financial Accounting Standards Board (FASB) Statement #34 states that interest costs during the construction period are considered part of the acquisition cost.

Land with Building to Be Demolished

When land is purchased with an existing building that will be demolished, the purchase may involve brokerage fees, recording fees, escrow fees, and title fees. Other expenses may involve fees for surveying, draining, grading, and clearing the property. All of these expenditures may be part of the acquisition cost. In addition, any delinquent taxes paid by the buyer are part of the acquisition cost.

Exhibit 1 illustrates the computation of the acquisition cost of land with a building that will be demolished. All of these expenditures are recorded in the Land account.

Land and Building for a Lump Sum

It is not uncommon for hospitality companies to purchase land with an existing building that will be used in the business. Generally, the selling price is stated as one lump sum for both the land and building. Land is a non-depreciable asset because it has an unlimited life in the normal course of business for hospitality companies; on the other hand, a building is a depreciable asset. When land and building are purchased with a lump sum, the acquisition cost must be allocated between two asset accounts, one entitled Land and another entitled Building. This allocation is usually computed on the basis of real estate appraisals or tax valuations.

For example, assume that land with a building is purchased for $350,000, but the real estate tax appraisals total $300,000 ($90,000 for the land, $210,000 for the building). The first step in determining amounts of the $350,000 purchase cost to allocate to the Land and Building accounts is to calculate allocation percentages on the basis of the appraisal values. This is accomplished by dividing the appraisal value of the land and the appraisal value of the building by the total appraisal value. The resulting allocation is as follows:

Land	$ 90,000	30%
Building	210,000	70%
Total appraisal	$300,000	100%

The allocation percentage for the cost of the land is 30% ($90,000 divided by $300,000), and the allocation percentage for the cost of the building is 70% ($210,000 divided by $300,000).

The next step is to apply the individual allocation percentages to the total acquisition cost of $350,000. The individual allocations, or cost bases, of the land and building are recorded in the general ledger accounts as follows:

Land ($350,000 × 30%)	$105,000
Building ($350,000 × 70%)	245,000
Total acquisition cost	$350,000

Equipment Requiring Special Installation

Certain equipment items (such as ovens, dishwashers, and air conditioning systems) may require special platforms or electrical wiring to make them ready for use. These special installation costs are considered part of the asset's acquisition cost.

Assume that a hospitality business purchases equipment that requires special wiring. The acquisition cost of the equipment would be calculated as follows:

Invoice price	$2,000
Freight	100
Sales tax	120
Installation	350
Special wiring	200
Total acquisition cost	$2,770

Land Improvements

Land improvements (such as driveways, parking lots, and fences) should not be charged to the Land account. Whether the land is owned or leased is a determining factor in how these improvements are recorded.

If the land is owned by the hospitality business, improvements may be charged to an account called Land Improvements and depreciated over the improvement's estimated useful life.

If the land is leased, improvements may be charged to an account called **Leasehold Improvements** and amortized over the improvement's estimated useful life or the life of the **lease,** whichever is shorter. The life of the lease may include renewable options if the probability of renewal is high. Most lease agreements state that any improvements made by the **lessee** (tenant) to the leased property become the property of the **lessor** (landlord) at the expiration of the lease.

Building Repairs and Improvements

After a building has been placed in use, the costs of ordinary repairs and maintenance are charged to the appropriate expense account. Ordinary repairs and maintenance costs are defined as recurring expenditures which are necessary in order to keep an asset in good operating condition. These costs include expenditures associated with routine repair and maintenance activities such as repairing broken windows and doors, cleaning, lubricating, and painting. These expenditures do not increase the future service potential of an asset. Instead, they allow the company to derive the intended benefits from the asset over the asset's estimated useful life. Therefore, ordinary repairs and maintenance expenditures are expensed.

Improvements to a building (sometimes called betterments) are capitalized. Improvements are expenditures that improve or increase the future service potential of an asset. For example, expenditures associated with replacing an old heating system with a more efficient heating system would be considered an improvement and not a repair. When an old building is purchased and requires extensive repairs and maintenance before it is ready for use, these expenditures should be capitalized to the Building asset account. Other kinds of expenditures that are treated as improvements and not as repairs are major reconditioning and overhaul expenditures that extend the asset's useful life beyond the original estimate. The term "addition" applies to a building expansion made to increase the building's service potential.

It is not always easy to distinguish between an improvement and a repair. However, it is important to be able to distinguish them because their accounting treatments are different: expenditures for repairs are expensed; expenditures for improvements are capitalized.

The amount capitalized to a fixed asset account depends on whether the building is owned or leased. **Capital expenditures** for a leased building should be charged to an asset account called Leasehold Improvements and amortized. Capital expenditures for an owned building should be charged to the Building account and depreciated.

China, Glassware, Silver, Uniforms, and Linen

There are several ways to account for the acquisition costs of china, glassware, and silver. Three common methods recommended by the American Institute of Certified Public Accountants (AICPA) are:

1. Capitalize/Depreciate/Expense
   a. Capitalize the acquisition cost.
   b. Depreciate the acquisition cost.
   c. Charge the cost of any replacements to an expense account.

2. Capitalize/Depreciate/Expense/Adjust
    a. Capitalize the acquisition cost.
    b. Depreciate the acquisition cost.
    c. Charge the cost of any replacements to an expense account.
    d. Adjust the asset account annually to correspond to a physical inventory.
3. Capitalize/Depreciate/Capitalize/Adjust
    a. Capitalize the acquisition cost.
    b. Depreciate the acquisition cost.
    c. Capitalize any replacements and adjust the cost basis accordingly.
    d. Adjust the asset account annually to correspond to a physical inventory.

Accounting for china, glassware, and silver is presented later in this chapter when depreciation is discussed in detail.

Hotels that rent uniforms or use a linen service simply record these expenditures as they are incurred, charging their costs to expense accounts entitled Uniforms Expense and Linen and Laundry Expense. If a hotel purchases its own uniforms and linen, such expenditures should be capitalized and depreciated.

Operating Leases and Capital Leases

A hotel may purchase its **fixed assets** or it may lease them. A hotel may lease land, building(s), office equipment, vehicles, or any other fixed asset through a leasing company.

A lease is a contract in which the lessor (landlord or leasing company) gives the lessee (tenant or user) the right to use an asset over a period of time in return for lease or rental payments. The lessor is the owner of the asset and the lessee is the person or company obtaining the right to use and possess the asset.

Real estate leasing contracts generally do not present any accounting problem because they are truly rental arrangements. However, leases of vehicles and other equipment items may be simple rental arrangements or may actually serve as long-term financing arrangements.

Operating leases are rental arrangements. An operating lease generally involves equipment which will be used by the lessee for a relatively short period of time. At the end of the lease term, the asset has a substantial remaining useful life and the lessor retains ownership rights. Operating leases do not contain bargain purchase options. A bargain purchase option provides the lessee with the right to buy the asset at the end of the lease term for a nominal amount or for an amount which is substantially less than the asset's fair market value. Unlike operating leases, some **capital leases** contain such options.

Capital leases are not simply rental arrangements; they actually serve as long-term financing arrangements which effectively transfer ownership of the leased asset from the lessor to the lessee at the end of the lease term. Even though title may not be transferred until the end of the lease, a capital lease is essentially regarded as the sale of an asset from the lessor to the lessee. In some cases, the term of a capital lease may be so long that the asset's economic life (period during which the asset has value) is nil at the end of the lease. These types of leases are also classified as capital leases even though the lessor retains ownership at the end of the lease term.

FASB Statement #13 provides criteria for distinguishing capital leases from operating leases for accounting purposes. According to the FASB, if any of the following four criteria are met, the lessee must classify and account for the lease as a capital lease:

1. The lease transfers ownership of the property to the lessee by the end of the lease term.

2. The lease contains a bargain purchase option.

3. The lease term is equal to 75% or more of the estimated economic life of the leased property.

4. The present value of the minimum lease payments is at least 90% of the fair market value of the leased property.

Based on FASB Statement #13, *only those leases that do not meet any of these criteria may be accounted for as operating leases.* In accounting for an operating lease, the lessee records the lease payments as a rental expense.

When equipment is acquired through a capital lease, the lessee should capitalize the cost to an asset account called Leased Equipment. In the same journal entry, a liability account called Lease Payment Obligation is credited for the present value of the future lease payments. The journal entry is as follows:

Leased Equipment	xxx	
Lease Payment Obligation		xxx

The asset account Leased Equipment is depreciated over the estimated useful life of the asset rather than the life of the lease.

When the lease payments are made, the following entry is recorded:

Lease Payment Obligation	xxx	
Interest Expense	xxx	
Cash		xxx

Depreciation of Property and Equipment

Depreciation spreads the cost of an asset over its estimated useful life. Except for land, all property and equipment is depreciated by gradually converting the cost of the asset into an expense in the periods during which the asset provides a service. With the exception of china, glassware, silver, uniforms, and linen, the entry to record depreciation is as follows:

Depreciation Expense	xxx	
Accumulated Depreciation		xxx

Depreciation Expense is an expense account containing the depreciation charges for the current year only. Separate depreciation expense accounts may be used for each type of depreciable asset. Since depreciation is based on estimation, depreciation expense may be rounded to the nearest dollar to avoid implying pinpoint accuracy.

Accumulated Depreciation is a contra-asset account and contains depreciation charges from the date of purchase (or from the date on which the asset is placed in service) to the present. These charges represent the expired cost of the asset. Assets may be purchased with the intent to use them several months after the purchase date. Since depreciation is the allocation of the cost of an asset over its estimated useful life, depreciation charges should commence only when the asset is put in use. Separate accumulated depreciation accounts may be used for buildings, furniture, equipment, and other depreciable assets.

It is important to stress that depreciating an asset is not an attempt to establish the market value of the asset. The market value is the value which the asset could bring if sold on the open market. Depreciation does not represent a decline in market value. The cost of an asset minus the amount of its accumulated depreciation is the net asset value, commonly called the "book value" of the asset.

The useful life may be estimated in terms of time or in terms of units of output. These concepts will be discussed later in the chapter. When estimating the useful life of an asset, the following factors must be considered:

- Past experience with similar assets
- Age of the asset when acquired
- Repair, maintenance, and replacement policies of the company
- Current technological trends
- Frequency of use
- Local conditions, such as weather

Salvage value, sometimes called residual value, refers to the estimated proceeds from the disposal of an asset less all removal and selling costs at the end of its useful life. Salvage values are usually subjective because they require estimates. Nominal salvage values may be ignored and assigned a value of zero. One approach is to set the salvage value of an asset at zero when the estimated salvage value amounts to 10% or less of the asset's original cost. It is possible for a building to actually have a salvage value of zero because the costs incurred in tearing down the building at the end of its useful life may approximate the sales value of the scrap materials.

When the book value of an asset equals the asset's estimated salvage value, the asset is fully depreciated and no further depreciation is recorded for that asset. As long as the asset remains in use, its original cost and fully accumulated depreciation remain on the books. When an asset is disposed of, entries are made to remove the original cost from the asset account and to remove its related accumulated depreciation from the accumulated depreciation account.

Several methods may be used to compute depreciation. Different depreciation methods may be used for different assets. For example, one method may be used to allocate the cost of a building and another method may be used to allocate the cost of a vehicle. Also, one method of computing depreciation may be used for allocating the cost of a particular vehicle and another method for allocating the costs of other vehicles. Moreover, the depreciation methods used for financial reporting purposes may differ from those used for tax reporting purposes.

While a company may use different depreciation methods for different assets, the generally accepted accounting principle of consistency requires that once a depreciation method is selected for a particular asset, it should be used throughout that asset's estimated useful life. However, a company may be justified in changing depreciation methods for a particular asset. Any changes must be disclosed in the footnotes to the financial statements as required by the disclosure principle.

Depreciation methods may be classified as time-factor methods or use-factor methods. Time-factor methods estimate useful life in terms of time. Use-factor methods estimate useful life in terms of units of output. Three time-factor methods used for financial accounting purposes are presented in this chapter: the straight-line method, the declining balance method, and the sum-of-the-years-digits method. An identical example is used for all three time-factor methods. The time-factor methods are then compared, and depreciation for partial periods is addressed. The section concludes with a discussion of a use-factor method: the productive-output method.

Straight-Line Method

The **straight-line method** of depreciation is the simplest and most popular time-factor method used in computing depreciation for financial reporting purposes. Under the straight-line method, an equal allocation of the cost of the asset less salvage value is assigned to each period. This spreads depreciation expense evenly throughout the asset's estimated useful life.

Annual straight-line depreciation is calculated by subtracting salvage value from the cost basis and dividing this amount by the estimated useful life. The computation of straight-line depreciation is expressed by the following formula:

$$\text{Annual Depreciation Expense} = \frac{\text{Cost} - \text{Salvage Value}}{\text{Years of Useful Life}}$$

For example, assume that a hospitality business buys equipment at the beginning of a year for $3,500; the salvage value of the equipment is estimated at $500; and its useful life is estimated to be five years. The straight-line method computes the annual depreciation expense as follows:

$$\text{Annual Depreciation Expense} = \frac{\text{Cost} - \text{Salvage Value}}{\text{Years of Useful Life}}$$

$$\text{Annual Depreciation Expense} = \frac{\$3,500 - \$500}{5 \text{ Years}} = \underline{\underline{\$600}}$$

Another approach to computing straight-line depreciation is to calculate an annual depreciation percentage by dividing 100% by the estimated useful life of the asset:

$$\text{Annual Depreciation Percentage} = \frac{100\%}{\text{Years of Useful Life}}$$

Multiplying the annual depreciation percentage by the asset's cost determines the annual depreciation expense. Given the same information as in the previous example, the annual depreciation percentage is 20% (100% divided by 5 years) and the annual depreciation expense is computed at $600 (20% × $3,000).

Exhibit 2   Depreciation Schedule: Straight-Line Method

Year	Computation	Depreciation Expense	Accumulated Depreciation	Cost	Book Value
	Upon Acquisition	—	—	$3,500	$3,500
1	$1/5 \times \$3,000$	$ 600	$ 600	3,500	2,900
2	$1/5 \times \$3,000$	600	1,200	3,500	2,300
3	$1/5 \times \$3,000$	600	1,800	3,500	1,700
4	$1/5 \times \$3,000$	600	2,400	3,500	1,100
5	$1/5 \times \$3,000$	600	3,000	3,500	500
		$3,000			

Exhibit 2 presents a depreciation schedule of the equipment purchased in the preceding example. The schedule illustrates the effect of straight-line depreciation over the useful life of the asset.

The matching principle requires that all expenses incurred during an accounting period be recorded in that accounting period. Since financial statements are generally issued on a monthly basis, depreciation expense must be recorded monthly. If the annual depreciation expense for a purchased equipment item is $600, the monthly depreciation expense would be $50 ($600 divided by 12 months). The entry to record this monthly depreciation is as follows:

Depreciation Expense   50
    Accumulated Depreciation   50

Declining Balance Method

The declining balance method is based on a percentage rate. Although any percentage rate may be used, the most common rate is twice the straight-line rate. The method associated with this doubled rate is called the **double declining balance method.** The double declining rate is computed by the following formula:

$$\text{Double Declining Rate} = \frac{100\%}{\text{Years of Useful Life}} \times 2$$

For example, assume again that a hospitality business purchases equipment at the beginning of a year for $3,500; the salvage value of the equipment is estimated at $500; and its useful life is estimated to be five years. The double declining rate is computed as follows:

$$\text{Double Declining Rate} = \frac{100\%}{\text{Years of Useful Life}} \times 2$$

$$\text{Double Declining Rate} = \frac{100\%}{5} \times 2 = 40\%$$

The declining balance method computes depreciation expense for the first year of an asset's estimated useful life by multiplying the annual depreciation rate by the

Exhibit 3   Depreciation Schedule: Double Declining Balance Method

Year	Computation	Depreciation Expense	Accumulated Depreciation	Cost	Book Value
	Upon Acquisition	—	—	$3,500	$3,500
1	40% × $3,500	$1,400	$1,400	3,500	2,100
2	40% × $2,100	840	2,240	3,500	1,260
3	40% × $1,260	504	2,744	3,500	756
4	(See *Note*)	256	3,000	3,500	500
5	Not Applicable	0	3,000	3,500	500
		$3,000			

Note: The allowable $256 depreciation expense is determined by computing the difference between the prior book value of $756 and the salvage value of $500.

cost of the asset. Each successive year's depreciation expense is determined by multiplying the annual depreciation rate by the beginning book value of the asset. With the declining balance method of computing depreciation, salvage value is not subtracted from the asset's cost; however, the book value may never fall below the salvage value. If depreciation computations result in a book value at the end of a year which is less than the asset's salvage value, depreciation expense is computed by subtracting the salvage value from the book value at the beginning of that year.

Exhibit 3 presents a depreciation schedule which illustrates the effect of declining balance depreciation over the estimated useful life of the asset. Depreciation expense for the first year is calculated at $1,400 (the double declining rate of 40% × $3,500 cost). The book value of the asset at the beginning of the second year is $2,100 ($3,500 cost − $1,400 accumulated depreciation); therefore, depreciation expense for the second year is calculated at $840 (40% × $2,100).

At the beginning of the fourth year, the book value of the asset is $756. When this amount is multiplied by the 40% annual depreciation rate, the resulting depreciation expense is $302. However, this amount cannot be used because the resulting book value for the end of the fourth year would be $454 ($3,500 cost − $3,046 accumulated depreciation), which is less than the asset's salvage value of $500. Therefore, the allowable depreciation expense for the fourth year is $256, which is computed by subtracting the salvage value ($500) from the book value at the beginning of that year ($756). The book value at the end of the fourth year becomes equal to the asset's salvage value ($3,500 cost − $3,000 accumulated depreciation). There is zero depreciation expense for the fifth year because, at the end of the fourth year, the asset's book value equals its salvage value.

Sum-of-the-Years-Digits Method

The **sum-of-the-years-digits method** uses a fraction in computing depreciation expense. The numerator of the fraction is the remaining years of the asset's estimated useful life. This figure changes with each year's computation of depreciation. The denominator of the fraction is the sum of the digits of the asset's estimated useful life. This figure remains constant with each year's computation of depreciation. Each year's depreciation expense is determined by multiplying this fraction by the asset's cost less its salvage value.

For example, assume again that a hospitality business purchases equipment at the beginning of a year for $3,500; the salvage value of the equipment is estimated at $500; and its useful life is estimated to be five years.

The numerator of the fraction used to compute depreciation expense changes each year to match the remaining years of the asset's estimated useful life. In the first year of the asset's five-year estimated useful life, the numerator is 5; in the second year, the numerator is 4, and so on. An easy way to determine the appropriate numerator for each year's computation of depreciation expense is to simply list the estimated years of the asset's useful life and then reverse them:

Year of Useful Life	Years Reversed (Numerator)
1	5
2	4
3	3
4	2
5	1

The denominator of the fraction used to compute depreciation expense remains constant and is the sum of the digits of the asset's estimated useful life. Since the asset's estimated useful life is five years, the denominator of the fraction is 15 (1 + 2 + 3 + 4 + 5 = 15). When the span of an asset's estimated useful life is short, the sum of the years' digits is easily computed. However, when longer time spans are involved, it may be easier to compute the sum of the years' digits by using the following procedure:

1. Square the number of years estimated as the asset's useful life.
2. Add the asset's useful life to the squared result.
3. Divide the resulting figure by 2.

For our five-year estimated useful life example, the procedure is as follows:

1. $5 \times 5 = 25$
2. $25 + 5 = 30$
3. 30 divided by 2 = 15 (the denominator)

Therefore, the fractions used to compute depreciation expense in our example are as follows:

Year 1: $5/15$
Year 2: $4/15$
Year 3: $3/15$
Year 4: $2/15$
Year 5: $1/15$

Exhibit 4   Depreciation Schedule: Sum-of-the-Years-Digits Method

Year	Year Reversed	Computation	Depreciation Expense	Accumulated Depreciation	Cost	Book Value
		Upon Acquisition	—	—	$3,500	$3,500
1	5	$5/15 \times \$3,000$	$ 1,000	$ 1,000	3,500	2,500
2	4	$4/15 \times \$3,000$	800	1,800	3,500	1,700
3	3	$3/15 \times \$3,000$	600	2,400	3,500	1,100
4	2	$2/15 \times \$3,000$	400	2,800	3,500	700
5	1	$1/15 \times \$3,000$	200	3,000	3,500	500
	15		$ 3,000			

For any particular year, depreciation expense is computed by using the following formula:

$$\text{Depreciation Expense} = \frac{\text{Remaining Years of Useful Life}}{\text{Sum-of-the-Years-Digits}} \times (\text{Cost} - \text{Salvage Value})$$

Exhibit 4 presents a depreciation schedule which illustrates the effect of the sum-of-the-years-digits depreciation over the useful life of the asset.

The previous computations assume that the asset was purchased at the beginning of the year. It is common for assets to be purchased throughout a year. If the sum-of-the-years-digits method is used, additional computations are necessary for any asset not purchased at the beginning of the year.

For example, assume that the equipment item was acquired on May 1. This means the asset will be in use for only 8 months in the first accounting period; therefore, only $8/12$ of the first year's depreciation calculation is allowed. In the second accounting year, the remaining $4/12$ of the first year's calculation is added to $8/12$ of the second year's calculation. A similar pattern is used for each accounting year during the asset's life. Exhibit 5 illustrates this procedure.

Comparison of Time-Factor Methods

The straight-line, double declining balance, and sum-of-the-years-digits methods are used to compute depreciation expense for financial accounting purposes. Exhibit 6 compares the results of these three time-factor methods for computing annual depreciation expense. The comparison is based on the preceding examples (depreciation for equipment purchased at the beginning of a year for $3,500, with an estimated salvage value of $500 and a useful life estimated at five years). Note that regardless of which depreciation method is used, the total depreciation expense amounts to $3,000 and the book value of the asset never falls below the asset's estimated salvage value. However, the methods differ in terms of the depreciation amounts computed for individual years.

The straight-line method results in equal depreciation charges each year of the asset's estimated useful life. The declining balance method and the sum-of-the-years-digits are called **accelerated depreciation methods** because they result in the

Exhibit 5   Sum-of-the-Years-Digits Depreciation Method—Additional Computations

Year	Allocation	Carryover	Allowable Depreciation (Rounded)
19X1:	$8/12 \times \$1,000$		$ 667
	$4/12 \times \$1,000$	$ 333	
	Depreciation expense for 19X1		$ 667
19X2:	$4/12$ carryover		$ 333
	$8/12 \times \$800$		533
	$4/12 \times \$800$	$ 267	
	Depreciation expense for 19X2		$ 866
19X3:	$4/12$ carryover		$ 267
	$8/12 \times \$600$		400
	$4/12 \times \$600$	$ 200	
	Depreciation expense for 19X3		$ 667
19X4:	$4/12$ carryover		$ 200
	$8/12 \times \$400$		$ 267
	$4/12 \times \$400$	$ 133	
	Depreciation expense for 19X4		$ 467
19X5:	$4/12$ carryover		$ 133
	$8/12 \times \$200$		133
	$4/12 \times \$200$	$ 67	
	Depreciation expense for 19X5		$ 266
19X6:	$4/12$ carryover		$ 67
Total depreciation over life of asset			$3,000

highest depreciation charges in the first year, with lower and lower charges in successive years. These accelerated methods allocate the largest portion of an asset's depreciable cost to the early years of the asset's estimated useful life. As reflected in Exhibit 6, the double declining balance method generally results in the highest depreciation expense for the early years of an asset's estimated useful life.

Depreciation for Partial Periods

The previous illustration of time-factor methods assumed that assets were purchased on the first day of the month. Of course, asset transactions may occur throughout a month. When these transactions occur, it is not necessary to carry depreciation precisely to the day or even the month because depreciation, after all, is not an exact science. For instance, the salvage value and the useful life used in depreciation calculations are not actual measurements, but simply estimates.

When an asset is purchased and a time-factor method is used to compute depreciation, company policy may state how depreciation for partial periods is to be

Exhibit 6   Comparison of Depreciation Methods

	Straight-Line	Double Declining Balance	Sum-of-the-Years-Digits
Acquisition Cost	$3,500	$3,500	$3,500
Depreciation: Year			
1	$ 600	$1,400	$1,000
2	600	840	800
3	600	504	600
4	600	256	400
5	600	0	200
Total	$3,000	$3,000	$3,000
Book Value	$ 500	$ 500	$ 500

determined. The following discussion presents possible options for depreciation involving partial periods.

Recognizing Depreciation to the Nearest Whole Month. Using this option, assets purchased from the 1st to the 15th of the month are depreciated as if they were purchased on the 1st of the current month. Any assets purchased from the 16th to the end of the month are treated as if they were purchased on the 1st of the following month.

Conversely, any assets sold from the 1st to the 15th of the month are not depreciated for that month. Any assets sold from the 16th to the end of the month are depreciated for the month.

Recognizing Depreciation to the Nearest Whole Year. Using this option, assets acquired during the first six months of the accounting year are considered held for the entire year. Assets acquired during the last six months are not depreciated in that accounting year.

Conversely, assets sold during the first six months of the accounting year are not depreciated for that year; those sold after the first six months are depreciated for the full year.

Other Options. Other options for depreciation involving partial periods are as follows:

• One-half year's depreciation is recognized on all assets acquired or sold during the year.

• No depreciation is recognized on any acquisitions during the year. Any asset sold during the year receives a full year's depreciation.

- A full year's depreciation is recognized on any acquisitions during the year. Any assets sold during the year receive no depreciation.

Productive-Output Method

This use-factor method allocates the depreciable cost of an asset on the basis of the asset's estimated useful output. When an asset is purchased, an estimate of its useful output is made. As expressed by the following formula, the cost of the asset minus its estimated salvage value is divided by its estimated useful output to arrive at depreciation per unit of output (unit depreciation factor):

$$\text{Unit Depreciation Factor} = \frac{\text{Cost} - \text{Salvage Value}}{\text{Estimated Useful Output}}$$

Depreciation expense is determined by multiplying the unit depreciation factor by the actual output of the asset during the depreciation period. This continues until the accumulated depreciation is the same as the asset's depreciable basis (cost minus salvage value).

Hospitality businesses may use the productive-output method to compute depreciation expense for vehicles. For example, assume that a vehicle is purchased for $25,000. The estimated output of the vehicle is 100,000 miles and its salvage value is estimated at $5,000. The unit depreciation factor is computed as follows:

$$\text{Unit Depreciation Factor} = \frac{\text{Cost} - \text{Salvage Value}}{\text{Estimated Useful Output}}$$

$$\text{Unit Depreciation Factor} = \frac{\$25,000 - \$5,000}{100,000 \text{ miles}}$$

$$\text{Unit Depreciation Factor} = 20\text{¢ per mile}$$

Assuming that the vehicle has traveled 1,500 miles in the current accounting month, the depreciation expense for the month would be $300 (1,500 miles times 20¢ per mile).

Depreciation of China, Glassware, and Silver

China, glassware, and silver may be depreciated using any of the depreciation methods presented earlier. However, no depreciation expense account or accumulated depreciation account is used to record the allocated acquisition costs of these assets. When depreciation is computed, the China, Glassware, and Silver asset account is directly reduced by the computed amount and the depreciation charge is made to the China, Glassware, and Silver expense account. The entry to record computed depreciation is as follows:

China, Glassware, and Silver (expense account)	xxx	
China, Glassware, and Silver (asset account)		xxx

For example, assume that a new restaurant purchases its original supply of china, glassware, and silver on April 1 at a cost of $9,000. The useful life is estimated at five years and the salvage value is estimated at $3,600. Assume further that straight-line depreciation has been selected to depreciate the acquisition cost. The restaurant policy regarding the depreciation of china, glassware, and silver is to capitalize the acquisition cost, depreciate on the basis of this cost, and charge the cost of any replacements to an expense account.

The journal entry to record the purchase is as follows:

China, Glassware, and Silver (asset account)	9,000	
Cash (or Accounts Payable)		9,000

One month's depreciation is computed as follows:

$$\text{Monthly Depreciation Expense} = \frac{\text{Cost} - \text{Salvage Value}}{\text{Months of Useful Life}}$$

$$\text{Monthly Depreciation Expense} = \frac{\$9,000 - \$3,600}{60 \text{ Months}} = \underline{\underline{\$90}}$$

On April 30, the adjusting entry to record depreciation for the month is as follows:

China, Glassware, and Silver (expense account)	90	
China, Glassware, and Silver (asset account)		90

Since the restaurant has chosen to expense any replacements, these replacements do not affect the depreciation calculation for the life of this asset. For example, the purchase of replacements is recorded as follows:

China, Glassware, and Silver (expense account)	xxx	
Cash (or Accounts Payable)		xxx

For the purpose of illustration, the depreciation of china, glassware, and silver were combined. Since these assets may have different salvage values and depreciation periods, they may require separate computations.

Amortization of Leaseholds and Leasehold Improvements

Amortization is a means of allocating the costs of certain intangible assets to those periods which benefit from their use. Intangible assets are long-lived assets that are useful to a business but have no physical substance. Financial accounting rules require that certain intangible assets be amortized over their useful lives, with a maximum amortization period of 40 years. The useful life of some intangible assets may be limited by law, competition, or contract, in which case the amortization period may be less than the 40 years allowable under generally accepted accounting principles.

Unlike depreciation, amortization does not require an accumulated account for expense. The usual accounting entry for amortization is a debit to amortization expense and a credit directly to the asset account. Some accountants will credit an accumulated amortization account instead of reducing the basis of the asset, but this practice is not prevalent.

Examples of assets that are amortized are **leaseholds,** leasehold improvements, and certain types of intangible assets. According to the *Uniform System of Accounts and Expense Dictionary for Small Hotels, Motels, and Motor Hotels,* leaseholds and leasehold improvements are classified as Property and Equipment on the balance sheet.

Leaseholds

The rights granted by a lease to the lessee (tenant or user) are called a leasehold. In addition to the periodic payments, some long-term leases require the lessee to make a substantial payment at the inception of the lease. This initial payment (if it is not a rental deposit) is recorded to a noncurrent asset account called Leasehold. The payment is amortized over the life of the lease for a period not to exceed 40 years.

For example, assume that on June 1 a hotel leases property for a 20-year period and makes an initial payment of $120,000 which is not considered a rental or security deposit. This payment is recorded as follows:

Leasehold	120,000	
Cash		120,000

The noncurrent asset account Leasehold is amortized over 20 years at the rate of $6,000 per year ($120,000 divided by 20 years). Therefore, the monthly amortization expense is $500 ($6,000 divided by 12 months). On June 30, the month-end entry is as follows:

Amortization Expense	500	
Leasehold		500

Sometimes a lease agreement requires an advance payment of the monthly rents. If the advance payments cover a period of one year or less, they are charged to Prepaid Rent and allocated to the proper accounting periods.

Security deposits are not classified as leaseholds; these deposits are recorded to a noncurrent asset which may be called Deposits or Security Deposits. These deposits remain on the books until refunded.

Leasehold Improvements

Any improvements made to leased property generally revert to the landlord (lessor) upon termination of the lease. Accordingly, the tenant (lessee) should record such improvements to a Leasehold Improvements account. Examples of leasehold improvements are expansion of a leased building, permanent partitions, or installation of any material fixtures which become a permanent part of the building.

A leasehold improvement should be amortized over its estimated useful life or over the remaining term of the lease (including renewal options that are highly likely to be exercised), whichever is shorter. However, the amortization period should not exceed 40 years.

Sale or Disposal of Property and Equipment

A business may sell its assets and receive cash from the transaction, or it may dispose of certain assets and receive no value in return. The gain or loss associated with such transactions is computed on the book value. As explained previously, the book value of an asset is the asset's cost less its accumulated depreciation. The book value of a fully depreciated asset with no salvage value would be zero, since its accumulated depreciation would equal its cost. The following sections explain how to account for the gain or loss on the sale of an asset.

Sale at a Price Above Book Value. Assume that equipment is sold for $2,000. Its original cost is $10,000 and its accumulated depreciation at the date of sale is $8,500. The gain is computed as follows:

Selling price	$2,000
Book value ($10,000 − $8,500)	1,500
Gain on disposal	$ 500

The entry to record the disposal of the equipment is as follows:

Cash	2,000	
Accumulated Depreciation—Equipment	8,500	
Equipment		10,000
Gain on Disposal of Equipment		500

Accumulated depreciation is a contra-asset account with a normal credit balance. It is credited with each period's computation of depreciation. When an asset is sold, it is necessary to remove all accumulated depreciation related to that asset by a debit entry. In the same entry, the asset account Equipment is credited to remove the original cost of the disposed asset from this account.

Sale at a Price Below Book Value. If the same asset had been sold for $1,200, the loss would be computed as follows:

Selling price	$1,200
Book value ($10,000 − $8,500)	1,500
Gain on disposal	$ 300

The entry to record the disposal of this asset would be as follows:

Cash	1,200	
Accumulated Depreciation—Equipment	8,500	
Loss on Disposal of Equipment	300	
Equipment		10,000

Sale at a Price Equal to Book Value. If the same asset had been sold for $1,500, there is neither a gain nor a loss:

Selling price	$1,500
Book value ($10,000 − $8,500)	1,500
Difference	$ 0

The entry to record the disposal of this asset would be as follows:

Cash	1,500	
Accumulated Depreciation—Equipment	8,500	
Equipment		10,000

Trade-In of Property and Equipment

New assets may be acquired by trading in old assets. Transportation equipment trade-ins are common in the hospitality industry. Accounting for trade-ins depends on the fair market value of the assets involved in the transaction. For our purposes, the basis for evaluating gain or loss on the trade-in of property and equipment will be the fair market value of the newly acquired asset.

Although uncommon, it is possible for a hospitality firm making a trade-in to receive cash (also called boot) in the transaction. This occurs when the asset traded in has a fair market value greater than the asset acquired. Whenever boot (cash) is involved, special procedures are necessary in computing gain or loss. These procedures are beyond the scope of our discussion; interested readers are referred to intermediate accounting texts for specific explanations.

Trade-ins may involve the exchange of like-kind assets or the exchange of dissimilar assets. The trade-in of one automobile for another is an example of an exchange of like-kind assets. The trade-in of an automobile for a computer is an example of an exchange of dissimilar assets. The following sections address accounting for gain or loss on each of these types of exchanges.

Exchange of Like-Kind Assets

Certain types of depreciable assets, such as vehicles, computers, copying machines, and other equipment items, are customarily traded in for new assets of the same kind (like-kind). For example, the exchange of a van for another van is considered an exchange of like-kind assets. According to accounting rules, when a book gain results from the exchange of like-kind assets, the gain is not recognized through an entry involving a general ledger revenue account. Instead, the acquisition cost of the newly acquired asset is reduced by the amount of the book gain. However, when a material book loss results from the exchange of like-kind assets (due to a trade-in allowance which is substantially below the book value of the asset), the book loss must be recognized. The following sections explain these accounting rules and procedures in greater detail.

Nonrecognition of Book Gain. There are two reasons why a book gain is not recognized when it results from an exchange of like-kind assets:

1. It is difficult to objectively measure the realistic book gain because the list price of the asset to be acquired may be set artificially high, allowing the dealer to grant an inflated trade-in allowance.

2. The substitution of like-kind assets should not be a means of generating income.

Due to these reasons, no book gain is realized when a depreciable asset is traded in for another like-kind asset. Any computed gain is used to reduce the cost basis of the newly acquired asset. For example, assume that old equipment with an original cost of $10,000 and accumulated depreciation of $8,500 is traded in for similar equipment. The new equipment has a list price of $14,000 and the dealer grants a trade-in allowance of $2,000 on the old equipment. The balance of $12,000 is paid in cash. The nonrecognized gain is computed as follows:

Trade-in allowance on old equipment	$2,000
Book value of old equipment ($10,000 − $8,500)	1,500
Nonrecognized gain (to reduce cost basis of new equipment)	$ 500

The cost basis of the new equipment is computed as follows:

List price of new equipment	$14,000
Less: Nonrecognized gain on trade-in of old equipment	500
Recorded cost basis of new equipment	$13,500

The journal entry to record this transaction is as follows:

Equipment (new)	13,500	
Accumulated Depreciation—Equipment (old)	8,500	
Equipment (old)		10,000
Cash		12,000

Another method may be used to determine the cost basis of an asset acquired in a like-kind exchange resulting in a nonrecognition of gain. Using this method, the cost of the acquired asset may be computed as follows:

New Asset Cost = Book Value of Asset Exchanged + Cash Paid Out

This alternate method produces the same results and journal entries as the previous method. Using the information from the previous example, the cost basis of the new equipment would be computed as follows:

Book value of old equipment ($10,000 − $8,500)	$ 1,500
Add: Cash payment for new equipment	12,000
Cost basis of new equipment	$13,500

Recognition of Book Loss. In financial accounting, a material loss resulting from a trade-in allowance substantially below book value must be recognized. For example, assume that old equipment with an original cost of $10,000 and accumulated depreciation of $8,500 is traded in for similar equipment. The new equipment has a list price of $14,000 and the dealer grants a trade-in allowance of $1,200 on the old equipment, which has a book value of $1,500. The balance of $12,800 is paid in cash. The recognized loss is computed as follows:

Trade-in allowance on old equipment	$1,200
Book value of old equipment ($10,000 − $8,500)	1,500
Recognized loss	$ 300

The journal entry to record this transaction is as follows:

Equipment (new)	14,000	
Accumulated Depreciation—Equipment (old)	8,500	
Loss on Disposal of Equipment	300	
Equipment (old)		10,000
Cash		12,800

A small loss (as defined by management) may be accounted for in a manner similar to that described for the exchange of assets under tax rules, which is discussed later in this chapter.

Exchange of Dissimilar Assets

Examples of exchanges involving dissimilar assets are the exchange of equipment for a vehicle, or the exchange of inventory for equipment. When dissimilar assets are exchanged, any gain or loss is recognized immediately.

For example, assume that old equipment with an original cost of $10,000 and accumulated depreciation of $8,500 is traded in for supplies inventory. The inventory has a list price of $14,000 and the dealer grants a trade-in allowance of $2,000 on the old equipment. The balance of $12,000 is paid in cash. The recognized gain is computed as follows:

Trade-in allowance on old equipment	$2,000
Book value of old equipment ($10,000 − $8,500)	1,500
Recognized gain	$ 500

The cost basis of the supplies inventory is simply the list price of $14,000, assuming that this is the fair market value. The journal entry to record the transaction is as follows:

Inventory	14,000	
Accumulated Depreciation—Equipment	8,500	
Equipment		10,000
Cash		12,000
Gain on Disposal of Equipment		500

Sometimes there will be an even exchange of dissimilar assets. An even exchange raises the question: which asset represents the more reliable indicator of fair market value? Assuming the acquired asset offers a more reliable indicator, this asset is recorded at its fair market value (current replacement cost in a market which is fair and reasonable in view of existing conditions); the resulting gain or loss is recognized as the difference between the fair market value of the new asset and the book value of the old asset.

For example, assume that equipment with an original cost of $25,000 and accumulated depreciation of $13,000 is exchanged for a vehicle having a fair market value of $12,500. The recognized gain is computed as follows:

Original cost of equipment traded in	$25,000
Less: Accumulated depreciation	13,000
Book value of equipment traded in	$12,000
Fair market value of vehicle received	12,500
Recognized gain	$ 500

The journal entry to record this transaction is as follows:

Autos and Trucks	12,500	
Accumulated Depreciation—Equipment	13,000	
Equipment		25,000
Gain on Disposal of Equipment		500

Tax Accounting for Exchange of Assets

Financial accounting records are used to prepare income tax returns. However, certain items require special treatment for reporting on tax returns. Exceptions resulting from tax accounting differences are not recorded in the financial records; they are accounted for either on the income tax returns or on supplementary schedules.

Differences between tax accounting and financial accounting affect the treatment of depreciation. A business may use one method of depreciation for financial statements and another method for income tax purposes. This may result in a different book value for an asset, which will affect the gain or loss when this asset is sold or exchanged.

For exchanges of dissimilar assets, the income tax rules are similar to the financial accounting rules. For exchanges of like-kind assets, however, the income tax rules do not allow the recognition of either gain or loss. A nonrecognized gain is treated similarly under both sets of rules, but financial accounting rules require the immediate recognition of any material loss. Tax accounting requires that any loss on a like-kind exchange be used to adjust the cost basis of the newly acquired asset.

For example, assume that old equipment with an original cost of $10,000 and accumulated depreciation of $8,500 is traded in for similar equipment. The new equipment has a list price of $14,000 and the dealer grants a trade-in allowance of $1,200 on the old equipment. The balance of $12,800 is paid in cash. The computation of nonrecognized loss is as follows:

Trade-in allowance on old equipment	$1,200
Book value of old equipment ($10,000 − $8,500)	1,500
Nonrecognized loss	$ 300

For income tax purposes, the loss is not deductible, but is instead used to increase the asset's cost basis. This adjusted cost, which will be the basis for depreciation, is computed as follows:

Book value of old equipment ($10,000 − $8,500)	$ 1,500
Add: Cash payment for new equipment	12,800
Cost basis of new equipment	$14,300

Another way of computing the cost basis of the new equipment for tax purposes is to add the unrecognized loss ($300) to the list price of the new equipment ($14,000). For income tax purposes, depreciation will be computed on the cost basis of $14,300; thus, the $300 loss will be prorated over the life of the equipment through higher depreciation charges.

In practice, many companies will not enter into a like-kind exchange that will result in a loss. Instead, they will sell the old asset first, then purchase the new asset. In this way, the loss will be deductible for tax purposes. On the other hand, if a like-kind exchange involves a gain, companies will make the trade so that the gain is not recognized or taxed.

Based on Accounting Principles Board Opinion #29, the top half of Exhibit 7 summarizes the recognition of gain or loss for exchanges involving like-kind and dissimilar assets. The income tax rules regarding this area are slightly different from those of financial accounting. The bottom half of Exhibit 7 summarizes the income tax rules relating to the recognition of gain or loss for exchanges involving like-kind and dissimilar assets.

Exhibit 7   Summary of Rules Relating to Like-Kind and Dissimilar Exchanges

	Financial Accounting	
	Like-Kind exchange	Dissimilar exchange
Gain on exchange	Not recognized, used to reduce basis of new asset	Recognized
Loss on exchange	Recognized	Recognized
	Tax Accounting	
	Like-Kind exchange	Dissimilar exchange
Gain on exchange	Not recognized, used to increase basis of new asset	Recognized
Loss on exchange	Not recognized, used to reduce basis of new asset	Recognized

Depreciation and Income Taxes

The depreciation methods discussed thus far are supported by generally accepted accounting principles. They are also accepted in the hospitality industry and approved by the FASB. However, the accounting rules established by the FASB may differ from the rules established by the Internal Revenue Service (IRS). In preparing financial statements, hospitality businesses must conform to generally accepted accounting principles; but in preparing tax returns, they must follow tax rules and regulations.

Tax laws are complex and frequently change. Tax depreciation methods have changed several times over the last decade. IRS Publication 534 contains detailed information about tax depreciation methods.

Modified Accelerated Cost Recovery System

In the preparation of federal income tax returns, the Internal Revenue Code (IRC) requires that businesses use the straight-line depreciation method or a special accelerated depreciation method called **Modified Accelerated Cost Recovery System (MACRS)**. MACRS is similar to the declining balance method except that salvage value is not taken into consideration. This means that the book value of an asset is fully depreciated down to zero. The appendix to this chapter explains MACRS in more detail.

Key Terms

accelerated depreciation method
accumulated depreciation

capital expenditure
capital lease

depreciation
double declining balance method
fixed assets
lease
leasehold improvements
leaseholds
lessee
lessor

modified accelerated cost recovery
   system
operating lease
property and equipment
straight-line method
sum-of-the-years-digits method
tangible asset
useful life

Review Questions

1. How are the following terms defined?

    a. Capital expenditure

    b. Revenue expenditure

    c. Acquisition cost

    d. Tangible asset

    e. Intangible asset

2. What is the major difference between a capital lease and an operating lease?

3. What is the major difference between the Depreciation account and the Accumulated Depreciation account?

4. What are three common time-factor depreciation methods?

5. What are three common methods which may be used to account for the acquisition and replacement of china, glassware, and silver?

6. Is the gain (or loss) recognized for the following transactions involving like-kind assets?

    a. For financial reporting purposes: a material loss on the exchange

    b. For tax reporting purposes: a loss on the exchange

    c. For financial reporting purposes: a gain on the exchange

    d. For tax reporting purposes: a gain on the exchange

7. Is the gain (or loss) recognized for the following transactions involving dissimilar assets?

    a. For financial reporting purposes: a loss on the exchange

    b. For tax reporting purposes: a loss on the exchange

    c. For financial reporting purposes: a gain on the exchange

    d. For tax reporting purposes: a gain on the exchange

Problems

Problem 1

Compute the land acquisition cost from the following information:

Purchase price: $150,000

Legal fees: $1,500

Brokerage fees: $15,000

Site grading: $28,000

Delinquent taxes paid by buyer: $7,000

Removal of existing building: $12,000

Salvage proceeds from scrap of existing building: $2,000

Problem 2

Land and a building are purchased for a lump sum price of $500,000. According to county tax records, the real estate is appraised as follows: land, $99,000; building, $341,000. What cost basis will be entered in the general ledger for the land and the building?

Problem 3

An asset's cost is $10,000; its salvage value is estimated at $2,000; and its useful life is estimated at 4 years. Using each of the following depreciation methods, compute the depreciation, accumulated depreciation, and book value for each year of this asset's estimated useful life.

a. Straight-line method

b. Declining balance method using a double declining rate

c. Sum-of-the-years-digits method

Problem 4

A depreciation policy of the hospitality business in this example is to recognize depreciation to the nearest whole month. Compute the straight-line depreciation of the first and second months for the following assets:

	Date Acquired	Cost	Salvage Value	Useful Life Years
Asset A	3/15	$11,100	$1,500	8
Asset B	5/18	11,100	1,500	8

Problem 5

Journalize the following transactions:

a. Depreciation on the building is $1,300.

b. Depreciation on china and glassware is $275.

c. Amortization of the leasehold is $300.

Problem 6

A truck is sold outright for $4,500. The financial records show that its cost was $12,500 and accumulated depreciation to the date of sale was $6,000. Journalize the entry to record the disposal of this asset. Trucks are recorded in an asset account called Transportation Equipment.

Problem 7

Journalize the entry for Problem 6 if the truck's accumulated depreciation to the date of sale was $9,200.

Problem 8

Journalize the entry for Problem 6 if the truck's accumulated depreciation to the date of sale was $8,000.

Problem 9

A computer with an original cost of $17,000 and accumulated depreciation of $15,000 is traded in for a new computer with a list price of $25,000. The dealer grants a trade-in allowance of $4,800 on the old computer. The balance of $20,200 is paid with $2,200 cash and a note for the balance. Journalize this transaction in accordance with generally accepted accounting principles. Computers are recorded in an asset account called Computer Equipment.

Problem 10

Journalize the entry for Problem 9 if the computer's accumulated depreciation was $10,000.

Problem 11

A computer with an original cost of $17,000 and accumulated depreciation of $15,000 is traded in for a new van with a list price of $25,000. The dealer grants a trade-in allowance of $4,800 on the old computer. The balance of $20,200 is paid with $2,200 cash and a note for the balance. Journalize this transaction in accordance with generally accepted accounting principles. Computers are recorded in the Computer Equipment account and vans are recorded in the Transportation Equipment account.

Problem 12

Journalize the entry for Problem 11 if the computer's accumulated depreciation was $10,000.

Appendix

Modified Accelerated Cost Recovery System (MACRS)

MACRS Rules

MACRS rules generally apply to tangible property placed in service after 1986. Property that cannot be depreciated using MACRS includes:

- Intangible property

- Motion picture film or videotape

- Sound recordings

- Property placed in service before 1987

- Property that the taxpayer chooses to exclude from MACRS because its depreciation method is not based on a term of years

Property Classes and Recovery Periods

Under MACRS, property is assigned to one of several property classes. Property classes designate the useful life (recovery period) of depreciable assets. Some examples of property classes are:

- **3-year property:** small tools, tractors

- **5-year property:** automobiles, computers, office machinery such as typewriters, calculators, and copiers

- **7-year property:** desks, files, safes, office furniture

- **10-year property:** vessels, barges, tugs

- **15-year property:** shrubbery, fences, roads, bridges

- **31.5-year property:** nonresidential real estate placed in service before May 13, 1993

- **39-year property:** nonresidential real estate placed in service after May 12, 1993

Conventions

Assets may be purchased throughout the year; therefore depreciation calculations generally cannot be performed for an entire year unless an asset was purchased at the beginning of a tax year. The term "convention" describes a company's standard practice for treating depreciable assets purchased during the year.

The most common convention is the half-year convention. The half-year convention treats all property placed in service or disposed of during a tax year as placed in service or disposed of at the midpoint of that tax year. This means that in the year of purchase, a half year of depreciation expense is taken; when the asset is disposed of, another half year of depreciation expense is taken.

For example, an asset purchased on February 10 would have a half year of depreciation expense in the year of purchase. In subsequent years a full year of depreciation expense would be taken. In the year of disposition, only a half year of depreciation expense would be allowed regardless of the month of disposition.

The same would be true for an asset purchased in December (assuming it is the last month of a tax year). In the year of purchase, a half year of depreciation expense would be taken. In subsequent years a full year of depreciation expense would be taken. If the asset were to be sold in January of a subsequent year, a half year of depreciation expense would be allowed for that year.

Calculating MACRS Depreciation

Depreciation expense is computed based on the tax basis (which is usually the cost) of a tangible asset. The straight-line method can be used for any property class. Other depreciation methods allowable for certain property classes under MACRS are:

- 200% declining balance method

- 150% declining balance method

Salvage values are ignored in calculating depreciation under MACRS. A depreciable asset is depreciated down to zero at the end of its recovery period.

MACRS Tables

The Internal Revenue Service (IRS) provides MACRS percentage tables that can be used instead of performing depreciation calculations. These tables are categorized by property recovery period and convention (half-year, mid-quarter, mid-month). IRS Publication 534 provides a complete set of MACRS tables.

For example, a 3-year recovery period, half-year convention table would provide the following depreciation percentages:

Year	Rate
1	33.33%
2	44.45%
3	14.81%
4	7.41%

Note that all the percentages for the recovery period add up to 100%; thus the asset is fully depreciated, leaving no salvage value. The four years in which the asset depreciates allow for the half-year convention. For a 3-year recovery period, the percentages have been computed using the 200% declining balance method.

To illustrate the use and effect of MACRS, the following example is provided.

Assume that assorted small tools amounting to $1,000 for the maintenance department of a new hotel are purchased in March of the current year.

Small tools are classified as 3-year recovery property. This hotel uses the half-year convention for all its depreciable assets.

Using the 3-year recovery period, half-year convention table, the depreciation expense over the life of this asset is computed as follows:

Year	Computation	Depreciation
1 (year of purchase)	(33.33% × $1,000)	$ 333
2	(44.45% × $1,000)	$ 445
3	(14.81% × $1,000)	$ 148
4	(7.41% × $1,000)	$ 74
Total		$1,000

REVIEW QUIZ

When you feel you have covered all of the material in this chapter, answer these questions. Choose the *best* answer. Check your answers with the correct ones found on the Review Quiz Answer Key at the end of this book.

True (T) or False (F)

T   F   1. When a property or equipment item is purchased, it is generally recorded at its market value.

T   F   2. If a hotel purchases its own uniforms and linen, such expenditures should be capitalized and depreciated.

T   F   3. The expense account Depreciation Expense records depreciation charges from the date of purchase (or the date on which the asset is placed in service) to the present.

T   F   4. Depreciation methods that result in the highest depreciation charges in the first year, with lower and lower charges in successive years, are referred to as accelerated depreciation methods.

Multiple Choice

5. Which of the following assets is non-depreciable?

    a. buildings
    b. land
    c. land improvements on property owned by the company
    d. china, glassware, and silver

6. Which of the following is *not* a criterion for identifying a lease arrangement as a capital lease?

    a. The lease transfers ownership of the property to the lessee by the end of the lease term.
    b. The lease contains a bargain purchase option.
    c. The lessee agrees to certain expenditures to improve the leased property or equipment.
    d. The lease term is equal to 75% or more of the estimated economic life of the leased property.

7. The cost of an asset minus the amount of its accumulated depreciation is called:

    a. market value.
    b. book value.
    c. salvage value.
    d. residual value.

8. The straight-line method of depreciation:

    a. is an accelerated depreciation method.
    b. is classified as a productive-output method of depreciation.
    c. results in the highest depreciation expense for the early years of an asset's estimated useful life.
    d. results in equal depreciation charges each year of an asset's estimated useful life.

9. Which of the following is true about improvements made to leased property?

    a. They should be recorded by the tenant to a Leasehold Improvements account.
    b. They do not revert to the landlord upon termination of a lease.
    c. They include the installation of all temporary partitions.
    d. They should be amortized over their estimated useful life or the remaining term of the lease, whichever is longer.

10. When an asset is sold at a price above its book value:

    a. there is a loss on the disposal of the item.
    b. it is necessary to credit the revenue account Gain or Loss on Disposal of Equipment for the amount of the gain.
    c. the gain is not recognized through an entry involving a general ledger revenue account.
    d. the contra-asset account Accumulated Depreciation is unaffected.

Chapter Outline

Intangible Assets
    Organization Costs
    Goodwill
    Franchises
    Trademarks and Tradenames
    Patents
    Copyrights
    Preopening Expenses
    Liquor Licenses
Cash Value Intangible Assets
    Security Deposits
    Cash Surrender Value of Life Insurance

Learning Objectives

1. Define intangible assets, and list common intangible assets discussed in this chapter. (pp. 251–253)

2. Define organization costs, and describe how they are amortized. (p. 253)

3. Explain the accounting term "goodwill," and describe how goodwill is amortized. (pp. 253–254)

4. Explain franchise agreements, and describe how the costs of such agreements are amortized. (p. 254)

5. Define trademarks and tradenames, and describe how they are amortized. (pp. 254–255)

6. Compare patents and copyrights, and describe how they are amortized. (pp. 255–256)

7. Define preopening expenses, and contrast them to organization costs. (pp. 256–257)

8. Describe the renewal and purchase of liquor licenses, and explain how their costs are amortized. (p. 257)

9. Define cash value intangible assets using security deposits as an example. (pp. 257–258)

10. Describe the two basic kinds of life insurance, pointing out their similarities and differences. (pp. 258–259)

8

Other Noncurrent Assets Accounting

LONG-LIVED ASSETS that lack physical existence are called **intangible assets.** Some common examples of intangible assets are franchise rights, trademarks, tradenames, goodwill, copyrights, and patents. These intangible assets provide significant benefits to a business and may be a major reason for its success.

The acquisition cost of certain intangible assets is spread over the asset's useful life by the process of amortization. In comparison with the benefits derived from tangible assets such as property and equipment, the benefits derived from intangible assets are less certain and less well-defined. The real value of intangible assets is dependent upon the earning power of the hospitality firm.

Intangible assets such as franchise rights, copyrights, and patents have a definite legal life. Frequently, the economic life of an intangible asset is shorter than its legal life; in such cases, the shorter life is used to compute amortization.

Some intangible assets do not have a limited legal life. For example, purchased goodwill may have a life that is beyond the scope of economic estimation. Generally accepted accounting principles require that the acquisition cost of intangible assets be allocated over a period not to exceed 40 years. Shorter periods are allowed for intangible assets with shorter economic or legal lives.

Sometimes an intangible asset will no longer have any economic value before the conclusion of its legal or useful life. In this case, the cost of the intangible asset should be written off when it is reasonably evident that the asset has become worthless. Some intangible assets continue to have value long after their legal or economic lives. Frequently, management decides that the amortization process will stop when the intangible asset's book value reaches one dollar. In these cases, the intangible asset's value is presented on the balance sheet as one dollar to serve as a reminder of the existence of an important but undervalued intangible asset of the business.

This chapter will address accounting for other noncurrent assets by answering such questions as:

1. How are the various intangible assets defined?

2. How is the acquisition cost of intangible assets determined?

3. How are intangible assets amortized?

4. What is a "covenant not to compete"?

251

The purpose of this chapter is to present accounting for the acquisition and amortization of intangible assets. The chapter begins by identifying common intangible assets and explains how they are recorded on the balance sheet. Next, each of these intangible assets is defined and the method of accounting for its acquisition and amortization is presented. The final section of the chapter discusses non-amortizable intangible assets such as security deposits, utility deposits, and the cash surrender value of life insurance.

Intangible Assets

Intangible assets are long-lived assets that are useful to a business but have no physical substance. All intangible assets provide benefits over the long term. Some intangible assets provide legal and economic rights by virtue of their ownership. Examples of intangible assets are:

* Organization costs

* Goodwill

* Franchises

* Trademarks and tradenames

* Patents

* Copyrights

* Preopening expenses

* Liquor licenses

Cost is used as the basis for recording intangible assets. Cost represents the acquisition cost of the asset. Some companies may have a valuable tradename or trademark which does not show on the financial records because it is the result of reputation or advertising, rather than a purchase transaction. Although a tradename and/or a trademark may be famous and valuable, neither of these intangible assets is recorded in the financial records or shown on the balance sheet unless an acquisition cost is involved.

Amortization is a means of allocating the costs of intangible assets to those periods which benefit from their use. While amortization and depreciation are similar in purpose, the salvage value of an asset is generally ignored in amortization computations. Also, an accumulated amortization account is generally not used. The amortized amount is generally a debit to amortization expense and a credit directly to the asset account. For example, the entry to amortize purchased goodwill is as follows:

Amortization Expense	xxx	
Goodwill		xxx

Financial accounting rules require that intangible assets be amortized over their useful lives, with a maximum amortization period of 40 years. The useful life of some intangible assets may be limited by law (as in the case of copyrights), by competition (as in the case of patents), or by contract (as in the case of franchise agreements). The useful life as limited by law, competition, or contract is used as the amortization period if it is less than the 40 years allowable under generally accepted accounting principles. However, some intangible assets (such as goodwill, tradenames, and trademarks) may have an indefinite useful life. In these cases, the amortization period may not exceed 40 years.

Long-term assets that cannot be classified as property, equipment, or investments are shown on the balance sheet in a section called Other Assets. This balance sheet section includes intangible assets. Sometimes, intangible assets will be classified on the balance sheet as Deferred Charges instead of Other Assets. A deferred charge is an expenditure that will generate benefits over a long-term period and is amortized over its useful life. Deferred charges may include items such as remodeling expenditures, moving expenses, and bond issuance costs.

This chapter makes no distinction between Other Assets and Deferred Charges, since both of these balance sheet classifications are noncurrent assets representing costs which will benefit a business in the long run and are amortized in accordance with generally accepted accounting principles.

Organization Costs

Certain costs are incurred to form a corporation. These costs include state incorporation fees, attorneys' fees, costs of printing stock certificates, and other costs related to the formation of a corporate entity.

These costs of incorporating are recorded to a noncurrent asset account called **Organization Costs** and are amortized over a period not to exceed 40 years. Income tax rules require a minimum amortization period of five years, and many companies choose to amortize organization costs over this five-year period.

For example, assume that the total organization costs for a newly formed corporation were $6,000; the journal entry to record this expenditure is as follows:

Organization Costs	6,000	
Cash		6,000

The monthly amortization of the organization costs can be computed by dividing the cost ($6,000) by 60 months (5 years × 12 months). Therefore, at the end of the first accounting month, the amortization entry is as follows:

Amortization Expense	100	
Organization Costs		100

Goodwill

The term "**goodwill**" may mean one thing to the general public and quite a different thing to an accountant. The general public usually thinks of goodwill as the excellent reputation that a business has with its customers. To an accountant, goodwill means the potential of a business to earn a rate of return in excess of the average rate of return for similar businesses in that industry. Goodwill is the result of competitive advantages, customer recognition, a favorable location, outstanding management, excellent employee relations, and other factors which a successful company continually develops.

Goodwill is recorded in the accounting records only if it is purchased. Any goodwill that a firm enjoys because of its reputation based on name recognition, product quality, or other factors is not recorded on the financial statements for accounting purposes. There are many well-known firms that do not show goodwill on their financial statements because it was not purchased in a business transaction.

When a business is purchased, the purchase price should stipulate the portion of the amount paid for assets purchased, for goodwill, and for any covenant not to compete. A covenant not to compete is an agreement by the seller not to operate a similar business in a certain geographical area for a specified number of years.

Financial accounting requires that goodwill be capitalized and amortized over a period not to exceed 40 years. However, companies may choose to amortize goodwill over a shorter period of time if appropriate. The purchase of goodwill is recorded as follows:

Goodwill	xxx	
Cash (or Notes Payable)		xxx

The monthly entry to amortize goodwill over its useful life is as follows:

Amortization Expense	xxx	
Goodwill		xxx

Franchises

A **franchise** is the exclusive right or privilege granted by the franchiser that allows the franchisee to sell certain services or products in a specified geographical area. A franchise agreement usually stipulates a period of time and establishes the conditions under which the franchise may be revoked. Examples of franchise operations include Ramada Inns, Sheraton Inns, McDonald's, Wendy's, Pizza Hut, and Dunkin' Donuts.

The cost of a franchise right includes the purchase price as well as legal fees and other costs associated with obtaining it. These costs may be substantial. The amortization period is based on the life of the franchise contract, but cannot exceed 40 years. The purchase of a franchise right is recorded as follows:

Franchise	xxx	
Cash (or Notes Payable)		xxx

The monthly entry to amortize the cost of a franchise right over its useful life is as follows:

Amortization Expense	xxx	
Franchise		xxx

A franchise right may be purchased for a lump sum plus periodic payments which may be based on sales volume or other criteria. In these cases, the initial lump sum is capitalized and amortized; the periodic payments are charged to an expense account called Franchise Expense.

Trademarks and Tradenames

The federal government provides legal protection for trademarks and tradenames if they are registered with the United States Patent Office. Once a trademark or tradename is registered, the company retains the right to it as long as it is continuously used. Distinctive trademarks and tradenames may be sold.

The cost of a trademark or tradename consists of the expenditures necessary to develop it as well as the filing and registry fees. If the costs are not material, they may be charged to an expense account. A purchased trademark or tradename is recorded at its purchase price.

Material costs associated with acquiring a trademark or tradename are capitalized to a noncurrent asset account called Trademarks and Tradenames. Even though a trademark or tradename may have an indefinite life, its cost must be amortized over its expected useful life, but for a period not to exceed 40 years. The purchase of a trademark or tradename is recorded as follows:

Trademarks and Tradenames	xxx	
Cash (or Notes Payable)		xxx

The monthly entry to amortize the cost of a trademark or tradename over its useful life is as follows:

Amortization Expense	xxx	
Trademarks and Tradenames		xxx

Patents

A **patent** is an exclusive right granted by the federal government to use, manufacture, sell, or lease a product or design. This right is granted for 17 years. The owner of a patent may sell a patent after it is granted. Patents that are purchased should be capitalized to a noncurrent asset account called Patents if the cost is material. (If the cost is not material, it should be charged to an expense account.) The cost of a patent is amortized over the course of either the 17-year legal life, the remaining years of its legal life, or the estimated useful life—whichever is shortest. The purchase of a patent is recorded as follows:

Patents	xxx	
Cash (or Notes Payable)		xxx

The monthly entry to amortize the cost of a patent over its useful life is as follows:

Amortization Expense	xxx	
Patents		xxx

The cost of a successful legal defense of patent rights may be capitalized to the cost of the patent and amortized over the remaining life of the patent. An unsuccessful defense might indicate that the patent is worthless, suggesting that the legal costs and unamortized patent costs should be expensed.

Copyrights

A **copyright** is an exclusive right granted by the federal government to produce and sell musical, literary, or artistic materials. The period of this right is equal to the life of the author plus 50 years.

The owner of a copyright may sell it after it is granted. Copyrights that are purchased should be capitalized to a noncurrent asset account called Copyrights if

Exhibit 1   Progression of Business Expenditures

Organization Stage	→	Preopening Stage	→	Operations
• State incorporation fees • Legal fees—incorporation • Stock issuance costs		• Feasibility studies • Expenses prior to opening • Grand-opening advertising		• Sales and ordinary business expenses

the cost is material. (If the cost is not material, it should be charged to expense.) The cost of a copyright is amortized over its useful life, but for a period not to exceed 40 years. The purchase of a copyright is recorded as follows:

Copyrights	xxx	
Cash (or Notes Payable)		xxx

The monthly entry to amortize the cost of a copyright over its useful life is as follows:

Amortization Expense	xxx	
Copyrights		xxx

The cost of a successful legal defense of a copyright may be capitalized to the cost of the copyright and amortized over its remaining life. An unsuccessful defense might indicate the copyright is worthless, suggesting that the legal costs and unamortized copyright costs should be expensed.

Preopening Expenses

Preopening expenses are costs associated with certain business activities which occur before a company is operational. They are sometimes called start-up costs. The following are examples of preopening expenses:

- Market and feasibility studies
- Travel costs for securing suppliers and customers
- Consultation fees
- Employee training costs
- Executive salaries
- Professional services
- Advertisements of the grand opening
- Labor costs associated with preparing for the grand opening

It is important to recognize the difference between organization costs and preopening expenses. While organization costs are expenditures incurred before a corporation legally exists, preopening expenses are expenditures incurred after the formation of a corporate entity but before it opens for business. Exhibit 1 illustrates the progression of a company's expenditures at various stages.

Although generally accepted accounting principles allow intangible assets to be amortized over a period as long as 40 years, it is unlikely that preopening expenses will benefit a company for such a long period of time. Therefore, it is not unusual for a company to amortize preopening expenses over a minimum five-year period.

Expenditures for preopening expenses are recorded as follows:

Preopening Expenses	xxx	
Cash (or Notes Payable)		xxx

The monthly entry to amortize preopening expenses is as follows:

Amortization Expense	xxx	
Preopening Expenses		xxx

Liquor Licenses

Fees for the renewal of licenses are generally recorded immediately to expense. Substantial annual fees should be recorded to a prepaid asset account. At the end of each month, an adjusting entry is recorded to expense the portion of the asset that has expired.

In some communities, liquor licenses may not be available from the local authority because of quota restrictions. In these cases, a business may have to purchase a liquor license from a current holder. This holder may be currently in business or may hold a license for sale.

In certain instances, liquor licenses have market values of $75,000 or more. Sometimes, a company will purchase a going business for the sole purpose of acquiring this business's liquor license and transferring it to another location. In this case, the cost of the liquor license is the total purchase price of the business less any proceeds on the subsequent sale of the property and equipment.

If the acquisition costs of a liquor license are material, they are recorded to a noncurrent asset account; a separate account called Liquor License may be used. The cost is amortized over a period not to exceed 40 years. The purchase of a liquor license is recorded as follows:

Liquor License	xxx	
Cash (or Notes Payable)		xxx

The monthly entry to amortize the cost of the liquor license over its useful life is as follows:

Amortization Expense	xxx	
Liquor License		xxx

Cash Value Intangible Assets

Not all intangible assets are amortized over their useful lives. Some intangible assets represent future sources of cash. For example, when a hotel pays a security deposit in order to obtain a certain service, this deposit creates an intangible asset. Common intangible assets representing cash values are security deposits and the cash surrender value of life insurance.

Security Deposits

A hospitality operation may be required to pay a security deposit before a landlord will permit occupancy, before a leasing company will allow the use of rented equipment, or before utility companies will render services. These deposits are not an advance payment for occupancy, equipment, or services. A security deposit serves as reimbursement should any damages occur to the property or equipment, or as compensation should the depositor not pay for eventual services. Many utility companies refund a security deposit after one year while others may retain it indefinitely.

Although security deposits have characteristics in common with accounts receivable, they cannot be treated as such because: (1) they may not be collectible for as long as the leasing agreement or utility arrangement remains in effect, or (2) they may be refundable only at the option of the provider of the service. Therefore, security deposits are recorded in a noncurrent asset account and are not amortized. The account remains indefinitely until the deposit is refunded.

Cash Surrender Value of Life Insurance

Two basic kinds of life insurance are term-life insurance and whole-life insurance. Both provide a payment to the beneficiary if the insured person dies. Term-life insurance does not build up any cash value and is worthless if it is canceled or if it is allowed to expire at the end of a specified termination date. On the other hand, whole-life insurance (sometimes called permanent insurance) combines death benefits with a cash value. A portion of the premiums paid for whole-life insurance is used to build up a cash value. The owner of the policy may redeem the policy for its cash value or may borrow against that value while the policy remains in force. Whole-life insurance premiums are significantly higher than those for term-life insurance, which is based solely on death benefit coverage. Therefore, if death benefits are the primary consideration, a $100,000 term-life insurance policy may be a better buy than a $100,000 whole-life policy.

Either the business will own the life insurance policy and be the beneficiary, or the employee will own the policy and have the right to name a beneficiary. When the employee owns the policy, this fringe benefit is an expense of the company. Under income tax rules, term-life insurance (not exceeding a specified amount) is not considered compensation to the employee and therefore is not taxable income to the employee. However, whole-life insurance provided as a fringe benefit to the employee is taxable income to the employee.

Fringe benefits are a business expense; for instance, any life insurance purchased for employees (who become the owners of these policies) is considered a business expense, not an asset of the business. However, in addition to life insurance purchased as fringe benefits to employees, it is not unusual for a company to insure the lives of its executives and retain ownership of the policy. For tax reporting, insurance premiums on company-owned policies are not a tax-deductible expense; on the other hand, the eventual collection of any death benefit or cash value is not taxable income. For financial reporting, insurance premiums are an expense and any collections are income.

Insurance premiums on company-owned whole-life policies are separated into two parts:

1. The portion representing life insurance coverage is an expense.

2. The portion that builds up cash value is an asset.

Most whole-life insurance policies provide for the payment of an annual cash dividend. Life insurance policy dividends are not income and should not be confused with dividends from investments. Life insurance policy dividends are really a return of the life insurance premium. In financial accounting, these dividends should be treated as a reduction in insurance expense.

Company-owned whole-life insurance premiums may be paid monthly, quarterly, semi-annually, or annually. Any premiums paid in advance are recorded as follows:

Prepaid Insurance	xxx	
Cash		xxx

At the end of each month, an adjusting entry is recorded as follows to expense the portion of the asset that has expired:

Insurance Expense	xxx	
Prepaid Insurance		xxx

Insurance policies generally contain a table showing cash values at various stages of the policy's life. The dividends may be guaranteed or stated as an expected dividend based on prior experience. The dividends may be left with the insurance company to accumulate and earn interest. This option will further increase the cash value of the policy.

There are several methods of accounting for the cash value of insurance policies and accounting for dividends. The end result of these methods is that the cash value of the life insurance is recorded as an intangible asset.

Key Terms

amortization	intangible assets
copyright	organization costs
franchise	patent
goodwill	preopening expenses

Review Questions

1. How are the following intangible assets defined?

   a. Preopening expenses

   b. Franchise cost

   c. Organization cost

   d. Liquor license cost

  e. Goodwill

  f. Covenant not to compete

2. What is the maximum write-off period for organization costs under generally accepted accounting principles?

3. What is the write-off treatment for goodwill under generally accepted accounting principles?

4. What is the major difference between term-life insurance and whole-life insurance?

5. In accounting for company-owned whole-life policies, which of the following are expensed and which are capitalized?

  a. Portion of premium representing life insurance coverage

  b. Portion of premium that builds cash value

  c. Cash dividend earned on insurance policy

Problems

Problem 1

Journalize the following expenditures:

  a. Purchase of $50,000 goodwill with cash
  b. Incorporation fees of $3,000
  c. Franchise right of $25,000
  d. Preopening expenses of $40,000

Problem 2

On July 1, goodwill was purchased for $60,000. This expenditure will be written off over 20 years.

  a. Journalize the July 31 adjusting entry.
  b. Journalize the August 31 adjusting entry.

Problem 3

On July 1, a new corporation was formed. The capitalized organization costs of $8,100 are to be written off over five years.

  a. Journalize the July 31 adjusting entry.
  b. Journalize the August 31 adjusting entry.

Problem 4

A $567 check is issued in payment of the employees' group insurance premium for the month. These policies are not company-owned. Journalize this expenditure.

Problem 5

The Prepaid Life Insurance account for company-owned policies shows a balance of $2,000. Of this balance, $300 represents a buildup of cash value and $800 represents expired premiums. Journalize the adjusting entry.

Problem 6

A $500 check representing an annual cash dividend on company-owned policies is received from the life insurance company. Journalize this transaction.

REVIEW QUIZ

When you feel you have covered all of the material in this chapter, answer these questions. Choose the *best* answer. Check your answers with the correct ones found on the Review Quiz Answer Key at the end of this book.

True (T) or False (F)

T   F   1. In cases where the economic life of an intangible asset is shorter than its legal life, the longer life is used to compute amortization.

T   F   2. A franchise is the exclusive right granted by the federal government that allows the franchisee to sell certain services or products in a specified geographical region.

T   F   3. If the costs of developing and registering a trademark are not material, they may be charged to an expense account.

T   F   4. Term-life insurance builds up cash value.

Multiple Choice

5. Which of the following is a means of allocating the costs of intangible assets to those periods that benefit from their use?

    a. acquisition
    b. expenditure optioning
    c. amortization
    d. assignment

6. Organization costs include:

    a. state incorporation fees.
    b. attorneys' fees.
    c. printing costs for stock certificates.
    d. all of the above.

7. When a business is purchased, the purchase price should stipulate the portion of the amount paid for:

    a. assets purchased.
    b. goodwill.
    c. a covenant not to compete.
    d. all of the above.

8. A patent right is granted for a period of:

    a. 5 years.
    b. 17 years.
    c. 40 years.
    d. indefinite length.

9. Preopening expenses include all of the following *except:*

    a. employee training costs.
    b. travel costs for securing suppliers and customers.
    c. costs incurred prior to formation of the corporation.
    d. executive salaries.

10. Which of the following is true of security deposits?

    a. They serve as reimbursement for damages to property or equipment.
    b. They are advance payments for occupancy, equipment, or services.
    c. They are always refunded after a year.
    d. They can be treated as accounts receivable.

Chapter Outline

The Importance of Inventory Valuation
The Gross Profit Method
Approaches to Inventory Valuation
The Specific Identification Approach to
    Inventory Valuation
    The Specific Identification Perpetual
       Method
    The Specific Identification Periodic
       Method
The FIFO Approach to Inventory Valuation
    The FIFO Perpetual Method
    The FIFO Periodic Method
The LIFO Approach to Inventory Valuation
    The LIFO Perpetual Method
    The LIFO Periodic Method
The Weighted Average Approach to
    Inventory Valuation
    The Weighted Average Perpetual
       Method
    The Weighted Average Periodic
       Method
A Comparison of Cost Allocation Methods
LIFO Analyzed

Learning Objectives

1. Describe how inaccurate inventory records can affect the financial statements. (pp. 266–268)

2. Explain the gross profit method of estimating inventory levels. (pp. 268–270)

3. Explain the basis of accounting for inventory, and differentiate between inventory valuation approaches according to their emphasis on product flow or cost flow. (pp. 270–271)

4. Describe the specific identification approach to inventory valuation. (pp. 271–274)

5. Explain the FIFO approach to inventory valuation and how it differs from the specific identification approach. (pp. 274–275)

6. Describe the LIFO approach to inventory valuation, and compare it with the FIFO approach. (pp. 275–277)

7. Describe the weighted average approach to inventory valuation and how it differs from the approaches previously discussed. (pp. 277–280)

8. Compare the three cost flow approaches to inventory valuation with respect to cost of sales and ending inventory. (pp. 280–281)

9. Summarize the benefits and drawbacks of the LIFO approach. (pp. 281–282)

9

Inventory Accounting

A HOSPITALITY OPERATION maintains inventories for both merchandise and operating supplies. Merchandise inventories include food, beverages, and other items primarily sold to guests. Operating supplies refer to cleaning supplies, office supplies, guest supplies, and other supply items consumed by a business in its day-to-day operations. While this chapter will concentrate on merchandise inventories, many of the concepts may be applied to supplies inventories.

Inventories influence the decision-making process in many areas of a hospitality organization. For example, food inventories are not just the concern of the food and beverage department. The marketing department is concerned that there be sufficient quantities of specific food items advertised as specials. The accounting department monitors food inventory costs related to financing, storage, insurance, and local inventory taxes.

Inventory accounting affects both the balance sheet and the income statement. The portion of inventory remaining at the end of the accounting period appears on the balance sheet as a current asset; the portion of inventory used during the accounting period appears on the income statement as Cost of Sales. Measuring the value of ending inventory and computing the cost of sales are significant tasks in merchandising operations. While taking a physical inventory is costly and time-consuming, the process is necessary to confirm the accuracy of the inventory amount reported on the financial statements.

This chapter addresses fundamental concepts related to inventory accounting by answering such questions as:

1. How do inventory errors affect reported income?

2. How is the gross profit method used to estimate ending inventories?

3. What is the distinction between product flow and cost flow?

4. How does the selection of an inventory valuation method affect the balance sheet and the income statement?

5. What are the advantages and disadvantages of the "last-in, first-out" approach to inventory valuation?

The purpose of this chapter is to present the concept of inventory valuation and its effect on the financial statements. The cumulative effect of inventory errors between two periods and the counterbalancing effect are explained. The gross profit method is demonstrated as a means of estimating ending inventories when a physical inventory is not available but financial statements must be prepared.

The discussion includes four approaches to **inventory valuation:** specific identification, "first-in, first-out" (FIFO), "last-in, first-out" (LIFO), and weighted average. These approaches are discussed with respect to the perpetual and periodic methods associated with their application. The chapter concludes with a comparison of the effects of each method on the balance sheet and income statement, and a critical analysis of LIFO.

The Importance of Inventory Valuation

Some companies adopt a perpetual inventory system and thus maintain perpetual records for all inventory items. Under this system, the acquisition of inventory is charged to an inventory account. During the sales period, the issues are costed and recorded by debiting a cost of sales account and crediting the appropriate inventory account. If a company adopts the perpetual inventory system, the general ledger inventory account reflects the inventory on hand at the end of an accounting period. However, the use of perpetual inventory cards is generally too time-consuming and expensive for a business to adopt this system on a universal basis.

If a company does not use a perpetual inventory system, the accounting department must use the periodic method to account for inventory in the financial records. Using the periodic inventory method, the acquisition of inventory is charged to a purchases account. Because there is no cost of sales account, no entry is made for cost of sales during the sales period. Since issues are not recorded by the storekeeper, this information is not available for accounting purposes. The inventory account is brought up to date only at the end of the accounting period through a physical inventory or an estimating procedure.

Of course, a company can use a combination of recordkeeping systems. Perpetual recordkeeping is often used for those items with high costs per unit. Items with low costs per unit might not require perpetual records, and would instead be accounted for using the periodic inventory method. The remainder of this section will focus on the periodic inventory method.

The measurement of inventory is a source of possible errors on the balance sheet. When inventory records are inaccurate, this not only affects the reporting of Inventory on the balance sheet, but also the computation of total current assets and total assets.

Inaccurate inventories also affect the income statement. Ending inventory is a primary factor in the cost of sales computation, which can be expressed in the following general format:

Cost of Sales = Beginning Inventory + Purchases − Ending Inventory

In order to perform this computation, a hospitality company must cost the items on hand at the end of an accounting period based on a physical inventory or an estimate. An inaccurate inventory measurement not only affects cost of sales on the income statement, but also distorts the net income on the statement. The distortion of net income will ultimately affect the equity section of the balance sheet.

Exhibit 1   Sample Report of Gross Profit

	Period 1	Period 2
Sales	$100,000	$90,000
Cost of Sales:		
Beginning Inventory	20,000	**30,000**
Purchases	42,000	26,000
Cost of Goods Available	62,000	56,000
Ending Inventory	**30,000**	22,000
Cost of Sales	$ 32,000	$34,000
Gross Profit	$ 68,000	$56,000

Exhibit 2   Computation of Gross Profit with Corrected Inventory

	Period 1	Period 2
Sales	$100,000	$90,000
Cost of Sales:		
Beginning Inventory	20,000	**27,000**
Purchases	42,000	26,000
Cost of Goods Available	62,000	53,000
Ending Inventory	**27,000**	22,000
Cost of Sales	$ 35,000	$31,000
Gross Profit	$ 65,000	$59,000

Because the ending inventory of one period is the beginning inventory for the next period, an error in measuring ending inventory will affect at least two periods. This is best understood by analyzing the effect of inventory amounts in the calculation of gross profit.

Gross profit on sales is calculated by subtracting cost of sales from the sales for the period. The gross profit must be large enough to cover payroll and other expenses. If gross profit is large enough to cover these expenses, the remainder represents income from operations; if gross profit is not large enough to cover these expenses, the difference represents a loss from operations. Exhibit 1 illustrates a calculation of gross profit on sales for two periods. Note that the ending inventory of Period 1 becomes the beginning inventory of Period 2.

Now assume that the reported ending inventory for Period 1 was erroneous; the ending inventory should have been reported as $27,000, not $30,000. Exhibit 2 shows the result of this correction in the calculation of gross profit on sales for Periods 1 and 2. Note that the corrected ending inventory becomes the beginning inventory of Period 2.

The effect of this inventory error on gross profit may be analyzed as follows:

Gross Profit

	As Reported	Should Have Been	Difference
Period 1	$ 68,000	$ 65,000	+3,000
Period 2	56,000	59,000	−3,000
Total	$124,000	$124,000	0

Gross profit is the element in the income statement from which operating expenses, fixed charges, and corporate income taxes are subtracted to arrive at net income. Therefore, differences noted for gross profit also apply to net income. Due to the ending inventory error in Period 1, net income reported for Period 1 would be overstated by $3,000; net income reported for Period 2 would be understated by $3,000.

Assuming no further errors, the cumulative effect is self-correcting; when the differences for the two periods are totaled, the errors counterbalance one another. While the individual figures for gross profit of each period differ, the sum of gross profits for both periods are equal ($124,000) irrespective of the inventory correction.

The Gross Profit Method

If inventories are accounted for using the periodic inventory accounting method, the financial records do not readily provide inventory information as is the case with the perpetual inventory accounting method. Using the periodic inventory accounting method, ending inventory is nonetheless an integral part of computing gross profit. Therefore, the preparation of financial statements requires an inventory amount at the end of the accounting period.

Tax laws and generally accepted accounting principles require that a physical inventory be taken at least once in the business year. As part of its inventory control practices, a hospitality business will perform physical inventories more often to gauge spoilage, quality, and disappearance. Alcoholic beverages and other attractive inventory items may be inventoried weekly. Low-cost items may be physically counted less frequently.

If a physical inventory has not been performed and financial statements are to be prepared, an estimating procedure is necessary. One acceptable estimating procedure is called the **gross profit method.** The gross profit method is also useful in estimating inventory losses from fire, theft, and other casualties.

The gross profit method uses an estimate of the gross profit percentage on sales. The percentage is calculated by dividing gross profit by net sales, which are obtained from previous financial statements. The accuracy of the estimated ending inventory depends on the accuracy of the gross profit percentage used. The gross profit percentage represents an average on all inventory items sold.

The sales mix affects the gross profit percentage. As a result, the sales mix may affect the reliability of this method. If the gross profit percentage on the financial statements is 65%, it implies that the sales mix generates an average of 65% gross profit on sales. If the products composing the sales mix lack a relatively standard

Exhibit 3   Steps in the Gross Profit Method

Sales (net)	Known	100%
Cost of Sales:		
Beginning Inventory	Known	
+ Purchases	Known	
Cost of Goods Available	Addition	
− Ending Inventory	(C)	
Cost of Sales	(B)	(A)
Gross Profit	(D)	Known

(A) Cost of Sales % = 100% − Gross Profit %
(B) Cost of Sales = Cost of Sales % × Net Sales
(C) Ending Inventory = Cost of Goods Available − Cost of Sales
(D) PROOF: 1. Gross Profit = Net Sales − Cost of Sales
           2. Gross Profit = Gross Profit % × Net Sales
           3. Answers in 1 and 2 must be equal.

markup or if the mix changes, the accuracy of this method may be affected. Gross profit percentages should be individually computed for food and beverages, and estimating procedures should be carried out separately for these two areas of inventory.

The gross profit method involves a number of basic assumptions and calculations. It assumes that the financial records provide the following information under a periodic inventory system:

- Sales for the period
- Last period's ending inventory
- Purchases for the period

Having determined the gross profit percentage through an analysis of previous financial statements, one can work back to a figure for the cost of sales percentage, which relates cost of sales expense to net sales. Since net sales is the basis or common denominator for an income or expense analysis, net sales is always 100%. The procedure can be demonstrated as follows:

		If	Then
Sales (net)	=	100%	100%
Cost of Sales	=	− ?	− 40%
Gross Profit	=	60%	60%

Using the cost of sales percentage, the cost of sales amount can be estimated. Net sales multiplied by the cost of sales percentage yields an estimate for cost of sales. This cost of sales estimate can, in turn, be used to solve for ending inventory.

Exhibit 3 demonstrates the steps involved in the gross profit method. This exhibit presents the basic procedure for estimating ending inventory. The steps are:

- Using the gross profit percentage (estimated through analysis of previous financial statements), solve for the cost of sales percentage.

- Using the cost of sales percentage, calculate the cost of sales from net sales.

- Estimate ending inventory by working back from the cost of sales and the cost of goods available.

- Check calculations by comparing gross profit (net sales minus cost of sales) with the result of multiplying the gross profit percentage by net sales.

For example, assume the accounting records provide the following information:

Sales for the period	$50,000
Ending inventory of prior period	8,000
Purchases for the period	14,000
Estimated gross profit percentage	60%

Based on this information, Exhibit 4 shows how the ending inventory for the period is estimated as $2,000. It provides a proof of the calculation by comparing figures for gross profit determined two different ways.

Approaches to Inventory Valuation

The primary basis of accounting for inventory is cost. Cost should include transportation charges unless such charges are not considered significant. In this case,

Exhibit 4   Estimating Inventory by the Gross Profit Method

Sales (net)	$50,000	100%
Cost of Sales:		
Beginning Inventory	8,000	
+ Purchases	14,000	
Cost of Goods Available	22,000	
− Ending Inventory	2,000 (C)	
Cost of Sales	$20,000 (B)	40% (A)
Gross Profit	$30,000 (D)	60%

(A)   Cost of Sales % = 100% − Gross Profit %
        Cost of Sales % = 100% − 60% = 40%
(B)   Cost of Sales = Cost of Sales % × Net Sales
        Cost of Sales = 40% × $50,000 = $20,000
(C)   Ending Inventory = Cost of Goods Available − Cost of Sales
        Ending Inventory = $22,000 − $20,000 = $2,000
(D)   PROOF: 1. Gross Profit   = Net Sales − Cost of Sales
                                      $50,000 − $20,000 = $30,000
              2. Gross Profit = Gross Profit % × Net Sales
                                      60% × $50,000 = $30,000
              3. Answers in 1 and 2 must be equal.

their omission from inventory cost may be justified in the interests of convenience and economy in the accounting system. Purchase discounts do not enter into the computation of cost of sales or inventory. Under the *Uniform System of Accounts and Expense Dictionary for Small Hotels, Motels, and Motor Hotels,* purchase discounts are recorded as revenue.

The costs of inventory items, especially produce and other food items, change on a more or less regular basis. Produce prices may change from week to week. A category of items purchased at a particular price on one occasion may have a different price on another occasion. The effect of price fluctuations raises some important questions related to inventory valuation:

- What is the cost of inventory on hand?

- Should the value of items in inventory reflect their actual purchase cost?

- Should the value of items in inventory reflect the most recent purchase cost?

Answering these questions requires a knowledge of the various approaches to costing issues and accounting for inventories.

An important distinction between inventory valuation approaches is whether the approach emphasizes the flow of the physical product (product flow) or the flow of costs (cost flow). Of the four inventory valuation approaches presented in this chapter, only the specific identification approach emphasizes the flow of the physical product and its identified cost. The FIFO approach, the LIFO approach, and the weighted average approach emphasize the flow of costs.

For each of the four approaches, the inventory valuation process is explained for both perpetual and periodic inventory accounting methods. To use the perpetual method, perpetual recordkeeping cards must be maintained to record issues and ending inventory. The periodic inventory accounting method requires a physical count or estimating procedure to determine inventory at the end of the accounting period.

Examples of the inventory valuation methods presented in this chapter will use the same basic illustrative case. We assume that transactions during the month of March are as follows:

Date	Inventory Transaction
3/1	Purchased 10 units at $1.00 per unit
3/2	Purchased 5 units at $1.02 per unit
3/3	Purchased 5 units at $1.05 per unit
3/6	Issued 3 units
3/10	Issued 11 units

These transactions will be processed for a new inventory item with a beginning balance of zero.

The Specific Identification Approach to Inventory Valuation ——

The **specific identification approach** uses the actual purchase cost of each unit of inventory as the basis for inventory valuation. In order to use this approach, all

Exhibit 5   Example of FIFO Perpetual Inventory Card

		PURCHASES			ISSUES			BALANCE ON HAND		
Date	Ref.	Units	Unit Cost	Total	Units	Unit Cost	Total	Units	Unit Cost	Total
3/1		10	1.00	10.00				10	1.00	10.00
3/2		5	1.02	5.10				10	1.00	
								5	1.02	15.10
3/3		5	1.05	5.25				10	1.00	
								5	1.02	20.35
								5	1.05	
3/6					3	1.00	3.00	7	1.00	
								5	1.02	17.35
								5	1.05	
3/10					7	1.00	7.00			
					4	1.02	4.08	1	1.02	6.27
					11		11.08	5	1.05	
TOTAL		20		20.35	14		14.08	6		6.27

items in the storeroom must be identified with their actual purchase costs. Thus, the specific identification approach is concerned with product flow, not cost flow. Supporters of this approach believe that the actual purchase price is the best measure for cost of sales and ending inventory.

Good inventory procedures require that the oldest products always be issued first. In other words, those products first in will be the products first out. This basic assumption underlies the FIFO approach to inventory valuation. The specific identification approach will produce the same result as the FIFO approach provided that the storekeeper always issues the oldest products first.

The specific identification approach to inventory valuation may be carried out by either of two methods: the specific identification perpetual method or the specific identification periodic method.

The Specific Identification Perpetual Method

Following the inventory procedures just described, the specific identification perpetual method produces the same result as the FIFO perpetual method. Therefore, it is possible to use the sample perpetual inventory card for the FIFO perpetual method (Exhibit 5) to explain the results of applying the specific identification perpetual method.

Note that for each of the three purchases (March 1, 2, and 3), entries are made within the Purchases and Balance on Hand sections of the inventory card. In the Purchases section, purchases are recorded by number of units, unit cost, and total cost (number of units multiplied by unit cost). In the Balance on Hand section, number of units and unit cost are recorded on an ongoing basis, and the overall balance is updated as purchases are made. This same basic format for recording purchases is used by all of the inventory methods except the weighted average method, which will be discussed later in the chapter.

The difference between the specific identification, FIFO, and LIFO approaches relates to the costing of issues. The specific identification approach uses the actual costs of individual groups or batches of items. When items are issued, the basis for costing will be the identified cost of the individual items. If similar items having different costs are received, they must be separately costed from existing items. Issues of the same items having different costs must be separately counted or weighed, and then costed.

On March 6, the storekeeper issues 3 items from the storeroom. Items from the oldest stock (purchased March 1) are issued first. These items had been purchased at a cost of $1.00 per unit. The 10 units at this cost are reduced by the issue of 3 units. The balance on hand is reduced by $3.00.

On March 10, the storekeeper issues 11 units. Seven of these units had been purchased at $1.00 per unit and 4 units had been purchased at $1.02. The balance on hand is adjusted to reflect this issue, leaving 1 unit on hand at $1.02 and 5 units at $1.05. The Balance on Hand section shows that the total cost of ending inventory is $6.27.

The mathematical accuracy of the ending balance on the perpetual inventory card may be verified by subtracting total issues for the period from goods available (beginning inventory + purchases) for the period. This procedure is as follows:

	Quantity	Cost
Beginning Inventory	0	$ 0
Purchases	20	20.35
Goods Available	20	20.35
Issues (Cost of Sales)	− 14	− 14.08
Ending Inventory	6	$ 6.27

With respect to the costing of issues, the specific identification perpetual method would differ from the FIFO perpetual method only if products are issued out of order. In this case, the identified cost would be the basis for costing using the specific identification perpetual method.

The Specific Identification Periodic Method

The use of the specific identification periodic method does not require the maintenance of perpetual inventory cards, but still requires that goods in inventory be identified by their actual purchase cost. Using this method, inventory valuation is based on the identified cost of items on hand at the end of a period. Thus, both the perpetual and periodic variations on this approach match the flow of recorded costs to the physical flow of goods.

As a periodic method, however, the specific identification periodic method has labor-saving benefits; issues are not costed and inventory recordkeeping cards need not be maintained. When provisions are purchased, the account Purchases is debited. Issues are not recorded during the selling period. At the end of the period, however, a physical inventory is required.

A physical inventory using specific identification techniques involves counting the quantity on hand at each specific purchase cost, then totaling the amounts derived from the individual counts. For the inventory item in the previous example, a physical count would produce the following results:

Physical Count	Marked Cost	Ending Inventory Cost
1	$1.02	$1.02
5	1.05	5.25
Total		$6.27

This procedure is followed for each item in inventory. After all items have been counted and costed, the total of all the inventory items represents the ending inventory for financial reporting.

Any specific identification method emphasizes the flow of physical products and their identified costs. However, the use of a specific identification method requires considerable attention to detail since inventory items must be specifically identified at their actual costs.

If using a specific identification method is not possible or practical for a company, then a cost flow method must necessarily be chosen. The question is whether to value the units in the ending inventory at the most recent costs (per the FIFO approach), the oldest costs (per the LIFO approach), or an average cost (per the weighted average approach).

The FIFO Approach to Inventory Valuation

In hospitality operations, good storeroom procedures require that products be used in the order of their purchase. From a product flow perspective, this means that those items first in the storeroom will be those items first out of the storeroom. Inventory transactions may also be viewed from a cost flow perspective. If products first in are those first out, then it follows that *costs* first in will be those first out.

FIFO is an acronym for **first-in, first-out.** This approach is not concerned with product flow, but instead concentrates on the sequence of costs in and out of inventory. The oldest cost in inventory will be the first to go out of inventory. Thus, FIFO produces results that approximate the physical flow of goods, although no effort is made to match an issued item with its specific cost as is required with a specific identification method.

Supporters of the FIFO approach emphasize that cost flow should parallel the typical flow of goods. Since the first-in (oldest) costs are used to cost issues, cost of sales will closely match actual purchase prices.

The FIFO approach to inventory valuation may be carried out by either of two methods: the FIFO perpetual method or the FIFO periodic method.

The FIFO Perpetual Method

Exhibit 5 is an example of a perpetual inventory card for the FIFO perpetual method. The same inventory transactions noted previously are the basis for purchases and issues represented on this card. The recording of purchases is identical to that described for the specific identification method under a perpetual system.

As issues are costed, the oldest cost represented within the Balance on Hand section is used first. The first issue of 3 items is costed at the oldest cost of $1.00 per unit. The second issue of 11 items allocates costs among the remaining 7 units on hand at $1.00 per unit and 4 units of the next batch at $1.02 per unit.

The Balance on Hand section reflects this costing process. After the first issue, the number of units at the oldest cost of $1.00 per unit is reduced by 3 units. After the second issue, all of the units costed at $1.00 per unit have been eliminated from inventory, and there is only one remaining unit at the next oldest cost of $1.02 per unit. All five units at the most recent cost of $1.05 per unit remain in inventory.

Whenever the total quantity issued exceeds the available balance on hand at the oldest cost, issues are costed for the remaining items at the oldest cost, then at the next oldest unit cost. This process is repeated until all of the units issued have been costed.

The mathematical accuracy of the ending balance on the perpetual inventory card may be verified using the procedure previously described for the specific identification perpetual method.

The FIFO Periodic Method

A company need not maintain perpetual inventory cards in order to take advantage of the cost flow features of the FIFO approach. Using the FIFO perpetual method just explained, the oldest costs in inventory are the first to go out of inventory. This process results in the most recent costs remaining in the inventory on hand. The FIFO periodic method costs ending inventory at these most recent costs.

To illustrate, consider the previous inventory transactions:

Date	Inventory Transaction
3/1	Purchased 10 units at $1.00 per unit
3/2	Purchased 5 units at $1.02 per unit
3/3	Purchased 5 units at $1.05 per unit

After a physical inventory of this particular item, it is determined that 6 units are on hand at the end of the accounting period. The 6 units in ending inventory are costed at the most recent costs. The most recent purchase (March 3) was for 5 units at $1.05 per unit. One more unit cost is necessary, which may be obtained by referring to the March 2 purchase at $1.02 per unit. The cost of the ending inventory is computed as follows:

5 units × $1.05	=	$5.25
1 unit × $1.02	=	1.02
Total ending inventory	=	$6.27

The FIFO periodic method produces the same results for ending inventory as the FIFO perpetual method.

The LIFO Approach to Inventory Valuation

LIFO is an acronym for **last-in, first-out.** It assumes that those costs *last* in inventory will be those costs first out of inventory. Like the FIFO approach, LIFO is concerned

Exhibit 6   Example of LIFO Perpetual Inventory Card

Date	Ref.	PURCHASES			ISSUES			BALANCE ON HAND		
		Units	Unit Cost	Total	Units	Unit Cost	Total	Units	Unit Cost	Total
3/1		10	1.00	10.00				10	1.00	10.00
3/2		5	1.02	5.10				10	1.00	15.10
								5	1.02	
3/3		5	1.05	5.25				10	1.00	20.35
								5	1.02	
								5	1.05	
3/6					3	1.05	3.15	10	1.00	17.20
								5	1.02	
								2	1.05	
3/10					2	1.05	2.10			
					5	1.02	5.10			
					4	1.00	4.00	6	1.00	6.00
					11		11.20			
TOTAL		20		20.35	14		14.35	6	1.00	6.00

with cost flow rather than product flow. Unlike the FIFO approach, LIFO uses the most recent costs as those first out of inventory.

Supporters of the LIFO approach believe that the cost of sales should reflect current replacement costs. Since the last-in (most recent) costs are used to cost issues, the cost of sales will more closely reflect the replacement costs compared to the FIFO approach.

The LIFO approach to inventory valuation may be carried out by either of two methods: the LIFO perpetual method or the LIFO periodic method.

The LIFO Perpetual Method

Exhibit 6 is an example of a perpetual inventory card for the LIFO perpetual method. The recording of purchases is identical to that described for previous perpetual methods. In costing issues, however, the LIFO perpetual method is strikingly different. The issues are costed at the last-in (most recent) costs rather than the oldest costs.

Note that the first issue of 3 items is costed at the most recent cost of $1.05 per unit. Costing the second issue of 11 items allocates costs among the 2 remaining items at the most recent cost of $1.05 per unit, all 5 items at the next most recent cost of $1.02 per unit, and 4 items at the oldest cost of $1.00 per unit.

The Balance on Hand section reflects this costing process. After the first issue, the number of units at the most recent cost of $1.05 is reduced by 3 units. After the second issue, all of the units at $1.05 and $1.02 (the most recent and next most recent costs per unit) have been eliminated from inventory. The remaining units are costed at $1.00 per unit (the oldest cost).

Whenever the total quantity issued exceeds the available balance on hand at the most recent cost, issues are costed for the remaining items at the most recent cost, then at the next most recent cost. This process is repeated until all of the units issued have been costed.

The mathematical accuracy of the ending balance on the perpetual inventory card may be verified using the procedure previously described for the specific identification perpetual method.

The LIFO Periodic Method

A company that does not use perpetual inventory cards may still use the cost flow features of the LIFO approach. Using the LIFO perpetual method, the most recent costs in inventory are the first costs to go out of inventory. This process results in the oldest costs remaining in the inventory on hand.

Since the oldest costs remain in inventory, the ending inventory can be costed on this basis. The cost of the ending inventory is computed by starting with the beginning inventory and then working down through the purchases until enough units have been costed to cover the units in the ending inventory.

To illustrate, consider the previous inventory transactions:

Date	Inventory Transaction
3/1	Purchased 10 units at $1.00 per unit
3/2	Purchased 5 units at $1.02 per unit
3/3	Purchased 5 units at $1.05 per unit

After a physical inventory of this particular item, it is determined that 6 units are on hand at the end of the accounting period. The 6 units in ending inventory are to be costed at the oldest costs coming into the inventory. The oldest purchase (March 1) was for 10 units at $1.00 per unit. This purchase has enough units to cost the ending inventory of 6 units. The ending inventory can be costed at $6.00 (6 units $\times$ $1.00 = $6.00).

It should be pointed out that ending inventory values obtained under the LIFO periodic method may differ from those values obtained under the LIFO perpetual method. The LIFO periodic method may not be realistic if the ending inventory drops below the beginning inventory. This topic is best reserved for an upper-level accounting text.

The Weighted Average Approach to Inventory Valuation ———

Like FIFO and LIFO, the **weighted average approach** concentrates on cost flow rather than product flow. Unlike FIFO and LIFO, the weighted average approach uses an average unit cost for inventory valuation purposes. Cost of sales (issues) and ending inventory are costed at this weighted average.

The weighted average approach to inventory valuation may be carried out by either of two methods: the weighted average perpetual method or the weighted average periodic method.

Exhibit 7   Example of Weighted Average Perpetual Inventory Card

		PURCHASES			ISSUES			BALANCE ON HAND		
Date	Ref.	Units	Unit Cost	Total	Units	Unit Cost	Total	Units	Total	Unit Cost
3/1		10	1.00	10.00				10	10.00	1.00
3/2		5	1.02	5.10				15	15.10	1.007
3/3		5	1.05	5.25				20	20.35	1.018
3/6					3	1.018	3.05	17	17.30	
3/10					11	1.018	11.20	6	6.10	
TOTAL		20		20.35	14		14.25	6	6.10	

The Weighted Average Perpetual Method

The weighted average method is based on the assumption that issues should be charged at an average unit cost, weighted by the number of units acquired at each price. Because a new average is computed after each purchase, the weighted average perpetual method is sometimes called the moving average method.

Computing a new average only after a purchase assumes that an issue from inventory does not affect the previous costs in inventory. If an average were to be computed after each issue, the average cost would not change with the exception of minor rounding differences. (Some users of the weighted average method compute a new average cost after every inventory transaction to resolve any rounding difference. For our purposes a new average will be computed only after a purchase transaction.)

Exhibit 7 is an example of a perpetual inventory card for the weighted average perpetual method. The same inventory transactions noted previously are the basis for purchases and issues represented on this card. Since this is a new inventory item, the first purchase (March 1) is recorded at its actual cost of $1.00 per unit. However, after the second purchase (March 2), the inventory on hand represents a quantity of items purchased at different prices. Therefore, a new weighted average must be computed as follows:

$$\text{Weighted Average} \; = \; \frac{\text{Total Cost of Inventory on Hand}}{\text{Total Units in Inventory}}$$

After a third purchase on March 3, a weighted average must again be computed.

This weighted average cost becomes the basis for costing items issued. Notice that the first issue of 3 items is costed at the weighted average of $1.018 per unit. The second issue of 11 items is also costed at the weighted average of $1.018 per unit. If items are purchased after these issues, a new weighted average would be computed.

At the end of the accounting period, the perpetual inventory card reflects 6 units on hand. The Balance on Hand section shows that the total cost of ending inventory is $6.10. The mathematical accuracy of the ending balance on the perpetual inventory card may be verified using the procedure previously described for the specific identification perpetual method.

The Weighted Average Periodic Method

Under a perpetual recordkeeping system, the weighted average is a moving average because it is recomputed after every purchase. Under a periodic inventory system, however, the weighted average is computed on the total goods available for the period. Therefore, the results produced by the weighted average periodic method will be slightly different from those produced by the weighted average perpetual method.

Using the weighted average periodic method, a weighted average is computed by the same formula as previously presented. However, instead of computing a new average after every purchase, the weighted average is computed only at the end of the accounting period. The procedure used to compute the weighted average and to cost inventory at the end of the accounting period can be summarized as follows:

1. List beginning inventory and purchases for the period and determine the total units and the total cost.

2. Using the total units and the total cost, compute a weighted average using the previous formula.

3. Multiply the ending inventory quantity by the weighted average to arrive at a value for the ending inventory.

For example, assume inventory valuation is to be accomplished using the weighted average periodic method. Transactions during the month are as follows:

Date	Inventory Transaction
3/1	Purchased 10 units at $1.00 per unit
3/2	Purchased 5 units at $1.02 per unit
3/3	Purchased 5 units at $1.05 per unit

In our example, no beginning inventory is carried over. Purchases are listed and totaled as follows:

	Unit Cost	Units	Cost
3/1 Purchase	$1.00	10	$10.00
3/2 Purchase	1.02	5	5.10
3/3 Purchase	1.05	5	5.25
Total		20	$20.35

Using the total units available during the period and the total cost of these units, a weighted average may now be computed:

$$\text{Weighted Average} = \frac{\text{Total Cost of Inventory on Hand}}{\text{Total Units in Inventory}}$$

$$\text{Weighted Average} = \frac{\$20.35}{20 \text{ units}} = \$1.0175$$

After a physical inventory on this particular item, it is determined that 6 units are on hand at the end of the accounting period. The ending inventory is costed by the following calculation:

$$\text{Ending Inventory} = \text{Number of Units} \times \text{Weighted Average}$$
$$\text{Ending Inventory} = 6 \text{ units} \times \$1.0175 = \$6.11$$

A Comparison of Cost Allocation Methods

Each of the cost flow methods previously discussed produces identical or nearly identical results using both perpetual and periodic inventory accounting methods. Therefore, the following discussion will compare results for the various perpetual methods discussed to this point. The comparison will demonstrate the effect of the various methods on the balance sheet and the income statement.

The previous examples used only one type of inventory item to demonstrate the costing of inventories. Ending inventory on the balance sheet is the result of costing and totaling all types of items on hand. For ease of presentation, our discussion is necessarily limited to one type of inventory product. This limitation is also true for the cost of sales comparisons.

Each of the cost flow methods will produce a different ending inventory amount on the balance sheet. Given our basic illustrative case involving a period of rising prices, the three cost flow methods produce the following values for ending inventory:

	Ending Inventory
FIFO	$6.27
LIFO	6.00
Weighted Average	6.10

During a period of rising prices, the FIFO method produces the highest ending inventory valuation on the balance sheet. Using the FIFO method, the most recent costs remain in inventory since issues are costed at the oldest costs. The LIFO method results in the lowest ending inventory on the balance sheet because the oldest costs remain in inventory. The weighted average method produces an ending inventory figure which is between those figures obtained using the FIFO and LIFO methods, as would be expected of any method using an average.

Each of the cost flow methods will produce a different cost of sales expense on the income statement. Based on the previous examples, the FIFO, LIFO, and weighted average methods produce the following amounts for cost of sales expense:

	Cost of Sales
FIFO	$14.08
LIFO	14.35
Weighted Average	14.25

During a period of rising prices, the LIFO method produces the highest cost of sales. Using the LIFO method, the most recent costs are the basis for costing issues. The FIFO method results in the lowest cost of sales because the oldest costs are used to cost the issues. Again, the weighted average method produces an ending inventory figure which is between those figures obtained using the FIFO and LIFO methods.

LIFO Analyzed

Unlike the FIFO approach or the specific identification approach, LIFO assumes a cost flow that is not compatible with typical storeroom procedures. If matching the physical flow of products with cost flow is an important criterion in choosing an inventory valuation method, then LIFO would not be a satisfactory choice.

On the other hand, if the major concern is to closely relate cost of sales to current costs, then LIFO is a better choice. Since the LIFO approach tends to produce a higher expense for cost of sales (assuming rising prices are typical), it has the advantage of deferring income taxes.

Generally, a company may use one method of accounting for financial reporting and another for tax reporting. For example, a company may select straight-line depreciation under generally accepted accounting principles and double declining depreciation for tax reporting. However, federal income tax laws require that, if a LIFO method is adopted for income tax purposes, it must also be used for financial reporting. Once a company elects to use a LIFO method for tax reporting, it must receive permission from the IRS to change valuation methods. Generally, a tax liability is created during the conversion.

Compared to the other inventory valuation methods, the major advantages of LIFO may be summarized as follows:

- LIFO provides a better measure of income. Because the most recent prices are used to cost issues, the cost of sales expense more closely reflects current costs.

- LIFO often has income tax benefits. A higher cost of sales expense reduces taxable income, resulting in a cash savings. A company may use these savings to produce revenue or to reduce debt and interest expense.

The disadvantages of using LIFO are not always obvious. Companies adopting LIFO sometimes realize too late the pitfalls of this method. Compared to the other inventory valuation methods, the major disadvantages may be summarized as follows:

- LIFO produces a lower figure for income. Investors and stockholders generally base their investment decisions on the net income of a company.

- LIFO produces a lower figure for inventory on the balance sheet. As a result, current assets, working capital, and the current ratio are all understated during periods of rising prices. This financial information is analyzed closely by investors, stockholders, and banks.

- The income tax benefits of LIFO are not guaranteed. Under certain circumstances, it is possible that LIFO will produce an increased tax burden.

- LIFO may not be practical for the hospitality industry, in which food and beverage inventories generally have a fast turnover. Compared to inventories maintained by manufacturing industries, hospitality inventories may never achieve significant levels. The increased costs associated with LIFO may not be worth the benefits.

Because of the added costs and potential problems associated with LIFO, serious and close scrutiny is necessary before selecting it as an inventory valuation method.

Key Terms

first-in, first-out (FIFO)
gross profit method
inventory valuation
last-in, first-out (LIFO)
specific identification approach
weighted average approach

Review Questions

1. Which bookkeeping account is used to record the acquisition of food inventory under the following methods?

   a. The periodic inventory accounting method
   b. The perpetual inventory accounting method

2. How many monthly periods will be affected by an error in ending inventory? Why are cost of sales and gross profit affected by an error in ending inventory?

3. What are the cost flow assumptions of the following approaches?

   a. FIFO
   b. LIFO
   c. Weighted average

4. Which approach to costing issues will result in the highest ending inventory valuation in times of rising prices?

5. Which approach to costing issues will result in the highest cost of sales in times of rising prices?

6. What are the advantages and disadvantages of LIFO?

Problems

Problem 1

A hospitality business uses the periodic inventory method. After reviewing the financial statements, the following determinations of gross profit were reported:

	Month of September	Month of October	Year-to-date October
Sales	$150,000	$130,000	$1,200,000
Cost of Sales:			
Beginning Inventory	18,000	17,000	15,000
Purchases	46,000	42,000	400,000
Cost of Goods Available	64,000	59,000	415,000
Ending Inventory	17,000	13,000	13,000
Cost of Sales	47,000	46,000	402,000
Gross Profit	$103,000	$ 84,000	$ 798,000

It is discovered that the ending inventory on September 30 should have been reported as $14,000. What are the corrected figures for gross profit in these periods?

Problem 2

Although monthly financial statements are due, management has decided not to take a physical inventory at the end of the month since several audits were performed during the month. The gross profit method will be used to estimate the ending inventory for financial statement purposes. Using this method, estimate the ending inventory for April 30 based on the following information:

Food inventory, March 31	$ 4,000
Food sales, April	31,000
Food purchases, April	12,000
Estimated gross profit percentage	64%

Problem 3

Purchases of a new inventory product during the month of April are as follows:

4/1	Purchased 15 units at $5.00 each
4/10	Purchased 10 units at $5.20 each
4/20	Purchased 8 units at $5.25 each

Since the facility uses a periodic inventory system, perpetual recordkeeping cards are not maintained and issues are not known. A physical inventory shows that 5 units are on hand at the close of business, April 30. Compute the dollar value of the ending inventory (to two decimal places) under the following valuation methods:

a. The FIFO periodic method

b. The LIFO periodic method

c. The weighted average periodic method (using a weighted average rounded to four decimal places)

REVIEW QUIZ

When you feel you have covered all of the material in this chapter, answer these questions. Choose the *best* answer. Check your answers with the correct ones found on the Review Quiz Answer Key at the end of this book.

True (T) or False (F)

T   F   1.   If the gross profit method is used, estimating procedures should be carried out separately for food and beverage inventories.

T   F   2.   Good inventory procedures require that the most recent products in the storeroom be the first products issued.

T   F   3.   The FIFO periodic method may produce results for ending inventory that differ from those produced by the FIFO perpetual method.

T   F   4.   The weighted average perpetual method is sometimes called the moving average method because a new average is computed after each purchase.

Multiple Choice

5.   Hospitality operations are likely to use a perpetual recordkeeping system for:

   a.   supply items only.
   b.   inventory items with low cost per unit.
   c.   inventory items with high cost per unit.
   d.   all inventory items.

6.   Inaccurate inventory measurements affect:

   a.   the current assets section of the balance sheet.
   b.   the equity section of the balance sheet.
   c.   the income statement.
   d.   all of the above

7.   Which of the following would *not* represent a valid consideration relating to the gross profit method?

   a.   A physical inventory has not been taken at the end of an accounting period.
   b.   The financial statements need to be prepared.
   c.   Inventory losses need to be assessed due to a recent theft.
   d.   Purchase discounts need to be tracked to achieve better cost savings.

8.   Which of the following is *not* an example of a cost flow approach to inventory valuation?

   a.   weighted average
   b.   specific identification
   c.   LIFO
   d.   FIFO

9. The FIFO approach to inventory valuation values units of ending inventory at:

    a. the oldest costs.
    b. the most recent costs.
    c. the highest costs.
    d. the average costs.

10. Which of the following approaches to inventory valuation produces cost of sales measurements that most closely reflect current costs?

    a. LIFO
    b. FIFO
    c. weighted average
    d. specific identification

Chapter Outline

Learning Objectives

1. Describe the two groups who use a hotel income statement and the formats available for presenting data to them, and explain the elements and conventions used in preparing an income statement. (pp. 287–292)

2. Explain the preparation and purposes of common-size and comparative income statements, and describe their analysis and interpretation. (pp. 292–301)

3. Describe the purpose of and information reported on the statement of retained earnings. (pp. 301–302)

10

Hotel Income Statements

T HE INCOME STATEMENT for a hotel shows the operating results of its departments and revenue from other sources. While all income statements present operating results, this information may be presented in a variety of formats. This chapter provides examples of different types of income statements so that the reader should be able to properly analyze any income statement issued by a hospitality business.

One reason for having various formats for financial statements is to best meet the needs of the two groups who use the statements: **internal users** and **external users**. Even users within these two groups have different requirements because some of them perform statistical analysis using percentages, comparative data, and ratios.

Internal financial statements are designed to include great detail and contain numerous supporting schedules to serve the needs of internal users like a company's board of directors, executives, managers, and supervisors.

External financial statements are designed to present information in a summarized format and emphasize company results. They are intended for external users like stockholders, creditors, and members of the investment community. These statements are reviewed or audited by independent certified public accountants.

In explaining hotel income statements, this chapter will address such questions as:

1. What are the basic elements and conventions used in the preparation of an income statement?

2. What is the difference between internal long-form and short-form hotel income statements?

3. What is an external income statement?

4. What is a common-size income statement?

5. What is a comparative income statement?

6. What is the relationship between an income statement and a statement of retained earnings?

Elements and Conventions

Over the years, the income statement has also been called the:

- Statement of operations
- Profit and loss statement

- Earnings statement

The purpose of the income statement is to report the results of operations of a hospitality business for a specific period of time. This period can be as short as one month or one quarter, but not longer than one year. For this reason, the accounting cycle for a hospitality business that is legally organized as a corporation is any consecutive 12-month period, called a **fiscal year**. At the end of a fiscal year, income statement bookkeeping accounts (revenue and expenses) are closed and set to zero. The start of the new fiscal year begins with entries pertaining only to that accounting period.

The elements that form the basis for preparation of the income statement can be represented by the following equation:

$$\text{Revenue} - \text{Expenses} = \text{Net Income}$$

Revenue. Revenue results from the sale of goods and services. Revenue also includes interest income, dividend income, and other items reported on the schedule of rentals and other income.

Expenses. Expenses are the costs of goods and services used in the process of creating revenue. Classifying expenditures as asset or expense is critical to the proper measurement of income or loss for a period. Some expenditures are assets when purchased but become expenses as they are used (food inventory, for example). A one-year fire insurance policy is an asset when purchased; as time expires, part of its cost also expires and becomes an expense.

Dividends are not a business expense. The declaration of dividends is a reduction of retained earnings, which is a balance sheet item. Dividends are explained in more detail in the section on the statement of retained earnings.

Conventions. All revenue and expenses are recorded using **accrual basis accounting.** The income statement recognizes all sales and other revenue in the time period in which they are earned and not when cash is received. Likewise, all expenses are recognized in the time period in which they are incurred and not when they are paid.

The **realization principle** of accounting dictates that revenue is recorded when a sale has been made *and* earned. The **matching principle** dictates that all expenses associated with the earning of revenue be recorded in the same accounting period as the revenue they helped generate.

Hotel Income Statement Formats

The income statement for a hotel combines all the financial data from its revenue centers, support centers, energy costs, fixed costs, and other items that are not reported in any departmental reports or schedules. For instance, the expense for income taxes is not allocated to any specific department. Also, gains and losses from the sale of assets such as marketable securities, investments (subsidiaries), property, and equipment may have occurred during the reporting period.

Many formats are available for presenting financial data on a hotel income statement. The following formats are described in this chapter:

- Internal long-form format

- Internal short-form format
- External formats

Net Income Is Not Cash Flow

As stated earlier, **net income** represents revenue less expenses for a period. Revenue is generated from both cash sales and sales on account. Likewise, expenses either are paid during the period or may still be due. However, the net income of a business does not necessarily cause a corresponding increase in the business's cash account.

While net income is the result of revenue minus expenses, not all expenses require a cash payment. For example, depreciation is an expense that is merely the write-off of the cost of a fixed asset over its useful life. While depreciation expense appears on the income statement as a reduction of net income, it does not involve any cash payment. Amortization is another expense that does not require any cash payment but appears on the income statement as a reduction of net income. Therefore, to properly reflect cash flow, items such as depreciation and amortization must be "added back" to net income to reflect net income as a source of cash. (Net income on the income statement is *not* affected by this procedure.)

On the other hand, some items requiring cash payments do not appear on the income statement. For example, principal payments on debt require cash payments, but never appear on the income statement. These payments must be subtracted from net income to properly reflect cash flow.

The difference between net income and cash flow can be best explained using the following business transactions during a given month:

	Effect on:	
	Income Statement	Cash Balance
Cash sales	+ 100,000	+ 100,000
Sales on account	+ 400,000	0
Total	+ 500,000	+ 100,000
Expenses purchased on account	− 200,000	0
Payment of last month's accounts payable	0	− 270,000
Total	+ 300,000	− 170,000
Depreciation	− 120,000	0
Total	+ 180,000	− 170,000
New bank loan	0	+ 50,000
Total	+ 180,000	− 120,000

The Hotel DORO's Income Statement

The fictitious Hotel DORO is used here to present the following example of an income statement for a hotel as a whole. To complete an income statement, it is necessary to include any gains or losses from the sale of assets and other items not related to revenue centers, support centers, energy costs, and fixed charges. Finally, income taxes must be entered to arrive at the net income for the hotel. During the

Exhibit 1   Internal Long-Form Income Statement—Hotel DORO

Hotel DORO, Inc.
Statement of Income
For the year ended December 31, 19X2   Schedule A

	Schedule	Net Revenue	Cost of Sales	Payroll and Related Expenses	Other Expenses	Income (Loss)
Operated Departments						
Rooms	A1	$ 897,500		$143,140	$ 62,099	$692,261
Food and Beverage	A2	524,570	$178,310	204,180	54,703	87,377
Telephone	A3	51,140	60,044	17,132	1,587	(27,623)
Other Operated Departments	A4	63,000	10,347	33,276	6,731	12,646
Rentals and Other Income	A5	61,283				61,283
Total Operated Departments		1,597,493	248,701	397,728	125,120	825,944
Undistributed Expenses						
Administrative and General	A6			97,632	66,549	164,181
Marketing	A7			35,825	32,043	67,868
Property Operation and Maintenance	A8			36,917	24,637	61,554
Energy Costs	A9				47,312	47,312
Total Undistributed Expenses				170,374	170,541	340,915
Income Before Fixed Charges		$1,597,493	$248,701	$568,102	$295,661	$485,029
Fixed Charges						
Rent	A10					28,500
Property Taxes	A10					45,324
Insurance	A10					6,914
Interest	A10					192,153
Depreciation and Amortization	A10					146,000
Total Fixed Charges						418,891
Income Before Income Taxes and Gain on Sale of Property						66,138
Gain on Sale of Property						10,500
Income Before Income Taxes						76,638
Income Taxes						16,094
Net Income						$ 60,544

reporting period under consideration, the Hotel DORO sold property, resulting in a gain of $10,500, and its income tax expense (state and federal) was $16,094.

Internal Formats

The following sections describe the two formats for internal income statements: the long form and the short form.

Long Form. The long-form income statement presents detailed information to the reader. Exhibit 1 illustrates the completed internal long-form income statement for the Hotel DORO. If there had been no gain on the sale of property, the line showing $66,138 would have been labeled as income before income taxes. Since there has been a gain on the sale of property, the line showing $66,138 must be labeled as income before income taxes and gain (loss) on sale of property. The $10,500 gain on

Exhibit 2   Internal Short-Form Income Statement—Hotel DORO

Hotel DORO, Inc.
Statement of Income
For the year ended December 31, 19X2   Schedule A

	Schedule		Income
Operated Departments			
Rooms	A1		$692,261
Food and Beverage	A2		$ 87,377
Telephone	A3		(27,623)
Other Operated Departments	A4		12,646
Rentals and Other Income	A5		61,283
Total Operated Departments			825,944
Undistributed Expenses			
Administrative and General	A6	164,181	
Marketing	A7	67,868	
Property Operation and			
Maintenance	A8	61,554	
Energy Costs	A9	47,312	
Total Undistributed Expenses			340,915
Income Before Fixed Charges			485,029
Fixed Charges			
Rent	A10	28,500	
Property Taxes	A10	45,324	
Insurance	A10	6,914	
Interest	A10	192,153	
Depreciation and Amortization	A10	146,000	
Total Fixed Charges			418,891
Income Before Income Taxes and			
Gain (Loss) on Sale of Property			66,138
Gain on Sale of Property			10,500
Income Before Income Taxes			76,638
Income Taxes			16,094
Net Income			$ 60,544

the sale of property is added to the $66,138 to arrive at income before income taxes of $76,638. The income taxes of $16,094 are then subtracted to arrive at the $60,544 net income.

Short Form. Sometimes a brief income statement format is required. Exhibit 2 illustrates the short-form income statement, which shows only summary information for revenue and support centers. Aside from this difference, both the long and short forms have the same general format; information appearing in the right-most column of the long-form income statement is identical to the information presented in the short-form version.

External Formats

There is no single standard format for external income statements, but all external statements must comply with the pronouncements of the American Institute of

Exhibit 3   External Income Statement—Hotel DORO

Hotel DORO, Inc. Income Statement For the year ended December 31, 19X2		Schedule A
Net Revenue		
Rooms	$ 897,500	
Food and Beverage	524,570	
Telephone	51,140	
Other Operated Departments	63,000	
Rentals and Other Income	61,283	
Total Operated Departments		$ 1,597,493
Costs and Expenses		
Rooms	205,239	
Food and Beverage	437,193	
Telephone	78,763	
Other Operated Departments	50,354	
Administrative and General	164,181	
Marketing	67,868	
Property Operation and Maintenance	61,554	
Energy Costs	47,312	
Rent, Property Taxes, and Insurance	80,738	
Interest Expense	192,153	
Depreciation and Amortization	146,000	
Total Costs and Expenses		1,531,355
Income Before Gain on Sale of Property		66,138
Gain on Sale of Property		10,500
Income Before Income Taxes		76,638
Income Taxes		16,094
Net Income		$ 60,544

Certified Public Accountants (AICPA) and the Financial Accounting Standards Board (FASB). These pronouncements are influenced by the Securities and Exchange Commission (SEC).

Exhibit 3 illustrates one type of external income statement for the Hotel DORO; this statement complies with generally accepted accounting principles. Its financial data can be traced back to Exhibit 1. The net revenue has been copied onto this statement, and each department's costs and expenses consist of the total of its cost of sales, payroll expenses, and other expenses from Exhibit 1.

Two additional popular ways to present financial information are common-size financial statements and comparative financial statements. The following sections describe common-size and comparative income statements.

Common-Size Income Statement

While an income statement is informative for reporting the operating results for a period, managers need more information to measure efficiency and investigate potential problem areas. To accommodate management, accountants have designed a common-size income statement.

A common-size financial statement shows the relationship of each item on the statement to a common base amount. Each dollar amount on the financial statement is converted to a percentage. In the case of the common-size income statement, the relationship of the items to net sales is expressed as a percentage.

Common-Size Analysis of an Income Statement. The importance of **common-size analysis** can be emphasized by the following example: If management has budgeted 1% of net sales for allowances (price adjustments), and the results for the period show allowances of 1.5%, then there may be a quality control problem. The potential problem has been brought to light because the actual allowances have exceeded those budgeted.

The computation to arrive at common-size percentages is expressed by the following formula:

$$\frac{\text{Line Amount}}{\text{Net Sales}} = \text{Common-Size Percentages}$$

The dividend is the dollar amount for any line of the income statement. The divisor is always net sales. Since every item is divided by net sales, the net sales figure will always have a common-size figure of 100%.

Common-size analysis is also referred to as **vertical analysis** because computations are made from top to bottom on an income statement using the same divisor.

Common-size percentages can be rounded to a whole number or shown with any number of decimal places. For example, 5 divided by 3 can be shown as 2 (rounded to a whole number), 1.7 (shown with one decimal), or 1.67 (shown with two decimals). Regardless of the decimal places used, common-size percentage calculations require rounding. To illustrate this concept, the following data will be used.

Food sales	$250,000
Cost of food sold	− 84,125
Gross profit	$165,875

The common-size percentages are computed and rounded to one decimal position as follows:

	Input	Calculator Display	Rounded
Food sales	$\dfrac{250,000}{250,000}$ =	100. =	100.0%
Cost of food sold	$\dfrac{84,125}{250,000}$ =	33.65 =	33.7%
Gross profit	$\dfrac{165,875}{250,000}$ =	66.35 =	66.4%

Putting the results of these computations in proper form results in the following:

Food sales	$250,000	100.0%
Cost of food sold	− 84,125	− 33.7
Gross profit	$165,875	66.4%

↑

Problem:
100.0 − 33.7 is not 66.4

Because of rounding, sometimes the technically accurate computations do not lend themselves to logical presentation. This is a dilemma that is resolved by different company policies.

Some companies follow a policy of *forcing* the computations as necessary to present logical results. One policy is to force the largest number (except sales or net income) up or down to accommodate the problems caused by rounding. Such a policy would produce the following results:

Food sales	$250,000	100.0%
Cost of food sold	− 84,125	− 33.7
Gross profit	$165,875	66.3%

Other companies have a policy of entering the computation regardless of any mathematical discrepancy. This policy is often used for computer-prepared statements since a computer cannot backtrack after it has printed a computed amount.

Any forced numbers presented in this chapter appear in bold print on the financial statements.

Common-size analysis is useful beyond examining the percentages for signs of potential problems. It is also useful for forecasting sales and expenses for budget purposes. For example, if supplies expense currently shows a common-size percentage of 10%, a quick and simple method for forecasting supplies expense is to apply that percentage to the forecasted revenue for a period. That is, if the marketing department is forecasting sales of $200,000 for a future period, then management could forecast the corresponding supplies expense to be $20,000.

Common-size percentages also provide data useful for preparing meaningful reports for management or for meetings. Generally, pictures depict outcomes or predictions better than words do. Common-size percentages can easily be converted into graphics, especially with the capabilities of today's computers and software. Graphic illustrations are very effective for delivering information in a dramatic fashion to emphasize highs, lows, and trends. One popular graphic device is the pie chart.

Pie charts. Pie charts quickly deliver an easy-to-understand message. A pie chart is a circular graph divided into sections, showing the size of each segment in proportion to the whole. Simply stated, a pie chart is a circle (called a "pie") that is divided into "slices." Each slice (item) represents a different portion of the pie. The larger the slice, the larger that portion is relative to the pie.

To construct a pie chart, one must know the relationship of each portion to the whole. Exhibit 4 shows an example of a pie chart, which shows that the Hotel DORO's food and beverage sales dollar generated a profit of about 9¢. (Refer to the food and beverage department income statement in Exhibit 5 to see how data there

Exhibit 4   Pie Chart—Hotel DORO's Food and Beverage Sales Dollar

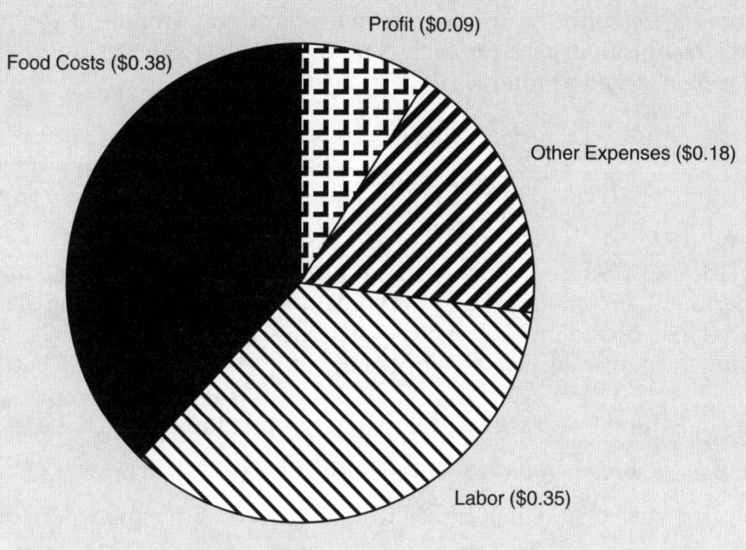

Exhibit 5   Common-Size Income Statement—Hotel DORO's Food and Beverage Department

Food Sales	$50,350	100.7%
Allowances	350	.7
Net Food Sales	50,000	100.0
Cost of Food Sold	19,000	38.0
Gross Profit	31,000	62.0
Expenses		
Payroll and Related Expenses	17,700	35.4
All Other Expenses	9,000	18.0
Total Expenses	26,700	53.4
Food Department Income	$ 4,300	8.6%

can be presented as the pie chart shown in Exhibit 4, including the impact of costs and expenses.)

Common-size analysis can be performed for the income statement of a hotel or individually for any department that has net sales, as explained in the following sections.

Common-Size Analysis—the Hotel DORO's Food and Beverage Department Income Statement. Exhibit 5 shows a common-size analysis of the Hotel DORO's food and beverage department income statement. Each dollar amount was divided by the net sales amount of $50,000 to arrive at the common-size percentages. All percentages were rounded to one decimal place; none required forcing up or down. The technical answer for each computation was entered, and the column footings were checked as follows:

100.7%	−	.7%	did equal	100.0%
100.0%	−	38.0%	did equal	62.0%
35.4%	+	18.0%	did equal	53.4%
62.0%	−	53.4%	did equal	8.6%

Interpretation of Common-Size Analysis—the Hotel DORO's Food and Beverage Department Income Statement. The data shown on a common-size income statement is interpreted in relationship to net sales. Interpretation can be simplified by restating the percentages as a component of the sales dollar (100% equaling one dollar).

Refer to Exhibit 5 to trace the following interpretation of the data:

- Allowances were less than 1% of net sales (.7%).

- Food cost was 38%, which can be restated as 38¢ on the food sales dollar (net sales).

- A 38% food cost resulted in a gross profit of 62%. This means that there was 62¢ left of the food sales dollar to cover payroll and all the other expenses.

- The total expenses amounted to 53.4% or about 53¢ on the food sales dollar. This means that the food cost and operating expenses of the food and beverage department totaled 91¢ (38¢ + 53¢) on the food sales dollar.

- The net income of 8.6% shows that the hotel enjoyed a profit of only about 9¢ for each dollar of food sales.

Common-Size Analysis—the Hotel DORO's Income Statement. Exhibit 6 illustrates a common-size income statement for the Hotel DORO. A common-size analysis for a hotel income statement uses the same procedures previously explained. Again, net revenue is used as the common divisor. Each amount on the statement is divided by net sales to arrive at a common-size percentage.

Internal and external hotel income statements may contain common-size percentages. To provide management with further information, an accountant may supplement the internal income statement with budgeted ratios and/or industry ratios.

Interpretation of the Hotel DORO's Common-Size Income Statement. The income statement in Exhibit 6 shows that the rooms department generated 56.3% of the hotel's total revenues of $1,597,493. This department's expenses were only 12.8% of revenues.

Total costs and expenses of the hotel were 95.9% or 96¢ on the sales dollar. The gain on the sale of property added about 1¢ and income taxes took away 1¢ of the sales dollar. The final result was that the hotel was able to keep only about 4¢ (3.8%) of each sales dollar.

Exhibit 6   Common-Size Income Statement—Hotel DORO

Hotel DORO, Inc.
Income Statement
For the year ended December 31, 19X2

Net Revenue		
Rooms	$ 897,500	**56.3%**
Food and Beverage	524,570	32.8
Telephone	51,140	3.2
Other Operated Departments	63,000	3.9
Rentals and Other Income	61,283	3.8
Total Departmental Revenue	1,597,493	100.0
Costs and Expenses		
Rooms	205,239	12.8
Food and Beverage	437,193	27.4
Telephone	78,763	4.9
Other Operated Departments	50,354	3.2
Administrative and General	164,181	10.3
Marketing	67,868	4.2
Property Operation and Maintenance	61,554	3.9
Energy Costs	47,312	3.0
Rent, Property Taxes, and Insurance	80,738	5.1
Interest Expense	192,153	12.0
Depreciation and Amortization	146,000	9.1
Total Costs and Expenses	1,531,355	95.9
Income Before Gain on Sale of Property	66,138	4.1
Gain on Sale of Property	10,500	.7
Income Before Income Taxes	76,638	4.8
Income Taxes	16,094	1.0
Net Income	$ 60,544	3.8%

Comparative Income Statement

A comparative financial statement presents financial data for two or more periods. The comparative data can be shown in the the form of dollar amounts or percentages that management finds useful in its planning and controlling functions. Because computations are made on a side-by-side basis, a **comparative analysis** is also known as a **horizontal analysis**. A comparative analysis does not use a common divisor. The divisor for each line is the prior period's data for that particular line.

A popular comparative income statement format is the following:

Current Year   Prior Year $ Change   % Change

The method for preparing a comparative income statement is outlined in the following discussion.

	19X4	19X3	$ Change	% Change
Net sales	$210,000	$200,000		
Cost of sales	80,000	82,000		

After the current and prior years' data have been entered as shown above, the steps required to complete the comparative income statement are:

1. The *dollar change* is computed by entering the current year's amount in a calculator and then subtracting the prior year's amount. The proper mathematical sign (positive or negative) will be provided by the calculator.

$210,000	$80,000
− 200,000	− 82,000
$ 10,000	$(2,000)

2. The *percentage change* is computed by dividing the dollar change amount by the prior year's amount. The mathematical sign of the percentage change is always the same as that for the dollar change.

$$\frac{10,000}{200,000} = 5.0\% \qquad \frac{(2,000)}{82,000} = (2.4)\%$$

Once the dollar changes and percentage changes have been computed, they can be entered in the appropriate columns as shown below.

	19X4	19X3	$ Change	% Change
Net sales	$210,000	$200,000	$10,000	5.0%
Cost of sales	80,000	82,000	(2,000)	(2.4)%

The preceding example shows the current year in the left-most column. Some companies prefer to have the prior year in the left-most column. The following example shows the different presentation of the current and prior year's data. Notice that this format has no effect on the changes between the periods.

	19X3	19X4	$ Change	% Change
Net sales	$200,000	$210,000	$10,000	5.0%
Cost of sales	82,000	80,000	(2,000)	(2.4)%

Always read the date headings so that the math is performed as this year's amount less last year's amount; otherwise, it is easy to make a mistake in signing the change as an increase or decrease.

Comparative Income Statement for the Hotel DORO. Exhibit 7 illustrates a comparative income statement for the Hotel DORO. The dollar change for each line item (including any total) was independently computed horizontally. The $72,100 for all departments was also a horizontal computation. It is possible to verify the accuracy of the $72,100 by vertically adding each department's dollar changes. (This *cross-checking* of all columns is standard procedure for producing an accurate statement.)

Exhibit 7   Comparative Income Statement—Hotel DORO

Hotel DORO, Inc.
Statement of Income
For the years ended December 31, 19X2 and 19X1

	19X2	19X1	$ Change	% Change
Income of Operated Departments				
Rooms	$692,261	$615,114	$77,147	12.5%
Food and Beverage	87,377	90,520	(3,143)	(3.5)
Telephone	(27,623)	(26,814)	(809)	(3.0)
Other Operated Departments	12,646	14,502	(1,856)	(12.8)
Rentals and Other Income	61,283	60,522	761	1.3
Total Departmental Income	825,944	753,844	72,100	9.6
Undistributed Expenses				
Administrative and General	164,181	140,812	23,369	16.6
Marketing	67,868	57,647	10,221	17.7
Property Operation and Maintenance	61,554	64,482	(2,928)	(4.5)
Energy	47,312	42,114	5,198	12.3
Total Undistributed Expenses	340,915	305,055	35,860	11.8
Income Before Fixed Charges	485,029	448,789	36,240	8.1
Fixed Charges				
Rent	28,500	28,500	0	0
Property Taxes	45,324	33,421	11,903	35.6
Insurance	6,914	4,900	2,014	41.1
Interest	192,153	193,814	(1,661)	(.9)
Depreciation and Amortization	146,000	128,000	18,000	14.1
Total Fixed Charges	418,891	388,635	30,256	7.8
Income Before Income Taxes and Gain on Sale of Property	66,138	60,154	5,984	9.9
Gain on Sale of Property	10,500		10,500	—
Income Before Income Taxes	76,638	60,154	16,484	27.4
Income Taxes	16,094	14,030	2,064	14.7
Net Income	$ 60,544	$ 46,124	$14,420	31.3%

Because the percentage changes are computed without a common divisor, it is not possible to add a column of percentages to verify any total percentage. For example, the 9.6% total change for the operating departments cannot be verified by adding the individual percentage changes for each department. Therefore, it is suggested that all percentage computations be rechecked for accuracy as follows:

- Verify that the mathematical sign of the percentage change is the same as that of the dollar change.

- Use a change of 10% as a mental guide when entering a percentage change. For example, the rooms department of the Hotel DORO had last year's income of

$615,114. A 10% change is $61,511 (simply drop the last digit, moving the decimal point one position to the left). The actual dollar change amount was $77,147, which is slightly more than 10%. If you had entered a percentage change of 125% or 1.3%, you would know there is a calculation error.

- Double-check the percentage change on those items that show a possible calculation error when the preceding procedure has been applied.

Interpretation of a Comparative Analysis. A specialized vocabulary is used to discuss changes in a comparative financial statement. If this year's data is larger than last year's data, the change is called an *increase* or simply stated as *up* or *upward*; it cannot be called a *gain* because a gain results from the sale of assets at a price exceeding book value. If this year's data is smaller than last year's data, the change is called a *decrease* or simply stated as *down* or *downward*; it cannot be called a *loss* because a loss results from the sale of assets at a price less than book value.

If this year's data is equal to last year's data, the situation is referred to as *no change*; it would be illogical to call it a zero change.

Sometimes it is impossible to calculate a *percentage change* because there is no last year's data, which means there is no divisor. In this case, the proper procedure is to indicate that the percentage change is *not measurable* by entering the symbol "—" or "n/m" in the applicable column.

When analyzing the changes, it is incorrect to concentrate only on the percentage changes because a large percentage change may not necessarily represent a large dollar change. The comparing of small numbers can produce a large percentage change for a minor dollar change. For example, a $50 change on last year's data of $20 results in a 250% change. Conversely, a small percentage change could represent a large dollar change. For example, if the dollar change is $500,000 on last year's data of $50,000,000, the percentage change is only 1%.

Interpretation of the Hotel DORO's Comparative Income Statement. The comparative income statement for the Hotel DORO in Exhibit 7 is used to make the following brief interpretation of its operating results based on a comparison of 19X2 (current year) with 19X1 (prior year).

- The resulting *increase* of 31.3% in net income is misleading because of the gain on the sale of property. Selling assets is not part of the hotel's normal business purpose. Ignoring the gain on the sale of property reveals that the hotel's normal course of business actually produced an *increase* of only 9.9% in profits before income taxes.

- The income for the rooms department showed an *increase* of 12.5%, but the food and beverage department had a *decrease* of 3.5%. This situation requires further study.

- The results of the telephone department are at first difficult to interpret. Consider that the income of an operating department is being analyzed. A larger loss this year causes a decrease to operating income. The $809 change is a *decrease* in income because this year's departmental loss of $27,623 is greater than last year's departmental loss of $26,814.

- At first glance, the 12.8% *decrease* in the income for the other operated departments is alarming. However, the dollar decrease is only $1,856. In any case, management would want to find out why this year's trend was *downward*.

- The rentals and other income increase of 1.3% appears to have followed the trend in rooms department income but at a lower rate.

- The administrative and general expenses had an increase of 16.6%. This increase needs management attention because it is out of proportion when compared with the 9.6% increase for the income of all revenue centers (operated departments).

- The increase in marketing expense might be related to the increase in room sales. Perhaps more money was spent on advertising, which increased room sales. In any case, management would investigate the reason for the marketing expense increase.

- The property operation and maintenance data is for an expense. If this year's expense is smaller than last year's expense, the change is a *decrease*.

- The data in the change column for rent expense is referred to as *no change*.

- The percentage change column for the gain on the sale of property cannot be computed because there is no divisor (no last year's data). Therefore, a dash is inserted.

Statement of Retained Earnings

The statement of retained earnings is prepared for any hospitality business legally organized as a corporation. The purpose of this statement is to provide updated information about the lifetime earnings retained by a corporation. These **retained earnings** represent the lifetime profits of a business that have not been declared as dividends to the shareholders.

Retained earnings are increased by the net income for the period and reduced by any dividends *declared* for the period. Dividends may be declared in one period and paid in the following period; thus, the distinction between *dividends declared* and *dividends payable* has important consequences for this statement.

Dividends are first declared by action of a corporation's board of directors. This declaration immediately becomes a reduction to retained earnings as shown by the following journal entry:

Retained Earnings (or Dividends Declared)	xxx	
Dividends Payable		xxx

When the dividends are paid, the entry now affects cash as shown by the following journal entry:

Dividends Payable	xxx	
Cash		xxx

The statement of retained earnings may be prepared as a separate statement or combined with the income statement. In either case, the ending retained earnings are brought forward to the equity section of the balance sheet.

Exhibit 8 Statement of Retained Earnings—Hotel DORO

Hotel DORO, Inc. Statement of Retained Earnings For the year ended December 31, 19X2	Schedule B
Retained Earnings at beginning of year	$278,118
Net Income for the year (Schedule A)	60,544
Total	338,662
Less Dividends Declared during the year	20,000
Retained Earnings at end of year	$318,662

Statement of Retained Earnings for the Hotel DORO

Exhibit 8 illustrates a separate statement of retained earnings for the Hotel DORO. Because the statement of retained earnings is generally prepared after the income statement, it is designated as Schedule B.

The computations for the statement of retained earnings are relatively simple. The beginning retained earnings are those of prior years, which represent the lifetime profits (net income) of the corporation less lifetime dividends declared as of the beginning of the period. For the Hotel DORO, retained earnings at the start of the year are $278,118. To this amount is added the net income for the period, $60,544, resulting in a total of $338,662. Dividends declared during the year, $20,000, are subtracted to arrive at the retained earnings of $318,662 at the end of the period. This amount will be carried over to the balance sheet of Hotel DORO.

Statement of Income and Retained Earnings for the Hotel DORO

Exhibit 9 illustrates retained earnings data combined with the income statement. This is a popular statement format because it readily shows the net income incrementing the retained earnings in one statement. In this combined statement, called the statement of income and retained earnings, the net income is not double-underlined. Instead it is added to the beginning retained earnings, and then the dividends declared are subtracted to arrive at ending retained earnings. End-of-year retained earnings are double-underlined to indicate the end of the statement.

Key Terms

accrual basis accounting
common-size analysis
comparative analysis
external financial statements
external users
fiscal year
horizontal analysis

internal financial statements
internal users
matching principle
net income
realization principle
retained earnings
vertical analysis

Exhibit 9 Statement of Income and Retained Earnings (External)—Hotel DORO

Hotel DORO, Inc.
Statement of Income and Retained Earnings
For the year ended December 31, 19X2

Net Revenue

Rooms	$ 897,500	
Food and Beverage	524,570	
Telephone	51,140	
Other Operated Departments	63,000	
Rentals and Other Income	61,283	
Total Departmental Revenue		$1,597,493

Costs and Expenses

Rooms	205,239	
Food and Beverage	437,193	
Telephone	78,763	
Other Operated Departments	50,354	
Administrative and General	164,181	
Marketing	67,868	
Property Operation and Maintenance	61,554	
Energy Costs	47,312	
Rent, Property Taxes, and Insurance	80,738	
Interest Expense	192,153	
Depreciation and Amortization	146,000	
Total Costs and Expenses		1,531,355
Income Before Gain on Sale of Property		66,138
Gain on Sale of Property		10,500
Income Before Income Taxes		76,638
Income Taxes		16,094
Net Income		60,544
Retained Earnings at beginning of year		278,118
Less Dividends Declared during the year		20,000
Retained Earnings at end of year		$ 318,662

Review Questions

1. What is the purpose of the income statement?
2. What are some other names used for the income statement?
3. What are the components of revenue for a hotel?
4. What are the financial components of a hotel income statement?
5. Why is net income *not* the same as cash flow?
6. What is a common-size income statement?
7. What is a comparative income statement?

8. What is the purpose of the statement of retained earnings?

9. What is a statement of income and retained earnings?

Problems

Problem 1

Prepare an internal short-form income statement based on the following data for Hotel Sivad, Inc.

The data is for the year ended September 30, 19XX.

Income of Revenue Centers:	
Rooms	$776,786
Food and Beverage	119,726
Telephone	(15,610)
Vending Machine Commissions	1,500
Cash Discounts Earned	2,700
Interest Income	800
Expenses of Support Centers:	
Administrative and General	158,684
Marketing	48,209
Property Operation and Maintenance	88,296
Other Expenses:	
Energy Costs	81,420
Rent	135,225
Property Taxes	55,650
Insurance	9,986
Interest	52,148
Depreciation and Amortization	115,860
Income Taxes	48,707

Problem 2

Prepare a statement of retained earnings based on the following data for Hotel Carbob, Inc.

The data is for the year ended June 30, 19X9.

Dividends paid this year	$ 40,000
Dividends declared this year	60,000
Income before income taxes	140,424
Income taxes	48,707
Retained earnings July 1, 19X8	122,930

Problem 3

Prepare a common-size income statement for the Garden Bistro, Inc. The rules for rounding are as follows:

a. Show all answers to one decimal, rounded (for example, 7,900 divided by 170,000 equals 4.6%).

b. If a series of computed percentages do not add up to the computed total, force the largest number in the series up or down as necessary.

c. The net income percentage is not to be forced up or down.

The Garden Bistro, Inc.
Income Statement
For the Year Ended December 31, 19X8

REVENUE	
Food Sales	$171,000
Allowances	1,000
Net Revenue	170,000
Cost of Food Sold	53,000
Gross Profit	117,000
OPERATING EXPENSES	
Payroll	55,000
Payroll Taxes and Employee Benefits	7,900
China, Glassware	300
Kitchen Fuel	900
Laundry and Dry Cleaning	2,100
Credit Card Fees	1,500
Operating Supplies	5,000
Advertising	2,000
Utilities	3,800
Repairs and Maintenance	1,900
Total Operating Expenses	80,400
Income Before Fixed Charges and Income Taxes	36,600
FIXED CHARGES	
Rent	6,000
Property Taxes	1,500
Insurance	3,600
Interest	3,000
Depreciation	5,500
Total Fixed Charges	19,600
Income Before Income Taxes	17,000
Income Taxes	2,000
Net Income	$ 15,000

Problem 4

Prepare a comparative analysis from the following income statement. Show all percentages to one decimal, rounded.

The Garden Bistro, Inc.
Income Statement
For the Years Ended December 31, 19X8 and 19X7

	19X8	19X7	$ Change	% Change
REVENUE				
Food Sales	$171,000	$ 160,800		
Allowances	1,000	800		
Net Revenue	170,000	160,000		
Cost of Food Sold	53,000	51,000		
Gross Profit	117,000	109,000		
OPERATING EXPENSES				
Payroll	55,000	56,000		
Payroll Taxes and Employee Benefits	7,900	7,500		
China, Glassware	300	300		
Kitchen Fuel	900	600		
Laundry and Dry Cleaning	2,100	1,800		
Credit Card Fees	1,500	0		
Operating Supplies	5,000	5,200		
Advertising	2,000	1,400		
Utilities	3,800	3,000		
Repairs and Maintenance	1,900	1,000		
Total Operating Expenses	80,400	76,800		
Income Before Fixed Charges and Income Taxes	36,600	32,200		
FIXED CHARGES				
Rent	6,000	6,000		
Property Taxes	1,500	1,200		
Insurance	3,600	3,600		
Interest	3,000	2,800		
Depreciation	5,500	4,700		
Total Fixed Charges	19,600	18,300		
Income Before Income Taxes	17,000	13,900		
Income Taxes	2,000	1,600		
Net Income	$ 15,000	$ 12,300		

Problem 5

Determine the effects on an income statement and cash flow from the following data. Show the effect of each item and indicate the total effect.

| | | Effect on: | |
		Income Statement	Cash Balance
Cash sales	$200,000		
Sales on account	500,000		
Expenses purchased on account	300,000		
Payment of last month's accounts payable	200,000		
Depreciation	80,000		
Amortization	15,000		
New bank loan	25,000		
Payment of mortgage principal	60,000		

Problem 6

You have been asked to perform forensic accounting to discover financial information missing due to fraud within a company. It has been determined that sales for the period were $791,000. Your assignment is to determine the following items based on the average common-size percentages typical for this company. Round your answers to the nearest dollar.

Cost of sales	61.9%
Selling expenses	22.8
Administrative and general expenses	6.8

Format your answer as follows:

Sales	_____
Cost of sales	_____
Gross profit	_____
Selling expenses	_____
Administrative and general expenses	_____
Income before income taxes	_____

Problem 7

Due to destruction of certain records by fire, you have been hired by a firm to perform forensic accounting to discover missing financial information. Fill in the following blanks based on the information provided.

19X9	19X8	$ Change	% Change
_____	20,269	16,231	80.1
3,450	_____	733	27.0
_____	2,100	(200)	(9.5)
3,000	_____	0	0
4,000	_____	4,000	n/m
48,000	_____	1,807	_____
_____	50,000	_____	10.0

Problem 8

Computer Assignment: Prepare a pie chart showing the disposition of the sales dollar based on the following information.

Net food sales	100.0%
Cost of food sold	32.0
Labor costs	37.0
Other operating costs	13.2
Fixed costs	13.3
Income taxes	.8
Net income	3.7

REVIEW QUIZ

When you feel you have covered all of the material in this chapter, answer these questions. Choose the *best* answer. Check your answers with the correct ones found on the Review Quiz Answer Key at the end of this book.

True (T) or False (F)

T   F   1. The major difference between internal and external financial statements is the intended audience.

T   F   2. The expense for a hotel's income taxes is *not* allocated to any specific department.

T   F   3. A common-size income statement converts the dollar amount for each line item into a percentage of net sales.

T   F   4. A common-size financial statement presents financial data for two or more periods.

Multiple Choice

5. Which of the following is *not* an example of an internal user of a company's financial statements?

   a. member of the board of directors
   b. department head
   c. stockholder
   d. top-level manager

6. Which of the following is the correct form of the equation that is the basis for preparing the income statement?

   a. Revenue = Expenses − Net Income
   b. Revenue − Expenses = Net Income
   c. Line Amount ÷ Net Sales = Common-Size Percentage
   d. Sales − Cost of Sales = Gross Profit

7. An external income statement must comply with the pronouncements of which of the following?

   a. American Institute of Certified Public Accountants
   b. Financial Accounting Standards Board
   c. Percentage Change Board of Review
   d. a and b

8. Interpretation of data shown on a common-size income statement can be simplified by:

   a. zeroing out the income statement bookkeeping accounts.
   b. classifying dividends as a business expense.
   c. restating the percentages as a component of the sales dollar.
   d. redesigning the statement.

9. Which of the following sentences about the statement of retained earnings is *true*?

    a. It is not prepared for incorporated businesses.
    b. It uses common-size percentages rounded to one decimal place.
    c. It is never combined with the income statement.
    d. It may be combined with the income statement.

10. The first major financial statement to be prepared is generally:

    a. the income statement.
    b. the statement of retained earnings.
    c. the balance sheet.
    d. the statement of changes in financial position.

Chapter Outline

Ratio Analysis of the Income Statement
    Prior-Period Ratios
    Industry and Trade Association Ratios
    Budgeted Ratios
Popular Income Statement Ratios
    Profitability Ratios
    Activity Ratios
    Operating Ratios
    Occupancy Ratios
    Stock Valuation Ratios
Rooms Department Ratios
    Profit Margin Ratio
    Labor Cost Percentage
    Average Room Rate
    Occupancy Percentage
Food and Beverage Department Ratios
    Profit Margin Ratio
    Labor Cost Percentage
    Food Cost Percentage
    Prime Cost Percentage
    Beverage Cost Percentage
    Average Food Check
    Average Beverage Check
    Average Total Check
    Inventory Turnover Ratio
    Days' Inventory on Hand Ratio
Hotel Ratios
    Profit Margin Ratio—Hotel
    Profit Margin Ratio—Corporation
    Labor Cost Percentage
    Return on Equity Ratio
    Earnings per Share Ratio
    Price Earnings Ratio
Other Income Statement Ratios
    Number of Times Interest Earned Ratio
    Return on Assets Ratio
Reference List of Ratio Formulas

Learning Objectives

1. Explain the use of ratios in the analysis of a hospitality business income statement, and list the advantages and limitations of their use. (pp. 313–314)

2. Summarize the general categories of popular income statement ratios. (pp. 314–316, 332–333)

3. List the ratios typically used to analyze a hotel rooms department, and describe their formulas and interpretation. (pp. 317–320)

4. List the ratios typically used to analyze a food and beverage department, and describe their formulas and interpretation. (pp. 320–327)

5. List the ratios typically used to analyze a hotel, and describe their formulas and interpretation. (pp. 327–332)

11

Ratio Analysis of the Income Statement

A DETAILED ANALYSIS of an income statement is important because the long-term success of a hospitality business depends upon the realization of profits. Common-size and comparative analysis of an income statement is not sufficient because the results cannot be compared against standard or expected criteria.

The volume of sales reflects the dynamic activity of a hospitality business. An increase in sales volume is not necessarily favorable for profits, and a decrease in sales volume may not be unfavorable in the measurement of profits. The analysis of an income statement requires an in-depth study of the relationships between sales and expenses and a comparison of these relationships with benchmarks.

Ratios express a direct relationship between two relevant items for a period; they are calculated by dividing one figure by another, both for the same accounting period. The use of ratios makes it possible to convert an absolute dollar amount to a number that can be used as a basis to measure against benchmarks of prior years, industry standards, and goals of management. The goals of management are interpreted by the use of forecasts and budgets. The proper use of ratios requires an understanding of the advantages and limitations of ratio analysis.

Advantages of ratio analysis include:

- Ratios are easy to compute and use.
- Ratios provide a basis of comparison against benchmarks established by management and industry studies.
- Ratios can point to problem areas.
- Ratios provide a basis for establishing trends.

Limitations of ratio analysis include:

- A ratio standing alone cannot be properly evaluated.
- Ratios do not solve problems.
- Ratios must be properly interpreted.
- Income statements contain estimates that may influence results.
- A change in accounting procedures may influence ratios.

Any single management tool has limitations; therefore, financial analysis requires the use of dollar income statements that show only absolute amounts, data of prior periods, percentages, and ratios. This chapter presents information about ratios based on financial information from the fictitious Hotel DORO and answers the following questions:

1. What are ratios, and how are they used?
2. What are the advantages and limitations of prior-period ratios, trade association ratios, and budgeted ratios?
3. Which ratios are most commonly used to analyze an income statement?

Ratio Analysis of the Income Statement

Good financial management requires more than common-size or comparative income statements. Therefore, in addition to these different income statements, the accountant provides managers with a number of ratios that will assist them in studying the results of operations.

A ratio is the relationship of one item to another expressed as a number. For example, the relationship of food sales of $358,300 and food covers (customers) of 37,716 results in a $9.50 average food check ($358,300 ÷ 37,716 = $9.50). Ratios may be expressed as percentages, decimals, dollars and cents, or other indices customary to the hospitality industry.

Ratios are a critical part of financial analysis because they point to potential problem areas. A ratio by itself does not give a complete picture. For example, knowing that the average food check is $9.50 is insufficient unless another comparative ratio is provided. When ratios are interpreted, the determination of a favorable or unfavorable condition cannot be made unless there are other measuring devices or standards of comparison. Meaningful ratios that can be used for comparisons are:

- Prior-period ratios
- Industry and trade association ratios
- Budgeted ratios

Prior-Period Ratios

Prior-period ratios provide a basis for comparison with the current period's ratio. For example, assume that the average food check ratios for a business are as follows:

	19X2	19X1	19X0
Average food check	$9.50	$9.45	$9.48

At first glance, the assumption might be that everything is normal. However, what if there had been 5% menu price increases in 19X1 and 19X2? This would mean that the average food check actually is declining. This example illustrates one danger of using results of prior periods for comparisons: the inefficiencies of prior periods may be carried over from one period to the next and remain undetected.

Industry and Trade Association Ratios

Hospitality industry ratios and statistics are published by PKF Consulting, Arthur Andersen, Smith Travel Research, and the National Restaurant Association (for stand-alone restaurants).

Hospitality industry ratios are useful because they represent the average of similar businesses and provide management with uniform ratios that can be used as another measurement tool.

However, industry ratios are not meant to be relied upon as a "yardstick." The timeliness of industry ratios is affected by the delay in collecting the data, then the extensive time for assembling the data, publishing, and distribution.

Furthermore, some members of the industry are in excellent financial condition and have favorable operating results while others are not. Industry ratios come from composite statements and might be affected by the extreme figures of the most successful or unsuccessful companies unless these wide swings are eliminated. (For example, if five companies have a net income of $100,000 each and five other companies have a net income of $10,000 each, the average net income is $55,000. However, only half of the companies are very profitable, and the other half are barely surviving.) Finally, the use of these standards is affected by geographic and demographic factors.

Budgeted Ratios

Budgeted ratios represent the goals of management. They are developed as part of the planning process and are used to measure against actual results. Budgeted ratios are the best form of measurement when they are properly developed.

The validity of budgeted ratios depends on the source of data used in preparing the budget. If only prior years' averages are used, the inconsistencies of the prior periods will be built into the budget. The proper development of a budget requires a study of operating results and up-to-date forecasting techniques and data. Some companies use a budgeting process called **zero base budgeting.** Under this concept, all expenditures are reviewed and must be justified from a starting point of zero. But even zero base budgeting has limitations because of its large volume of paperwork and the difficulties in describing and identifying resources and activities.

Popular Income Statement Ratios

Many ratios are used to analyze the results of operations for operating departments and a hotel as a whole. Some ratio formulas are applicable to all areas (for example, the profit margin ratio) while others can only be used in one department (for example, average room rate). There are differences in the form in which a ratio is expressed, but this dissimilarity does not affect the accuracy or usage of ratio analysis.

The use of a ratio to evaluate items on an income statement requires knowledge of what a ratio measures. Ratios relative to the income statement are used to measure profitability, activity, and operations. The following sections classify ratios according to what they measure and list some of the popular ratios in each classification.

Profitability Ratios

Profitability ratios reflect the effectiveness of management in producing income. Some of the popular ratios used to measure profitability in the hospitality industry are:

- Profit margin ratio (net income to net sales ratio)
- Return on equity ratio

Activity Ratios

Activity ratios measure the effectiveness with which management uses the assets of a hospitality business. Activity ratios are also called *asset management ratios.* Some of the popular ratios used to measure asset management in the hospitality industry are:

- Inventory turnover ratio
- Days' inventory on hand ratio

Operating Ratios

Operating ratios measure the effectiveness with which management controls expenses and the efficiency of operations. Some of the popular ratios used to measure operating efficiency in the hospitality industry are:

- Average room rate
- Food cost percentage
- Labor cost percentage
- Prime cost percentage
- Average food check

Occupancy Ratios

Occupancy ratios measure the success of rooms management in selling the primary product of the hotel or motel. Occupancy ratios can be computed for *paid occupancy, complimentary occupancy, average occupancy,* and *multiple occupancy.* For our purposes, this chapter will work with the paid occupancy ratio and call it:

- Occupancy percentage

Stock Valuation Ratios

Stock valuation ratios are used by investors to determine if they should *buy, hold,* or *sell* the stock of a hospitality corporation. Sometimes these ratios are classified as profitability ratios. However, they are classified separately in this chapter because they only apply to corporations and are used by the investment community. Department managers and executive managers do not use these ratios in their planning, organizing, and controlling functions.

Investors use many tools in deciding the merits of investing in any stock listed on a major stock exchange. The two popular measurements of a stock's value are:

- Earnings per share ratio
- Price earnings ratio

Exhibit 1   Rooms Department Income Statement—Hotel DORO

Hotel DORO, Inc.
Rooms Department Income Statement
For the year ended December 31, 19X2

Revenue

Room Sales	$900,000	
Allowances	2,500	
Net Revenue		$897,500

Expenses

Salaries and Wages	$120,000	
Employee Benefits	23,140	
Total Payroll and Related Expenses		143,140
Other Expenses		
Commissions	2,500	
Contract Cleaning	5,285	
Guest Transportation	10,100	
Laundry and Dry Cleaning	7,000	
Linen	11,000	
Operating Supplies	11,125	
Reservation Expense	9,950	
Uniforms	2,167	
Other Operating Expenses	2,972	
Total Other Expenses		62,099
Total Expenses		205,239
Departmental Income (Loss)		**$692,261**

Rooms Department Ratios

The rooms department ratios in this chapter are computed from the Hotel DORO's departmental income statement illustrated in Exhibit 1. The popular ratios used in analyzing any rooms department are:

* Profit margin ratio
* Labor cost percentage
* Average room rate
* Occupancy percentage

Profit Margin Ratio

The profit margin ratio, also called the **net income to sales ratio**, is used as a measure of *profitability*. It provides the net income on each sales dollar. It is computed by dividing the net income by net sales and is expressed as a *percentage*.

Formula. The profit margin ratio is computed as follows:

$$\frac{\text{Departmental Income}}{\text{Net Sales}}$$

The profit margin ratio for the Hotel DORO's rooms department is computed as follows:

$$\frac{692,261}{897,500} = 77.1\%$$

Interpretation. The average dollar of sales in the rooms department is generating a profit of 77.1%, or it could be stated that the rooms department income is 77¢ on the sales dollar. This profit might seem high, but be aware that building depreciation is charged to the schedule of fixed charges, building maintenance is charged to the property operation and maintenance department, and electricity, water, and heat are charged to the energy costs reporting department.

This ratio should be compared with a benchmark profit margin ratio. If this ratio is *equal* to or *greater* than the benchmark, a preliminary and general assumption is that the condition appears *favorable*. For example, comparing the result of 77.1% with a budgeted profit margin ratio of 75% would indicate that the rooms department has generated the desired profit margin return and has done slightly better.

Labor Cost Percentage

One of the largest expenses for hotels and motels is labor. Labor expense includes total payroll costs and all related expenses, such as benefits and payroll taxes. The **labor cost percentage** is used as a measure of *operating* efficiency and provides the labor cost on each sales dollar.

Formula. The labor cost percentage is computed as follows:

$$\frac{\text{Total Payroll and Related Expenses}}{\text{Net Sales}}$$

The labor cost percentage for the Hotel DORO's rooms department is computed as follows:

$$\frac{143,140}{897,500} = 15.9\%$$

Interpretation. The average labor cost in the rooms department is 15.9% of the sales dollar, or it could be stated that 16¢ of the sales dollar is used to pay labor costs.

This ratio should be compared with a benchmark labor cost ratio. If this ratio is *equal* to or *less* than the benchmark, a preliminary and general assumption is that the condition appears *favorable*. For example, comparing the result of 15.9% with a budgeted ratio of 16% would indicate that the desired goal for operating efficiency has been achieved.

Average Room Rate

While room rates vary depending on the type of room, number of guests, and other factors, it is important to measure the *average selling price,* which is also called **average room rate (ARR)**. This ratio provides the average rate charged per paid room occupied. The ARR is used as a measure of *operations.*

Formula. The ARR is computed as follows:

$$\frac{\text{Net Room Sales}}{\text{Paid Rooms Occupied}}$$

An income statement is not sufficient to calculate ARR, which is also called **average daily rate (ADR)**. Statistics not appearing on the income statement must be maintained separately for the paid rooms occupied during the related period. There were 17,950 total paid rooms occupied for the Hotel DORO during the year 19X2. The ARR for the Hotel DORO's rooms department is computed as follows:

$$\frac{897,500}{17,950} = \$50.00$$

Interpretation. Taking all rooms into consideration, the average selling price was $50.00, with some rooms selling for more and others for less.

This ratio should be compared with a benchmark ratio. If this ratio is *equal* to or *greater* than the benchmark, a preliminary and general assumption is that the condition appears *favorable.* For example, comparing the result of $50.00 with a budgeted ratio of $48.00 would indicate that the average selling price has improved; this could be attributable to factors such as less discounting, selling more higher-priced rooms, better economic conditions, and other factors.

Occupancy Percentage

The **occupancy percentage** is important because it measures rooms sales in terms of the hotel's capacity to generate rooms sold. This *occupancy* percentage requires a hotel or motel to keep separate statistical information during a period for data such as rooms available to sell, complimentary rooms, and paid rooms occupied.

Formula. The paid occupancy percentage is computed as follows:

$$\frac{\text{Paid Rooms Occupied}}{\text{Rooms Available}}$$

The Hotel DORO is a 75-room hotel. All these rooms were available for sale during the year. The hotel is not a resort hotel. Its operations calendar is 365 days. There were 17,950 paid rooms occupied for the hotel during the year 19X2. The paid occupancy percentage for the Hotel DORO's rooms department is computed as follows:

$$\frac{17,950}{75 \times 365} = \frac{17,950}{27,375} = 66\%$$

Exhibit 2   Food and Beverage Department Income Statement—Hotel DORO

	Food	Beverage	Total
Hotel DORO, Inc.			
Food and Beverage Department Income Statement			
For the year ended December 31, 19X2			

	Food	Beverage	Total
Revenue	$360,000	$160,000	$520,000
Allowances	1,700	130	1,830
Net Revenue	358,300	159,870	518,170
Cost of Sales:			
Beginning Inventory	5,800	3,000	
Purchases	145,600	40,310	
Available	151,400	43,310	
Ending Inventory	7,000	2,800	
Cost of Goods Used	144,400	40,510	184,910
Cost of Employee Meals	9,200		9,200
Cost of Goods Sold	135,200	40,510	175,710
Net Other Income			3,800
Gross Profit			346,260
Operating Expenses:			
Total Payroll and Related Expenses			204,180
Total Other Operating Expenses			54,703
Departmental Income			$ 87,377

Interpretation. The result shows that the Hotel DORO rented 66% of its room nights available. As with any average calculation, care must be taken in interpreting the information. The occupancy percentage of any hotel varies from day to day and month to month. Any average statistical information tends to disguise these variations.

This ratio should be compared with a benchmark ratio. If this ratio is *equal* to or *greater* than the benchmark, a preliminary and general assumption is that the condition appears *favorable*. For example, comparing the result of 66% with a budgeted ratio of 60% would indicate that occupancy has improved. This could be due to an effective advertising program, local special tourist attractions, better economic conditions, and other factors.

Food and Beverage Department Ratios

The food and beverage (F&B) department ratios in this chapter are computed from the Hotel DORO's departmental income statement illustrated in Exhibit 2. The popular ratios used in analyzing any F&B department are:

- Profit margin ratio
- Labor cost percentage

- Food cost percentage
- Prime cost percentage
- Beverage cost percentage
- Average food check
- Average beverage check
- Average total check
- Inventory turnover ratio
- Days' inventory on hand ratio

Profit Margin Ratio

The profit margin ratio for the F&B department is calculated in the same manner as that discussed for the rooms department and provides the same measurement of *profitability*. However, net sales of the F&B department needs definition. Does net sales include only food and beverage sales, or should it also include other revenue such as cover charges, souvenirs, and candy? It is not important how net sales is defined providing that the definition is used consistently and the benchmarks are composed of the same elements.

Formula. The profit margin ratio is computed as follows:

$$\frac{\text{Departmental Income}}{\text{Net Sales}}$$

The Hotel DORO excludes other revenue from its F&B departmental net sales. The profit margin ratio for the hotel's F&B department is computed as follows:

$$\frac{87,377}{518,170} = 16.9\%$$

Interpretation. The average dollar of sales in the F&B department is generating a profit of 16.9%, or it could be stated that F&B departmental income is 17¢ on the sales dollar. This profit cannot be measured against a stand-alone restaurant because an independent restaurant operation has the following expenses on its income statement: depreciation, repairs and maintenance, electricity, water, heat, administrative and general (A&G), marketing, and fixed charges.

This ratio should be compared with a benchmark profit margin ratio. If this ratio is *equal* to or *greater* than the benchmark, a preliminary and general assumption is that the condition appears *favorable*. For example, comparing the result of 16.9% with a budgeted profit margin ratio of 16% would indicate that the F&B department has generated the desired profit margin return and has done slightly better.

Labor Cost Percentage

The labor cost percentage for the F&B department is calculated in the same manner as that discussed for the rooms department and provides the same *operating* measurement.

Formula. The labor cost percentage is computed as follows:

$$\frac{\text{Total Payroll and Related Expenses}}{\text{Net Sales}}$$

The Hotel DORO excludes other revenue from its departmental net sales. The labor cost percentage for the hotel's F&B department is computed as follows:

$$\frac{204,180}{518,170} = 39.4\%$$

Interpretation. The average labor cost in the F&B department is 39.4% of the sales dollar, or it could be stated that 40¢ of the sales dollar is used to pay labor costs.

This ratio should be compared with a benchmark labor cost ratio. If this ratio is *equal* to or *less* than the benchmark, a preliminary and general assumption is that the condition appears *favorable*. For example, comparing the result of 39.4% with a budgeted ratio of 40% would indicate that the desired goal for operating efficiency has been achieved.

Food Cost Percentage

The **food cost percentage** for the F&B department is calculated in nearly the same manner as the labor cost percentage except that food cost is the numerator in the formula. The food cost ratio excludes beverage costs and beverage sales.

This ratio shows the cost of food per dollar of sales. It is a key *operating* ratio popular with most food service managers for evaluating and controlling food costs.

Formula. The food cost percentage is computed as follows:

$$\frac{\text{Cost of Food Sold}}{\text{Net Food Sales}}$$

The food cost percentage for the Hotel DORO's F&B department is computed as follows:

$$\frac{135,200}{358,300} = 37.7\%$$

Interpretation. The average cost of food used to serve guests is 37.7% of the sales dollar, or it could be stated that 38¢ of the sales dollar is used to pay for food prepared for guest consumption.

This ratio should be compared with a benchmark food cost ratio. If this ratio is *equal* to or *less* than the benchmark, a preliminary and general assumption is that the condition appears *favorable*. For example, comparing the result of 37.7% with a budgeted ratio of 38% would indicate that the desired goal for operating efficiency has been achieved.

However, caution is necessary when judging if results are favorable or unfavorable. It is possible for this ratio to be manipulated even if the actual sales volume is identical to the forecasted sales volume. Substituting a lower-quality product or reducing portion size will lower the food cost ratio. A high food cost ratio could be the result of poor portion control, poor purchasing practices at high costs, spoilage, or theft. Another factor affecting the food cost ratio is menu pricing. With no changes in quality or food costs, the food cost ratio can be reduced merely by increasing menu prices.

Prime Cost Percentage

Prime costs refer to the total labor and materials used in the production or selling process. Prime costs for the F&B department are total labor costs and total cost of sales. This *operating* measurement is more meaningful if it is prepared separately for food prime costs. However, this is not always possible because of the difficulties of separating labor applicable to food and labor applicable to beverages.

The Hotel DORO does not separate food labor from beverage labor. However, the consistent application of this percentage will lend itself to proper measurement and interpretation for the hotel.

Formula. The prime cost percentage is computed as follows:

$$\frac{\text{Total Cost of Sales } + \text{ Total Payroll and Related Expenses}}{\text{Net Sales}}$$

The prime cost percentage for the Hotel DORO's F&B department is computed as follows:

$$\frac{157,710 + 204,180}{518,170} = 73.3\%$$

Interpretation. The prime costs for labor and food used to provide guest service are 73.3% of the sales dollar, or it could be stated that 73¢ of the sales dollar is used to pay prime costs, leaving 27¢ of the sales dollar to cover kitchen fuel, laundry, menus, uniforms, china, and other operating expenses.

This ratio should be compared with a benchmark ratio. If this ratio is *equal* to or *less* than the benchmark, a preliminary and general assumption is that the condition appears *favorable*. For example, comparing the result of 73.3% with a budgeted ratio of 75% would indicate that the desired goal for operating efficiency has been achieved.

Beverage Cost Percentage

The **beverage cost percentage** is calculated in the same manner as the food cost percentage except that only costs and sales applicable to beverages are in the formula. This *operating* measurement for beverage cost does not include any food costs or food sales.

Formula. The beverage cost percentage is computed as follows:

$$\frac{\text{Cost of Beverages Sold}}{\text{Net Beverage Sales}}$$

The beverage cost percentage for the Hotel DORO's F&B department is computed as follows:

$$\frac{40,510}{159,870} = 25.3\%$$

Interpretation. The average cost of beverages used to serve guests is 25.3% of the sales dollar, or it could be stated that 25¢ of the sales dollar goes to materials used in preparing guest beverages.

This ratio should be compared with a benchmark beverage cost ratio. If this ratio is *equal* to or *less* than the benchmark, a preliminary and general assumption is that the condition appears *favorable*. For example, comparing the result of 25.3% with a budgeted ratio of 26% would indicate that the desired goal for operating efficiency has been achieved.

The cautions involved in interpreting the food cost percentage also apply to this ratio. Quality is a factor in the preparation of alcoholic beverages because of the wide price variation between well brands (lower-cost, lesser-known brands of liquor) and call brands (higher-priced and specifically ordered by the guest). Portion control is also an important issue in a bar operation and an integral part of any food and beverage operations management course.

Average Food Check

The **average food check** for a food service operation represents the average sale per **cover**. The term "covers" refers to the number of guests served in a food service operation during a specific period. This *operating* ratio should be computed separately for the dining room, cafeteria, snack bar, and other facilities because of the wide variations in menu prices at these locations within a hotel.

Formula. The average food check is computed as follows:

$$\frac{\text{Net Food Sales}}{\text{Covers}}$$

The number of guests served during 19X2 in the Hotel DORO's food service operation was 37,716. The average food check for the hotel is computed as follows:

$$\frac{358,300}{37,716} = \$9.50$$

Interpretation. The average food check for the period was $9.50, which did not include any alcoholic beverage sales.

This ratio should be compared with a benchmark ratio. If this ratio is *equal* to or *greater* than the benchmark, a preliminary and general assumption is that the condition appears *favorable*. For example, comparing the result of $9.50 with a budgeted ratio of $9.25 would indicate that the desired goal for operating efficiency has been achieved. This could be due to menu price increases or guests selecting more expensive menu items.

Average Beverage Check

The procedure for computing the average beverage check is identical to that explained for the average food check except that beverage sales is substituted for food sales.

Average Total Check

The average total check includes the sales of food and beverages for a cover. Its computation is identical to that explained for the average food check except that the total of food and beverage sales is substituted for food sales.

Inventory Turnover Ratio

The **inventory turnover ratio** indicates how fast inventory moves through a hospitality business. The inventory turnover ratio shows *activity* by measuring the number of times inventory turns over relative to demand and is a good *asset management* tool. Turnover should be computed separately for the food inventory and the beverage inventory.

The food inventory turnover is an average turnover of all items such as perishables, canned goods, and frozen foods. Since some of these products move faster than others, an *average* inventory turnover may seem high for some items and low for others. However, this limitation can be overcome by comparing this period's turnover with prior-period ratios, budgeted ratios, and industry standards.

Similarly, the separately computed beverage turnover is an average turnover of all alcoholic beverages including expensive wines that might not move as rapidly as beer, house wines, and liquor.

The inventory turnover ratio is an indication of how well the funds invested in food and beverage inventories are being managed. A decrease in inventory turnover might indicate that the size of the inventory relative to sales is increasing unnecessarily. Having an inventory larger than required to meet sales demand ties up funds and may also increase food cost due to spoilage and other factors.

Formula. The inventory turnover ratio formula uses an average of the inventories for the period. The average inventory is computed by adding the beginning and ending inventories and then dividing this total by 2. If the beginning and ending inventories are not shown on the F&B department income statement, it will be necessary to find these on the cost of sales supplementary schedule, balance sheet, or footnotes to the balance sheet. In using inventory figures, one must be careful to ensure that the food inventory amount is stated separately from the beverage inventory amount. The F&B department income statement shown in Exhibit 2 does show the required inventory data.

If *cost of food used* is not available, then the *cost of food sold* may be used. Because employee meals are a small part of food used, either number may be used without distorting the inventory turnover for a period. Regardless of which number is used, it should be used consistently.

The average food inventory turnover ratio is computed as follows:

$$\frac{\text{Cost of Food Used}}{\textit{Average} \text{ Food Inventory}}$$

The food inventory turnover ratio for the Hotel DORO's F&B department is computed as follows:

$$\frac{144,400}{(5,800 + 7,000) \div 2} = \frac{144,400}{6,400} = 23 \text{ Times}$$

The beverage inventory turnover ratio for the Hotel DORO's F&B department is computed as follows:

$$\frac{\text{Cost of Beverages Used}}{\textit{Average} \text{ Beverage Inventory}}$$

$$\frac{40,510}{(3,000 + 2,800) \div 2} = \frac{40,510}{2,900} = 14 \text{ Times}$$

Interpretation. Notice that the inventory turnover figures have a label of "Times." The term "times" refers to the number of times the *complete* inventory, on average, has been *purchased* and *used* (sold). It takes both the purchase and use to equal a cycle of 1 time.

Interpreting any inventory turnover ratio requires careful attention to the time period involved. One must know if the data used results in an inventory turnover ratio for a month, year, or other period.

In the case of the Hotel DORO, the data was from the year ended; therefore, the ratios represent the average food and beverage inventory turnovers for the current year. The annual beverage inventory turnover of 14 times divided by 12 converts to an average monthly turnover of 1 time.

If management requests information about a specific month's turnover, the computation is performed by dividing the food used for that month by the average of the inventories (beginning inventory for that *month* plus the ending inventory of the period divided by 2).

Generally, a high inventory turnover ratio indicates a favorable condition because it shows that less investment in the inventory is required. However, a high turnover might also mean that too little inventory is carried and frequent stock-outs will occur. A stock-out results in poor guest service and in the long run may prove costly because of loss of repeat business. A low turnover might mean that excessive stock is on hand relative to sales demand, resulting in unnecessary use of cash and possibly increased spoilage.

What is the best inventory turnover ratio? The answer depends on the kind of food service operation, management's policy on customer service, and the use of fresh goods versus canned and frozen goods. Therefore, budgeted ratios based on these factors appear to be the best benchmarks for any particular hospitality business. A new restaurant operation might refer to industry standards, also called "norms," as a guide in setting turnover goals.

Hospitality Industry Turnover Norms. The Hotel DORO's food inventory turnover of 23 times for the year converts to a turnover of 2 times per month. At first glance, one might consider this turnover to be too low. However, the hotel's management has a policy of quality service and quality food at its fine-dining restaurant. A ratio of 2 times per month falls within the low end of the industry norm.

Fine dining restaurants will have low turnovers. A quick-service restaurant will have extremely high food inventory turnovers, sometimes in excess of 200 times in a year (17 times a month). The industry norms for hotels having several types of restaurants are as follows:

	Per Year	Per Month
Food inventory turnover	48	4
Beverage inventory turnover	15	1

These turnovers are generally considered satisfactory to maintain sales levels at reasonable cost. However, there are always exceptions. In addition to type of service, type of menu, and customer service policies, another factor a food service operation must consider is the frequency of delivery by suppliers. This is especially true of remote resort locations and franchised operations.

Days' Inventory on Hand Ratio

This ratio measures the average number of days that inventory is on hand before being used. This ratio is calculated simply by dividing 365 days (or less for seasonal operations) by the annual inventory turnover ratio. The days' inventory on hand ratio provides another way of evaluating inventory activity for proper asset management.

Formula. The days' inventory on hand ratio is computed as follows:

$$\frac{365 \text{ Days}}{\text{Annual Inventory Turnover Ratio}}$$

The average number of days the food inventory was in stock for the Hotel DORO can be calculated by referring to the annual food inventory turnover previously calculated and computing as follows:

$$\frac{365}{23} = 16 \text{ Days}$$

Interpretation. Generally, a low number of days' inventory on hand is desired. However, the same considerations discussed for the inventory turnover ratio apply to the measurement of the days' inventory on hand ratio.

Hotel Ratios

A hotel may be only one of several properties that make up a business corporation. There are ratios to measure the activities of a single property and other ratios to measure the activities of a corporation (the sum of all its locations). Ratios used to measure corporate activities cannot be applied to a single property because it is the corporation that issues stock.

The popular ratios used in analyzing any single hotel property are:

- Profit margin ratio
- Labor cost percentage

The popular ratios used in analyzing any hotel corporation are:

- Profit margin ratio
- Return on equity ratio

Exhibit 3   Long-Form Income Statement—Hotel DORO

Hotel DORO, Inc.
Statement of Income
For the year ended December 31, 19X2

	Schedule	Net Revenue	Cost of Sales	Payroll and Related Expenses	Other Expenses	Income (Loss)
Operated Departments						
Rooms	A1	$ 897,500		$143,140	$ 62,099	$ 692,261
Food and Beverage	A2	524,570	$178,310	204,180	54,703	87,377
Telephone	A3	51,140	60,044	17,132	1,587	(27,623)
Other Operated Departments	A4	63,000	10,347	33,276	6,731	12,646
Rentals and Other Income	A5	61,283				61,283
Total Operated Departments		1,597,493	248,701	397,728	125,120	825,944
Undistributed Expenses						
Administrative and General	A6			97,632	66,549	164,181
Marketing	A7			35,825	32,043	67,868
Property Operation and Maintenance	A8			36,917	24,637	61,554
Energy Costs	A9				47,312	47,312
Total Undistributed Expenses				170,374	170,541	340,915
Income Before Fixed Charges		$1,597,493	$248,701	$568,102	$295,661	$ 485,029
Fixed Charges						
Rent	A10					28,500
Property Taxes	A10					45,324
Insurance	A10					6,914
Interest	A10					192,153
Depreciation and Amortization	A10					146,000
Total Fixed Charges						418,891
Income Before Income Taxes and Gain on Sale of Property						66,138
Gain on Sale of Property						10,500
Income Before Income Taxes						76,638
Income Taxes						16,094
Net Income						$ 60,544

- Earnings per share ratio
- Price earnings ratio

The Hotel DORO is a single property in a one-property corporation. Therefore, our discussion will cover all of the listed single-property and corporate ratios. The ratios for the Hotel DORO will be computed from its income statement, illustrated in Exhibit 3.

Profit Margin Ratio—Hotel

The profit margin ratio for a hotel is computed in a procedure identical to those previously discussed for individual departments. In the case of a hotel, the ratio provides a mixed measure of *profitability* because it is based on sales of all revenue centers and its income is the result of all departments of the hotel.

Formula. The profit margin ratio for a hotel is computed as follows:

$$\frac{\text{Net Income}}{\text{Net Sales}}$$

The profit margin ratio for the Hotel DORO is computed as follows:

$$\frac{60{,}544}{1{,}597{,}493} = 3.8\%$$

Interpretation. The hotel's average dollar of sales from all revenue centers is generating a profit of 3.8%, or it could be stated that the hotel keeps about 4¢ of each sales dollar. Unlike the amount in a departmental analysis, this amount is after income taxes.

This ratio should be compared with a benchmark profit margin ratio. If the ratio is *equal* to or *greater* than the benchmark, a preliminary and general assumption is that the condition appears *favorable.*

Profit Margin Ratio—Corporation

The profit margin ratio for a corporation is computed using the same formula as for a hotel. Since the Hotel DORO is a single-property corporation, both the hotel profit margin ratio and corporate profit margin ratio would be identical.

Labor Cost Percentage

One of the largest expenses for hotels and motels is labor. Labor expense includes total payroll costs and all the related expenses such as benefits and payroll taxes. The labor cost percentage for a hotel is computed using a procedure identical to that previously discussed for the individual departments. In the case of a hotel, the ratio gives a mixed measure of labor costs because it is based on sales of all revenue centers and its labor cost is the result of all departments of the hotel.

Formula. The labor cost percentage is computed as follows:

$$\frac{\text{Total Payroll and Related Expenses}}{\text{Net Sales}}$$

The labor cost percentage for the Hotel DORO includes the labor costs of revenue centers and support centers. It is computed as follows:

$$\frac{568{,}102}{1{,}597{,}493} = 35.6$$

Interpretation. The average labor cost for the hotel is 35.6% of the sales dollar, or it could be stated that 36¢ of the sales dollar is used to pay labor costs.

This ratio should be compared with a benchmark labor cost ratio. If this ratio is *equal* to or *less* than the benchmark, a preliminary and general assumption is that the condition appears *favorable.*

Exhibit 4   Equity Section of Balance Sheet—Hotel DORO

	December 31	
	19X2	19X1
SHAREHOLDERS' EQUITY		
Common Stock Issued, $1 Par	$ 50,000	$ 50,000
Additional Paid-In Capital	700,000	700,000
Retained Earnings	318,662	278,118
Total Shareholders' Equity	$1,068,662	$1,028,118

Return on Equity Ratio

The return on equity ratio measures the profit after taxes of the hospitality corporation relative to the equity of its owners (shareholders). **Equity** represents the retained earnings of the corporation and proceeds from its sale of stock (common stock issued + paid-in capital). The equity amount comes from the *balance sheet.* Therefore, the computation of this ratio requires both an income statement and a balance sheet.

Formula. The formula for this ratio depends on the capitalization of the corporation, which might consist of both common and preferred stock. If only common stock is issued, the following formula is used:

$$\frac{\text{Net Income}}{\textit{Average} \text{ Equity}}$$

Average equity is the equity at the beginning of the year added to the equity at the end of the year, divided by 2. Remember that balance sheet data at the end of a year becomes the beginning data for the next year.

The equity section of the Hotel DORO's balance sheet is shown in Exhibit 4. It is used with the net income shown in Exhibit 3, the corporation's income statement. The return on equity ratio for the hotel is computed as follows:

$$\frac{60,544}{(1,068,662 + 1,028,118) \div 2} = \frac{60,544}{1,048,390} = 5.8\%$$

Interpretation. The rate of return after taxes using shareholders' equity is 5.8%, which is almost a 6% return. This amount is after taxes. If a comparison is made to money market rates, the stated money market rates must be reduced by the effect of income taxes (state and federal).

This ratio should be compared with a benchmark profit margin ratio. Like any other type of *profitability ratio,* if this ratio is *equal* to or *greater* than the benchmark, a preliminary and general assumption is that the condition appears *favorable.*

Formula if Preferred Stock Is Issued. If preferred stock is issued, the formula is modified to measure the *return on common stockholders' equity.* The formula is modified as follows:

$$\frac{\text{Net Income Less Preferred Dividends}}{\text{Average Common Shareholders' Equity}}$$

The Hotel DORO has only common stock issued, and this calculation is not necessary.

Earnings per Share

The **earnings per share (EPS) ratio** is a corporation's net income divided by the number of common shares issued and outstanding. For the moment, the EPS ratio will be discussed in its simplest form.

Formula. The EPS is computed as follows:

$$\frac{\text{Net Income}}{\textit{Average} \text{ Common Stock Outstanding}}$$

The Hotel DORO's common shares issued represent common stock outstanding because there is no treasury stock. Also, the common stock outstanding has not changed between January 1, 19X2 and December 31, 19X2 (see the equity section of the balance sheet shown in Exhibit 4). The hotel's common stock is $1 par value, thus there are 50,000 common shares issued and outstanding.

The EPS for the Hotel DORO is computed as follows:

$$\frac{60{,}544}{50{,}000} = \$1.21$$

Interpretation. Each share of the Hotel DORO's stock earned $1.21 after taxes. Investors expect a *growth* company to have increasing EPS in each successive reporting period. The significance of the use of EPS in measuring a stock's value will become apparent when the price earnings ratio is discussed.

Complications in Computing. Computing EPS for the Hotel DORO is quick and easy because it has a *simple capital structure,* meaning that the corporation has no convertible preferred stock, convertible bonds, or options. If the holders of convertible securities and options exercise their conversion privileges, the number of outstanding common shares will increase. Corporations that have convertible securities or options have a *complex capital structure.*

A corporation with a complex capital structure will eventually incur a dilution to its EPS because more common stock will eventually be issued. Therefore, the EPS formula must be modified to account for diluted earnings per share. These calculations are very technical, lengthy, and complex. Their computation is best left to the professional accountant.

Price Earnings Ratio

The **price earnings (PE) ratio** is a popular ratio used by the investment community to evaluate whether a stock is reasonably priced. This ratio is computed for both current earnings and forecasted earnings. Investment reports, financial periodicals, and financial sections of newspapers widely use and display the PE ratio.

Formula. The PE ratio is computed as follows:

$$\frac{\text{Market Price per Share}}{\text{Earnings per Share}}$$

Previously, the EPS for the Hotel DORO was computed at $1.21 per share. Assume the stock is listed on a major stock exchange at $15.00 per share. The PE ratio for the hotel's stock is computed as follows:

$$\frac{15.00}{1.21} = 12$$

Interpretation. While not conclusive, any PE ratio higher than that of other companies in the same industry might indicate that a stock is fully priced or possibly overpriced. In the case of the Hotel DORO, if the stocks of other similar companies listed on the stock exchange are selling at a PE ratio of 15, then the hotel might be considered an attractive *buy* situation, assuming there is a growth pattern to earnings or other fundamental factors that might benefit earnings.

The EPS and PE ratios are only some of the measurements used by investment analysts and investors. Even though the use of these ratios might prove attractive, investing in the stock market requires specialized knowledge of technical factors and other considerations.

Considerations in Calculating. Typically, the net income should exclude extraordinary items that are not recurring in the normal course of business. In the case of the Hotel DORO, earnings were inflated by the gain on the sale of property. Therefore, the investment community would calculate the EPS and PE ratios in the following ways:

- Based on total net income

- Based on income before extraordinary items

The allocation of income taxes becomes a problem in these computations, and the necessary technical procedures are best left to the professional accountant.

Other Income Statement Ratios

The study of ratios can be never-ending because ratios are the relationships between two numbers. This chapter has presented the more popular and common ratios. However, the chapter would not be complete without presenting other ratios that are used in evaluating the income statement.

Number of Times Interest Earned Ratio

The **number of times interest earned ratio** shows the number of times the interest expense is covered by earnings. Although a business may be heavily financed by debt, its earnings may be adequate to pay the interest expense.

Formula. This ratio is computed as follows:

$$\frac{\text{Net Income} + \text{Income Taxes} + \text{Interest}}{\text{Interest Expense}}$$

The number of times interest earned ratio for the Hotel DORO is computed as follows:

$$\frac{60{,}544 + 16{,}094 + 192{,}153}{192{,}153} = \frac{268{,}791}{192{,}153} = 1.4 \text{ Times}$$

Interpretation. A ratio of less than 1 would indicate that the current earnings are not sufficient to meet interest expense.

Return on Assets Ratio

The **return on assets (ROA) ratio** measures how productively the assets have been used to generate net income.

Formula. This ratio is computed as follows:

$$\frac{\text{Net Income}}{\text{Average Total Assets}}$$

The total assets from the balance sheet (not shown) for the Hotel DORO are $3,292,371 on December 31, 19X1 and $3,247,412 on December 31, 19X2. The ROA would be calculated as follows:

$$\frac{60{,}544}{(3{,}292{,}371 + 3{,}247{,}412) \div 2} = 1.9\%$$

Interpretation. The corporation generates a profit after taxes of 1.9% for each dollar of its assets (at book value). Depreciation policies will affect the comparability of this ratio because *total* assets is a base. This ratio should be compared with prior-period ratios or budgeted ratios.

Reference List of Ratio Formulas

This list shows the major ratios and their formulas and is intended to be a convenient source of reference.

Average Food Check	$\dfrac{\text{Net Food Sales}}{\text{Covers}}$
Average Room Rate	$\dfrac{\text{Net Room Sales}}{\text{Paid Rooms Occupied}}$
Days' Inventory on Hand Ratio	$\dfrac{365 \text{ Days (or operating year)}}{\text{Annual Inventory Turnover Ratio}}$
Earnings per Share Ratio	$\dfrac{\text{Net Income}}{\textit{Average} \text{ Common Stock Outstanding}}$

Food Cost Percentage

$$\frac{\text{Cost of Food Sold}}{\text{Net Food Sales}}$$

Food Inventory Turnover Ratio

$$\frac{\text{Cost of Food Used}}{\textit{Average} \text{ Food Inventory}}$$

Beverage Inventory Turnover Ratio

$$\frac{\text{Cost of Beverages Used}}{\textit{Average} \text{ Beverage Inventory}}$$

Labor Cost Percentage

$$\frac{\text{Total Payroll and Related Expenses}}{\text{Net Sales}}$$

Number of Times Interest Earned Ratio

$$\frac{\text{Net Income} + \text{Income Taxes} + \text{Interest}}{\text{Interest Expense}}$$

Occupancy Percentage

$$\frac{\text{Paid Rooms Occupied}}{\text{Rooms Available}}$$

Price Earnings Ratio

$$\frac{\text{Market Price per Share}}{\text{Earnings per Share}}$$

Prime Cost Percentage

$$\frac{\text{Cost of Sales} + \text{Payroll and Related Expenses}}{\text{Net Sales}}$$

Profit Margin Ratio

$$\frac{\text{Net Income (or Departmental Income)}}{\text{Net Sales}}$$

Return on Assets Ratio

$$\frac{\text{Net Income}}{\text{Average Total Assets}}$$

Return on Equity Ratio

$$\frac{\text{Net Income}}{\textit{Average} \text{ Equity}}$$

Key Terms

average daily rate (ADR)
average food check
average room rate (ARR)
beverage cost percentage
cover
earnings per share (EPS) ratio
equity
food cost percentage
inventory turnover ratio

labor cost percentage
net income to sales ratio
number of times interest earned ratio
occupancy percentage
price earnings (PE) ratio
prime costs
ratios
return on assets (ROA) ratio
zero base budgeting

Review Questions

1. What is a ratio?

2. What are the advantages and limitations of ratio analysis?

3. How can a ratio be used to determine if a condition is favorable or unfavorable?

4. Which specific ratios can be used by a rooms department manager to evaluate profitability, operations efficiency, and asset management?

5. Which specific ratios can be used by a food service manager to evaluate profitability, operations efficiency, and asset management?

6. Which two ratios are most frequently used to measure a stock's value?

7. How is a rooms department profit margin ratio of 72% interpreted?

8. How is a food cost percentage of 30% interpreted?

9. What do the acronyms "ARR" and "ADR" represent?

10. What factors may reduce a food cost percentage?

11. What are prime costs?

12. What are covers?

13. What is the monthly inventory turnover for a food service operation that has experienced an annual inventory turnover ratio of 60 times?

14. What is the formula for each of the following ratios as applicable to a rooms department analysis?

    Average room rate
    Labor cost percentage
    Occupancy percentage
    Profit margin ratio

15. What is the formula for each of the following ratios as applicable to a food service department analysis?

    Average food check
    Inventory turnover ratio
    Days' inventory on hand ratio
    Food cost percentage
    Labor cost percentage
    Prime cost percentage
    Profit margin ratio

16. What is the formula for each of the following ratios as applicable to a corporate income statement analysis?

    Earnings per share ratio
    Price earnings ratio
    Profit margin ratio
    Return on equity ratio

17. Which of the following ratios is expressed as a percentage?

   Average food check
   Average room rate
   Days' inventory on hand ratio
   Earnings per share ratio
   Food cost percentage
   Inventory turnover ratio
   Labor cost percentage
   Occupancy percentage
   Price earnings ratio
   Profit margin ratio
   Return on equity ratio

Problems

Problem 1

Compute the food cost percentage (with two decimals) from the following information:

Food sales	$345,000
Allowances	3,000
Cost of food sold	95,000

Problem 2

Compute the beverage cost percentage (with two decimals) from the following information:

	Food	Beverage
Sales	$596,000	$150,000
Allowances	3,000	1,000
Cost of sales	170,000	30,000

Problem 3

Compute the food inventory turnover ratio (with one decimal) from the following information:

Food sales		$345,000
Allowances		3,000
Net sales		342,000
Cost of food sold:		
Beginning inventory	$ 2,800	
Purchases	105,000	
Available	107,800	
Ending inventory	1,600	
Food used	106,200	
Employee meals	2,200	
Cost of food sold		104,000
Gross profit		238,000

Problem 4

What was a hotel's current labor expense if its labor cost percentage was 40% and its net sales were $800,000?

Problem 5

What was the gross profit percentage if a food service operation had a food cost of 28%?

Problem 6

What was a hotel's current net income if its profit margin ratio was 8% and its net sales were $2,000,000?

Problem 7

The following supplementary information and income statement is provided for The Garden Bistro, Inc. for its year ended December, 19X8.

    Supplementary Information
        Food covers: 21,250
        Common stock issued and outstanding: 25,000 shares (all year)
        Common stock quotation, end of year: $12.00 per share
        Inventory 12/31/X7: $2,100
        Inventory 12/31/X8: $2,400
        Shareholders' equity 12/31/X7: $83,000
        Shareholders' equity 12/31/X8: $98,000

The Garden Bistro, Inc.
Income Statement
For the year ended December 31, 19X8

Net Food Sales		$170,000
Cost of Food Used	$54,000	
Employee Meals	1,000	
Cost of Food Sold		53,000
Gross Profit		117,000
Operating Expenses:		
Payroll	55,000	
Payroll Taxes and Benefits	7,900	
Laundry	2,100	
Supplies	1,500	
Advertising	2,000	
Utilities	3,800	
Repairs	1,900	
Other	6,200	
Total Operating Expenses		80,400

Income Before Fixed Charges and Income Taxes	36,600
Fixed Charges	19,600
Income Before Income Taxes	17,000
Income Taxes	2,000
Net Income	$ 15,000

Instructions:

1. Compute the following ratios.
2. Unless the ratio result is stated in dollars and cents, show the computed result with one decimal, properly rounded (xx.x).

Average food check	Inventory turnover ratio
Food cost percentage	Days' inventory on hand ratio
Labor cost percentage	Earnings per share ratio
Prime cost percentage	Price earnings ratio
Profit margin ratio	
Return on equity ratio	

Problem 8

A 120-room hotel with a 365-day year sold 25,864 rooms (paid occupancy of $1,463,902)for the year. Compute its occupancy ratio (as a whole number) and average room rate for that year.

Problem 9

A hotel had 400 rooms available for sale on February 21. The paid room occupancy was $18,077 on 289 rooms sold for that evening. Compute the following ratios for February 21:

Occupancy percent (show answer as a whole number)
Average room rate

Problem 10

In July, a hotel had a daily capacity of 540 rooms available for sale. The paid room occupancy was $506,340 on 8,730 room nights sold. Compute the occupancy percent (as a whole number) based on rooms available to sell for the month of July.

Problem 11

Executive managers of the Dermonel National Hotels, Inc. have completed analyzing the income statement for the current period. Compare the results against the budgeted goals and indicate whether the results are favorable or unfavorable. Do not consider any other factors but the ratio numbers provided.

	Actual	Budget
Average room rate	$120.00	$118.00
Occupancy percentage	68%	72%
Average food check	$12.00	$11.15

	Actual	Budget
Food cost percentage	31%	32%
Labor cost percentage	34%	34%
Inventory turnover ratio	48	41
Profit margin ratio	12%	10%
Return on equity ratio	18%	22%

REVIEW QUIZ

When you feel you have covered all of the material in this chapter, answer these questions. Choose the *best* answer. Check your answers with the correct ones found on the Review Quiz Answer Key at the end of this book.

True (T) or False (F)

T   F   1. Activity ratios reflect management's ability to use a property's assets.

T   F   2. One of the largest expenses for hotels and motels is labor.

T   F   3. Fine dining restaurants generally have low inventory turnover.

T   F   4. Ratios are used to measure only the activities of a single property.

Multiple Choice

5. Hospitality industry ratios:

   a. are the most up-to-date ratios available.
   b. are affected by the delay in collecting data and distribution.
   c. deal primarily with occupancy percentages.
   d. a and c

6. Which of the following types of ratios represent the goals of management?

   a. prior-period ratios
   b. industry ratios
   c. budgeted ratios
   d. stock valuation ratios

7. The occupancy percentage is computed by:

   a. dividing paid rooms occupied by rooms available.
   b. dividing rooms available by paid rooms occupied.
   c. dividing paid rooms occupied by net room sales.
   d. dividing net room sales by paid rooms occupied.

8. Which of the following terms refers to the total labor and materials used in a production or selling process?

   a. benchmarks
   b. prime costs
   c. equity
   d. expense margin

9. The inventory turnover ratio formula uses:

   a. the beginning inventory amount.
   b. the ending inventory amount.
   c. the number of days in the operating year.
   d. an average of inventories for the period.

10. Which of the following ratios is popular with the investment community for evaluating whether a stock is reasonably priced?

    a. industry ratio
    b. return on equity ratio
    c. price earnings ratio
    d. earnings per share ratio

Chapter Outline

Elements and Conventions
Assets
    Current Assets
    Noncurrent Assets
Liabilities
    Current Liabilities
    Long-Term Liabilities
Equity
Hotel Balance Sheet Formats
The Hotel DORO's Balance Sheet
    Common-Size Balance Sheet
    Comparative Balance Sheet
The Statement of Retained Earnings

Learning Objectives

1. Describe the purpose, general content, and users of a hotel balance sheet, and explain the elements and conventions used in preparing a balance sheet. (pp. 343–344)

2. Explain assets, and identify current and noncurrent assets. (pp. 344–346)

3. Explain liabilities, and identify current and long-term liabilities. (pp. 346–347)

4. Describe the items that might appear in the equity section of a balance sheet. (p. 348)

5. Differentiate between the account and report formats and the internal and external formats for a balance sheet. (pp. 348–349)

6. Explain the preparation and purposes of common-size and comparative balance sheets, and describe their analysis and interpretation. (pp. 349–357)

7. Explain the relationship between the statement of retained earnings and the balance sheet. (p. 357)

12

Hotel Balance Sheets

T HE BALANCE SHEET shows a hotel's assets, liabilities, and owner's equity for a particular date. The balance sheet is a property or corporate statement; it is not a financial tool directed to supervisors and departmental managers. It is useful to executives, the board of directors, shareholders, creditors, and the investment community.

The content of all balance sheets is fairly consistent because of the reporting requirements established by the Financial Accounting Standards Board (FASB) and generally accepted accounting principles (GAAP). This standardization results in very similar formats. Like hotel income statements, balance sheets can be prepared in internal or external formats.

A balance sheet is very important because it presents the "financial health" of a company on a certain date. An income statement shows what happened in the past but does not give an indication of the company's ability to continue in business.

The income statement shows the profit for a period of time, while the balance sheet shows what a company *owns* and *owes* on a given date. It is possible that a profitable company could go out of business because of its debt service load.

In presenting the hotel balance sheet, this chapter will address the following questions:

1. What are the basic elements and conventions used in the design of a balance sheet?

2. What is the difference between internal and external balance sheets?

3. What is a common-size balance sheet?

4. What is a comparative balance sheet?

5. What is the relationship between the balance sheet and the statement of retained earnings?

Elements and Conventions

The balance sheet is also called the *statement of financial position*. Its purpose is to report a company's resources and commitments as of a specified date. For example, a balance sheet dated December 31 does not cover the month or the year ended December 31; it reports financial balances as of the close of business for the day ended December 31. To clarify, a company issuing its annual statements on a calendar basis would use the following headings on its financial reports:

Katygard Motel, Inc.   Katygard Motel, Inc.
Income Statement   Balance Sheet
For the year ended December 31, 19XX   December 31, 19XX

Elements. The basic elements of the balance sheet are represented by the following accounting equation:

$$\text{Assets} = \text{Liabilities} + \text{Equity}$$

Because liabilities and equity are claims on the assets of the business, the equation can be stated as follows:

$$\text{Assets} = \text{Claims}$$

The accounting equation can be restated in the form of a financial equation as follows:

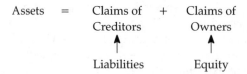

Conventions. The *going concern principle* and *historical cost principle* dictate that assets be shown at amounts not greater than their cost; this allows the reader to measure the use of resources. In the case of accounts receivable, inventories, marketable securities, and investments, the *principle of conservatism* dictates that these assets be shown at the lesser of their cost or current market value.

Assets

An **asset** is anything of monetary value that is owned by a business. To qualify as an asset, an item must provide future economic benefit or provide certain rights or claims. For example, the acquisition of a franchise right is capitalized (recorded as an asset instead of an expense) because the "right" will be a benefit over an extended period of time. The assets of a hospitality business can be classified as:

- Current assets
- Noncurrent assets

Current Assets

Current assets include cash and other assets that will be converted to cash within 12 months of the balance sheet date. Also included in current assets are prepayments of expenditures expected to benefit operations over the next 12 months from the balance sheet date. Current assets are listed on the balance sheet in descending order of liquidity and consist of:

- Cash
- Marketable securities
- Accounts receivable

- Inventories

- Prepaid expenses

Cash. Cash consists of cash in checking and savings accounts, cash in house banks, and certificates of deposit. However, money held in a bank account that has a *restricted use* is shown as a noncurrent asset and listed under the other assets classification.

Marketable Securities. Marketable securities are short-term investments that are readily marketable and can be converted into cash. With marketable securities, management's intention is to invest in other companies for potential gain and not for control of or affiliation with these companies.

Accounts Receivable. In a hotel operation, accounts receivable include the guest ledger and the city ledger. An *Allowance for Doubtful Accounts* is used to estimate potential bad debts. This allowance is listed as a deduction from the face value of the receivables.

Inventories. Inventories include food, beverages, guestroom supplies, office supplies, cleaning supplies, and other reserve stocks of operating supplies that are on hand on the balance sheet date.

Prepaid Expenses. Prepaid expenses are expenditures paying in advance for services that will benefit the hospitality company for a period up to 12 months from the balance sheet date. Typical examples of prepaid expenses are insurance, interest, property taxes, rent, and service contracts.

Noncurrent Assets

Noncurrent assets are those assets that will not be converted to cash within 12 months of the balance sheet date. Categories of noncurrent assets include noncurrent receivables, investments, property and equipment, and other assets.

Noncurrent Receivables. Noncurrent receivables represent accounts and notes that are not expected to be collected during the next 12 months. Amounts due from owners, officers, employees, and affiliated entities should be shown separately, unless insignificant. If any noncurrent receivables are estimated to be uncollectible, an allowance for doubtful noncurrent receivables should be established.

Investments. In accounting, the term "investments" applies to investments in other companies that are made with an objective of control or affiliation. Investments do not meet any or all of the conditions of marketable securities.

Property and Equipment. Assets grouped under property and equipment are long-lived, tangible assets which may also be called fixed assets. These assets include land, buildings, vehicles, china, glassware, silver, linen, uniforms, machinery, rooms department furniture, food and beverage department furniture, and all other furniture and equipment necessary for a hotel to do business.

Also included in property and equipment are leaseholds, leasehold improvements, construction in progress, and assets held under a capital lease (a lease that is in essence a purchase of an asset).

Accumulated depreciation, the sum of all depreciation charges over a period of time, is subtracted from cost to arrive at the net book value of the assets in this category. (Land is not depreciated in the hospitality industry.)

Other Assets. This noncurrent asset classification includes intangible assets and deferred charges. Examples of intangible assets in this category are organization costs, preopening expenses, franchise rights, goodwill, trademarks, tradenames, security deposits, patents, copyrights, and cash surrender value of officers' life insurance.

These intangible assets must have been *acquired.* They are carried at cost and *amortized* over their expected life (not to exceed 40 years). Amortization reduces the book value of the intangible asset, and the amortization expense appears on the income statement.

Deferred charges are similar to prepaid expenses since both are temporary assets that become expenses over a period of time. However, while a prepaid expense benefits the next 12 months, a deferred expense has a benefit beyond 12 months. For example, assume a hotel signs up for a three-year service contract to get a discounted rate. At any time, 12 months of contract costs are a prepaid expense and any remaining contract costs are a deferred expense.

Liabilities

Liabilities represent amounts owed to creditors. They are classified as:

- Current liabilities
- Long-term liabilities

Current Liabilities

Current liabilities are liabilities that must be paid within 12 months of the balance sheet date. Current liabilities include the current portion of long-term loans such as bank loans and mortgages. Also included in current liabilities are *deferred credits.* Two examples of deferred credits are:

- Unearned revenue
- Deferred income tax

Unearned Revenue. Unearned revenue results when a hotel collects room deposits or banquet deposits from guests before any services have been rendered. Unearned revenue may appear on the balance sheet under other names such as advance deposits, deposits and credit balances, or customer deposits.

Deferred Income Tax. Deferred income tax represents the amount of a hotel's potential income tax obligation that results from differences in financial reporting and income tax reporting. This situation is not uncommon. For example, the depreciation methods approved by the FASB are not accepted by the Internal Revenue Service. Therefore, there will be a difference between book income and taxable income. This can be shown as follows:

	Books	Tax Return
Sales	$100,000	$100,000
Expenses before depreciation	− 70,000	− 70,000
Income before depreciation	30,000	30,000
Depreciation	3,000	10,000
Income for tax computation	27,000	20,000
Income tax at 30%	8,100	6,000

In filing its income tax return, the company will have a tax liability of $6,000. However, its financial statements will show a tax liability of $8,100 based on its book income. The above data is recorded by the following journal entry:

Income tax expense	8,100	
Income tax payable		6,000
Deferred income tax		2,100

Deferred income taxes relating to a specific asset or liability are usually classified as current or long-term depending on the classification of the asset or liability. Deferred income taxes relating to depreciation are generally classified as long-term liabilities.

Deferred income taxes arise because accounting for income and expenses under generally accepted accounting principles generally differs from income tax procedures and regulations. It is not unusual for the taxable income on the financial statements to be different from the taxable income on the income tax return. These differences are classified as *permanent differences* and *timing differences.*

A **permanent difference** occurs when a revenue or expense appears on the income statement but does not appear on the income tax return. For example, qualifying municipal bond interest income is recorded on the books as income but receives favorable tax treatment in that it is never taxed.

Timing differences, also called temporary differences, occur when revenue or expense amounts on the income statement differ from the amounts entered on the income tax return for a given year; but over a period of several years, the totals of these amounts will eventually be equal. A timing difference occurs when the tax depreciation method differs from the book depreciation method. While the depreciation expense may vary from year to year, the *total* expense at the end of the asset's life is the same.

Permanent differences do not cause deferred income taxes. A deferred tax liability is attributable to nontaxable temporary differences. The calculation of deferred income taxes is technical and complex; it is a task best left to a professional accountant.

Long-Term Liabilities

Long-term liabilities are debts and commitments that are due beyond 12 months of the balance sheet date.

Equity

The equity section of a corporation is called *shareholders' equity* or *stockholders' equity*. Its content depends on the type of equity transactions that have occurred. Some corporations have simple capital structures while others have complex structures. The types of items that might appear in the equity section of a balance sheet are:

- Common stock issued
- Preferred stock issued
- Additional paid-in capital
- Retained earnings
- Donated capital
- Treasury stock

Common Stock Issued. This item represents the amount of common stock issued shown at par value.

Preferred Stock Issued. This item represents the amount of preferred stock issued shown at par value.

Additional Paid-In Capital. When stock is issued at an amount in excess of par value, the stock has been issued at a premium which is recorded as additional paid-in capital.

Retained Earnings. This item includes the net income and net losses of the business since its inception, reduced by any *dividends declared* since inception.

Donated Capital. Sometimes corporations receive assets (such as land) as gifts from states, cities, or private benefactors to increase local employment or encourage business activity in a locality. In such cases, the asset is recorded (debited) to its proper asset account, and instead of crediting cash or a liability, the donated capital account is credited for the asset's fair market value (FMV) on the date of the gift.

Treasury Stock. A corporation may reacquire shares (at market price) of its previously issued stock to reduce the number of outstanding shares. When stock is reacquired, it is called **treasury stock**. The possession of treasury stock does not give the corporation any voting rights. Some common reasons why a corporation may acquire its own stock are as follows:

- To increase earnings per share by reducing outstanding shares
- To reduce outside ownership
- To block takeover attempts

Treasury stock is not an asset. The purchase cost of treasury stock is shown as as a contra item in the equity section. However, the amount of issued and outstanding stock is generally not changed.

Hotel Balance Sheet Formats

The balance sheet can be designed in either the *account format* or the *report format*. The **account format** lists the asset accounts on the left side of the statement. The more popular balance sheet design is the **report format,** which lists the assets, liabilities, and owners' equity in columns. Exhibit 1 illustrates a balance sheet in the report format.

The Hotel DORO's Balance Sheet

Exhibit 2 shows an internal balance sheet, and Exhibit 3 shows an external balance sheet for the fictitious Hotel DORO. Compared with the internal format, the external format is more condensed. For example, notice the differences for cash, accounts receivable, and long-term debt. In any case, these slight format differences do not have any effect on the mathematical result of the balance sheet.

Common-Size Balance Sheet

While a balance sheet reports a company's financial position on a given data, management needs more information to measure financial growth and determine potential problem areas. To accommodate management, accountants have designed a **common-size balance sheet** to measure the relationship of each item on the balance sheet to *total assets.* The relationship of the components of the balance sheet to total assets is expressed as a percentage.

Common-Size Analysis of a Balance Sheet. Since every item on the balance sheet is divided by total assets, the percentage listed next to total assets will always be 100%. Also, since the total liabilities and shareholders' equity line is always the same as total assets, that line will likewise be 100%. The computation to arrive at common-size percentages can be expressed by the following formula:

$$\frac{\text{Line Amount}}{\text{Total Assets}} = \text{Common-Size Percentage}$$

As with any *vertical analysis,* the components of a series can be added to cross-check the computed percentages for their total. Because these computations are rounded, it might be necessary to "force" certain results.

In the exhibits in this chapter, forced numbers are shown in bold print.

Common-Size Analysis—the Hotel DORO's Balance Sheet. Either an internal or external balance sheet may contain common-size percentages. To provide management with further information, an accountant may supplement the internal balance sheet with budgeted and/or industry ratios.

Interpretation of Hotel DORO's Common-Size Balance Sheet. The balance sheet in Exhibit 4 tells us that the claims on the assets are as follows:

$$\text{Assets} = \text{Liabilities} + \text{Owners' Equity}$$
$$100\% = 67.1\% + 32.9\%$$

Obviously, the Hotel DORO has substantial debt because about 67% of its assets have creditor claims. However, financial decisions should not be based on one ratio alone. In addition to comparing any ratio with budgeted ratios and industry ratios, it is necessary to determine if the company is using its debt favorably to generate

Exhibit 1   Balance Sheet—Report Format

BALANCE SHEET

Assets

	Date	
	19___	19___

Current Assets
   Cash
      House Banks $ $
      Demand Deposits
      Temporary Cash Investments
         Total Cash
   Marketable Securities
   Receivables
      Accounts Receivable—Trade
      Notes Receivable
      Other
         Total Receivables
      Less Allowance for Doubtful Accounts
         Net Receivables
   Inventories
   Prepaid Expenses
   Other
         Total Current Assets

Noncurrent Receivables, Net of Current Maturities

Investments

Property and Equipment
   Land
   Buildings
   Leaseholds and Leasehold Improvements
   Construction in Progress
   Furnishings and Equipment
   China, Glassware, Silver, Linen, and Uniforms
   Less Accumulated Depreciation and Amortization
         Net Property and Equipment

Other Assets
   Security Deposits
   Preopening Expenses
   Deferred Charges
   Other
         Total Other Assets

Total Assets $ $

Exhibit 1 *(continued)*

BALANCE SHEET (continued)

Liabilities and Owners' Equity

Current Liabilities
Notes Payable $ $
Current Maturities of Long-Term Debt
Accounts Payable
Federal, State, and City Income Taxes
Deferred Income Taxes
Accrued Expenses
Advance Deposits
Other
         Total Current Liabilities

Long-Term Debt
Notes and Other Similar Liabilities
Obligations Under Capital Leases

Less Current Maturities
         Total Long-Term Debt

Other Long-Term Liabilities

Deferred Income Taxes

Commitments and Contingencies

Owners' Equity
Preferred Stock, Par Value $_____
       Authorized _____ Shares
       Issued _____ Shares
Common Stock, Par Value $_____
       Authorized _____ Shares
       Issued _____ Shares
Additional Paid-In Capital
Retained Earnings
         Total Owners' Equity

Total Liabilities and Owners' Equity $ _____ $ _____

See the accompanying notes to financial statements.

Source: *Uniform System of Accounts and Expense Dictionary for Small Hotels, Motels, and Motor Hotels,* 4th ed. (East Lansing, Mich.: Educational Institute of the American Hotel & Motel Association, 1987), pp. 4–5.

earnings growth. Therefore, a complete ratio analysis requires a reader to study both the income statement and balance sheet.

Further interpretations of the common-size balance sheet are possible by studying the components of the various subdivisions of the balance sheet. For example, cash represents about 2% of assets; current assets represent 4.6% of assets. While this might seem minor, notice that the current liabilities are only 3.8% of assets. It is not unusual for fixed assets to compose the largest percentage of assets.

Exhibit 2   Balance Sheet (Internal)—Hotel DORO

Hotel DORO, Inc.
Balance Sheet
December 31, 19X2   Schedule C

ASSETS

Current Assets

Cash—House Banks	$ 3,500	
Cash—Demand Deposits	55,000	
Total Cash		$ 58,500
Marketable Securities		25,000
Accounts Receivable	41,216	
Less Allowance for Doubtful Accounts	1,020	40,196
Inventories		11,000
Prepaid Expenses		13,192
Total Current Assets		$ 147,888

Property and Equipment

Land	850,000	
Building	2,500,000	
Furniture and Equipment	475,000	
Total	3,825,000	
Less Accumulated Depreciation	775,000	
Total	3,050,000	
Leasehold Improvements (net)	9,000	
China, Glassware, and Silver (net)	36,524	
Total Property and Equipment		3,095,524

Other Noncurrent Assets

Security Deposits	1,000	
Preopening Expenses (net)	3,000	
Total Other Assets		4,000
Total Assets		$3,247,412

LIABILITIES

Current Liabilities

Accounts Payable	$ 13,861	
Current Portion of Long-Term Debt	70,000	
Federal and State Income Taxes Payable	16,545	
Accrued Payroll	11,617	
Other Accrued Items	7,963	
Deposits and Credit Balances	3,764	
Total Current Liabilities		$ 123,750

Long-Term Debt

Mortgage Payable	2,125,000	
Less Current Portion	70,000	
Total Long-Term Debt		2,055,000
Total Liabilities		2,178,750

SHAREHOLDERS' EQUITY

Common Stock, par value $1, authorized and issued 50,000 shares	50,000	
Additional Paid-in Capital	700,000	
Retained Earnings	318,662	
Total Shareholders' Equity		1,068,662
Total Liabilities and Shareholders' Equity		$3,247,412

Exhibit 3 Balance Sheet (External)—Hotel DORO

Hotel DORO, Inc.
Balance Sheet
December 31, 19X2   **Schedule C**

ASSETS

Current Assets
Cash	$ 58,500	
Marketable Securities	25,000	
Accounts Receivable (net)	40,196	
Inventories	11,000	
Prepaid Expenses	13,192	
Total Current Assets		$ 147,888

Property and Equipment
Land	850,000	
Building	2,500,000	
Furniture and Equipment	475,000	
Total	3,825,000	
Less Accumulated Depreciation	775,000	
Total	3,050,000	
Leasehold Improvements	9,000	
China, Glassware, and Silver (net)	36,524	
Total Property and Equipment		3,095,524

Other Noncurrent Assets
Security Deposits	1,000	
Preopening Expenses (net)	3,000	
Total Other Assets		4,000

Total Assets | | $3,247,412

LIABILITIES

Current Liabilities
Accounts Payable	$ 13,861	
Current Portion of Long-Term Debt	70,000	
Federal and State Income Taxes Payable	16,545	
Accrued Payroll	11,617	
Other Accrued Items	7,963	
Unearned Revenue	3,764	
Total Current Liabilities		$ 123,750

Long-Term Debt
Mortgage Payable, less current portion		2,055,000

Total Liabilities | | 2,178,750

SHAREHOLDERS' EQUITY

Common Stock, par value $1, authorized and issued 50,000 shares	50,000	
Additional Paid-in Capital	700,000	
Retained Earnings	318,662	
Total Shareholders' Equity		1,068,662

Total Liabilities and Shareholders' Equity | | $3,247,412

Comparative Balance Sheet

A **comparative balance sheet** presents financial data for two or more periods. The comparative data can be in the the form of dollars or percentages that management

Exhibit 4 Common-Size Balance Sheet—Hotel DORO

Hotel DORO, Inc.
Balance Sheet
December 31, 19X2

ASSETS

Current Assets		
Cash	$ 58,500	**1.9%**
Marketable Securities	25,000	.8
Accounts Receivable (net)	40,196	1.2
Inventories	11,000	.3
Prepaid Expenses	13,192	.4
Total Current Assets	147,888	4.6
Property and Equipment		
Land	850,000	26.2
Building	2,500,000	77.0
Furniture and Equipment	475,000	14.6
Total	3,825,000	117.8
Less Accumulated Depreciation	775,000	23.9
Total	3,050,000	93.9
Leasehold Improvements	9,000	.3
China, Glassware, and Silver (net)	36,524	1.1
Total Property and Equipment	3,095,524	95.3
Other Noncurrent Assets		
Security Deposits	1,000	—
Preopening Expenses (net)	3,000	.1
Total Other Assets	4,000	.1
Total Assets	$3,247,412	100.0%

LIABILITIES

Current Liabilities		
Accounts Payable	$ 13,861	.4%
Current Portion of Long-Term Debt	70,000	2.2
Federal and State Income Taxes Payable	16,545	.5
Accrued Payroll	11,617	.4
Other Accrued Items	7,963	.2
Unearned Revenue	3,764	.1
Total Current Liabilities	123,750	3.8
Long-Term Debt		
Mortgage Payable, less current portion	2,055,000	63.3
Total Liabilities	2,178,750	67.1

SHAREHOLDERS' EQUITY

Common Stock, par value $1, authorized		
and issued 50,000 shares	50,000	1.5
Additional Paid-in Capital	700,000	21.6
Retained Earnings	318,662	9.8
Total Shareholders' Equity	1,068,662	32.9
Total Liabilities and Shareholders' Equity	$3,247,412	100.0%

finds useful in its planning and controlling functions. Because computations are made on a side-by-side basis, a comparative analysis is also known as a *horizontal analysis.*

A popular comparative balance sheet is in the following format:

Current Year	Prior Year	$ Change	% Change

After the current and prior years' data have been entered, the steps to complete a comparative statement are as follows:

1. The *dollar change* is computed by entering the current year's amount in a calculator and then subtracting the prior year's amount. The proper mathematical sign (positive or negative) will be provided by the calculator.

2. The *percentage change* is computed by dividing the dollar change amount by the *prior year's amount*. The sign of the percentage change (either positive or negative) is always the same as that for the dollar change. A comparative analysis does not use a common divisor. The divisor for each line is the prior period's data for that particular line item.

Comparative Balance Sheet for the Hotel DORO. Exhibit 5 presents a comparative balance sheet for the Hotel DORO. The dollar change for each line item is independently computed using a horizontal process. The $234 for the total dollar change is also a horizontal computation. It is possible to verify the accuracy of the $234 by adding the dollar changes of each current asset. The cross-checking of all columns is a standard procedure that produces an accurate statement.

After the dollar changes are computed and cross-checked, the next step is to compute the percentage changes. This is accomplished by dividing the dollar change by the prior year's amount. For example, the change for cash of $(3,006) is divided by the 19X1 amount of $61,506 to arrive at a (4.9)% change.

Because the percentage changes are computed without a common divisor, it is not possible to add a column for percentages to verify any total percentage. Therefore, it is suggested that all percentage computations be rechecked for accuracy.

Interpretation of a Comparative Analysis. A specialized vocabulary is used to discuss changes in a comparative financial statement. If this year's data is larger than last year's data, the change is called an *increase* or simply stated as *up* or *upward;* it cannot be called a *gain* because a gain results from the sale of assets at a price exceeding book value. If this year's data is smaller than last year's data, the change is called a *decrease* or simply stated as *down* or *downward;* it cannot be called a *loss* because a loss results from the sale of assets at a price less than book value.

If this year's data is equal to last year's data, the situation is referred to as *no change;* it would be illogical to call it a zero change.

Sometimes it is impossible to calculate a *percentage change* because there is no last year's data, which means there is no divisor. In this case, the proper procedure is to indicate that the percentage change is *not measurable* by entering the symbol "—" or "n/m" in the applicable column.

When analyzing the changes, it is incorrect to concentrate only on the percentage changes because a large percentage change may not necessarily represent a large dollar change. The comparing of small numbers can produce a large percentage change for a minor dollar change. For example, a $50 change on last year's data of $20 results in a 250% change. Conversely, a small percentage change could represent a large dollar change. For example, if the dollar change is $500,000 on last year's data of $50,000,000, the percentage change is only 1%.

Exhibit 5   Comparative Balance Sheet—Hotel DORO

Hotel DORO, Inc.
Comparative Balance Sheet
December 31, 19X2 and December 31, 19X1

ASSETS	19X2	19X1	$ Change	% Change
Current Assets				
Cash	$ 58,500	$ 61,506	$ (3,006)	(4.9)%
Marketable Securities	25,000	25,000	0	0
Accounts Receivable (net)	40,196	38,840	1,356	3.5
Inventories	11,000	10,143	857	8.4
Prepaid Expenses	13,192	12,165	1,027	8.4
Total Current Assets	147,888	147,654	234	.2
Property and Equipment				
Land	850,000	792,000	58,000	7.3
Building	2,500,000	2,500,000	0	0
Furniture and Equipment	475,000	427,814	47,186	11.0
Total	3,825,000	3,719,814	105,186	2.8
Less Accumulated Depreciation	775,000	640,000	135,000	21.1
Total	3,050,000	3,079,814	(29,814)	(1.0)
Leasehold Improvements	9,000	10,000	(1,000)	(10.0)
China, Glassware, and Silver	36,524	49,403	(12,879)	(26.1)
Total Property and Equipment	3,095,524	3,139,217	(43,693)	(1.4)
Other Noncurrent Assets				
Security Deposits	1,000	1,000	0	0
Preopening Expenses (net)	3,000	4,500	(1,500)	(33.3)
Total Other Assets	4,000	5,500	(1,500)	(27.3)
Total Assets	$3,247,412	$3,292,371	$(44,959)	(1.4)
LIABILITIES				
Current Liabilities				
Accounts Payable	$ 13,861	$ 18,642	$ (4,781)	(25.6)%
Current Portion of Long-Term Debt	70,000	70,000	0	0
Federal and State Income Taxes	16,545	24,619	(8,074)	(32.8)
Accrued Payroll	11,617	9,218	2,399	26.0
Other Accrued Items	7,963	10,899	(2,936)	(26.9)
Unearned Revenue	3,764	5,875	(2,111)	(35.9)
Total Current Liabilities	123,750	139,253	(15,503)	(11.1)
Long-Term Debt				
Mortgage Payable	2,055,000	2,125,000	(70,000)	(3.3)
Total Liabilities	2,178,750	2,264,253	(85,503)	(3.8)
SHAREHOLDERS' EQUITY				
Common Stock Issued	50,000	50,000	0	0
Additional Paid-In Capital	700,000	700,000	0	0
Retained Earnings	318,662	278,118	40,544	14.6
Total Shareholders' Equity	1,068,662	1,028,118	40,544	3.9
Total Liabilities and Shareholders' Equity	$3,247,412	$3,292,371	$(44,959)	(1.4)%

Interpretation of the Hotel DORO's Comparative Balance Sheet. The balance sheet for the Hotel DORO in Exhibit 5 is used to make the following interpretation of its financial position from a comparison of data on December 31, 19X2 with data on December 31, 19X1.

   1. The decrease to cash of 4.9% might first be a subject of concern. However, notice that current liabilities have decreased by 11.1%. This looks especially favorable

because it was accomplished without any new long-term debt, bank financing, or secondary issuance of common stock.

2. Receivables are up 3.5%. If the income statement were provided, it would show that sales are up over last year which might justify the increase in accounts receivable.

3. Inventories are up 8.4%. This matter should be investigated because the food and beverage department income decreased from last year.

4. The increase in prepaid expenses could be due to increases in insurance premiums and taxes which are typical from year to year.

5. The company has increased its land and furniture and equipment holdings. The reasons for these acquisitions should be explained.

6. Preopening expenses have decreased because of amortization. Unlike fixed assets, intangible assets do not have an accumulated depreciation account. The amortization expense appears on the income statement, and it is used to directly reduce the book value shown on the balance sheet. In time, the preopening expenses will be fully amortized and will no longer appear on the balance sheet.

7. The company has managed its resources to reduce all of its current liabilities and long-term debt.

8. The increase to retained earnings is due to the income from operations less any dividends declared. The company's net profit for the year was $60,544 and dividends declared were $20,000; thus retained earnings increased by $40,544.

The Statement of Retained Earnings

This statement was prepared with the income statement and serves as a "connecting link" between the income statement and balance sheet because it brings the computed retained earnings amount over to the balance sheet.

Exhibit 6 shows the statement of retained earnings that was prepared after the income statement was completed. Notice that the final amount representing retained earnings for the year just ended is brought over to the retained earnings line item of the balance sheet as of the end of the same period.

Exhibit 6 Statement of Retained Earnings—Hotel DORO

Hotel DORO, Inc. Statement of Retained Earnings For the year ended December 31, 19X2	Schedule B
Retained Earnings at beginning of year	$278,118
Net Income for the year (Schedule A)	60,544
Total	338,662
Less Dividends Declared during the year	20,000
Retained Earnings at end of year	$318,662

Key Terms

account format	long-term liabilities
asset	noncurrent assets
common-size balance sheet	permanent difference
comparative balance sheet	report format
current assets	timing difference
current liabilities	treasury stock
deferred income taxes	unearned revenue
liabilities	

Review Questions

1. What is the purpose of a balance sheet?

2. What is the time period covered by a balance sheet?

3. How can the accounting equation be restated to a financial equation?

4. What are the three major sections of a balance sheet?

5. How are the different assets of a hospitality business classified on a balance sheet?

6. What is the definition of a current asset? List the five major current assets in their descending order of liquidity.

7. What is the difference between marketable securities and investments on a balance sheet?

8. What is the difference between a prepaid expense and a deferred charge on a balance sheet?

9. What is unearned revenue on a balance sheet?

10. What does the line item Deferred Income Tax represent on a balance sheet?

11. What is a common-size balance sheet?

12. What is a comparative balance sheet?

Problems

Problem 1

A newly formed corporation issues 40,000 shares of its $1 par value common stock for $90,000. How will this appear on the balance sheet?

Problem 2

A hospitality corporation has some issued and outstanding common stock of $100,000. It recently reacquired 1,000 shares of its own stock for $20,000. What will be the amount of issued and outstanding common stock after this acquisition of treasury stock?

Problem 3

A company recently purchased land with a mortgage of $50,000, which will require monthly payments on the principal of $1,000. What will be the amount of long-term debt before any payments are made?

Problem 4

Prepare a balance sheet using the internal format for the Village Hotel, Inc. as of its year ended December 31, 19X9. The following are selected accounts from the worksheet necessary to prepare this statement.

	Balance Sheet	
	dr	cr
Cash—House Banks	10,000	
Cash—Regular Checking	37,148	
Cash—Payroll Checking	500	
Marketable Securities	10,000	
Guest Ledger (debit balances)	41,221	
City Ledge	20,616	
Allowance for Doubtful Accounts		1,523
Food Inventory	6,825	
Beverage Inventory	3,614	
Supplies Inventory	8,726	
Prepaid Insurance	12,819	
Prepaid Rent	3,000	
Furniture	475,000	
Equipment	450,000	
Allowance for Depreciation: Furniture		125,000
Allowance for Depreciation: Equipment		150,000
Leasehold Improvements	475,000	
China, Glassware, and Silver	42,119	
Security Deposits	2,500	
Accounts Payable		36,972
Income Taxes Payable		15,212
Accrued Payroll		21,316
Other Accrued Items		34,918
Guest Ledger Credit Balances		4,500
Notes Payable (see Note 1)		425,000
Common Stock (see Note 2)		30,000
Additional Paid-In Capital		600,000
Retained Earnings (as of 12/15/X9)		62,930

The following notes must be taken into account when preparing the balance sheet:

1. The item referred to as Notes Payable is a ten-year note. Of the $425,000 unpaid balance, $25,000 is due in the next 12 months.

2. There are 50,000 shares of $1 par common stock authorized; 30,000 shares have been issued.

3. The retained earnings of $62,930 are not the retained earnings as of the period ended December 31 and should be ignored. To compute the retained earnings for December 31, the following data is provided:

Retained earnings 1/1/X9	$122,930
Net income for the year ended 12/31/X9	91,717
Dividends declared during the year	60,000

4. For your convenience, a checkpoint amount for total assets is provided: $1,322,565.

Problem 5

Prepare a common-size income statement for Garden Bistro, Inc. as of December 31, 19X8. The rules for rounding are as follows:

a. Show all answers to one decimal, rounded (for example, 7,900 divided by 170,000 equals 4.6%).

b. If a series of computed percentages do not add up to the computed total, force the largest number in the series up or down as necessary.

The Garden Bistro, Inc.
Balance Sheet
December 31, 19X8

ASSETS

CURRENT ASSETS	
Cash	$ 34,000
Accounts Receivable	4,000
Food Inventory	2,400
Supplies Inventory	2,600
Prepaid Expenses	2,000
Total Current Assets	45,000
PROPERTY AND EQUIPMENT	
Land	$ 30,000
Building	60,000
Furniture and Equipment	52,000
China, Glassware, and Silver	8,000
Total	150,000
Less Accumulated Depreciation	40,000
Net Property and Equipment	110,000
OTHER ASSETS	
Security Deposits	1,500
Preopening Expenses (net)	2,500
Total Other Assets	4,000
TOTAL ASSETS	$159,000

LIABILITIES

CURRENT LIABILITIES
Accounts Payable	$ 11,000
Sales Tax Payable	1,000
Accrued Expenses	9,000
Current Portion of Long-Term Debt	6,000
Total Current Liabilities	27,000

LONG-TERM LIABILITIES
Mortgage Payable, net of current portion	34,000

SHAREHOLDERS' EQUITY

Paid-In Capital:
Common Stock, par value $1, authorized	
50,000 shares, issued 25,000 shares	25,000
Additional Paid-in Capital	15,000
Total Paid-in Capital	40,000
Retained Earnings, December 31, 19X8	58,000
TOTAL LIABILITIES AND SHAREHOLDERS' EQUITY	$159,000

Problem 6

Prepare a comparative analysis from the following balance sheet. Show all answers to one decimal, rounded.

The Garden Bistro, Inc.
Balance Sheet
December 31, 19X8 and December 31, 19X7

ASSETS

	19X8	19X7
CURRENT ASSETS		
Cash	$ 34,000	$ 36,500
Accounts Receivable	4,000	3,450
Food Inventory	2,400	2,100
Supplies Inventory	2,600	1,900
Prepaid Expenses	2,000	2,600
Total Current Assets	45,000	46,550
PROPERTY AND EQUIPMENT		
Land	$ 30,000	30,000
Building	60,000	60,000
Furniture and Equipment	52,000	48,000
China, Glassware, and Silver	8,000	8,300
Total	150,000	146,300
Less Accumulated Depreciation	40,000	35,000
Net Property and Equipment	110,000	111,300

LIABILITIES

CURRENT LIABILITIES

Accounts Payable	$ 11,000	25,400
Sales Tax Payable	1,000	950
Accrued Expenses	9,000	7,000
Current Portion of Long-Term Debt	6,000	6,000
Total Current Liabilities	27,000	39,350

LONG-TERM LIABILITIES

Mortgage Payable, net of current portion	34,000	40,000

SHAREHOLDERS' EQUITY

Paid-In Capital:

Common Stock, par value $1, authorized 50,000 shares, issued 25,000 shares	25,000	25,000
Additional Paid-In Capital	15,000	15,000
Total Paid-In Capital	40,000	40,000
Retained Earnings, December 31, 19X8	58,000	43,000
TOTAL LIABILITIES AND SHAREHOLDERS' EQUITY	$159,000	$162,350

REVIEW QUIZ

When you feel you have covered all of the material in this chapter, answer these questions. Choose the *best* answer. Check your answers with the correct ones found on the Review Quiz Answer Key at the end of this book.

True (T) or False (F)

T   F   1.   The balance sheet is also called the statement of financial position.

T   F   2.   Current assets are listed on the balance sheet in ascending order of liquidity.

T   F   3.   All liabilities are classified as unearned revenue or deferred income tax.

T   F   4.   A common-size balance sheet measures each item on the balance sheet in relation to total assets.

Multiple Choice

5.   Which of the following is *not* a major section of a hotel's balance sheet?

    a.   revenue
    b.   assets
    c.   liabilities
    d.   equity

6.   Among current assets, cash includes all of the following *except:*

    a.   checking and savings accounts.
    b.   bank accounts with restricted use.
    c.   certificates of deposit.
    d.   house banks.

7.   China, glassware, silver, and linen belong in which category of assets?

    a.   inventories
    b.   investments
    c.   property and equipment
    d.   other assets

8.   Which of the following is *true* of unearned revenue?

    a.   It is dependent upon the equity transactions that have occurred.
    b.   It results when a hotel collects room or banquet deposits from guests before any services have been rendered.
    c.   It may appear on a balance sheet under another name.
    d.   b and c

9.   Which of the following types of balance sheets presents data for two or more periods?

    a.   comparative
    b.   common-size
    c.   account format
    d.   report format

10. On a financial statement, if this year's data is larger than last year's data, the change is called:

   a. a gain.
   b. an increase.
   c. a cross-check.
   d. unearned revenue.

Chapter Outline

Ratio Analysis of the Balance Sheet
    Liquidity
    Asset Management
    Debt Management
Ratio Analysis of the Hotel DORO's Balance
    Sheet
Current Ratio
    Bank Standard
    Composition
Quick Ratio
    Bank Standard
Accounts Receivable Turnover Ratio
Average Collection Period Ratio
Inventory Turnover Ratio
Fixed Asset Turnover Ratio
Debt-to-Equity Ratio
Assets-to-Liabilities Ratio
Working Capital
    Computation of Working Capital
    Composition of Working Capital
    The Importance of Adequate Working
        Capital
    Causes of Inadequate Working Capital
    Causes of Excess Working Capital
Factors Affecting Working Capital
    Requirements
Reference List of Ratio Formulas

Learning Objectives

1. Describe the use of ratios in the analysis of a hospitality business balance sheet. (pp. 367–368)

2. Explain the purpose and use of the current ratio, and describe its formula and interpretation. (pp. 370–371)

3. Explain the purpose and use of the quick ratio, and describe its formula and interpretation. (pp. 371–372)

4. Explain the purpose and use of the accounts receivable turnover ratio, and describe its formula and interpretation. (p. 372)

5. Explain the purpose and use of the average collection period ratio, and describe its formula and interpretation. (p. 373)

6. Identify the formulas for food and beverage inventory turnover. (p. 373)

7. Explain the purpose and use of the fixed asset turnover ratio, and describe its formula and interpretation. (pp. 373–374)

8. Explain the purpose and use of the debt-to-equity ratio, and describe its formula and interpretation. (pp. 374–375)

9. Explain the purpose and use of the assets-to-liabilities ratio, and describe its formula and interpretation. (pp. 375–376)

10. Describe the computation, composition, and importance of working capital. (pp. 376–377)

13

Ratio Analysis of the Balance Sheet

Rₐₜᵢₒ ᴀɴᴀʟʏsɪs ᴏf ᴀ ʜᴏᴛᴇʟ's ʙᴀʟᴀɴᴄᴇ sʜᴇᴇᴛ is very useful to the hotel's board of directors, management, shareholders, and creditors, and to the investment community. Unlike the income statement, the balance sheet is not oriented toward departmental use; a balance sheet shows the overall financial condition of a hospitality property or corporation. It is important to know the financial condition of any business to determine its ability to stay in business.

The balance sheet uses historical costs to measure a hospitality company's use of its resources. While there is some debate over the use of market values on the balance sheet, these values can only be achieved if the company is sold. This value concept is contrary to the purpose of a going concern.

Balance sheet ratios are tools for analyzing and interpreting the financial soundness of a hospitality company. **Analysis** involves the calculating of percentages and ratios; **interpretation** involves comparing percentages and ratios to determine the meaning and significance of the analysis. Ratios that can be used in an interpretation are:

- Prior-period ratios

- Industry and trade association ratios

- Budgeted ratios

    This chapter will answer the following questions:

1. What do balance sheet ratios measure?

2. What are some of the popular ratios used in the analysis of a balance sheet?

3. What is working capital?

4. What is the significance of adequate and inadequate working capital?

Ratio Analysis of the Balance Sheet

Ratios are a critical part of financial analysis because they point to symptoms or potential problem areas when compared with budgeted ratios, prior-period ratios, and industry and trade association ratios. Hospitality industry ratios and statistics are published by PKF Consulting, Arthur Andersen, Smith Travel Research, and the National Restaurant Association (for stand-alone restaurants).

    Balance sheet ratios are used to measure the following financial factors:

- Liquidity
- Asset management
- Debt management

Liquidity

A company's ability to pay its current liabilities is a measurement of **liquidity**. Creditors and the investment community are especially interested in knowing whether a company can pay its current obligations without the need to borrow money not intended to finance future growth. Liquidity ratios assume that current assets are the major source of funds to pay current liabilities. The two most popular ratios in evaluating liquidity are:

- Current ratio
- Quick ratio

Asset Management

The financial soundness and success of a company depend on how the company's assets are managed. Asset management involves controlling the level of assets according to company policies and sales volume. As a business grows, it is not uncommon to find growth in its accounts receivable, inventory, and fixed assets. However, sales growth should not produce unjustified increases in these assets. The most popular ratios in evaluating asset management are:

- Accounts receivable turnover ratio
- Average collection period ratio
- Inventory turnover ratio
- Fixed asset turnover ratio

Debt Management

In addition to measuring a company's ability to pay its current debt, a company's ability to service its total debt (short-term and long-term) must be determined. Debt management is a measure of **solvency**, which refers to a company's ability to meet its long-term obligations. A hotel, motel, or other hospitality business is solvent when its assets are greater than its liabilities. The most popular ratios in evaluating the solvency of a company are:

- Debt-to-equity ratio
- Assets-to-liabilities ratio

Ratio Analysis of the Hotel DORO's Balance Sheet ─────────

The Hotel DORO's balance sheet illustrated in Exhibit 1 will be used as a model to explore the ratios that measure liquidity, asset management, and debt management. Each ratio presentation will include a brief description of the ratio, its formula, and its specific application to the Hotel DORO.

Exhibit 1   The Hotel DORO's Balance Sheet

Hotel DORO, Inc.
Comparative Balance Sheet
December 31, 19X2 and December 31, 19X1

	19X2	19X1	$ Change	% Change
ASSETS				
Current Assets				
Cash	$ 58,500	$ 61,506	$ (3,006)	(4.9)%
Marketable Securities	25,000	25,000	0	0
Accounts Receivable (net)	40,196	38,840	1,356	3.5
Inventories	11,000	10,143	857	8.4
Prepaid Expenses	13,192	12,165	1,027	8.4
Total Current Assets	147,888	147,654	234	.2
Property and Equipment				
Land	850,000	792,000	58,000	7.3
Building	2,500,000	2,500,000	0	0
Furniture and Equipment	475,000	427,814	47,816	11.0
Total	3,825,000	3,719,814	105,186	2.8
Less Accumulated Depreciation	775,000	640,000	135,000	21.1
Total	3,050,000	3,079,814	(29,814)	(1.0)
Leasehold Improvements	9,000	10,000	(1,000)	(10.0)
China, Glassware, and Silver	36,524	49,403	(12,879)	(26.1)
Total Property and Equipment	3,095,524	3,139,217	(43,693)	(1.4)
Other Noncurrent Assets				
Security Deposits	1,000	1,000	0	0
Preopening Expenses (net)	3,000	4,500	(1,500)	(33.3)
Total Other Assets	4,000	5,500	(1,500)	(27.3)
Total Assets	$ 3,247,412	$ 3,292,371	$ (44,959)	(1.4)%
LIABILITIES				
Current Liabilities				
Accounts Payable	$ 13,861	$ 18,642	$ (4,781)	(25.6)%
Current Portion of Long-Term Debt	70,000	70,000	0	0
Federal and State Income Taxes	16,545	24,619	(8,074)	(32.8)
Accrued Payroll	11,617	9,218	2,399	26.0
Other Accrued Items	7,963	10,899	(2,936)	(26.9)
Unearned Revenue	3,764	5,875	(2,111)	(35.9)
Total Current Liabilities	123,750	139,253	(15,503)	(11.1)
Long-Term Debt				
Mortgage Payable	2,055,000	2,125,000	(70,000)	(3.3)
Total Liabilities	2,178,750	2,264,253	(85,503)	(3.8)
SHAREHOLDERS' EQUITY				
Common Stock Issued	50,000	50,000	0	0
Additional Paid-In Capital	700,000	700,000	0	0
Retained Earnings	318,662	278,118	40,544	14.6
Total Shareholders' Equity	1,068,662	1,028,118	40,544	3.9
Total Liabilities and Shareholders'				
Equity	$ 3,247,412	$ 3,292,371	$ (44,959)	(1.4)%

At the conclusion of each ratio discussion will be an interpretation of the results of that specific ratio and other factors critical for application in the actual business environment.

Current Ratio

The current ratio shows the relationship of current assets to current liabilities. It is also called the *working capital ratio* because working capital is the excess of current assets over current liabilities. The current ratio is one of the most popular ratios used by the banking industry and investment community.

Formula. The current ratio formula is as follows:

$$\frac{\text{Current Assets}}{\text{Current Liabilities}}$$

The Hotel DORO's current ratio for 19X2 is calculated as follows:

$$\frac{147,888}{123,750} = 1.20$$

Interpretation. The current ratio is 1.20 to 1; it is sometimes expressed as follows:

$$1.20{:}1$$

This result indicates that there is $1.20 of current assets for every $1 of current liabilities. Another way of stating the result is: The current assets are 1.2 times larger than the current liabilities.

The larger the current ratio, the less difficulty a company should have in paying its current obligations. Therefore, a *favorable* condition occurs when the ratio is *equal* to or *greater* than prior-period or budgeted ratios.

The current ratio can be manipulated by borrowing long-term funds. The cash would become a current asset and the bank loan would not appear as a current liability.

Bank Standard

Banks generally use a guide that a current ratio should be 2.0 as a prerequisite for the approval of loans. While this bank standard of 2.0 is arbitrary, the investment community has also adopted it as a standard of measure.

The bank standard was developed in the evaluation of retail stores and manufacturing companies, which are characterized by large amounts of inventory and receivables. The operation of a hotel or restaurant does not require large amounts of inventory with a low turnover; therefore its current assets are generally more liquid. The receivables of hotels and restaurants are mostly from credit cards that are more dependable for collection than the high customer billings experienced by many other types of industries.

Composition

The interpretation of the current ratio requires more than comparison with other ratios and the bank standard. Two different companies can have identical current ratios, and yet one company's assets will not be as *liquid* as the other's. The following example shows how identical current ratios can be deceiving when comparing two different companies.

	Company A	Company B
Cash	$100,000	$ 20,000
Marketable securities	25,000	0
Accounts receivable	20,000	75,000
Inventories	40,000	90,000
Prepaid expenses	15,000	15,000
Total current assets	$200,000	$200,000
Total current liabilities	$100,000	$100,000
Current ratio	2:1	2:1

Even though both companies have 2:1 current ratios, Company A is in a better liquid position with larger amounts of cash and marketable securities. Company B is burdened by its heavy commitment in accounts receivable and inventories.

To overcome this limitation of the current ratio, the quick ratio was developed. This ratio does not use inventories and prepaid expenses in the evaluation of liquidity.

Quick Ratio

The quick ratio, also called the **acid-test ratio**, is a more refined version of the current ratio. In computing the quick ratio, the numerator includes only highly liquid current assets that are more quickly converted to cash. It excludes the less liquid current assets such as inventories and prepaid expenses.

Formula. The quick ratio formula is as follows:

$$\frac{\text{Cash} + \text{Marketable Securities} + \text{Receivables (Net)}}{\text{Current Liabilities}}$$

Hotel DORO's quick ratio for 19X2 is calculated as follows:

$$\frac{58,500 + 25,000 + 40,196}{123,750} = 1.00$$

Interpretation. The quick ratio is 1.00 to 1; it is sometimes expressed as follows:

1.00:1

This result indicates that there is $1 of highly liquid (quick) assets for every $1 of current liabilities. Another way of stating the result is: The quick assets are equal to the current liabilities.

The larger the quick ratio, the less difficulty a company should have in paying its current obligations. Therefore, a *favorable* condition occurs when the ratio is *equal* to or *greater* than prior-period or budgeted ratios.

Bank Standard

Banks generally use a guide that a quick ratio should be 1.0 as a prerequisite for the approval of loans. When the Hotel DORO is analyzed, its quick ratio of 1.0 is satisfactory under the bank standard even though its current ratio fails the 2.0 bank standard. These contradictory results emphasize the importance of not making any decisions on the basis of analyzing a limited number of ratios.

Relationship of Current Ratio Results to Quick Ratio Results. The current ratio for the Hotel DORO is 1.2 and its quick ratio is 1.0; both ratios are very close. This is typical for companies in the hospitality industry because of the industry's low inventory requirements.

Accounts Receivable Turnover Ratio

The accounts receivable turnover ratio measures the number of times, on average, that receivables are collected during a period. The data used in calculating this ratio are *sales* and *accounts receivable*. This ratio would not apply to a hospitality company whose sales are entirely on cash or bank credit cards. In those cases where a company sells for cash and credit, only those sales on credit should be used. If the separation of cash and credit sales is not possible, the accounts receivable turnover ratio will be of value if its basis for calculation is consistent. A low receivables-to-sales ratio is the result for any hospitality company that has mostly cash sales.

The accounts receivable turnover ratio requires the use of two financial statements: the income statement (to get the sales figure) and the balance sheet (to get the beginning and ending balances of the accounts receivable). The accounts receivable (after subtracting the allowance for doubtful accounts) are averaged by adding the beginning and ending balances for the period and dividing by 2.

Formula. The accounts receivable turnover ratio formula is as follows:

$$\frac{\text{Net Revenue}}{\text{Average Accounts Receivable (Net)}}$$

The net sales for the Hotel DORO in 19X2 were $1,597,493. The hotel's accounts receivable turnover ratio for 19X2 is calculated as follows:

$$\frac{1,597,493}{(38,840 + 40,196) \div 2} = \frac{1,597,493}{39,518} = 40 \text{ Times}$$

Interpretation. The accounts receivable have turned over 40 *times* on average. This high number indicates that the Hotel DORO's sales are mostly on bankcards and cash. A *favorable* condition occurs when the ratio is *equal* to or *greater* than prior-period or budgeted ratios.

The ratio takes on more meaning when it is restated in *days;* the conversion is made possible by computing the average collection period ratio.

Average Collection Period Ratio

The average collection period ratio can be used to evaluate a company's credit and collection policy. If the policy states that all billings are payable in 30 days, then the average collection period result should reflect that policy.

The accounts receivable turnover ratio can be converted to days (average collection period) by dividing the business year stated in days by the turnover.

Formula. The accounts receivable average collection period ratio formula is as follows:

$$\frac{365}{\text{Accounts Receivable Turnover}}$$

The average collection period for the Hotel DORO in 19X2 is calculated as follows:

$$\frac{365}{40} = 9 \text{ Days}$$

Interpretation. The average collection period for accounts receivable was 9 *days* or approximately every week. Another interpretation is that the accounts receivable balance consists of 9 days of sales.

A *favorable* condition occurs when the ratio is *equal* to or *less* than prior-period or budgeted ratios.

Inventory Turnover Ratio

Notice that the Hotel DORO's balance sheet shows a total for all inventories, including food, beverage, and operating supplies on hand. The footnotes to the balance sheet or information from other schedules would be necessary to compute the ratio.

The food inventory turnover is computed as follows:

$$\frac{\text{Cost of Food Used}}{\text{Average Food Inventory}}$$

The beverage inventory turnover is computed as follows:

$$\frac{\text{Cost of Beverages Used}}{\text{Average Beverage Inventory}}$$

Fixed Asset Turnover Ratio

The fixed asset turnover ratio measures management's effectiveness in using fixed assets (property and equipment) to generate revenue. This ratio requires the use of two financial statements: the income statement (to get the sales figure) and the balance sheet (to get the average of the fixed assets).

Formula. The fixed asset turnover ratio formula is as follows:

$$\frac{\text{Net Revenue}}{\text{Average Fixed Assets}}$$

The Hotel DORO's fixed asset turnover ratio for 19X2 is calculated as follows:

$$\frac{1,597,493}{(3,139,217 + 3,095,524) \div 2} = \frac{1,597,493}{3,117,371} = 0.5 \text{ Times}$$

Interpretation. The Hotel DORO's revenue was less than 1 time its average total fixed assets for the period. A *favorable* condition occurs when the ratio is *equal* to or *greater* than prior-period or budgeted ratios.

Limitation. Any ratio that uses fixed assets or total assets is subject to wide variations because of the effect of depreciation. In the case of the fixed asset turnover ratio, the fixed assets are at net of accumulated depreciation. Therefore, newer hotels or hotels with conservative depreciation policies will experience lower fixed asset turnover ratios.

Fixed assets are a significant part of any hotel company. The fixed asset turnover ratio ignores the market value of assets. As a result, the ratio could unfairly penalize newer hotels that were built at higher costs.

Debt-to-Equity Ratio

The debt-to-equity ratio compares the total debt of a hotel company with the total equity of its shareholders (owners). It shows the extent to which the company has borrowed from suppliers and banks and reveals whether the creditors or owners are financing most of the corporate assets. Creditors are interested in this ratio because it provides an indicator of risk: the higher the ratio, the higher the risk for those extending credit to the company.

Formula. The debt-to-equity ratio formula is as follows:

$$\frac{\text{Total Liabilities}}{\text{Total Equity}}$$

The Hotel DORO's 19X2 debt-to-equity ratio for 19X2 is calculated as follows:

$$\frac{2,178,750}{1,068,662} = 2.04$$

Interpretation. A *favorable* condition occurs when the ratio is *equal* to or *less* than prior-period or budgeted ratios. The result of 2.04 tells us that the creditors have financed $2.04 for every $1 the company (owners) has invested in the assets. A ratio higher than 1.00 indicates that the hotel is using debt financing more than equity financing to operate or expand its business. This is known as using **financial leverage.**

The significance of this leverage can be more clearly illustrated by applying the financial equation to the Hotel DORO as follows:

Assets		Claims of Creditors		Claims of Owners
Assets	=	Claims of Creditors	+	Claims of Owners
$3.04	=	$2.04	+	$1.00

The financial equation can be restated in percentages to show the proportion of who is financing most of the assets. This is done by dividing each claim by the total assets of $3.04 and results in the following:

Assets	=	Claims of Creditors	+	Claims of Owners
100%	=	67%	+	33%

Creditors have financed 67% of the assets while shareholders are bearing only 33% of the risk.

Significance. Each corporation has its own optimal credit and debt structure. Properly used financial leverage can maximize growth. Therefore, a high debt ratio is not necessarily unfavorable as long as the company is capable of timely servicing its debt (paying the interest and principal).

A high ratio could indicate the probability of a company becoming insolvent, especially if the company cannot service its debt. If a bank feels that a company has a high debt ratio, a higher rate of interest may be demanded on any new loans and/or collateral to support the loan in case of default by the company.

Assets-to-Liabilities Ratio

The assets-to-liabilities ratio is also called the **solvency ratio.** It compares total assets to total liabilities. A hospitality business gives the appearance of being solvent when its assets are greater than its liabilities. Therefore, the result of this ratio should be greater than 1.00.

Formula. The assets-to-liabilities ratio formula is as follows:

$$\frac{\text{Total Assets}}{\text{Total Liabilities}}$$

The Hotel DORO's assets-to-liabilities ratio for 19X2 is calculated as follows:

$$\frac{3,247,412}{2,178,750} = 1.49$$

Interpretation. A *favorable* condition occurs when the ratio is *equal* to or *greater* than prior-period or budgeted ratios. The result of 1.49 tells us that there is $1.49 of assets for each $1 of liabilities.

Interpreting this ratio is more meaningful if the financial equation is applied as follows:

Assets	=	Claims of Creditors	+	Claims of Owners
$1.49	=	$1.00	+	$.49
100%	=	67%	+	33%

Notice that when this ratio is converted to percentages, it gives the same result as the debt-to-equity ratio percentages.

Variation of the Assets-to-Liabilities Ratio. There are several variations of ratios used to measure solvency, but they all produce the same result. For example, some analysts use a ratio called the *debt-to-assets ratio* (or liabilities-to-assets ratio), which would produce the following result when applied to the Hotel DORO:

$$\frac{\text{Total Liabilities}}{\text{Total Assets}} = \frac{2,178,750}{3,247,412} = 67\%$$

The use of one or more solvency ratios depends on the particular likes or dislikes of management. The analyst or accountant will select those ratios that management favors and is experienced with when evaluating solvency.

Working Capital

A study of working capital is important because of its close relationship to day-to-day operations. One of the leading causes of business failures is the mismanagement of working capital.

Computation of Working Capital

Working capital is computed as follows:

$$
\begin{array}{l}
\text{Current Assets} \\
- \ \underline{\text{Current Liabilities}} \\
\text{Working Capital}
\end{array}
$$

If current liabilities exceed current assets, a net working capital *deficit* occurs. Working capital cannot be manipulated by loans from banks or extension of credit by suppliers. The immediate availability of working capital depends upon the composition of its current assets, especially cash, marketable securities, and receivables.

Composition of Working Capital

In addition to comparing the amount of current assets to current liabilities, the components of working capital can be converted to percentages by dividing each current asset by the total current assets. In the example below, each current asset of Company A was divided by $200,000.

	Company A	
Cash	$100,000	50.0%
Marketable securities	25,000	12.5
Accounts receivable	20,000	10.0
Inventories	40,000	20.0
Prepaid expenses	15,000	7.5
Total current assets	$200,000	100.0%
Total current liabilities	$100,000	
Working capital	$100,000	

The Importance of Adequate Working Capital

Working capital should be sufficient to enable a company to conduct its business and meet emergencies without danger of financial disaster. Adequate working capital provides the following benefits to a hospitality company:

• Makes it possible to take advantage of cash discounts

- Permits the company to pay all interest and debt when due

- Maintains the company's good credit rating

- Permits the carrying of inventories at quantities that will provide the highest level of customer service

- Enables the company to extend credit on open account to expand sales growth

- Allows the company to operate more efficiently because there are no delays in receiving goods or services, and items are not delivered C.O.D. (collect on delivery)

- Provides a margin of safety for the company during economic recessions

Causes of Inadequate Working Capital

It is not necessary to have a working capital deficit to suffer inadequate working capital. A common ailment of companies is to have a working capital balance that is positive but inadequate for the company's needs. Inadequate working capital may be caused by the following:

- Large or numerous operating losses because of lower sales volume and/or increased costs

- Losses due to theft or casualty losses that were uninsured or under-insured

- Failure of management to obtain the necessary funds

- Excessive investment in fixed assets

Causes of Excess Working Capital

Adequate working capital is desirable, but excess working capital may result if:

- Fixed assets were purchased with excessive borrowings or issuance of capital stock. (These tactics permit the company to purchase long-term assets without using current funds.)

- Fixed assets were sold and not replaced.

- Shareholders are deprived of their fair share of earnings in the form of dividends.

Factors Affecting Working Capital Requirements

Many factors affect working capital requirements. The hospitality industry, which is characterized by small inventories and minor sales on open account, can survive on smaller working capital than the manufacturing industry. The following are some determinants of working capital requirements:

- Time from purchase of goods to sale (inventory turnover)

- Profit margins (return on assets, return on equity)

- Credit policies (receivables turnover)

- Debt load (debt-to-equity, assets to liabilities)

Reference List of Ratio Formulas

This list shows the major balance sheet ratios and their formulas and is intended to be a convenient source of reference.

Accounts Receivable Turnover Ratio $$\dfrac{\text{Net Revenue}}{\text{Average Accounts Receivable (Net)}}$$

Assets-to-Liabilities Ratio $$\dfrac{\text{Total Assets}}{\text{Total Liabilities}}$$

Average Collection Period Ratio $$\dfrac{365}{\text{Accounts Receivable Turnover}}$$

Beverage Inventory Turnover $$\dfrac{\text{Cost of Beverages Used}}{\text{Average Beverage Inventory}}$$

Current Ratio $$\dfrac{\text{Current Assets}}{\text{Current Liabilities}}$$

Debt-to-Assets Ratio $$\dfrac{\text{Total Liabilities}}{\text{Total Assets}}$$

Debt-to-Equity Ratio $$\dfrac{\text{Total Liabilities}}{\text{Total Equity}}$$

Fixed Asset Turnover Ratio $$\dfrac{\text{Net Revenue}}{\text{Average Fixed Assets}}$$

Food Inventory Turnover $$\dfrac{\text{Cost of Food Used}}{\text{Average Food Inventory}}$$

Quick Ratio $$\dfrac{\text{Cash + Marketable Securities + Receivables (Net)}}{\text{Current Liabilities}}$$

Key Terms

acid-test ratio
analysis
financial leverage
interpretation

liquidity
solvency
solvency ratio

Review Questions

1. What is the difference between the terms "analysis" and "interpretation"?

2. Define the terms "liquidity," "asset management," and "debt management."

3. Which ratios are used to measure liquidity?

4. Which ratios are used to evaluate asset management?

5. Which ratios are used to evaluate debt management?

6. How would a current ratio result of 3.12 be interpreted?

7. How would a quick ratio result of 1.55 be interpreted?

8. What is financial leverage?

9. Write the formulas for the following ratios:

    a. Current ratio

    b. Quick ratio

    c. Accounts receivable turnover

    d. Average collection period

    e. Food inventory turnover ratio

    f. Fixed asset turnover

    g. Debt-to-equity ratio

    h. Assets-to-liabilities ratio

10. How is working capital computed?

11. What is the importance of adequate working capital?

12. What are some causes of inadequate working capital?

13. What are some causes of excess working capital?

14. What are some factors affecting working capital requirements?

Problems

Problem 1

The result of a debt-to-equity ratio is .75 at the end of a hospitality corporation's current year.

    a. State this result in the form of the financial (accounting) equation.

    b. Restate this result using percentages (rounded to a whole number) in the financial equation.

    c. Who is financing most of the assets?

Problem 2

The result of an assets-to-liabilities ratio is 2.33 at the end of a hospitality corporation's current year.

    a. State this result in the form of the financial (accounting) equation.

    b. Restate this result using percentages (rounded to a whole number) in the financial equation.

    c. Who is financing most of the assets?

Problem 3

Compute the percentage composition of the current asset section of the Pikalou Hotel from the information provided below. Carry your answers to one decimal.

Cash	$150,000
Marketable securities	40,000
Accounts receivable	12,000
Inventories	20,000
Prepaid expenses	5,000
Total current assets	$227,000

Problem 4

Executive management of the Dav-Elen National Hotel have completed analyzing the hotel's balance sheet for the current period. Compare the results against the budgeted goals and indicate whether the results are favorable or unfavorable. Do not consider any other factors but the ratio numbers provided.

	Actual	Budget
Current ratio	3.5	3.9
Quick ratio	1.6	1.2
Accounts receivable turnover ratio	25.3	30.0
Fixed asset turnover ratio	3.0	2.5
Debt-to-equity ratio	2.5	2.2
Assets-to-liabilities ratio	1.4	1.5

Problem 5

Compute the following ratios and working capital for 19X8 from the Garden Bistro's balance sheet and supplementary information presented below. Show all ratio results carried to two decimals, rounded.

a. Current ratio

b. Quick ratio

c. Accounts receivable turnover ratio

d. Average collection period ratio

e. Fixed asset turnover ratio

f. Debt-to-equity ratio

g. Assets-to-liabilities ratio

h. Working capital

Supplementary Information:

Selected information from the income statement for the 365-day operating year ended December 31, 19X8:

Sales	$171,000
Allowances	− 1,000
Net Sales	$170,000

The Garden Bistro, Inc.
Balance Sheet
December 31, 19X8 and December 31, 19X7

ASSETS

CURRENT ASSETS	19X8	19X7
Cash	$ 34,000	$ 36,500
Accounts Receivable	4,000	3,450
Food Inventory	2,400	2,100
Supplies Inventory	2,600	1,900
Prepaid Expenses	2,000	2,600
Total Current Assets	45,000	46,550
PROPERTY AND EQUIPMENT		
Land	$ 30,000	30,000
Building	60,000	60,000
Furniture and Equipment	52,000	48,000
China, Glassware, and Silver	8,000	8,300
Total	150,000	146,300
Less Accumulated Depreciation	40,000	35,000
Net Property and Equipment	110,000	111,300
OTHER ASSETS		
Security Deposits	1,500	1,500
Preopening Expenses	2,500	3,000
Total Other Assets	4,000	4,500
TOTAL ASSETS	$159,000	$162,350

LIABILITIES

CURRENT LIABILITIES		
Accounts Payable	$ 11,000	25,400
Sales Tax Payable	1,000	950
Accrued Expenses	9,000	7,000
Current Portion of Long-Term Debt	6,000	6,000
Total Current Liabilities	27,000	39,350
LONG-TERM LIABILITIES		
Mortgage Payable, net of current portion	34,000	40,000
TOTAL LIABILITIES	61,000	79,350

SHAREHOLDERS' EQUITY

Paid-In Capital:		
Common Stock, par value $1,		
authorized 50,000 shares,		
issued 25,000 shares	25,000	25,000
Additional Paid-In Capital	15,000	15,000
Total Paid-In Capital	40,000	40,000

Retained Earnings, December 31, 19X8	58,000	43,000
TOTAL SHAREHOLDERS' EQUITY	98,000	83,000
TOTAL LIABILITIES AND SHAREHOLDERS' EQUITY	$159,000	$162,350

REVIEW QUIZ

When you feel you have covered all of the material in this chapter, answer these questions. Choose the *best* answer. Check your answers with the correct ones found on the Review Quiz Answer Key at the end of this book.

True (T) or False (F)

T   F   1.   A balance sheet shows the specific financial condition of each department in a hospitality business.

T   F   2.   Banks generally require that a business's ratio of current assets to current liabilities be 2.0 before approving a loan.

T   F   3.   The quick ratio is also called the acid-test ratio.

T   F   4.   Every corporation has the same optimal credit and debt structure.

Multiple Choice

5.   Which of the following ratios indicates the ability of a company to meet its short-term obligations?

    a.   current ratio
    b.   debt-to-equity ratio
    c.   fixed asset turnover ratio
    d.   return on shareholders' equity ratio

6.   The fixed asset turnover ratio requires the use of which of the following financial statements?

    a.   income statement
    b.   working capital worksheet
    c.   balance sheet
    d.   a and c

7.   A ratio that measures total debt in relation to the investment by owners is called the:

    a.   return on shareholders' equity ratio.
    b.   debt-to-equity ratio.
    c.   current ratio.
    d.   quick ratio.

8.   Working capital is computed by:

    a.   adding current assets to current liabilities.
    b.   dividing total assets by total liabilities.
    c.   subtracting current assets from current liabilities.
    d.   subtracting current liabilities from current assets.

9.   Excess working capital may result if:

    a.   shareholders have been deprived of their dividends.
    b.   fixed assets have been sold and not replaced.
    c.   fixed assets have been sold and replaced.
    d.   a and b

Chapter Outline

Learning Objectives

14

Statement of Cash Flows

E$_{\text{VERY}}$ $_{\text{HOSPITALITY}}$ $_{\text{BUSINESS}}$ needs to predict **cash flow** to ensure that it has sufficient funds to finance its current operations and growth. The income statement,
balance sheet, and statement of retained earnings are not designed to provide information about cash inflows and cash outflows. These financial statements are
prepared using the accrual basis of accounting, in which all revenues are recorded
when realized and all expenses are recorded when incurred, whether or not cash
was involved at the time of the business transaction.

The income statement and balance sheet provide information that can be used
to prepare another statement called the statement of cash flows (SCF). The SCF reflects the cash inflows and outflows of a business for a period of time.

The procedures for preparing the SCF are relatively simple, but obtaining certain information requires a complex analysis of the general ledger and journal entries. An accounting department is responsible for performing the analysis and
preparing the SCF. The responsibility of a hospitality professional is to understand
how an SCF is prepared and know how to read and interpret the SCF in order to
make intelligent management decisions. It is not necessary to be an expert in the
analytical effort.

In order to provide the hospitality professional with sufficient background to
read an SCF, this chapter uses a unique approach to explain the preparation of the
SCF:

1. The format of the SCF is described.

2. The information for preparing the SCF is provided.

3. The procedures for preparing the SCF are explained.

4. For those desiring more knowledge about the accountant's approach to the
   SCF, the appendix to this chapter describes how the data is obtained.

   This chapter also answers such questions as:

1. What is the purpose of the SCF?

2. What is the relationship of the SCF to the other major financial statements?

3. What format may be used to prepare the SCF?

4. How are cash inflows and outflows classified?

5. How is the SCF prepared?

The Purpose of the Statement of Cash Flows

The major purpose of the **statement of cash flows** is to provide relevant information about the cash receipts and cash payments of a hospitality business for a stated

period of time. The time period covered by the SCF is identical to that of the accompanying income statement.

The Financial Accounting Standards Board (FASB) is responsible for establishing standards of financial accounting and reporting. Its major function is to study accounting issues and produce Statements of Financial Accounting Standards (SFAS or FAS). The FASB has issued SFAS 95 (FAS 95), which mandates that the SCF be included with the income statement, balance sheet, and statement of retained earnings as part of the information a company provides to external users. The income statement reports on the results of operations, the balance sheet reveals the financial position, and the SCF shows the sources and uses of cash. The SCF answers such questions as:

1. How much cash was generated from operations?

2. How much cash was received from borrowings?

3. How much cash was received from the issuance of common stock or sale of treasury stock?

4. How much cash was received from the sale of property, equipment, investments, and marketable securities?

5. What amount of cash was used to pay back current loans and long-term debt?

6. What amount of dividends were paid?

7. What amount of cash was used to acquire property and equipment?

8. What amount of cash was used to make investments?

The major users of the SCF are:

- Management
- Creditors
- Investors

Management uses the SCF to judge the company's ability to meet its debt obligations, estimate future borrowings, invest excess funds, plan for growth of facilities or locations, and determine dividend policy.

Creditors and investors use the SCF to judge the company's abilities to meet its debt obligations and pay dividends, and assess the company's financial soundness.

Cash and Cash Equivalents

Because the SCF explains the changes in cash for a period of time, it is important to define which items represent cash. The management of a company must establish a policy outlining which items are to be treated as cash in preparing the SCF. In addition to cash in savings and checking accounts, there are certain types of financial instruments that can be equivalent to cash even though they are not in the form of cash.

To qualify as a cash equivalent, a financial instrument must be:

1. Readily convertible to cash, and

2. Be so near its maturity that there is virtually no risk of decline in value due to changes in the market interest rates.

Cash equivalents are highly liquid investments such as:

- United States treasury bills
- Commercial paper
- Money market funds

U.S. treasury bills are borrowings by the United States government from investors. In the investment community, they are called U.S. T-bills or simply T-bills. T-bills are issued weekly at public auction through regional federal reserve banks. They can also be purchased through commercial banks and brokers for a small processing fee. The minimum T-bill purchase is $10,000, with the amount increasing in $1,000 increments. The minimum maturity period is 13 weeks from the date of original issue. There is a secondary market for selling these T-bills for holders who find that they cannot wait for the maturity date.

Commercial paper is unsecured short-term obligations of major corporations issued through brokers or directly by corporations.

A **money market fund** is a mutual fund that invests primarily in U.S. T-bills, commercial paper, and other financial instruments offering attractive interest rates. Investors in money market funds may redeem their holdings directly through the mutual fund or a broker.

Funds in marketable securities such as common and preferred stock of other companies are not classified as cash equivalents because these securities do not have a maturity date and may be subject to significant fluctuations in market value.

Format of the Statement of Cash Flows

Cash flow is the net result of cash receipts and cash payments. If cash receipts are greater than cash payments, the result is a positive cash flow, also called a **cash inflow**. A negative cash flow, also called a **cash outflow**, is the result of cash payments being greater than cash receipts.

Exhibit 1 shows the major sections of an SCF. The cash flows are classified in three major activities:

- Operating activities
- Investing activities
- Financing activities

If the cash inflows exceed the cash outflows, the net total of the section is labeled *net cash provided by (name of activity)*. If the cash outflows exceed the cash inflows, the net total of the section is labeled *net cash used in (name of activity)*.

The amount entered on the line labeled *increase (decrease) in cash for the period* is the net total of the three activities sections.

Exhibit 1   Format of the Statement of Cash Flows

Cash flows from operating activities:
> Net cash provided by operating activities
> *or*
> Net cash used in operating activities

Cash flows from investing activities:
> Net cash provided by investing activities
> *or*
> Net cash used in investing activities

Cash flows from financing activities:
> Net cash provided by financing activities
> *or*
> Net cash used in financing activities

Increase (decrease) in cash for the period
Cash balance at beginning of period
Cash balance at end of period

Footnotes:

The beginning cash balance is the ending balance from the previous period's SCF. As an alternative, the appropriate comparative balance sheet also provides the beginning cash balance for the SCF.

The ending cash balance for this period is the result of totaling the increase (decrease) in cash for the period and the beginning cash balance for the period. The ending cash balance on the SCF must agree with the amount shown on the balance sheet for the same date.

Income from Operating Activities

Operating activities refer to a hospitality company's primary revenue-generating activities. For a hotel, revenue from all its operating centers less expenses of operating centers, support centers, energy costs, and fixed charges is classified as income from operating activities. Interest income and dividends income are also included in income from operating activities.

Income from operating activities, also called income from operations, can be summarized as follows:

> + Sales: revenue centers
> + Interest income
> + Dividends income
> − Expenses: revenue centers

 - Expenses: support centers and energy costs
 - Fixed charges
 - Income taxes
 = Income from operations

Cash flows from the sale of property, equipment, and long-term investments are not considered to be from operating activities because these transactions are not part of a hotel's primary business purpose or day-to-day operations.

Marketable Securities

Showing the cash flows from the sale of marketable securities as an operating activity depends upon how the securities are categorized according to SFAS 115 (FAS 115). The classification criteria are technical and are explained in the appendix to this chapter.

The abstract of SFAS 115 is that cash flows from the sale of marketable securities categorized as trading securities should be included in the operating activities section of the SCF. Trading securities are characterized by frequent and heavy trading. If the marketable securities are not categorized as trading securities, then the gains or losses are shown in the investment activities section of the SCF, which is explained later in this chapter.

It is unlikely that a busy general manager of a hotel attending to its critical and demanding day-to-day management has the time to devote to heavy trading of securities. Therefore, this chapter will not classify marketable securities as trading securities.

Cash flows from the sale of marketable securities appear in the investing activities section of the statement of cash flows throughout this chapter.

A typical hotel income statement in condensed form is shown in Exhibit 2. The $151,000 net income amount is not income from operating activities because it contains a $10,000 gain from the sale of investments. Since the $10,000 was originally added to the hotel's income, nonoperating income of this type must be subtracted to eliminate the effect of a gain.

Net income	$151,000
Less gain on sale of investment	10,000
Income from operations	$141,000

Cash Flow from Operating Activities

While the $141,000 (as adjusted) is *income from operations*, it is not the *cash flow from operations*. Remember that the SCF is based on cash transactions and not on accrual accounting for income and expenses. The reason the $141,000 is not cash flow from operating activities is that not all sales were for cash and not all expenses were paid in the period reported. To explain this, the following summary of accrual accounting is presented:

- Sales can be for cash or on account (accounts receivable).

- Purchases can be for cash or on account (accounts payable).

Exhibit 2   Condensed Hotel Income Statement (Example)

Room sales	$600,000
Food and beverage sales	100,000
Interest and dividends income	1,000
Total revenue	$701,000
Less depreciation	50,000
Less other expenses	450,000
Income before income taxes and gain on sale of investments	$201,000
Gain on sale of investments	10,000
Income before income taxes	$211,000
Income taxes	60,000
Net income	$151,000

- Expenses such as depreciation and amortization never require a cash outlay because this type of expense is derived from adjusting entries that merely allocate the historical cost of a long-lived asset over an estimated useful life.

The two methods for computing the cash flows from operating activities are:

- Direct method
- Indirect method

Direct Method

One approach to preparing the operating activities section of the SCF is the direct method. Under the direct method, a thorough analysis of various general ledger accounts is required to determine cash receipts and cash disbursements from operations. A logical account to start with is the Cash account because all cash receipts and disbursements flow through this account. However, there are two major complications:

1. The volume of transactions posted to the Cash account is substantial, making it impractical to analyze all of them.
2. The individual postings to the Cash account and other accounts generally do not contain a sufficient description of the transaction.

Most hospitality companies do not use the direct method; instead they elect the faster and easier indirect method. Both methods produce an identical amount to represent cash flows from operating activities. Therefore, this chapter concentrates on the indirect method. The appendix to this chapter contains more information on the direct method for interested readers.

Indirect Method

The indirect method for preparing the operating activities section of the SCF is simple and efficient because it utilizes the existing income statement and balance sheet. The indirect method begins with net income as shown on the income state-ment, adjusts net income for noncash items, continues with the elimination of non-operating gains and losses, and concludes with the conversion from accrual accounting to cash basis accounting. This conversion is accomplished by adding or subtracting changes in certain current asset and current liability accounts.

Adjustments for Noncash Items. Under the indirect approach, cash flows from operating activities are determined in part by adjusting the net income shown on the income statement for any items that appear in it but do not have an effect on cash. Depreciation expense and amortization expense are noncash expenses that never affect cash flows. Since they were originally deducted on the income state-ment to arrive at net income, these noncash expenses are added back to eliminate them. Thus, the procedure to adjust operating net income to operating cash flow begins as follows:

$$\begin{array}{ll} & \text{Net income} \\ + & \text{Depreciation and amortization} \end{array}$$

Adjustments for Nonoperating Gains and Losses. The gains and losses from the sale of assets are the result of selling or disposing of property, equipment, invest-ments, and marketable securities. Since a gain had previously increased net in-come as shown on the income statement, it must now be subtracted to eliminate this transaction. Conversely, losses were deducted to arrive at net income, thus the elimination adjustment requires adding back the amount of loss. The procedure to adjust operating net income to operating cash flow continues as follows:

$$\begin{array}{ll} & \text{Net income} \\ + & \text{Depreciation and amortization} \\ - & \text{Gains from sale of assets} \\ + & \text{Losses from sale of assets} \end{array}$$

Adjustments for Changes in Current Assets and Current Liabilities. Adjust-ments are necessary to convert from accrual basis accounting to cash basis account-ing. Some of the sales on the income statement may not have been cash sales, and certain expenses may not yet be paid. Exhibit 3 shows how sales of $120,000 actu-ally result in only $100,000 of cash received. This is because, of the $120,000 total sales, $20,000 were on accounts receivable and $100,000 were cash sales.

Eliminating the need to analyze many ledger accounts, the indirect method employs logic to adjust accrual accounting to cash basis accounting. Exhibit 3 shows that it is possible to "squeeze" the amount representing cash sales using logic. Notice that sales and accounts receivable increased. Accounts receivable is a result of the selling process. Therefore, an increase to accounts receivable results in an increase to sales without a corresponding increase to cash. Accordingly, the in-crease of $20,000 in accounts receivable is subtracted from the total sales of $120,000 to arrive at cash sales of $100,000.

To present the basis of the logic involved, we will analyze three items that usually appear on a balance sheet: accounts receivable, inventory, and accounts payable.

Exhibit 3   Accrual Accounting versus Cash Basis Accounting

Transaction: Cash sales are $100,000.

Cash	Accounts Receivable	Sales
100,000		100,000

Transaction: Additional sales of $20,000 were on account.

Cash	Accounts Receivable	Sales
100,000	20,000	100,000
		20,000
		120,000

Result:

Accrual accounting shows sales of:	$120,000
However, cash received is:	$100,000

Reconciliation to cash received:

Total sales	$120,000
Less: Increase in accounts receivable	(20,000)
Cash received	$100,000

Assume a balance sheet shows the following comparative data for accounts receivable.

Accounts receivable:	
This year's ending balance	$40,000
Last year's ending balance	30,000
Increase to accounts receivable	$10,000

The data on accounts receivable shows that this year had a beginning balance of $30,000 and an ending balance of $40,000, meaning that accounts receivable increased by $10,000. An *increase* to accounts receivable delays a sale's conversion to cash. It could be stated that the customers of the company are using its money. Refer again to Exhibit 3, and notice that the increase to accounts receivable was used as a deduction from sales to arrive at cash received.

Assume a balance sheet shows the following comparative data for inventory.

Inventory:	
This year's ending balance	$3,000
Last year's ending balance	2,000
Increase to inventories	$1,000

The data on inventory shows that this year had a beginning balance of $2,000 and an ending balance of $3,000, meaning that inventory increased by $1,000. An increase to inventory is equivalent to a cash outflow because the increase is due to purchases that ultimately require cash payment.

Observe that *increases* in these *current asset* accounts caused a *decrease* to *cash flow.* Therefore, it is logical to assume that increases in a current asset account are a cash outflow and, conversely, decreases in a current asset account result in a cash inflow.

Current asset exceptions. The increase or decrease effects in *cash* and *marketable securities* are ignored for purposes of the operating activities section because these accounts are presented elsewhere in the SCF.

The procedure to adjust operating net income to operating cash flow continues as follows:

> Net income
> + Depreciation and amortization
> − Gains from sale of assets
> + Losses from sale of assets
> − Increases to certain current asset accounts
> + Decreases to certain current asset accounts

Our analysis of the logic used in the cash conversion procedure now turns to current liabilities. Assume a balance sheet shows the following comparative data for accounts payable.

> Accounts payable:
>
> | | |
> |---|---:|
> | This year's ending balance | $25,000 |
> | Last year's ending balance | 18,000 |
> | Increase to accounts payable | $ 7,000 |

The data on accounts payable shows that this year had a beginning balance of $18,000 and an ending balance of $25,000, meaning that accounts payable increased by $7,000. An *increase* to accounts payable is equivalent to a *cash inflow* because the use of credit to purchase inventory and other items results in the use of "other people's money," which is similar to borrowings of cash.

Using logic regarding accounts payable, we can conclude that increases in current liability accounts are a cash inflow. Increases in current liabilities preserve cash in the business. Conversely, decreases in a current liability account result in a cash outflow. *Notice that the increases and decreases to current liabilities are exactly the opposite of those stated for current assets.* This adds validity to the logic, because liabilities always have an effect opposite to that of assets, including the selection of debits and credits to record these transactions.

Current liability exceptions. The increase or decrease effects in *loans due to cash borrowings, dividends payable,* and *current portion of long-term debt* are ignored for purposes of the operating activities section because these accounts are presented elsewhere in the SCF.

The procedure to adjust operating net income to operating cash flow can now be completed as follows:

> Net income
> + Depreciation and amortization
> − Gains from sale of assets

+ Losses from sale of assets
− Increases to certain current asset accounts
+ Decreases to certain current asset accounts
+ Increases to certain current liability accounts
− Decreases to certain current liability accounts

Procedures reference chart. The various steps in the indirect method for adjusting net income from operations to cash flows from operating activities are listed in the procedures reference chart in Exhibit 4. This exhibit is a comprehensive procedures chart that can be used to prepare all sections of the SCF. Refer to the operating activities section of this chart, which summarizes how to convert net income to cash flow from operations.

Investing Activities

The investing activities section is the second cash activities section of the SCF. Investing activities generally involve cash transactions that affect marketable securities and noncurrent assets such as investments and property, plants, and equipment.

The purchase of these assets is a decrease to cash flow (cash outflow) for the amount of cash disbursed at the time of acquisition. The proceeds from the sale of these assets is an increase to cash flow (cash inflow) whether there was a gain or a loss in the selling transaction. The following comparison explains why the emphasis is on *proceeds* (selling price) instead of the gain or loss.

	Investment A	Investment B
Proceeds (cash received)	$100,000	$100,000
Cost basis	80,000	120,000
Gain (loss)	$ 20,000	$ (20,000)

Regardless of the gain or loss, the sale of either investment generated a cash inflow of $100,000, which is classified as an investing activity. The gain or loss is not relevant to the SCF.

Purchases of property and expensive equipment are seldom transacted with only a cash payment. Quite often, a cash down payment and debt such as a mortgage payable or note payable are used to complete the purchase. For example, land might be purchased as follows:

Acquisition cost	$80,000
Mortgage	60,000
Cash down payment	$20,000

The SCF reflects only cash inflows and cash outflows. Therefore, only the $20,000 cash payment will appear in the investing activities section of the SCF. Because this transaction also involves noncash investing and financing activities, it would be fully disclosed in the footnotes to the SCF. (Footnotes and disclosures are discussed later in this chapter.)

The items entered in the investing activities section of the SCF can be summarized as follows:

Cash inflows:
>   Proceeds from sale of marketable securities
>   Proceeds from sale of investments
>   Proceeds from sale of property and equipment

Cash outflows:
>   Cash used to acquire marketable securities
>   Cash used to acquire investments
>   Cash used to acquire property and equipment

While the investing activities section is relatively simple to complete, obtaining the data requires a thorough knowledge of accounting and bookkeeping procedures. Since the readers of this chapter are probably not accountants, the procedures for obtaining the data are explained in the appendix for those interested in that knowledge.

The steps for preparing the investing activities section are summarized in the procedures chart in Exhibit 4.

Financing Activities

The financing activities section is the third and final cash activities section of the SCF. The financing activities section deals with equity and debt transactions. It explains how cash was obtained from investors (equity financing) and from creditors (debt financing). For example, cash can be obtained by issuing capital stock or borrowings. These financing activities ultimately require paying the debt principal, paying dividends, and possibly reacquiring stock (treasury stock).

The items entered in the financing activities section of the SCF can be summarized as follows:

Cash inflows:
>   Issue capital stock (common or preferred)
>   Issue bonds
>   Sell treasury stock
>   Cash borrowings

Cash outflows:
>   Payment of dividends
>   Purchase of treasury stock
>   Payment of principal on debt (mortgages, loans, bonds)

While the financing activities section is relatively simple to complete, obtaining the data requires a thorough knowledge of accounting and bookkeeping procedures. Since the readers of this chapter are probably not accountants, the procedures for obtaining the data are explained in the appendix for those interested in that knowledge.

The steps for preparing the financing activities section are summarized in the procedures chart in Exhibit 4.

Footnotes and Disclosures

Since the three activities sections of the SCF present only those activities that are cash basis oriented, it is usually necessary to provide disclosures either in narrative form or summarized in a schedule. These disclosures and **footnotes** may be on the same page as the SCF or reported on an attachment page. Footnotes and disclosures are required for the following transactions:

- Income taxes and interest paid in the period

- Accounting policy regarding cash

- Noncash investing and financing transactions

Income Taxes and Interest Paid

The FASB requires that the amount paid for income taxes and interest be disclosed on the SCF if the indirect method of presenting cash flow from operating activities is used. This information is generally not found on the income statement because these expenses are recorded on the accrual basis. Therefore, an analysis of the bookkeeping accounts for income taxes expense and interest expense is necessary. The cash expenditure for income taxes and interest is most conveniently shown as a footnote on the SCF as follows:

Interest paid for the period	$xxx
Income taxes paid for the period	$xxx

Accounting Policy Regarding Cash

The footnote for the *disclosure of accounting policy* explains the reporting of cash flows based on cash, cash equivalents, and cash on hand.

Noncash Investing and Financing Transactions

Noncash investing and financing transactions are transactions during a period that affect long-term assets, equity, or debt but do not result in cash receipts or payments.

Examples of noncash investing and financing transactions are converting debt to equity, acquiring assets by part cash and part mortgage, obtaining an asset by entering into a capital lease, and the exchange of noncash assets or liabilities for other noncash assets or liabilities. Some specific examples of these transactions are:

- Issuing stock to settle a note payable

- Executing a new note to settle a note that became due

- Acquiring an auto via a three-year lease

- Exchanging vacant land for vacant land owned by another party

- Purchasing an asset with a cash down payment and the balance financed by a mortgage or note payable. In this case, only the cash down payment would show in the investing activities section of the SCF. This transaction would require disclosure, which might take the following form:

Acquisition cost of land	$80,000
Cash down payment	20,000
Balance financed by mortgage	$60,000

Demonstration Problem

Now that the logic and principles underlying the SCF have been presented, they can be applied to perform the procedure shown in Exhibit 4, the procedures reference chart for the SCF. This chart will be used along with Exhibit 5, which presents the financial statements (income statement and comparative balance sheet) of the Demonstration Hotel. The results of assembling this information are presented in Exhibit 6, which is the completed SCF.

The SCF will be prepared in the following sequence:

1. Operating activities section
2. Investing activities section
3. Financing activities section
4. Computation of ending cash balance
5. Footnotes and disclosures

Preparing the Operating Activities Section

Preparing the operating activities section requires an analysis of the balance sheet and the income statement, which are shown in Exhibit 5. The results of this analysis are presented in Exhibit 6. The objectives of this section are to convert net income, which has been computed on the accrual basis, to cash flow income and also to eliminate nonoperating gains and losses to arrive at cash flows from operations.

The starting point in preparing the operating activities section of the SCF is the net income of $9,000. To this amount are added back the $18,000 depreciation and $500 amortization noncash expenses.

Next are the adjustments to reconcile (convert) net income to net cash flows from operating activities. The nonoperating gains and losses are eliminated; the $1,000 gain is subtracted and the $1,200 loss is added back.

The final step to complete the operating activities section of the SCF is using the balance sheet to enter the increases and decreases in certain current asset and current liability accounts. These increases and decreases are processed as follows:

- *Increases* in current assets are *subtracted.*
- *Increases* in current liabilities are *added.*

It then follows that decreases in current assets and current liabilities require opposite mathematical functions than those stated for increases.

The current asset accounts for cash and marketable securities are bypassed because these items are processed elsewhere in the SCF. The $9,500 *increase* in accounts receivable is subtracted, the $2,000 *decrease* in inventories is added, and the $1,000 *increase* in prepaid expenses is subtracted.

The current liability accounts are now processed. The $1,500 *decrease* in accounts payable is added, and the $800 *increase* in sales tax payable is subtracted. The current liability accounts for dividends payable and current portion of mortgage are bypassed because these items are processed elsewhere in the SCF.

The adjustments total $8,200, which is added to the net income of $9,000. This results in a positive cash flow of $17,200, which is labeled *net cash provided by operating activities.*

Preparing the Investing Activities Section

The objective of the investing activities section is to show cash receipts and payments involving marketable securities and noncurrent assets such as investments, property, plant, and equipment.

Obtaining the information for the investing activities section requires technical accounting knowledge. Otherwise, analyzing the balance sheet changes can result in misleading information. For example, the balance sheet shows a $60,000 increase to property and equipment. It would be erroneous to assume that this increase applies only to a purchase of property and equipment. In actuality, the $60,000 increase is a combination of many transactions as follows:

Equipment purchased ($43,000 cash paid)	$43,000
Land purchased ($8,000 cash paid)	40,000
Equipment disposed of ($6,000 cash proceeds)	(8,000)
Accumulated depreciation (adjusting entry)	(18,000)
Accumulated depreciation (disposed asset)	3,000
Net change	$60,000

The analysis required to obtain the information for this section is provided in the appendix to this chapter for those readers interested in the detailed and technical expertise required in the process. We will only be concerned here with the types of cash transactions that are entered in the investing activities section as listed in the reference chart.

The investing activities section for the Demonstration Hotel shows a net cash outflow of $41,200, which is labeled *net cash used in investing activities*. This cash outflow is the result of the following cash investing transactions:

- $6,000 proceeds from the sale of equipment

- $3,800 proceeds from the sale of marketable securities

- $43,000 cash purchase of equipment

- $8,000 down payment for the purchase of land. The land acquisition cost was $40,000, but only the $8,000 cash paid is entered because the balance was financed by a mortgage (a noncash investing activity that is explained in the footnotes and disclosures section of the SCF).

Preparing the Financing Activities Section

The objective of the financing activities section is to show how cash was obtained from investors and creditors and how cash was used to pay the debt principal and dividends and purchase treasury stock.

Obtaining the information for this section involves the same degree of complexity mentioned in the investing activities section. We will only be concerned here with the types of cash transactions that are entered in the financing activities section as listed in the reference chart.

The financing activities section for the Demonstration Hotel shows a net cash inflow of $18,000, which is labeled *net cash provided by financing activities*. This cash inflow is the result of the following cash financing transactions:

- $30,000 proceeds from borrowings by a note payable to a bank
- $9,000 proceeds from the sale of no-par stock
- $1,000 cash payment for dividends declared and paid this year
- $20,000 cash paid out to reacquire its own stock to buy out a dissident shareholder

Areas that should be studied are the current portion of long-term debt and long-term debt lines shown on the balance sheet. In the demonstration problem, the current portion of the mortgage payable is $5,000 and the long-term portion is $27,000. These amounts are not shown in two bookkeeping accounts. There is only one bookkeeping account called Mortgage Payable. In this case, its balance would be $32,000 which is allocated by the accountant into its current and long-term portions. The general ledger account and presentation of this "mixed" debt is illustrated in Exhibit 7.

The debit side of the mortgage payable or other liability account generally indicates the payments on this debt. These payments are verified by their reference to a cash disbursements entry.

Computing the Ending Cash Balance

The $17,200 cash inflow from the operating activities section, the $41,200 cash outflow from the investing activities section, and the $18,000 cash inflow from the financing section result in a $6,000 *decrease* in cash for the year.

The balance sheet shows that the cash balance on 12/31/X1 was $45,000, which became the beginning cash balance on 1/1/X2. Subtracting the decrease of $6,000 results in a cash balance of $39,000 at the end of the year. This number is verified by referring to the balance sheet, which also shows cash on 12/31/X2 of $39,000.

Preparing the Footnotes and Disclosures

It is necessary to show the amounts paid for interest expense and income taxes. The amounts shown on the income statement are accounted for on the accrual basis and do not necessarily reflect the actual cash paid. The cash payments of $1,000 for interest expense and $2,000 for state and federal income taxes were determined by analyzing the respective general ledger bookkeeping accounts.

Transactions that affect assets, liabilities, or equity but did not involve cash are disclosed in a supplemental schedule called noncash investing and financing activities. The acquisition of land by cash and mortgage by the Demonstration Hotel has been explained earlier.

To comply with the disclosure on accounting policy, the Demonstration Hotel describes its cash and cash equivalents policy.

Key Terms

cash flow	footnotes
cash inflow	money market fund
cash outflow	statement of cash flows
commercial paper	U.S. treasury bills

Exhibit 4   Procedures Reference Chart—Statement of Cash Flows

Operating Activities Section

	Effect	
Net income (starting point)	+	
Adjustments for noncash items:		
Depreciation	+	
Amortization	+	
Adjustments for nonoperating gains and losses:		
Gain on sale of assets	−	
Loss on sale of assets	+	
Adjustments for changes in current assets:		

	Increase	Decrease
Cash	NA	NA
Marketable securities	NA	NA
Receivables	−	+
Inventories	−	+
Prepaids	−	+
Adjustments for changes in current liabilities:		

	Increase	Decrease
Loans for cash borrowings	NA	NA
Dividends payable	NA	NA
Current portion of long-term debt	NA	NA
Accounts payable	+	−
Accrued liabilities	+	−
Other current liability accounts	+	−

> **LEARNING TIP**
>
> The mathematical signs of the changes in current liabilities stay the same on the SCF. For example, a change that is an increase (+) is also an increase (+) on the SCF. It then follows that the changes in current assets would be reversed.

Investing Activities Section

	Effect
Proceeds from sale of marketable securities	+
Proceeds from sale of investments	+
Proceeds from sale of property and equipment	+
Cash used to acquire marketable securities	−
Cash used to acquire investments	−
Cash used to acquire property and equipment	−

Financing Activities Section

	Effect
Issue capital stock	+
Issue bonds	+
Sell treasury stock	+
Cash borrowings	+
Payment of dividends	−
Purchase of treasury stock	−
Payment of principal on debt	−

NA = Not applicable

Exhibit 5   Demonstration Problem—Income Statement and Balance Sheet

Income Statement
Demonstration Hotel
For the year ended 12/31/X2

Sales		$310,000
Depreciation	$ 18,000	
Amortization	500	
Other expenses	277,300	
Total expenses		295,800
Income before nonoperating gains (losses)		14,200
Gain on sale of equipment		1,000
Loss on sale of marketable securities		(1,200)
Income before income taxes		14,000
Income taxes		5,000
Net income		$ 9,000

Balance Sheet
Demonstration Hotel
12/31/X2 and 12/31/X1

	19X2	19X1	Increase (Decrease)
Cash	$ 39,000	$ 45,000	$ (6,000)
Marketable securities	0	5,000	(5,000)
Accounts receivable (net)	28,000	18,500	9,500
Inventories	10,000	12,000	(2,000)
Prepaid expenses	3,000	2,000	1,000
Total current assets	$ 80,000	$ 82,500	$ (2,500)
Property and equipment (net)	190,000	130,000	60,000
Other assets (net)	5,000	5,500	(500)
Total assets	$275,000	$218,000	$ 57,000
Accounts payable	$ 88,000	$ 89,500	$ (1,500)
Sales tax payable	2,000	1,200	800
Accrued expenses	6,000	7,300	(1,300)
Dividends payable	3,000	0	3,000
Current portion of mortgage	5,000	0	5,000
Total current liabilities	$104,000	$ 98,000	$ 6,000
Mortgage payable (net)	27,000	0	27,000
Note payable due 2/1/X4	30,000	0	30,000
Capital stock issued (no par)	117,000	108,000	9,000
Treasury stock	(20,000)	0	(20,000)
Retained earnings	17,000	12,000	5,000
Total liabilities and equity	$275,000	$218,000	$ 57,000

Exhibit 6   Demonstration Problem—Statement of Cash Flows

Statement of Cash Flows
Demonstration Hotel
For the year ended 12/31/X2

Cash Flows from Operating Activities:

Net income	$ 9,000	
Adjustments to reconcile net income to net cash flows from operating activities:		
Depreciation expense	18,000	
Amortization expense	500	
Gain on sale of equipment	(1,000)	
Loss on sale of marketable securities	1,200	
Increase in accounts receivable	(9,500)	
Decrease in inventories	2,000	
Increase in prepaid expenses	(1,000)	
Decrease in accounts payable	(1,500)	
Increase in sales tax payable	800	
Decrease in accrued expenses	(1,300)	8,200
Net cash provided by operating activities		17,200

Cash Flows from Investing Activities:

Proceeds from sale of equipment	6,000	
Proceeds from sale of marketable securities	3,800	
Purchase of equipment	(43,000)	
Down payment on purchase of land	(8,000)	
Net cash used in investing activities	(41,200)	

Cash Flows from Financing Activities:

Cash proceeds from note payable due 2/1/X4	30,000	
Proceeds from issuance of no par capital stock	9,000	
Dividends declared and paid this year	(1,000)	
Purchase of treasury stock	(20,000)	
Net cash provided by financing activities		18,000
Increase (decrease) in cash for the year		(6,000)
Cash at the beginning of the year		45,000
Cash at the end of the year		$ 39,000

Supplemental Disclosures of Cash Flow Information
Cash paid during the year for:

Interest	$ 1,000
Income taxes	$ 2,000

Supplemental Schedule of Noncash Investing and Financing Activities
A parcel of land was purchased in December 19X2 as follows:

Acquisition cost of land	$40,000
Cash down payment	8,000
Balance financed by mortgage	$32,000

Disclosure of Accounting Policy
For purposes of the statement of cash flows, the Company considers all highly liquid debt instruments purchased with a maturity of three months or less to be cash equivalents.

Exhibit 7   Current and Long-Term Portion Presentation

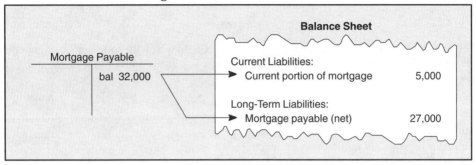

Review Questions

1. What is the purpose of the statement of cash flows (SCF)?

2. What kinds of questions are answered by the SCF?

3. How does the management of a hotel use the SCF?

4. What are some examples and brief descriptions of cash equivalents?

5. Why aren't marketable securities considered to be cash equivalents in the SCF?

6. What are the three sections of the SCF?

7. What is meant by the term "operating activities"?

8. Why aren't gains and losses from the sale of property, equipment, and investments considered to be a part of operating activities?

9. Why can't the net income from the income statement be used as cash flow from operating activities?

10. What are the two major noncash expenses?

11. What are nonoperating gains and losses?

12. What kinds of transactions would be entered in the investing activities section of the SCF?

13. What kinds of transactions would be entered in the financing activities section of the SCF?

14. What are three types of transactions that can appear in the footnotes and disclosures section of the SCF?

15. How would the acquisition of land at a cost of $100,000, purchased with a $30,000 down payment and the balance financed with a mortgage, be shown in the SCF?

Problems

Problem 1

Indicate the section of the statement of cash flows (SCF) in which the following items would be entered. Assume the operating activities section is prepared according to the indirect method.

	Operating Activities	Investing Activities	Financing Activities
Amortization	_____	_____	_____
Proceeds from sale of marketable securities	_____	_____	_____
Payment of principal on debt	_____	_____	_____
Cash used to acquire investments	_____	_____	_____
Depreciation	_____	_____	_____
Gain on sale of assets	_____	_____	_____
Increase or decrease in accrued liabilities	_____	_____	_____
Cash borrowings	_____	_____	_____
Proceeds from sale of property and equipment	_____	_____	_____
Increase or decrease in prepaid expenses	_____	_____	_____
Issue capital stock	_____	_____	_____
Cash used to acquire marketable securities	_____	_____	_____
Loss on sale of assets	_____	_____	_____
Increase or decrease in receivables	_____	_____	_____
Net income	_____	_____	_____
Payment of dividends	_____	_____	_____
Proceeds from sale of investments	_____	_____	_____
Increase or decrease in inventory	_____	_____	_____
Purchase of treasury stock	_____	_____	_____
Proceeds from sale of treasury stock	_____	_____	_____
Cash used to acquire property and equipment	_____	_____	_____
Increase or decrease in accounts payable	_____	_____	_____

Problem 2

Indicate the mathematical function (+ or −) in the proper activities section of the SCF for the following items. Assume the operating activities section is prepared according to the indirect method.

	Operating Activities	Investing Activities	Financing Activities
Amortization	_____	_____	_____
Proceeds from sale of marketable securities	_____	_____	_____
Payment of principal on debt	_____	_____	_____
Cash used to acquire investments	_____	_____	_____
Depreciation	_____	_____	_____
Gain on sale of assets	_____	_____	_____
Increase in accrued liabilities	_____	_____	_____

Decrease in accrued liabilities	_____	_____	_____
Cash borrowings	_____	_____	_____
Proceeds from sale of property and equipment	_____	_____	_____
Increase in prepaid expenses	_____	_____	_____
Decrease in prepaid expenses	_____	_____	_____
Issue capital stock	_____	_____	_____
Cash used to acquire marketable securities	_____	_____	_____
Loss on sale of assets	_____	_____	_____
Increase in accounts receivable	_____	_____	_____
Decrease in accounts receivable	_____	_____	_____
Net income	_____	_____	_____
Payment of dividends	_____	_____	_____
Proceeds from sale of investments	_____	_____	_____
Increase in inventory	_____	_____	_____
Decrease in inventory	_____	_____	_____
Purchase of treasury stock	_____	_____	_____
Proceeds from sale of treasury stock	_____	_____	_____
Cash used to acquire property and equipment	_____	_____	_____
Increase in accounts payable	_____	_____	_____
Decrease in accounts payable	_____	_____	_____

Problem 3

Prepare the operating activities section of the SCF for the Davdeg Motel using the indirect method.

Income Statement		
Sales		$500,000
Depreciation	$ 40,000	
Other expenses	400,000	440,000
Operating income		60,000
Loss on sale of equipment		(12,000)
Gain on sale of investments		5,000
Net income		$ 53,000

Changes in balance sheet accounts:	Increase (Decrease)
Cash	$ 20,000
Accounts receivable	(10,000)
Inventories	3,000
Prepaid expenses	1,000
Property and equipment	36,000
Accounts payable	7,000
Taxes payable	(1,000)
Current portion of long-term debt	3,000
Long-term debt	9,000
Equity accounts	32,000

Problem 4

Prepare the operating activities section of the SCF for the Lizdale Bistro using the indirect method.

Income Statement		
Sales		$200,000
Depreciation	$ 10,000	
Other expenses	170,000	180,000
Income from operations		20,000
Gain on sale of equipment		2,000
Gain on sale of marketable securities		3,000
Net income		$ 25,000

Changes in balance sheet accounts:	Increase (Decrease)
Cash	$ (7,000)
Marketable securities	4,000
Accounts receivable	15,000
Inventories	(2,000)
Prepaid expenses	(1,000)
Property and equipment	(9,000)
Accounts payable	(8,000)
Accrued payables	3,000
Dividends payable	3,000
Current portion of long-term debt	(5,000)
Long-term debt	(6,000)
Equity accounts	13,000

Problem 5

Prepare the operating activities section of the SCF for the Bessdoon Restaurant using the indirect method.

Income Statement		
Sales		$300,000
Depreciation	$ 8,000	
Other expenses	284,000	292,000
Operating income		8,000
Loss on sale of equipment		(1,000)
Loss on sale of marketable securities		(2,000)
Net income		$ 5,000

Changes in balance sheet accounts:	Increase (Decrease)
Cash	$ 10,000
Marketable securities	(5,000)
Accounts receivable	18,000
Inventories	5,000
Prepaid expenses	(2,000)

Property and equipment	10,000
Accounts payable	(6,000)
Accrued payables	1,000
Dividends payable	2,000
Current portion of long-term debt	12,000
Long-term debt	24,000
Equity accounts	3,000

Problem 6

Prepare the operating activities section of the SCF for the Walkam Ristorante using the indirect method.

Income Statement	19X2
Sales	$900,000
Cost of sales	300,000
Gross profit	600,000
Depreciation	80,000
Amortization	10,000
Other expenses	430,000
Operating income	80,000
Gain on sale of investments	4,000
Income before income taxes	84,000
Income taxes	30,000
Net income	$ 54,000

Balance Sheet	19X2	19X1
Cash	$ 30,000	$ 42,000
Marketable securities	10,000	0
Accounts receivable	120,000	90,000
Inventories	50,000	55,000
Prepaid expenses	7,000	9,000
Total current assets	$217,000	$196,000
Property and equipment (net)	500,000	420,000
Total assets	$717,000	$616,000
Accounts payable	$110,000	$ 90,000
Wages payable	30,000	37,000
Current maturities of long-term debt	24,000	12,000
Total current liabilities	$164,000	$139,000
Long-term debt	200,000	178,000
Total liabilities	$364,000	$317,000
Shareholders' equity	353,000	299,000
Total liabilities and equity	$717,000	$616,000

Problem 7

Prepare a complete SCF for the Manellian Bistro using the indirect method for the operating activities section.

Income Statement	19X2
Sales	$780,000
Cost of sales	250,000
Gross profit	530,000
Depreciation	50,000
Other expenses	445,000
Operating income	35,000
Gain on sale of investments	30,000
Income before income taxes	65,000
Income taxes	25,000
Net income	$ 40,000

Balance Sheet	December 31		
	19X2	19X1	Change
Cash	$ 32,000	$ 50,000	$ (18,000)
Marketable securities	40,000	35,000	5,000
Accounts receivable	140,000	90,000	50,000
Inventories	30,000	35,000	(5,000)
Prepaid expenses	3,000	2,000	1,000
Total current assets	$245,000	$212,000	$ 33,000
Property and equipment (net)	299,000	330,000	(31,000)
Total assets	$544,000	$542,000	$ 2,000
Accounts payable	$ 60,000	$ 70,000	$ (10,000)
Wages payable	10,000	8,000	2,000
Bank loan payable	15,000	0	15,000
Current maturities of long-term debt	14,000	14,000	0
Total current liabilities	$ 99,000	$ 92,000	$ 7,000
Long-term debt	65,000	100,000	(35,000)
Total liabilities	$164,000	$192,000	$ (28,000)
Shareholders' equity	380,000	350,000	30,000
Total liabilities and equity	$544,000	$542,000	$ 2,000

Supplementary information:

1. Marketable securities transactions during the year were as follows: sold securities with original cost of $15,000 for $45,000; cash purchase of new securities at a cost of $20,000.

2. Sold old equipment with a basis of $13,000 for $13,000; cash purchase of new equipment for $32,000.

3. In the last month of the year, transacted a cash borrowing of $15,000, which is classified as a bank loan payable in the balance sheet.

4. Cash payments of $35,000 were made on the long-term loan.

5. Dividends of $25,000 were declared and paid this year.

6. Treasury stock was purchased at a cost of $3,000.

7. The issuance of no-par common stock resulted in $18,000 being received.

Problem 8

Shown below are totals of the three sections from the SCF for the Sivad Motel for the year just ended. Analyze this information and prepare a report indicating your opinion regarding its sources and uses of funds and their impact on the future of the company. Your conclusions and recommendations should be supported with proper explanations and assumptions.

Statement of Cash Flows

Net cash provided by operating activities	$10,000
Net cash used by investing activities	(15,000)
Net cash used by financing activities	(5,000)
Decrease in cash for the year	(10,000)
Cash at beginning of year	15,000
Cash at end of year	$ 5,000

Problem 9

Shown below are totals of the three sections from the SCF for the Nanood Motel for the year just ended. Analyze this information and prepare a report indicating your opinion regarding its sources and uses of funds and their impact on the future of the company. Your conclusions and recommendations should be supported with proper explanations and assumptions.

Statement of Cash Flows

Net cash provided by operating activities	$ 5,000
Net cash used by investing activities	(50,000)
Net cash provided by financing activities	$100,000
Increase in cash for the year	55,000
Cash at beginning of year	15,000
Cash at end of year	$ 70,000

Problem 10

Shown below are totals of the three sections from the SCF for the Nanged Motel for the year just ended. Analyze this information and prepare a report indicating your opinion regarding its sources and uses of funds and their impact on the future of the company. Your conclusions and recommendations should be supported with proper explanations and assumptions.

Statement of Cash Flows

Net cash provided by operating activities	$ 505,000
Net cash provided by investing activities	150,000
Net cash used by financing activities	(50,000)
Increase in cash for the year	605,000
Cash at beginning of year	500,000
Cash at end of year	$1,105,000

Problem 11

Shown below is the SCF for the Nimak Steakhouse Chain for the year just ended. Analyze this statement and prepare a report indicating your opinion regarding its sources and uses of funds and their impact on the future of the company. Your conclusions and recommendations should be supported with proper explanations and assumptions.

Statement of Cash Flows

Cash Flows from Operating Activities

Net income		$ 4,000
Adjustments to reconcile net income to net cash flow:		
Depreciation	$ 6,000	
Loss on sale of equipment	10,000	
Decrease in accounts receivable	25,000	
Decrease in inventories	3,000	
Decrease in prepaid expenses	1,000	
Increase in accounts payable	18,000	63,000
Net cash provided by operating activities		$ 67,000
Cash Flows from Investing Activities		
Proceeds from sale of store equipment	$32,000	
Proceeds from sale of office equipment	5,000	
Net cash provided by investing activities		37,000
Cash Flows from Financing Activities		
Cash borrowings	$20,000	
Payment on cash borrowings	(5,000)	
Net cash provided by financing activities		15,000
Increase in cash for the year		$119,000
Cash at beginning of year		3,000
Cash at end of year		$122,000

Appendix

The purpose of this appendix is to provide additional information regarding the preparation of the statement of cash flows (SCF). The material is arranged by topics and concludes with a presentation of the direct method of preparing the operating activities section of the SCF.

Cash and Cash Equivalents. Generally, the maturity date of cash equivalents must be three months or less from the date of purchase. For example, a three-month treasury bill and a three-year treasury note purchased three months from maturity qualify as cash equivalents.

Commercial Paper. These corporate short-term promissory notes are generally issued in minimum units of $25,000. Finance companies such as General Motors Acceptance Corporation (GMAC) issue commercial paper directly instead of going through banks or brokers; this type of paper is called finance paper or direct paper. The commercial paper that is issued through dealers is called dealer paper.

Treasury Bills. These U.S. government issues mature in one year or less and are issued in three-month, six-month, and one-year maturities. The minimum purchase is $10,000, with the size increasing in $1,000 increments. Typically, the longer the maturity, the higher the interest rate paid to the holder. T-bill interest comes "up front." For example, a $10,000 T-bill selling at 6% discount means that the buyer pays $9,400 to purchase the T-bill and collects $10,000 at maturity.

Treasury Notes. These U.S. government issues are typically sold with maturities of two, three, five, and ten years. The two- and three-year notes have a $5,000 minimum investment, with $1,000 increments above that level. There is a $1,000 minimum investment for five- and ten-year notes, which generally pay interest twice a year.

Treasury Bonds. These U.S. government issues have maturities of more than ten years. It is not unusual for them to have a maturity of thirty years. They may be purchased in multiples of $1,000, with interest paid twice a year.

Marketable Securities

Statement of Financial Accounting Standards (SFAS) 115 arranges debt and equity investments into three categories:

- Trading securities
- Available for sale securities
- Held to maturity securities

Trading Securities. These are bought primarily to sell in the short term; they reflect active and frequent buying and selling. If marketable securities do not meet these requirements, they are treated as available for sale securities.

Available for Sale Securities. These are securities that are not classified as trading securities or held to maturity securities.

Held to Maturity Securities. These can only consist of debt securities because, unlike equity securities, they are characterized by a maturity date. However, if management has a positive intent to dispose of a debt security prior to its maturity, the debt security can be classified as available for sale.

SFAS 115 specifies the treatment of these three categories of securities as follows:

Trading securities	Operating activity
Available for sale securities	Investing activity
Held to maturity securities	Investing activity

Cash Flows from Investing Activities

According to SFAS 95 (FAS 95) issued by the Financial Accounting Standards Board, additional cash inflows that could appear in this section are receipts from collection or sales of loans by the enterprise and other entities' debt instruments (other than cash equivalents and certain debt instruments that are acquired specifically for resale) that were purchased by the enterprise.

Cash outflows would be the result of disbursements for loans made by the enterprise and payments to acquire debt instruments of other entities (other than cash equivalents and certain debt instruments that are acquired specifically for resale).

Cash Flow per Share

Financial statements shall not report an amount of cash flow per share. Neither cash flow nor any component of it is an alternative to net income as an indicator of an enterprise's performance, as reporting per share amounts might imply. [FAS 95, ¶33]

Foreign Currency Cash Flows

A statement of cash flows of an enterprise with foreign currency transactions or foreign operations shall report the reporting currency equivalent of foreign currency cash flows using the exchange rates in effect at the time of the cash flows. An appropriately weighted average exchange rate for the period may be used for translation if the result is substantially the same as if the rates at the dates of the cash flows were used. The statement shall report the effect of exchange rate changes on cash balances held in foreign currencies as a separate part of the reconciliation of the change in cash and cash equivalents during the period. [FAS 95, ¶25]

Obtaining Data for the Investing Activities Section

Preparation of the investing activities section requires an analysis of the long-term asset accounts and also any transactions affecting short-term investment accounts (marketable securities). Specifically, any account that contains any transactions for the sale or purchase of property, equipment, investments, and marketable securities requires careful scrutiny.

For example, analyzing investment transactions requires an analysis of the Investments account and related journal entries. The following explains the basic procedure:

Investments	
beg bal 8,000	J1 Sale 8,000
J2 Pur 5,000	
end bal 5,000	

The beginning balance in the account was $8,000. All these investments were sold. The investing activities section is not concerned with gain or loss. The proceeds from the sale, which represent a cash inflow, can only be determined by referring to J1. Later, the company made additional investments that cost $5,000, which represents a cash outflow.

J1: Cash 12,000
    Investments 8,000
    Gain on sale of securities 4,000

Analyzing Journal 1 shows that the cash inflow from the sale of investments was $12,000, which would be entered in the investment activities section of the SCF.

It is necessary to analyze Journal 2 to ascertain that the $5,000 purchase of new investment was indeed paid in cash and did not involve a noncash exchange of other assets or the company's stock.

J2: Investments 5,000
    Cash 5,000

Analyzing Journal 2 shows that the cash outflow from the purchase of investments was $5,000, which would be entered in the investment activities section of the SCF.

Obtaining Data for the Financing Activities Section

Preparation of the financing activities section requires an analysis of any account that contains transactions for short-term borrowings, long-term debt, and stockholders' equity accounts. Cash dividends paid may be determined by analyzing their declaration as a debit to retained earnings and tracing their ultimate payment as a debit to dividends payable.

The activity for dividends may be analyzed as follows:

Retained Earnings		Dividends Payable	
J4 Dec 2,000	beg bal 50,000	J5 Pay 2,000	beg bal 0
J5 Dec 3,000	end bal 45,000		J4 Dec 2,000
			J5 Dec 3,000
			end bal 3,000

Dividends declared total $5,000, as indicated by the debits to retained earnings and credits to dividends payable. However, the debit to dividends payable shows that only $2,000 of the dividends have been paid. Thus, $2,000 would be entered as a cash outflow in the financing activities section of the SCF.

Direct Method for Preparing the Operating Activities Section

The procedure for preparing the operating activities section of the SCF using the direct method differs from that using the indirect method. Under the direct method, the operating activities section does not begin with net income; instead, it shows cash collected from customers and cash used for various operating expenses.

Obtaining cash basis information requires an analysis of the transactions of each income and expense account or a conversion of year-end information from the accrual basis to cash basis accounting.

A typical operating activities section prepared under the direct method might appear as follows:

Statement of Cash Flows

Cash Flow from Operating Activities:	
Cash receipts	
from customers	$xxx
from interest and dividends	xxx
Cash payments	
to suppliers	$xxx
for operating expenses	xxx
for interest expense	xxx
for income taxes	xxx
Net cash provided (used) by operating activities	$xxx

Preparing the investing and financing activities sections is the same whether the direct or indirect method is used for the operating activities section.

When the direct method of reporting cash flows from operating activities is used, a separate schedule must be provided to reconcile the net income to net cash flow from operating activities. This supporting schedule is prepared according to the indirect method.

REVIEW QUIZ

When you feel you have covered all of the material in this chapter, answer these questions. Choose the *best* answer. Check your answers with the correct ones found on the Review Quiz Answer Key at the end of this book.

True (T) or False (F)

T   F   1. U.S. treasury bills are considered to be cash equivalents.

T   F   2. Cash flows from the sale of property, equipment, and long-term investments are considered to be from a hotel's operating activities.

T   F   3. The direct and indirect methods for preparing the operating activities section of the statement of cash flows produce identical results.

T   F   4. Acquiring an auto under a three-year lease is an example of a noncash investing/financing transaction.

Multiple Choice

5. Which of the following financial statements provides information about cash receipts and cash payments?

    a. income statement
    b. balance sheet
    c. statement of cash flows
    d. statement of retained earnings

6. Cash equivalents are highly liquid investments such as:

    a. marketable securities, such as common and preferred stock.
    b. commercial paper.
    c. money market funds.
    d. b and c

7. Which of the following transactions requires footnotes and/or disclosures?

    a. income taxes and interest paid in the period
    b. the company's accounting policy regarding cash
    c. noncash investing and financing transactions
    d. all of the above

8. Exchanging vacant land for vacant land owned by another party is an example of:

    a. cash received from borrowings.
    b. a noncash investing/financing transaction.
    c. equity financing.
    d. a marketable security transaction.

Chapter Outline

Role of the Independent Certified Public
   Accountant
Audit Service
     Purpose of an Audit
     Scope of an Audit
     Auditor's Report
     Example of a Standard Auditor's
      Report
Review Service
     Purpose of a Review
     Scope of a Review
     Review Report
     Example of a Standard Review Report
Compilation Services
     Purpose of a Compilation
     Scope of a Compilation
     Compilation Report
     Example of a Standard Compilation
      Report
Consolidated Financial Statements
     Minority Interest
     Purpose of Consolidated Financial
      Statements
     Intercompany Transactions
     Investment in Subsidiary Account
     Consolidated Worksheet
Annual Reports
     Content of an Annual Report
     Auditor's Report
     How to Read an Annual Report
     Financial Statements in an Annual
      Report
     Conclusion of an Annual Report
     Investor Relations Department

Learning Objectives

1. Summarize the role of and criteria for an independent certified accountant. (pp. 417–418)

2. Explain the purpose and scope of an audit, and describe an auditor's report. (pp. 418–420)

3. Explain the purpose and scope of a review, and describe a review report. (pp. 420–422)

4. Explain the purpose and scope of a compilation, and describe a compilation report. (pp. 422–423)

5. Describe the purpose and preparation of consolidated financial statements. (pp. 423–426)

6. Explain the purpose and content of an annual report, and describe how a reader can find and interpret information in the report. (pp. 426–431)

15

Interim and Annual Reports

CORPORATIONS THAT HAVE ISSUED STOCK to the public and are listed on a major stock exchange are required to keep their shareholders informed of the company's financial status. This is accomplished by issuing condensed financial statements during the year **(interim reports)** and a comprehensive information package at the end of the year **(annual report).** The Securities and Exchange Commission (SEC) requires that annual reports be audited by an independent certified public accounting firm. Because audits are very time-consuming and expensive, interim reports do not require an audit; however, they must be reviewed by an independent certified public accountant.

Interim and annual reports are also issued to creditors, especially when a company is seeking a bank loan. Not all creditors require audited financial statements. Many accept financial statements that have been reviewed or compiled by an independent certified public accountant.

Corporations generally produce extravagant annual reports because the reports also serve as marketing tools to the investment community. Expensive annual reports are printed on glossy paper, contain many color photos, and have as many pages as a small magazine.

The annual report is designed and arranged based on its "selling" philosophy and not for the convenience of the analyst. An annual report can be intimidating to a reader who is not familiar with the report's financial data, letters, and illustrations.

In presenting interim and annual reports, this chapter will address the following questions:

1. What is the role of a certified public accountant in the issuance of reports to shareholders, creditors, and other third parties?

2. What are the differences among the audit, review, and compilation services provided by certified public accountants?

3. What are consolidated financial statements?

4. What is the content of an annual report?

5. How does one read an annual report?

Role of the Independent Certified Public Accountant

An independent certified public accountant (CPA) is in public practice and is expected to perform all services with impartiality. The demonstration of bias toward any client may influence the independence of the CPA. To provide guidelines for the independence of CPAs, the American Institute of Certified Public Accountants

(AICPA) has established a *Code of Professional Conduct.* Violation of the code can result in the revocation of a license or suspension from public practice. The following are some of the criteria used to judge whether a CPA is independent:

- The CPA cannot be an employee of the client.

- The CPA must be free of any substantial financial interest in the client.

- The CPA must be free of any obligation to the client.

- The CPA must avoid any situation that may lead outsiders to doubt his or her independence. (For example, a presumption that independence is impaired arises from a significant financial interest, directorship, or close kin relationship with the client firm.)

When interim or annual reports are issued to shareholders, creditors, or other third parties, the financial statements are accompanied by a letter from the independent CPA explaining the *scope* of the service performed and the degree of responsibility assumed by the CPA.

The CPA may attach to the financial statements a letter called an **accountant's report.** The report varies based on whether the service provided was an *audit,* a *review,* or a *compilation.*

Audit Service

Auditing is the most recognized service that CPAs provide. Publicly owned companies are required to issue annual financial statements audited by an independent CPA. Audits are performed in accordance with *generally accepted auditing standards,* which are technical guidelines established by the AICPA in cooperation with the SEC. These standards ensure that an audit is conducted competently, ethically, and professionally.

Purpose of an Audit

The purpose of an audit is to ensure that financial statements *present fairly* and are *in conformity with generally accepted accounting principles.*

The phrase "present fairly" means that:

- The accounting principles used by the company have general acceptance.

- The financial statements and accompanying notes are informative and not misleading as to their use, understanding, and interpretation.

- The financial information is neither too detailed nor too condensed.

- The financial data is within a range of acceptable limits that are reasonable and practicable to attain in the preparation of any financial statements.

- The financial statements represent the financial position, results of operations, and cash flows for the period.

"**Generally accepted accounting principles (GAAP)**" is a technical accounting term that includes broad guidelines and detailed procedures relating to the conventions and rules that define the accepted accounting practice of a particular industry and the certified public accounting profession.

An audit is not designed to express judgment on the competence of management, the merits of investing in the company, or extending the company any credit; it is the responsibility of the reader to interpret the financial data and make these evaluations. The auditing process might also detect fraud or illegal acts, but there is no guarantee that all *irregularities* will be discovered. (CPA services do provide specialized audits solely for the purpose of detecting fraud and other irregularities.)

Scope of an Audit

Before an audit begins, the independent CPA must have or obtain a working knowledge of the client company and its industry. During the audit, the CPA will investigate and examine account balances and certain transactions. Not all accounts or transactions are examined; instead, samples are randomly selected and tested.

An audit is the only service that is a comprehensive investigation and examination of the items that appear on the financial statements and the accompanying footnotes (notes). The following are some functions that a CPA must perform during an audit:

- Observe the physical inventory-taking by the client company and test the reliability of the counts, condition, and cost valuation of the inventory

- Confirm the receivables with the company's customers

- Confirm the payables with the company's creditors

- Verify the existence of the marketable securities and their valuation at market

- Review the minutes of the corporate meetings

- Communicate with management, the board of directors, and outside legal counsel of the company

After completing an audit, the independent CPA expresses an *opinion* as to the fairness of the financial statements; this opinion is called the **auditor's report.** The report is in letter form and will accompany the financial statements.

Auditor's Report

The auditor's report (letter) should be read carefully because it contains the conclusion of the auditor as to the fairness of the financial statements and the consistent application of generally accepted accounting principles.

The standard auditor's report consists of three paragraphs. The first paragraph introduces the financial statements that were audited. The second paragraph describes what an audit is, and the third paragraph contains the auditor's opinion regarding the fairness of the financial statements and consistent application of GAAP.

The auditor's opinion is an important part of the auditor's report. A favorable opinion is called a "clean opinion." A clean opinion clearly states that the financial statements are presented fairly and in accordance with GAAP. Sometimes the opinion paragraph may contain a "qualified opinion" that reveals any "except for" conditions that might be significant. This opinion might state minor departures

Exhibit 1   Auditor's Report for the Hotel DORO

To Hotel DORO, Inc., The Board of Directors, and Shareholders:

We have audited the accompanying balance sheet of Hotel DORO, Inc. as of December 31, 19X2 and the related statements of income, retained earnings and cash flows for the year then ended. These financial statements are the responsibility of the Company's management. Our responsibility is to express an opinion on these financial statements based on our audits.

We conducted our audits in accordance with generally accepted auditing standards. Those standards require that we plan and perform the audit to obtain reasonable assurance about whether the financial statements are free of material misstatement. An audit includes examining, on a test basis, evidence supporting the amounts and disclosures in the financial statement. An audit also includes assessing the accounting principles used and significant estimates made by management, as well as evaluating the overall financial statement presentation. We believe that our audits provide a reasonable basis for our opinion.

In our opinion, the financial statements referred to above present fairly, in all material respects, the financial position of Hotel DORO, Inc. as of December 31, 19X2 and the results of its operations and its cash flows for the year then ended in conformity with generally accepted accounting principles.

from GAAP, uncertainties due to insufficient evidential matter, lack of consistency in the financial statements, or inadequate disclosures.

Worse than a qualified opinion is an *adverse opinion,* which states that the financial statements do not present fairly and are not in conformity with GAAP. Most distressing is when the opinion paragraph contains a *disclaimer of opinion.* A disclaimer of opinion states that the auditor is not expressing an opinion because he or she was unable to conduct a sufficient audit.

Example of a Standard Auditor's Report

An example of a standard auditor's report for the fictitious Hotel DORO is shown in Exhibit 1. Notice that the report states a clean opinion.

Review Service

An audit of financial statements is expensive and time-consuming for the client company's staff. Physical inventories can disrupt operations, customers are contacted, staff is interviewed, and the company's accounting department is constantly asked to supply financial records. It is not unusual for an audit to take several months, starting well in advance of the date of the financial statements. Because the auditing process is a burden on a company's finances and operations, the audit of quarterly (interim) statements is not required. To ensure that interim financial statements provide shareholders with timely, relevant financial information, the SEC has approved the issuance of *reviewed* financial statements during the year.

Reviews are performed in accordance with *standards for accounting and review services,* which are technical standards for *unaudited* financial statements. Established by the AICPA, these standards ensure that a review is conducted competently, ethically, and professionally.

Purpose of a Review

The objective of a review differs significantly from the objective of an audit, which is to express an opinion. The purpose of a review is to express *limited assurance* that no material changes to the financial statements are necessary for them to be consistent with generally accepted accounting principles.

Scope of a Review

Before a review begins, the independent CPA must have or obtain a working knowledge of the client company and its industry. A review does not require a comprehensive investigation of the company's financial records. Instead, the CPA makes inquiries and performs analytical procedures to form a reasonable basis for expressing limited assurance.

The following are some examples of the CPA's inquiries and analytical procedures:

- Inquiries concerning the client company's accounting principles, practices, and methods

- Inquiries regarding the procedures for classifying and recording business transactions

- Analytical procedures for business transactions, account balances, or other items that appear to be unusual

- Inquiries concerning actions taken at meetings of shareholders, the board of directors, or other committees that may affect the financial statements

- Reading financial statements

A review is not designed to express an opinion as to the fairness of the financial statements. The CPA does not confirm receivables or payables, observe the inventory, seek other corroborative evidential matter, or perform the other tests demanded of an audit service. A review may bring to the CPA's attention significant matters affecting the financial statements, but its procedures are not designed to provide assurance that the CPA will become aware of these matters.

Review Report

After completing a review, the independent CPA does not express an opinion but gives what is called a level of *negative assurance*. In other words, in the CPA's view, no modifications to the financial statements are necessary. This *limited assurance* is part of the review report that is in letter form and will accompany the financial statements.

The review report contains three paragraphs. The first paragraph introduces the financial statements that were reviewed. The second paragraph describes what a review is, and the third paragraph contains the CPA's level of assurance as to the conformity of the financial statements with GAAP.

A favorable third paragraph in a review report would include a "clean review" absent of any "except for" statements or other qualifying statements.

Exhibit 2   Review Report for the Hotel DORO

To Hotel DORO, Inc., The Board of Directors, and Shareholders:

We have reviewed the accompanying balance sheets of Hotel DORO, Inc. as of December 31, 19X2 and the related statements of income, retained earnings and cash flows for the year then ended in accordance with standards established by the American Institute of Certified Public Accountants. All information included in these financial statements is the representation of the management of Hotel DORO, Inc.

A review consists principally of inquiries of company personnel and analytical procedures applied to financial data. It is substantially less in scope than an examination in accordance with generally accepted auditing standards, the objective of which is the expression of an opinion regarding the financial statements taken as a whole. Accordingly, we do not express such an opinion.

Based on our review, we are not aware of any material modifications that should be made to the accompanying financial statements in order for them to be in conformity with generally accepted accounting principles.

Example of a Standard Review Report

An example of a standard review report for the Hotel DORO is shown in Exhibit 2. Notice that the report gives a clean level of assurance.

Compilation Services

Even though reviewed financial statements are less expensive than audited financial statements, the review services performed by a CPA are still costly. As a result, a lesser alternative might be acceptable to creditors or other third parties. Compiled financial statements, also referred to as *compilations*, are the least expensive and lowest level of financial statement services provided by a CPA.

Compilations are performed in accordance with *standards for accounting and review services,* which are technical standards for *unaudited* financial statements. These standards, established by the AICPA, ensure that a compilation is conducted competently, ethically, and professionally.

Purpose of a Compilation

The purpose of a compilation is to present in the form of financial statements information that is the representation of client company management. The CPA does not express an opinion or any level of assurance on the statements.

Scope of a Compilation

Before a compilation begins, the independent CPA must have or obtain a working knowledge of the client company and its industry. A compilation does not require the CPA to make inquiries or perform other procedures to verify or review information supplied by the client company.

In a compilation, the CPA becomes familiar with a company's bookkeeping procedures and then compiles the financial data into a professional format.

Exhibit 3   Compilation Report for the Hotel DORO

> To Hotel DORO, Inc., The Board of Directors, and Shareholders:
>
> We have compiled the accompanying balance sheets of Hotel DORO, Inc. as of December 31, 19X2 and the related statements of income, retained earnings and cash flows for the year then ended in accordance with standards established by the American Institute of Certified Public Accountants.
>
> A compilation is limited to presenting, in the form of financial statements, information that is the representation of management. We have not audited or reviewed the accompanying financial statements and, accordingly, do not express an opinion or any other form of assurance on them.

The CPA should possess a general understanding of the company's business transactions, its form of accounting records, and the qualifications of its accounting personnel. Based on this understanding, the CPA might consider it necessary to perform other services such as assistance in determining adjusting entries or consulting on accounting matters for the proper presentation of the financial statements.

Compilation Report

After completing a compilation, the independent CPA does not express an opinion as to the fairness of the financial statements or express any level of assurance.

The compilation report contains three paragraphs. The first paragraph introduces the financial statements that were compiled. The second paragraph describes what a compilation is, and the third paragraph simply states that the financial statements were prepared on the basis of information provided by management without audit or review and disclaims any level of assurance by the CPA.

A favorable third paragraph would include a "clean compilation" absent of any "except for" statements or other qualifications. However, since a compilation is a very limited service, the absence of any qualifications should provide little certainty.

Example of a Standard Compilation Report

An example of a standard compilation report for the Hotel DORO is shown in Exhibit 3.

Consolidated Financial Statements

The big business environment is characterized by large corporations operating in many locations. To further expand their earning power, corporations may seek the acquisition route. By acquisition, a corporation may own 100 percent of another corporation's voting stock or own a majority (more than 50 percent) of the voting stock of another corporation. The company owning the controlling interest is called the **parent company** and the controlled company is called a **subsidiary.**

A parent-subsidiary relationship does not affect the issued and outstanding common stock. Each corporation's stock remains issued and listed on any stock exchange as it was before the parent company purchased the stock of the subsidiary.

Minority Interest

When a parent corporation owns less than 100 percent of a subsidiary's stock, the portion of the outstanding shares not owned is considered to be owned by a **minority interest**.

Because they are separate corporations, the parent and its subsidiaries maintain separate accounting records. The parent must issue **consolidated financial statements,** which include the financial data of the parent and its subsidiaries. It should be noted that when a minority interest exists, financial statements for the subsidiary must be issued separately because consolidated statements rarely present specific information useful to minority interest shareholders.

Purpose of Consolidated Financial Statements

Consolidated financial statements are issued so that investors and other interested parties get complete information about all resources and operations under the control of the parent company. Consolidated financial statements combine the parent and subsidiaries into a single reporting economic entity.

All the financial data from these separate corporations is combined on a consolidated worksheet; entries are not made in the general ledger of any company.

Intercompany Transactions

An **intercompany transaction** is any transaction between a parent and any of its subsidiaries, or transactions among the subsidiaries of the parent. Before any amounts from the parent and its subsidiaries are combined on the consolidated financial statements, all intercompany transactions must be eliminated so that the parent and subsidiaries are represented as one economic entity.

Even though intercompany transactions do in fact occur, they must be eliminated from the financial statements because it would not be logical for a single entity to buy and sell from itself, especially since these transactions inflate the true sales of the single reporting entity. For example, if a parent sells $100,000 of merchandise to its subsidiary, the following book transactions occur:

Books of Parent	
Sales	$100,000

Books of Subsidiary	
Purchases	$100,000

When the consolidated income statement is prepared, the intercompany sales and purchases are offset (eliminated) to properly reflect the operating results of a single economic unit.

Intercompany transactions involving the lending or borrowing of money between a parent and subsidiary are likewise eliminated from the financial statements because it is not logical for a single entity to borrow from itself and owe itself. For example, if a parent loans $50,000 to its subsidiary, the following book transactions occur:

<u>Books of Parent</u>
Loan receivable from subsidiary $50,000

<u>Books of Subsidiary</u>
Loan payable to parent $50,000

When the consolidated balance sheet is prepared, the loan receivable from the subsidiary is offset (eliminated) by the loan payable to the parent.

Investment in Subsidiary Account

The parent company's purchase cost of the subsidiary's stock is recorded to an account called *Investment in Subsidiary*. For consolidated financial statement purposes, this cost is eliminated by allocating it against the subsidiary's common stock, retained earnings, and possibly some assets and liabilities. The allocation procedure is determined by whether the parent purchased the stock at book value or at fair market value. Obviously, very few companies are purchased at book value. *Eliminating the investment in subsidiary accounts is the first elimination entry on the consolidated worksheet.*

Consolidated Worksheet

The preparation of consolidated worksheets is highly technical and very complex. For example, a purchase at fair market value may generate goodwill, which requires tedious computations and special processing on the worksheet; there are several different methods used to eliminate the investment in subsidiary accounts on the worksheet; the existence of any minority interest complicates the worksheet procedures because the parent does not own 100 percent of the subsidiary; and there are alternate accounting procedures to perform the elimination allocation, in addition to many other technical accounting procedures.

A different kind of accounting arises depending on the stock purchase. If the stock purchase involves, among other factors, an exchange of the parent's stock, it qualifies for "pooling" accounting. Stock purchases can also be accounted for under the purchase method of accounting.

Because the consolidated worksheet is so complex, several chapters would be necessary to present the levels of worksheet preparation. Therefore, this chapter will provide only basic knowledge about preparing a consolidated worksheet. To simplify the discussion, the following conditions will be established:

- The parent has only one subsidiary.
- The parent owns 100 percent of the subsidiary.
- The parent purchased the subsidiary's stock at book value.
- The purchase of the subsidiary's stock was a cash purchase.
- The parent method of accounting will be used.
- No dividends have been declared by the parent or subsidiary.
- There are no intercompany sales or purchases.

In addition, the example that follows will use a partial trial balance including only selected accounts necessary to explain the consolidation procedures.

Exhibit 4   Trial Balances of Parent and Subsidiary

Trial Balance of Parent:

	Debit	Credit
Cash	$100,000	$ 30,000
Accounts receivable	80,000	40,000
Receivable from subsidiary	20,000	
Investment in subsidiary	70,000	
Common stock		80,000
Retained earnings		140,000
Sales		500,000

Trial Balance of Subsidiary:

	Debit	Credit
Cash	$30,000	
Accounts receivable	40,000	
Payable to parent		20,000
Common stock		30,000
Retained earnings		40,000
Sales		200,000

Exhibit 4 shows the separate trial balances of the parent and subsidiary before consolidation begins. Exhibit 5 shows the first step in the consolidation process. This step involves entering the trial balance information on a consolidated worksheet. (Instead of debit or credit columns, credits will be indicated by parentheses.)

The next step is to perform the elimination entries. These are shown in Exhibit 6. The first elimination entry is to allocate the $70,000 in the investment in subsidiary account. In this example, this is very simple since the subsidiary was purchased at book value; the $70,000 is allocated to the subsidiary's common stock of $30,000 and retained earnings of $40,000. The effect of this entry is to eliminate the parent's cost and the subsidiary's equity section.

Next, the intercompany loan transaction is eliminated. The receivable of $20,000 from the subsidiary and the $20,000 payable to the parent by the subsidiary are eliminated since they cancel each other under the single economic entity concept.

After all elimination entries are completed, the trial balance and elimination entry columns of the worksheet are combined and entered in the consolidated column as shown in Exhibit 6. The consolidated worksheet is then used to prepare the consolidated financial statements.

Annual Reports

Annual reports are issued by companies whose stock is publicly held. These reports contain more than just the company's annual statements. They also contain historical summaries, financial data, statistics, information about the company and its markets, and even illustrations and pictures.

Exhibit 5   Starting the Consolidated Worksheet

	Parent	Subsidiary	Elimination	Consolidated
Cash	$100,000	$ 30,000		
Accounts receivable	80,000	40,000		
Receivable from subsidiary	20,000			
Investment in subsidiary	70,000			
Payable to parent		(20,000)		
Common stock	(80,000)	(30,000)		
Retained earnings	(140,000)	(40,000)		
Sales	(500,000)	(200,000)		

Exhibit 6   Completing the Consolidated Worksheet

	Parent	Subsidiary	Elimination	Consolidated
Cash	$100,000	$ 30,000		$130,000
Accounts receivable	80,000	40,000		120,000
Receivable from subsidiary	20,000		(20,000)	–
Investment in subsidiary	70,000		(70,000)	
Payable to parent		(20,000)	20,000	–
Common stock	(80,000)	(30,000)	30,000	80,000
Retained earnings	(140,000)	(40,000)	40,000	140,000
Sales	(500,000)	(200,000)		(700,000)

Some companies spend considerable amounts of money to produce an annual report that is printed in color on glossy paper and is big enough to resemble a magazine. While these reports promote the image of a company, some shareholders do not like them because of their expense. The production and printing costs are paid out of profits, and some shareholders believe that profits should be targeted only for growth or payment of dividends.

Some companies produce annual reports that are printed in black and white and contain few or no pictures. While these reports are not as impressive as the more expensive annual reports, their reporting content is equally good.

Content of an Annual Report

Shareholders, creditors, and the investment community are more interested in the financial content of annual reports, not the fancy pictures and covers. A good typical annual report might contain the following components:

- Message to the shareholders
- Corporate profile
- Overview of the past year
- Historical summaries
- Stock price range

- Segmentation
- Financial statements
- Notes to the financial statements
- Auditor's report

Message to the Shareholders. The message to the shareholders is in the form of a letter from the CEO (chief executive officer) of the corporation. The letter informs the shareholders of pertinent business facts, reviews the past year, and presents the focus of management regarding the future plans of the company.

Corporate Profile. The corporate profile explains the business purpose of the company and its operating philosophy. It provides a brief description of the company's market, customers, type of operations, and diversity of products and services.

Overview of the Past Year. This section contains condensed financial data and statistics showing the company's financial condition and results of operations. It might explain the effect of competition, inflation, or other economic factors on the company's business. Comparison to prior years may be included to show the progression of sales, expenses, and income over the years.

Historical Summaries. Some companies may include a section that shows 5- or 10-year highlights of sales, expenses, and income. This presentation is usually in the form of condensed financial data and might be supplemented with graphs or trend analyses.

Stock Price Range. This section describes on which stock exchange the stock is listed and the stock's trading range of highs and lows for a certain number of periods. It may also provide information on cash dividends, stock splits, and other relevant data.

Segmentation. Many large and complex corporations engage in a variety of business operations that have little relationship to each other. For example, a company that operates hotels may have one subsidiary that manufactures computers and other subsidiaries that manufacture or sell other kinds of products or services. Such companies are called **conglomerates** or diversified companies. These conglomerates are required to provide *segment reporting* information to their shareholders in the annual report.

These conglomerates must show details of their activities in each major line of business or geographical area. This report should disclose revenue, operating profit, and identifiable assets for each significant industry segment of the company.

Financial Statements. This section must contain the following financial statements:

- Balance sheet
- Income statement
- Statement of cash flows

The balance sheet reports on the company's financial condition, the income statement reports on the results of operations, and the statement of cash flows shows the sources and uses of cash for the period. If there is a parent-subsidiary relationship, the parent company must present these statements in the form of consolidated financial statements. The appendix at the end of this chapter reproduces the financial statements for the Hilton Hotels Corporation from a recent annual report.

Notes to the Financial Statements. The notes are an integral part of the financial statements because they provide valuable information; the absence of this information might make the financial statements incomplete or misleading. Notes serve as **disclosures** for items on the financial statements by doing the following:

- Explaining the composition of certain line amounts on the financial statements

- Explaining the meaning or calculation of certain line items on the financial statements

- Explaining critical company facts that cannot be conveniently shown in the body of statements due to limitations of financial statement formats

- Explaining critical events that have affected or might affect the company

The disclosure of information must be sufficient so that the reader can make an informed judgment or decision. Disclosure is not limited only to financial statement data. Any fact that would affect the readers's judgment must be disclosed. For example, if a company has lost a customer that represented a significant portion of its sales, that information must be disclosed. The disclosure must state the percentage of business represented by that customer and its potential effect on the business.

Sometimes the numbers shown on the financial statements do not provide complete information. For example, the balance sheet may show accounts receivable on one line at net realizable value. The notes will disclose the amount the company has estimated for bad debts (allowance for doubtful accounts) so that the reader is properly informed.

Notes to the financial statements may consist of several pages; it is not unusual for notes to constitute more of an annual report than the financial statements. Notes cover a variety of items, including the following.

Accounting policies. This should be the first note. A description of all significant accounting policies such as depreciation and amortization methods, inventory valuation, and accounting principles specific to the industry must be disclosed.

Lease information. Financial statements do not indicate the long-term dollar commitment of operating lease contractual obligations. Therefore, this type of note discloses the lease period and payments required under the leases.

Discontinued operations. This type of note discloses any business segment that has been disposed of or is the subject of a formal plan for disposal. The particular business segment may be a product line or a subsidiary.

Contingent liabilities. This type of note explains an existing condition, situation, or circumstance involving uncertainty as to possible loss which cannot be determined until a future event occurs or fails to occur. Some examples of **contingent liabilities** that may need disclosure are pending lawsuits, possible tax assessments, future commitments, and loan guarantees.

Contingent liabilities for which the amount can be *estimated* and the loss is *probable* are shown in the financial statements and also explained in this type of note.

Liabilities for which the amount cannot be estimated and the loss is probable or *possible* are explained in the notes but do not appear in the financial statements.

If a contingency is *remote*, it is not shown in the financial statements and there is no requirement for disclosure in the notes to the financial statements unless the contingency applies to a loan guarantee. Sometimes a company may enter into a contract that guarantees payment of a loan for another company. This other company could be a subsidiary, supplier, or a favored customer. This type of guarantee obligates the guarantor to pay the loan should the borrower default. Even if the likelihood of the borrower not paying the note is remote, disclosure is required.

Auditor's Report

The certified public accounting firm that audited the financial statements includes a letter to the shareholders and company management explaining the financial statements that were audited, the scope of the audit, and the CPA's *opinion*. This letter was previously explained in this chapter.

How to Read an Annual Report

Many people have trouble understanding annual reports because they attempt to read them as they would read a book. The information in annual reports is scattered, and there is no standard format or sequence. The annual report of one company may be totally different from the report of another company.

Starting Point. The experienced reader *starts* with the *auditor's report*. The auditor's report is usually found just after the footnotes and just before the back cover of the annual report. The reader may proceed immediately to the third paragraph and look for a *clean opinion*. A paragraph with "except for" or other qualifying statements might signal serious trouble. Auditors are sometimes reluctant to use straightforward, strong language because of the client relationship. While they do make the qualification, they often use a subtle approach. Therefore, if the third paragraph does not contain a clean opinion, it may be a warning, and care should be taken in studying the complete annual report.

The President's Letter. Some experienced readers save reading the president's letter until they are nearly finished with the annual report. Others prefer to read it before proceeding to the financial statements because they feel it serves as a prelude to what the statements might reveal. A careful reading of this letter can be useful because the president reviews the past year, unveils new products or new company developments, or discusses the targeting of new markets.

Financial Statements in an Annual Report

The set of audited statements and accompanying footnotes tells the story of the company's financial success or failure. Some experienced readers claim that they get more from the financial statements if they first read the footnotes and then the financial statements. Other readers prefer to move back and forth between the financial statements and the footnotes. The method of reading an annual report is a matter of personal preference. In any case, it is probably not advisable to concentrate solely on the financial statements without reference to the footnotes.

The financial statements consist of the following:

- **Balance Sheet.** The balance sheet, also called the statement of financial condition, reveals the financial health of a company by showing its assets (what it owns), its liabilities (what it owes), and the shareholders' equity (stock issued and retained earnings).

- **Income Statement.** The income statement, sometimes called the results of operations, shows the revenue and expenses with the resulting profit or loss for the period.

- **Statement of Cash Flows.** The statement of cash flows shows the changes in the cash balance for the period by explaining the sources and uses of cash.

Conclusion of an Annual Report

The annual report may provide trends for the last 5 or 10 years and selected statistical information that requires careful reading. The sequence of reading this data varies with the skills and interests of the reader.

If key ratios are not provided, the reader will need to calculate the ratios and interpret the results.

After studying an annual report and analyzing ratios, it is not unusual for a reader to go back and read the report again. Reading the report a second time allows the reader to focus more on individual details and content.

Investor Relations Department

Most corporations make a sincere effort to communicate with their shareholders and the investment community. They will gladly send copies of their annual reports, answer questions, advise of the next shareholders' meeting, and respond to other investor-related concerns. The address and telephone number of the corporation's investor relations department is usually found on the inside of the back cover of the annual report.

Key Terms

accountant's report
annual report
auditor's report
conglomerate
consolidated financial statements
contingent liabilities
disclosure

generally accepted accounting
   principles (GAAP)
intercompany transaction
interim report
minority interest
parent company
subsidiary

Review Questions

1. What is an interim financial statement?

2. What is meant by the term "independent certified public accountant"?

3. What professional standards are used by the CPA to perform an audit service?

4. What is the purpose of an audit?

5. What is the scope of an audit?

6. What is an auditor's report? Describe each paragraph of the auditor's report.

7. What professional standards are used by the CPA to perform a review service?

8. What is the purpose of a review?

9. What is the scope of a review?

10. What professional standards are used by the CPA to perform a compilation service?

11. What is the purpose of a compilation?

12. What is the scope of a compilation?

13. Under what conditions are consolidated financial statements required?

14. What is the general content of annual reports?

15. What is segment reporting?

16. What are some of the disclosures that might appear in the notes to the financial statements?

17. What is a contingent liability? Give examples.

Problems

Problem 1

Complete a consolidated worksheet from the following supplementary information and worksheet data:

1. The period is for the year ended 12/31/X9.

2. The parent company's name is Don-Bess, Inc., and the subsidiary's name is Deb-Mar, Inc.

3. The parent owns 100% of Deb-Mar's voting stock. There is no preferred stock.

4. The subsidiary was purchased for cash in 19X9 at the book value of its assets and liabilities.

5. There were no sales and purchase transactions between the parent and subsidiary in 19X9.

6. No dividends were declared by either the parent or subsidiary.

	Parent	Subsidiary	Elimination	Consolidated
Cash	$ 70,000	$ 10,000		
Accounts receivable	50,000	20,000		
Inventories	30,000	15,000		
Receivable from subsidiary	10,000			
Prepaid expenses	3,000	1,000		
Investment in subsidiary	90,000		(1) (90,000)	
Land	70,000	30,000		
Building	150,000	92,000		
Equipment	30,000	20,000		
Accounts payable	(10,000)	(23,000)		
Payable to parent		(10,000)		
Accrued items	(8,000)	(6,000)		
Current portion of long-term debt	(20,000)	(12,000)		
Long-term debt (net of CP)	(60,000)	(30,000)		
Stock issued	(200,000)	(50,000)	(1) 50,000	
Retained earnings 1/1	(95,000)	(40,000)	(1) 40,000	
Sales	(400,000)	(100,000)		
Cost of sales	100,000	28,000		
Labor cost	120,000	32,000		
Other operating expenses	40,000	10,000		
Fixed expenses	28,000	12,000		
Income taxes expense	2,000	1,000		
Total	0	0		

Problem 2

Using the completed worksheet from Problem 1, prepare the three consolidated financial statements: income statement, statement of retained earnings, and balance sheet.

Appendix

Hilton Hotels Corporation and Subsidiaries

(in millions, except per share amounts)	Year Ended December 31,	1993	1992	1991
Revenue	Rooms	$ 440.2	386.7	345.0
	Food and beverage	236.8	216.2	204.4
	Casino	502.1	438.8	392.4
	Management and franchise fees	85.1	79.0	76.2
	Other	93.8	82.5	64.4
	Operating income from unconsolidated affiliates	35.5	26.4	30.3
		1,393.5	1,229.6	1,112.7
Expenses	Rooms	152.5	131.9	119.9
	Food and beverage	202.4	180.3	168.4
	Casino	217.5	195.6	200.1
	Other costs and expenses	554.4	476.9	416.4
	Corporate expense	26.8	25.0	23.1
		1,153.6	1,009.7	927.9
Operating Income		239.9	219.9	184.8
	Interest and dividend income	21.8	16.4	11.3
	Interest expense	(80.4)	(66.9)	(58.1)
	Interest expense, net, from unconsolidated affiliates	(14.6)	(11.2)	(15.6)
	Property transactions, net	(4.5)	.9	.5
	Foreign currency losses	(1.3)	—	—
Income Before Income Taxes		160.9	159.1	122.9
	Provision for income taxes	58.2	55.2	38.6
Income Before Cumulative Effect of Accounting Changes		102.7	103.9	84.3
	Cumulative effect of accounting changes, net	3.4	—	—
Net Income		$ 106.1	103.9	84.3
Income Per Share	Before cumulative effect of accounting changes	$ 2.14	2.17	1.76
	Cumulative effect of accounting changes, net	.07	—	—
Net Income Per Share		$ 2.21	2.17	1.76

See notes to consolidated financial statements

CONSOLIDATED BALANCE SHEETS   **Hilton Hotels Corporation and Subsidiaries**

(in millions)	December 31,	1993	1992
ASSETS			
Current Assets	Cash and equivalents	$ 380.4	348.5
	Temporary investments	98.1	162.4
	Other current assets	248.5	164.6
	Total current assets	727.0	675.5
Investments, Property and	Investments in and notes from		
Other Assets	unconsolidated affiliates	410.4	391.6
	Other investments	71.7	168.8
	Property and equipment, net	1,417.5	1,374.2
	Other assets	48.2	49.3
	Total investments, property and other assets	1,947.8	1,983.9
Total Assets		$2,674.8	2,659.4

LIABILITIES AND STOCKHOLDERS' EQUITY

Liabilities	Current liabilities	$ 277.9	364.9
	Long-term debt	1,112.6	1,087.1
	Deferred income taxes	140.6	147.2
	Insurance reserves and other	87.0	57.7
	Total liabilities	1,618.1	1,656.9
Stockholders' Equity	Preferred stock, none outstanding	—	—
	Common stock, 47.8 million and 47.7 million		
	shares outstanding, respectively	127.6	127.6
	Additional paid-in capital	1.9	4.4
	Cumulative translation adjustment	(1.5)	—
	Retained earnings	1,097.8	1,049.0
		1,225.8	1,181.0
	Less treasury stock, at cost	169.1	178.5
	Total stockholders' equity	1,056.7	1,002.5
Total Liabilities and			
Stockholders' Equity		$2,674.8	2,659.4

See notes to consolidated financial statements

436 *Chapter 15*

CONSOLIDATED STATEMENTS OF CASH FLOWS		Hilton Hotels Corporation and Subsidiaries		
(in millions) Year Ended December 31,		1993	1992	1991
Operating Activities	Net income	$ 106.1	103.9	84.3
	Adjustments to reconcile net income to net cash provided by operating activities:			
	Depreciation and amortization	118.9	109.3	104.8
	Change in working capital components:			
	Inventories	.7	(2.3)	.8
	Accounts receivable	(17.9)	(2.6)	32.7
	Other current assets	(19.9)	(10.0)	2.9
	Accounts payable and accrued expenses	(8.2)	53.1	7.8
	Income taxes payable	(9.2)	(1.0)	(17.0)
	Decrease in deferred income taxes	(6.6)	(14.4)	(4.2)
	Change in other liabilities	29.4	(11.8)	1.8
	Unconsolidated affiliates' distributions in excess of earnings	20.1	11.2	24.7
	Loss (gain) from property transactions	4.5	(.9)	(.5)
	Other	9.0	(7.8)	(14.5)
	Net cash provided by operating activities	226.9	226.7	223.6
Investing Activities	Capital expenditures	(156.8)	(220.9)	(78.5)
	Additional investments	(104.7)	(53.6)	(100.1)
	Change in long-term marketable securities	91.2	(154.8)	—
	Change in temporary investments	64.3	(127.4)	11.8
	Payments on notes receivable	4.5	5.4	4.0
	Proceeds from property transactions	—	4.7	4.1
	Other	1.4	1.4	2.4
	Net cash used in investing activities	(100.1)	(545.2)	(156.3)
Financing Activities	Change in short-term borrowings	(54.2)	65.0	—
	Long-term borrowings	56.0	373.5	344.2
	Reduction of long-term debt	(46.3)	(32.2)	(94.8)
	Issuance of common stock	6.9	2.9	2.2
	Cash dividends	(57.3)	(57.1)	(57.0)
	Net cash (used in) provided by financing activities	(94.9)	352.1	194.6
Increase in Cash and Equivalents		31.9	33.6	261.9
Cash and Equivalents at Beginning of Year		348.5	314.9	53.0
Cash and Equivalents at End of Year		$ 380.4	348.5	314.9

See notes to consolidated financial statements

CONSOLIDATED STATEMENTS OF STOCKHOLDERS' EQUITY   **Hilton Hotels Corporation and Subsidiaries**

(in millions, except per share amounts)	Number of Shares Outstanding	Common Stock	Additional Paid-in Capital	Cumulative Translation Adjustment	Retained Earnings	Treasury Stock	Total Stock-holders' Equity
Balance, December 31, 1990	47.5	$ 127.6	10.8	—	974.9	(190.0)	923.3
Exercise of stock options	—	—	(2.2)	—	—	4.4	2.2
Net income	—	—	—	—	84.3	—	84.3
Dividends ($1.20 per share)	—	—	—	—	(57.0)	—	(57.0)
Balance, December 31, 1991	47.5	127.6	8.6	—	1,002.2	(185.6)	952.8
Exercise of stock options	.2	—	(4.2)	—	—	7.1	2.9
Net income	—	—	—	—	103.9	—	103.9
Dividends ($1.20 per share)	—	—	—	—	(57.1)	—	(57.1)
Balance, December 31, 1992	47.7	127.6	4.4	—	1,049.0	(178.5)	1,002.5
Exercise of stock options	.1	—	(2.5)	—	—	9.4	6.9
Cumulative translation adjustment, net of deferred tax benefit of $.8 million	—	—	—	(1.5)	—	—	(1.5)
Net income	—	—	—	—	106.1	—	106.1
Dividends ($1.20 per share)	—	—	—	—	(57.3)	—	(57.3)
Balance, December 31, 1993	47.8	$ 127.6	1.9	(1.5)	1,097.8	(169.1)	1,056.7

See notes to consolidated financial statements

REVIEW QUIZ

When you feel you have covered all of the material in this chapter, answer these questions. Choose the *best* answer. Check your answers with the correct ones found on the Review Quiz Answer Key at the end of this book.

True (T) or False (F)

T   F   1.   An independent CPA may be an employee of his or her client.

T   F   2.   An audit is designed to express a judgment on the merits of investing in the company being audited.

T   F   3.   In a compilation, the CPA is required to make inquiries to verify information supplied by the client.

T   F   4.   Annual reports are issued by companies whose stock is publicly held.

Multiple Choice

5.   Violation of the AICPA *Code of Professional Conduct* can result in _____ for a CPA.

   a.   revocation of license
   b.   suspension from public practice
   c.   limited assurance
   d.   a and b

6.   In a compilation, the CPA _____ an opinion or level of assurance on the financial statements.

   a.   expresses
   b.   does *not* express
   c.   formally guarantees
   d.   asks his or her manager to express

7.   An intercompany transaction is:

   a.   any transaction between a parent and subsidiary.
   b.   any transaction between subsidiaries.
   c.   any transaction reported on an interim report.
   d.   a and b

8.   Which of the following parts of an annual report explains the business purpose of a company and its operating philosophy?

   a.   message to the shareholders
   b.   corporate profile
   c.   overview of the past year
   d.   historical summaries

9. In the notes to financial statements, information about which of the following should appear first?

   a. long-term contractual obligations for operating leases
   b. discontinued operations
   c. significant accounting policies
   d. diversified corporate activities

10. Examples of contingent liabilities that may need disclosure on financial statements include:

    a. pending lawsuits.
    b. possible tax assessments.
    c. loan guarantees.
    d. all of the above

Glossary

A

A&G

An abbreviation for the administrative and general department.

ACCELERATED DEPRECIATION METHOD

A depreciation method that produces relatively high depreciation expenses in the early years and smaller amounts in later years. However, at the end of the asset's useful life, total depreciation charges do not exceed the amount that the straight-line method would have produced. The double declining balance and sum-of-the-years-digits methods are both accelerated depreciation methods.

ACCOUNT

A form on which financial data are accumulated and summarized.

ACCOUNT BALANCE

A summary of an account in terms of its resulting monetary amount; specifically, the difference between the total debits and the total credits of an account.

ACCOUNT FORMAT

An arrangement of a balance sheet that lists the asset accounts on the left side of the page and the liability and owners' equity accounts on the right side.

ACCOUNT NUMBER

A numeric identification code assigned to an account; account numbers are crucial to computerized bookkeeping systems.

ACCOUNT NUMBERING SYSTEM

A system by which each account is numbered, reflecting its relationship to the company's chart of accounts. An account numbering system is designed to improve clerical accuracy and efficiency. Computers use account numbers to identify each account by department or major balance sheet classification, and by the type of information stored in it.

ACCOUNTANT'S REPORT

See Auditor's Report.

ACCOUNTING

The process by which quantitative information, primarily financial in nature, about economic entities is provided to external and internal users in order to aid decision-making.

ACCOUNTING CYCLE

The sequence of accounting procedures for a fiscal year; the accounting cycle comprises daily, monthly, and end-of-year activities.

ACCOUNTING EQUATION

The equation that states that assets equal liabilities plus equity.

ACCOUNTING SYSTEM

All the forms and procedures used to process business transactions—the ultimate objective of which is to produce reliable financial statements.

ACCOUNTING SYSTEMS DESIGN

The branch of accounting that focuses primarily on the information system of a hospitality organization.

ACCOUNTS PAYABLE

Unpaid invoices due to creditors from whom a firm receives merchandise or services in the ordinary course of business; they are also referred to as trade payables.

ACCOUNTS PAYABLE JOURNAL

A special journal used to record the receipt of all invoices, regardless of whether they will be paid immediately or at some later date; for some operations, entries to the accounts payable journal consist of only those invoices to be paid at a later date.

ACCOUNTS PAYABLE SUBSIDIARY LEDGER

A subsidiary ledger that provides detailed information about amounts owed by the business to its suppliers; it is also referred to as the creditors ledger.

ACCOUNTS RECEIVABLE

Amounts owed to a firm by its guests, usually through open account arrangements or nonbank credit cards.

ACCOUNTS RECEIVABLE SUBSIDIARY LEDGER

A subsidiary ledger that provides detailed information on amounts due the business from its customers; common types include the guest ledger, the city ledger, and the banquet ledger.

ACCRUAL BASIS ACCOUNTING

System of reporting revenue and expenses in the period in which they are considered to have been earned or incurred, regardless of the actual time of collection or payment.

ACCRUED EXPENSES

Unrecorded expenses that, at the end of an accounting period, have been incurred but not yet paid.

ACCUMULATED DEPRECIATION

A contra-asset account representing the depreciation on assets from the point at which they were acquired or first put into use until they are sold or disposed of.

ACID-TEST RATIO

See Quick Ratio.

ADDITIONAL PAID-IN CAPITAL

The premium paid for stock in excess of its par value.

ADJUSTED TRIAL BALANCE

Original trial balance amounts and adjustments are combined into one amount and entered in this worksheet section.

ADJUSTING ENTRIES

End-of-month entries in the general journal that are necessary to comply with the matching principle (accrual basis of accounting); adjusting entries are required for expired assets, unrecorded expenses, unrecorded revenue, and unearned revenue.

ADVANCE DEPOSIT

Amount paid to the business for goods and/or services it has not yet provided; an advance deposit represents a liability until the service is performed.

ALLOWANCE FOR DOUBTFUL ACCOUNTS

A contra-asset account providing an estimate of total potential bad debts. On the balance sheet, this amount is deducted from Accounts Receivable to show the amount expected to be collected in the future. Also called Allowance for Uncollectible Accounts.

ALLOWANCE METHOD

A method for estimating and recording bad debts before they are actually incurred. The estimate is recorded in Allowance for Doubtful Accounts and Uncollectible Accounts Expense. If the income statement approach is used, the estimate increases the Allowance for Doubtful Accounts balance. If the balance sheet approach is used, the estimated amount becomes the new balance in Allowance for Doubtful Accounts.

ALLOWANCES

A contra-revenue account for sales allowances such as rebates or price adjustments made after billing. On the income statement, this account is deducted from gross sales (gross revenue) to arrive at net sales (net revenue).

AMORTIZATION

The systematic transfer of the partial cost of an intangible long-lived asset (such as purchased goodwill, franchise rights, trademarks, tradenames, and preopening expenses) to an expense called amortization. The asset cost is generally reduced and shown at its remaining cost to be amortized.

ANALYSIS

Using amounts from financial statements to calculate percentages and ratios.

ANNUAL REPORT

A comprehensive information package regarding a company's financial status that is issued at the end of the fiscal year.

ANNUITY

When several future amounts (such as a hotel's future loan payments) are equal amounts occurring at equal intervals over a given period of time, the series of future amounts is called an annuity.

ASSET

Anything a business owns that has commercial or exchange value.

ATTEST FUNCTION

Reporting on the fairness and reliability of a company's financial statements—a function performed by independent certified public accountants.

AUDIT

A comprehensive investigation of the items that appear on the financial statements and in any accompanying notes that express an opinion on the financial statements.

AUDITING

The branch of accounting most often associated with the independent, external financial audit, as conducted by independent certified public accountants.

AUDITOR'S REPORT

A report, prepared by an independent auditor, that accompanies the financial statements and explains the degree of responsibility assumed by the auditor for those financial statements. Also referred to as the accountant's report.

AVERAGE DAILY RATE (ADR)

A key rooms department operating ratio obtained by dividing rooms revenue by number of rooms sold. Also called average room rate.

AVERAGE FOOD CHECK

A ratio comparing the revenue generated during a meal period with the number of guests served during the period. It is calculated by dividing total food revenue by number of food covers sold during a period. This ratio should be calculated for different dining areas and/or meal periods.

AVERAGE ROOM RATE (ARR)

See Average Daily Rate (ADR).

B

BAD DEBT

An expense incurred because of failure to collect accounts receivable.

BALANCE SHEET

A statement reporting on the financial position of a business by presenting its assets, liabilities, and equity on a given date.

BEGINNING INVENTORY

The inventory at the start of an accounting period. If the accounting data is for the year-to-date, the beginning inventory is the amount on hand as of the first day of the accounting year (same as the last year's ending inventory). If the accounting data is for the month, the beginning inventory is the amount on hand as of the first day of the month (same as the last month's ending inventory).

BEVERAGE COST PERCENTAGE

A ratio that shows beverage cost as a percentage of beverage sales; calculated by dividing the cost of beverages sold by beverage sales.

BONDS

Certificates of indebtedness sold by businesses to buyers known as bondholders. A legal agreement, called a trust indenture, identifies all the terms and conditions of the company's bond issue. The agreement states the interest rate that the company will pay to bondholders. This stated interest rate is commonly known as the contract interest rate. The agreement also states the maturity date of the bonds, which is the date on which the issuing company guarantees that it will buy back the bonds from the individual bondholders.

BOOK VALUE

The cost of an asset minus the amount of its accumulated depreciation; it is sometimes referred to as net asset value. When the book value of an asset equals the asset's estimated salvage value, the asset is fully depreciated; no further depreciation is recorded for that asset.

BOOKKEEPING

The routine aspects of recording, classifying, and summarizing business transactions—only one part of the overall accounting function.

BUSINESS SEGMENTATION

The division of work into specialized areas of responsibility. Business segmentation starts at the top echelons of a corporation and extends downward to the most detailed aspects of its operations. Various accounting reports reflect the efficiency and/or profitability of each specific area of responsibility. See Responsibility Accounting.

BUSINESS TRANSACTION

The exchange of merchandise, property, or services for cash or a promise to pay; business transactions initiate the accounting process.

C

CAPITAL ACCOUNT

A cumulative account that contains investments made by the owner in the business, plus the net income from operations of the business, less any net loss from operations of the business, less withdrawals of assets from the business by the owner for personal use.

CAPITAL EXPENDITURE

An expenditure recorded to an asset account and not directly to expense.

CAPITAL LEASE

A long-term financing arrangement that grants present or future ownership of the leased property to the lessor.

CAPITAL STOCK

Collective term for various classes of common and preferred stock.

CAPTION

An item on a financial statement representing one account or several accounts. Also referred to as a line item.

CASH

A category of current assets consisting of cash in house banks, cash in checking and savings accounts, and certificates of deposit.

CASH ACCOUNTING METHOD

The method by which the results of business transactions are recorded only when cash is received or paid out. See Accrual Basis Accounting.

CASH DISCOUNT

A discount offered for a specific time period by a seller on the amount of an invoice in order to encourage prompt payment. Also referred to as a purchase discount.

CASH EQUIVALENTS

Short-term, highly liquid investments such as U.S. Treasury Bills and money market accounts.

CASH FLOW

A stream of receipts (inflows) and disbursements (outflows) resulting from operational activities or investments.

CASH INFLOW

Cash received by the hospitality organization during the accounting period.

CASH OUTFLOW
Cash disbursed by the hospitality organization during the accounting period.

CASH PAYMENTS JOURNAL
A special journal used to record checks issued from the regular checking account.

CERTIFIED PUBLIC ACCOUNTANT (CPA)
A professional accountant who has met academic qualifications, satisfied state requirements, and passed the national CPA exam.

CHART OF ACCOUNTS
A list of all accounts (and account numbers) used by a business in its bookkeeping system.

CITY LEDGER
The accounts receivable subsidiary ledger used for all nonregistered guests. The billings for guests who have checked out and charged their bills are transferred from the guest ledger to the city ledger. The accounting department is responsible for maintaining the city ledger.

CLASSIFYING
The process of assembling the numerous business transactions encountered by a business into related categories.

CLOSING ENTRIES
End-of-year entries that set all revenue and expense accounts to a zero balance and transfer the resulting profit or loss to an equity account. In a corporation, net income or loss is recorded in Retained Earnings. In a proprietorship (or partnership), net income or loss is recorded in a Capital account; the Withdrawals account is set to zero and charged to the Capital account.

COMMERCIAL PAPER
Unsecured short-term securities or promissory notes issued by the largest and strongest corporations in our economy. Generally has a maturity of less than 270 days.

COMMISSIONS
Payments to authorized agents who secure business for the hotel. Commissions also include amounts paid to rental agents for permanent rooms business. Commissions are generally accounted for as a rooms department expense. A separate expense account may be used to account for the cost of reservation services.

COMMITMENTS
Anticipated expenditures evidenced by a contract or a purchase order. For example, a large resort may sign a contract in January committing itself to pay a well-known entertainer $300,000 to perform at the hotel during the first week of April.

COMMON STOCK
Stock issued by a corporation that gives ownership interest and voting rights.

COMMON-SIZE ANALYSIS

An analytical procedure in which each item amount is stated as a percentage of a base amount. The base amount for a common-size income statement is net sales (net revenue), and that for a common-size balance sheet is total assets. Also called vertical analysis because comparisons on common-size financial statements are made from top to bottom.

COMMON-SIZE BALANCE SHEET

A type of balance sheet that presents two sets of figures for each balance sheet line item. One set of figures is from the current balance sheet; the other set is from the balance sheet of a previous period. All amounts are reduced to percentages of their account classification.

COMPARATIVE ANALYSIS

An analytical procedure performed on comparative statements showing the actual and percentage change from the prior period. Also called horizontal analysis because comparisons are made from left to right.

COMPARATIVE BALANCE SHEET

A type of balance sheet that presents two sets of figures for each balance sheet line item. One set of figures is from the current balance sheet; the other set is from the balance sheet of a previous period. Changes in amounts of line items from one period to the next are reported both in absolute terms (in dollars) and in relative terms (as percentage changes).

COMPARATIVE FINANCIAL STATEMENT

A financial statement showing two or more periods of financial information.

COMPENSATING BALANCE

A minimum amount that must be maintained in a checking account in connection with a borrowing arrangement.

COMPILATION

A report limited to considering financial statements for form, application of accounting principles, and mathematical accuracy—without expressing an opinion or any other form of assurance on them.

COMPOUND INTEREST

Interest computed on the principal *and* on the interest accumulated from the preceding period(s). See Simple Interest.

COMPUTER PROGRAM

A sequence of instructions that commands a computer system to perform a useful task.

CONCESSIONAIRE

An individual or company given the right by the hotel to operate special sales activities on the premises.

CONGLOMERATE

A company that acquires and/or manages several corporate brands or independent unbranded hotels.

CONSERVATISM

The principle asserting that assets and income should be fairly presented and not overstated, especially for those situations that involve doubt.

CONSISTENCY

The principle stating that once an accounting method has been adopted, it should be followed without variance from period to period.

CONSOLIDATED FINANCIAL STATEMENTS

The merging of the financial information of the parent company and its subsidiaries into one set of financial statements representing one economic entity.

CONTINGENT LIABILITIES

A liability that is conditioned upon a future occurrence which may or may not take place; until such event, the liability is only contingent.

CONTRA ACCOUNT

An account that functions in an opposite manner to the regular classification with which it is associated; for instance, a fixed asset account is reduced by its associated Accumulated Depreciation account (a contra-asset account).

CONTRIBUTED CAPITAL

Funds provided by external sources.

CONTROL ACCOUNT

A term describing either the Accounts Receivable account or the Accounts Payable account in the general ledger; the term refers to the relationship between the balances of these accounts and the totals of their associated subsidiary ledgers.

CONTROLLING

(1) The management process of comparing actual performance with established standards and, when necessary, taking corrective action to bring performance up to standards in order to protect assets and income. (2) Safeguarding the operation's property and income.

COPYRIGHT

An exclusive right granted by the federal government to reproduce and sell an artistic or published work.

CORPORATION

An incorporated business—a separate legal entity organized under law and distinct from its owners.

CORRECTING ENTRIES

Entries in the general journal used to correct previous entries which were erroneous.

COST ACCOUNTING

The branch of accounting that relates to the recording, classification, allocation, and reporting of current and prospective costs.

COST OF SALES

The cost of food and beverage merchandise or other materials held for resale and used in the sales process, not including any cost for labor or operating supplies.

COVENANT NOT TO COMPETE

An agreement by the seller of a business not to operate a similar business in a certain geographical area for a specified number of years. Such an agreement requires separate cash consideration, either actual or implied. If stated in the purchase agreement, the cost basis of the covenant is the amount paid for it. Under tax rules, a covenant not to compete may be amortized over the life of the agreement or 40 years, whichever is less.

COVER

A meal served in a restaurant or at a food function; term used when counting the volume of business.

CREDIT

To record an amount on the right side of an account, or it may refer to the amount itself; a credit is used to increase a liability, equity, or revenue account, and to decrease an asset or expense account.

CROSSFOOTING

The process of horizontally adding or subtracting numbers.

CURRENT ASSETS

Cash or assets that are convertible to cash within 12 months of the balance sheet date; to be considered a current asset, an asset must be available without restriction for use in payment of current liabilities.

CURRENT LIABILITIES

Those liabilities expected to be satisfied by the use of a current asset or to be replaced by another current liability within 12 months of the balance sheet date.

CURRENT RATIO

A ratio of total current assets to total current liabilities. A current ratio indicates the ability of a company to meet its current obligations (current liabilities).

D

DAILY CASHIERS REPORT
An accounting document used to record cash register readings, cash count, bank deposits, and other transactions handled by the cashier.

DAILY ROOM REPORT
Listing of rooms occupied by registered guests. Also called the room rack report.

DAILY TRANSCRIPT
A documentation of guest ledger activity that serves as an essential reconciliation and audit tool.

DATA
Facts and/or figures to be processed into useful information. Three types of data are alpha data, numeric data, and alphanumeric data.

DEBIT
To record an amount on the left side of an account; a debit is used to increase an asset or expense account, and to decrease a liability, equity, or revenue account.

DEBT-TO-EQUITY RATIO
A ratio that measures the total debt (current and long-term liabilities) in relation to the investment by the owners (total shareholders' equity). Creditors are interested in this ratio because it provides an indicator of risk; the higher the ratio, the higher the risk for those extending credit to the business.

DEFERRED INCOME TAXES
When the income taxes on the statement of income exceed the amount of liability to government tax agencies for the year, the business records the excess as deferred income taxes. This difference generally represents timing differences with respect to payment dates of taxes.

DEPARTMENTAL INCOME
The difference between an operating department's revenue and direct expenses.

DEPARTMENTAL REVENUE REPORT
A sales log individually prepared for each department. Its main purpose is to summarize data that will be useful to management; it is not used for input to the general ledger. A departmental revenue report may be the basis for sales reports and statistical analyses.

DEPRECIATION
The systematic transfer of part of a tangible long-lived asset's cost to an expense called depreciation. The asset cost is generally not reduced, but is offset by an entry to the accumulated depreciation account which represents the depreciation recorded on an asset from the point at which it was acquired. Depreciation is usually associated with assets classified as property and equipment, but not with land.

DIRECT EXPENSE

An expense directly related to the department incurring the expense. Examples are cost of sales, payroll and payroll related expenses, and other expenses that can be readily identified as associated with a specific department.

DIRECT METHOD

With regard to the statement of cash flows, one of two methods for converting net income to cash flow from operations. This method shows cash receipts from sales and cash disbursements for expenses and requires that each item on the net income statement be converted from an accrual basis to a cash basis. Compare Indirect Method.

DIRECT PURCHASE

Food purchased for immediate use that is delivered directly to the kitchen instead of to the storeroom.

DIRECT WRITE-OFF METHOD

A method of accounting for uncollectibles by which bad debt expense is recorded only after a particular account has been judged worthless and is to be written off the books. Also called the direct charge-off method.

DISCLOSURE

An explanation of a financial statement item or any fact about a company's financial condition.

DIVIDEND

A distribution of earnings to owners of a corporation's stock. See Stock Dividends.

DOUBLE DECLINING BALANCE METHOD

See Accelerated Depreciation Method.

DOUBTFUL ACCOUNTS

An account used to record the portion of accounts receivable judged to be uncollectible.

DUE BACK

The amount "due back" to the house bank for a dip in the imprest of the house bank. A dip occurs when the front office, as a result of making cash advances and cashing guest checks, pays out more cash in a day than it receives.

E

EARNINGS PER SHARE (EPS) RATIO

A ratio that serves as a general indicator of corporate profitability by comparing net income of the corporation with the average common shares outstanding. If preferred stock has been issued for the operation, then preferred dividends are subtracted from net income before EPS is calculated. Calculated by dividing net income by average common shares outstanding.

EMPLOYEE EARNINGS RECORD

An individual record kept for each employee during the calendar year which indicates gross wages earned and amounts withheld and deducted. At the end of the year, an employee's earnings record is used to prepare IRS Form W-2, which is sent to federal and state agencies and to the employee.

EOM (END OF MONTH)

A modification of discount terms specifying that the cash discount period begins after the end of the month in which the invoice is dated. According to business practice, if an invoice with EOM terms is dated on or after the 26th day of a month, the cash discount period extends to the *second* month after the month of the invoice date (as if the invoice were dated for the beginning of the next month).

EQUITY

The claims of owners to assets of the business; equity represents the residual amounts after liabilities are deducted from assets.

EXPENSE

The cost of items consumed in the process of generating revenue or that expire due to the passage of time. Examples include cost of sales, payroll, taxes, supplies, advertising, utilities, repairs, rent, depreciation, and other operating and fixed expenses.

EXPENSE ACCOUNTS

Income statement accounts used to record expenditures made in the process of generating revenue including cost of sales, payroll, utilities, advertising, rent, and similar business expenses.

EXPENSE DICTIONARY

A special dictionary designed to enable controllers to classify expense items according to the proper account or expense group.

EXTERNAL FINANCIAL STATEMENTS

Statements designed to inform outside parties of the results of operations (as reported by the income statement), the financial position of the company as a whole (as reported by the balance sheet), or other pertinent information. These statements present information in a summarized format and emphasize company results. They are typically audited and certified by independent CPAs.

EXTERNAL USERS

Groups outside the business who require accounting and financial information; external users include suppliers, bankers, stockholders, and investors.

F

F&B
An abbreviation for the food and beverage department.

FACE VALUE
The issued amount of a bond.

FAIR LABOR STANDARDS ACT (FLSA)
A federal law that regulates such areas as minimum wage, overtime pay, and equal pay provisions. This federal law's provisions can be superseded by any state or contractual provision that is more generous to the employee. Also commonly known as the federal wage and hour law.

FEDERAL INCOME TAX
The income taxes calculated on a firm's taxable income and reported on the income statement.

FEDERAL INCOME TAX WITHHELD
Taxes withheld from employees' gross pay that must be paid to the federal government. This constitutes part of the system under which most persons pay their income tax during the year in which income is received or earned.

FEDERAL INSURANCE CONTRIBUTIONS ACT (FICA)
The federal law governing the national social security system, which imposes a payroll tax on the employee and the employer.

FEDERAL UNEMPLOYMENT TAX ACT (FUTA)
A federal law imposing a payroll tax on the employer for the purpose of funding national and state unemployment programs.

FINANCIAL ACCOUNTING
The branch of accounting primarily concerned with recording and accumulating accounting information to be used in the preparation of financial statements for external users.

FINANCIAL ACCOUNTING STANDARDS BOARD (FASB)
An independent, non-governmental body that develops and issues statements of financial accounting standards.

FINANCIAL LEVERAGE
The use of debt in place of equity dollars to finance operations and increase the return on the equity dollars already invested.

FINANCIAL REPORTING CENTER
An area of responsibility for which separate cost information must be collected; this information is then used to prepare financial reports. Financial reporting centers

are classified according to three basic types: revenue centers, support centers, and other financial reporting centers (i.e., energy costs and fixed charges).

FINANCIAL STATEMENT

Formal medium for communicating various kinds of accounting information to both internal and external users; examples include balance sheet, income statement, and statement of retained earnings.

FIRST-IN, FIRST-OUT (FIFO)

An inventory costing method that assumes the first units purchased are the first units used. The result is that ending inventory consists of the most recent costs, and the oldest costs are in cost of sales.

FISCAL YEAR

The business year; may or may not differ from the calendar year but is always a twelve-month period.

FIXED ASSETS

See Property and Equipment.

FIXED CHARGES

Expenses incurred regardless of sales volume of the hotel. Examples are rent, property taxes, property insurance, interest, depreciation, and amortization. Also referred to as occupancy costs.

FLOWCHART

Diagrams the flow of documents through an organization and reveals the origin, processing, and final deposition of each document. Flowcharting is useful because it provides a concise overview of the internal control system, enabling management to identify weaknesses for corrective action.

FOB (FREE ON BOARD)

Part of a freight term used to specify either the point of origin or the point of destination. Its specification determines whether the buyer or seller pays the additional freight charges required to complete delivery. Two common freight terms are FOB factory (in which case, the buyer pays) and FOB destination (in which case, the seller pays).

FOOD COST

The cost of food used in the production of a menu item; the cost of food served to guests in the revenue process.

FOOD COST PERCENTAGE

A ratio calculated by dividing cost of food sales by net food sales. Food cost percentages vary from company to company depending on such factors as service level, menu prices, and food quality.

FOOD PURCHASES ACCOUNT

An account used to record purchases of food provisions (direct and storeroom) under the periodic inventory method.

FOOTING

The process of totaling a column.

FOOTNOTES

Footnotes provide financial information which cannot be easily presented in the financial statements. Also called Notes to the Financial Statements.

FRANCHISE

An agreement by which the franchisee undertakes to conduct a business or sell a product or service in accordance with methods and procedures prescribed by the franchisor; the franchise may encompass an exclusive right to sell a product or service or conduct a business in a specified territory.

FRANCHISE AGREEMENT

The exclusive right or privilege granted by the franchisor that allows the franchisee to sell certain services or products in a specified geographical area. A franchise agreement usually stipulates a period of time and establishes the conditions under which the franchise may be revoked. The amortization period is based on the life of the franchise contract, but cannot exceed 40 years.

FUNDS

All of the financial resources of a hospitality business. Changes in these resources result in changes in a property's financial position. Major transactions which may create sources of funds include income from operations, decreases in noncurrent assets, increases in noncurrent liabilities (long-term debt), and increases in contributed capital. Major transactions which may create uses of funds include increases in noncurrent assets, decreases in noncurrent liabilities (long-term debt), and decreases in owners' equity.

FUTURE VALUE OF A SINGLE AMOUNT

The future worth of an amount invested today. Determining the future value of a single amount answers the following question: given a specific amount of funds to invest at a stated rate of interest, what will be the future value of the investment after a specified period of time?

G

GENERAL JOURNAL

A two-column, general purpose journal; since each entry in a general journal requires individual posting, this journal is impractical for large volumes of repetitive transactions.

GENERAL LEDGER

Collective form of the bookkeeping accounts; in a manual system, the general ledger is composed of a separate page for each account.

GENERALLY ACCEPTED ACCOUNTING PRINCIPLES (GAAP)

Professional accounting standards that have received substantial authoritative support and approval from professional accounting associations and governmental agencies.

GOING-CONCERN ASSUMPTION

The assumption that a business will continue indefinitely and thus carry out its commitments; it is also known as continuity of the business unit.

GOODWILL

In simple terms, goodwill is an intangible asset which is recorded if a business is purchased at a price greater than the value of its property and equipment. The difference (or premium) is the amount recorded in goodwill.

GROSS PAY

The total amount of pay before any payroll deductions. Also referred to as gross earnings.

GROSS PROFIT

The profit on the sale of material or merchandise excluding labor and other operating expenses. It is computed as follows: net sales less cost of sales.

GROSS PROFIT METHOD

A method of estimating the ending inventory based on the assumption that the rate of gross profit remains relatively constant.

GROSS RECORDING METHOD

A method of recording cash discounts that uses the full invoice amount as the basis of a journal entry. If the discount is realized, it may be treated as a reduction of the account originally debited (nonrevenue treatment) or as other income (revenue treatment).

GUEST CHECK

A document used for sales control designed to record a customer's order, requisition merchandise from the kitchen or bar, and serve as the guest bill.

GUEST FOLIO

A statement of the guest's account that records guest transactions and shows a perpetual balance.

GUEST LEDGER

A type of ledger comprising individual records (called folios) of the hotel's registered guests. The guest ledger provides current status on guest charges and payments; the front office is responsible for summarizing these transactions during a guest's stay. A guest ledger may also be referred to as a front office ledger, transient ledger, or room ledger.

H

HARDWARE
The physical components that make up a computer system. Also referred to as computer equipment.

HISTORICAL COST
The principle stating that the value of merchandise or services obtained through business transactions should be recorded in terms of actual costs, not current market values.

HORIZONTAL ANALYSIS
See Comparative Analysis.

HOUSEKEEPER'S REPORT
A report prepared each morning on the basis of reports from each room attendant; one of its purposes is to prevent intentional omissions from room sales. The status of a room (occupied, out of order, baggage, etc.) is shown in symbols on the housekeeper's report.

HUMAN RESOURCES DEPARTMENT
The personnel department of a hotel.

I

IMPREST
A predetermined, fixed amount of funds (for example, a cashier's initial funds or a payroll checking account balance) maintained or replenished as part of typical control procedures.

INCOME STATEMENT
A financial statement of the results of operations that presents the sales, expenses, and net income of a business entity for a stated period of time. Also called Statement of Income.

INCOME SUMMARY ACCOUNT
A temporary account into which the balances of the revenue and expense accounts are closed; the resulting balance represents the net income or loss of the business. The balance in Income Summary is also closed and transferred to an equity account. See also Closing Entries.

INDIRECT EXPENSES
Expenses that cannot be related directly to any specific department; generally, indirect expenses benefit the hotel as a whole.

INDIRECT METHOD

With regard to the statement of cash flows, one of two methods for converting net income to net cash flow from operations. This method starts with net income and then adjusts for noncash items included on the income statement.

INFORMATION

The end result of data processing and electronic data processing by which pieces of data are organized or manipulated into significant output.

INTANGIBLE ASSETS

Noncurrent assets that do not have physical substance; their value is derived from rights or benefits associated with their ownership. Examples include trademarks, patents, copyrights, purchased goodwill, and purchased franchise rights.

INTERCOMPANY TRANSACTION

A transaction between a parent company and any of its subsidiaries.

INTEREST

An amount based on the principal, the specific rate, and the time period of a loan. Simple interest is interest computed only on the original principal. Compound interest is interest computed on the principal and on interest accumulated from the preceding period(s).

INTEREST EXPENSE

The charge for borrowing funds; the difference between the amount borrowed and the amount paid over the life of a loan.

INTEREST INCOME

The reward for lending funds; the difference between the amount loaned and the amount received over the lending period.

INTERIM FINANCIAL STATEMENTS

Financial statements prepared during the business year; for instance, quarterly or monthly statements.

INTERIM REPORT

Condensed financial statement issued during the period between annual reports. Also called an interim statement.

INTERNAL CONTROL

The policies, procedures, and equipment used in a business to safeguard its assets and promote operational efficiency. Internal control allows employees to prove that they are performing their duties with efficiency and integrity.

INTERNAL CONTROL QUESTIONNAIRE

A form listing a series of questions about controls in each area of a business. This provides a way of identifying weaknesses in the internal control system.

INTERNAL FINANCIAL STATEMENTS

Financial statements intended for internal users. These statements present detailed information on each responsibility area and the hotel as a whole. Management uses the information in monitoring the profitability of operations and in long-range planning.

INTERNAL REVENUE CODE (IRC)

A codification of income tax statutes and other federal tax laws, whose objectives are guided by large-scale political, economic, and social concerns.

INTERNAL USERS

Groups inside the hospitality business who require accounting and financial information, e.g., the board of directors, the general manager, departmental managers, and other staff.

INTERPRETATION

Comparing percentages and ratios to determine the meaning and significance of an analysis.

INVENTORY

Stocks of food and beverage merchandise held for resale, stocks of operating supplies, and other supplies held for future use.

INVENTORY ACCOUNTING METHODS

The bookkeeping accounts and accounting procedures used for inventories; the recordkeeping is performed by the accounting department.

INVENTORY SYSTEM

The actual receipt and issue of products in the storeroom.

INVENTORY TURNOVER PERIOD

The average number of days that inventory is on hand. Any turnover ratio can be converted to a turnover period by dividing 365 days by the number of turnover times in a year.

INVENTORY TURNOVER RATIO

A ratio representing the number of times that the inventory is turned over (sold and replaced) during the period under consideration. This ratio is calculated by dividing the cost of sales by average inventory on hand.

INVENTORY VALUATION

Inventory valuation does not refer to market value but to the cost of inventory as determined by a costing inventory method such as FIFO, LIFO, or weighted average.

INVESTMENTS

Stocks or bonds failing to meet any or all of the conditions associated with marketable securities; investments also include cash restricted for use in connection with long-term borrowing arrangements and long-term notes receivable.

INVOICE
Statement issued by a seller containing relevant information about a purchase, including: parties involved; the transaction date; the method of shipment; and quantities, descriptions and prices of goods.

ISSUING
The process of distributing food and beverages from the storeroom to authorized individuals by the use of formal requisitions.

J

JOURNAL
An accounting document used to record business transactions.

JOURNALIZING
The process of recording transactions in a journal.

L

LABOR COST PERCENTAGE
Often referred to as labor cost to sales ratio, the percentage of sales that is used to pay labor, including salaries, wages, bonuses, payroll taxes, and fringe benefits. Calculated by dividing total labor costs by total revenue. This ratio should be calculated for each operated department. Sometimes used by international hotels to measure comparative operational advantages among properties in different countries.

LAPPING
A common fraudulent practice that may occur when cash handling and accounts receivable duties are not segregated. Lapping occurs when an accounts receivable clerk steals cash received on account. The next day, cash received from a second account is posted to the account which was not credited the previous day, and so on.

LAST-IN, LAST-OUT (LIFO)
An inventory costing method that assumes the most recent units purchased are the first units used. The result is that ending inventory consists of the oldest costs and the most recent costs are in cost of sales.

LEADING
The process of motivating employees toward the achievement of organizational goals and objectives. Leading is one of the basic functions of management.

LEASE
A contract by which the use of property or equipment is granted by the lessor to the lessee.

LEASEHOLD IMPROVEMENTS

Capital expenditures made to improve leased property by the lessee. The costs of these improvements are recorded in this account because the improvements become part of the leased property and thus revert to the lessor upon the lease's termination.

LEASEHOLDS

The right to use property or equipment by virtue of a lease.

LEGAL LIFE

The life of some intangible assets as defined by law. For example, a patent is an exclusive right granted by the federal government to use, manufacture, sell, or lease a product or design for a period of 17 years. Frequently, the economic life of an intangible asset is shorter than its legal life; in such cases, the shorter life is used to compute amortization.

LESSEE

The person or company that uses leased property or equipment under the terms of a lease.

LESSOR

The person or company that leases property or equipment to a lessee.

LIABILITIES

The claims of outsiders (such as creditors) to assets of the business; liabilities are sometimes called creditors' equities.

LIFE INSURANCE

Two basic kinds of life insurance are term-life insurance and whole-life insurance. Both provide a payment to the beneficiary if the insured person dies. Term-life insurance does not build up any cash value and is worthless if it is canceled or if it is allowed to expire at the end of a specified termination date. A portion of the premiums paid for whole-life insurance is used to build up a cash value. The owner of the policy may redeem the policy for its cash value or may borrow against that value while the policy remains in force.

LIMITED PARTNER

A partner who does not actively participate in the management of the business, and is basically an investor whose liability may be restricted according to the terms of the partnership agreement.

LIQUIDITY

The ability of a hospitality operation to meet its short-term (current) obligations by maintaining sufficient cash and/or investments easily convertible to cash.

LIQUIDITY RATIO

Ratio that shows the ability of a business to satisfy short-term obligations (current liabilities).

LONG-TERM LIABILITIES
Debts *not* due within 12 months of the balance sheet date.

M

MANAGEMENT INFORMATION SYSTEM (MIS)
A system that encompasses the collection, preparation, and communication of the information that management requires in maintaining and improving the operational efficiency of a business. A major purpose of a management information system (MIS) is to provide management with timely and useful financial information. As part of MIS, reporting areas may summarize financial data by means of reports on such matters as daily sales, receivables, and cash balances.

MANAGERIAL ACCOUNTING
The branch of accounting primarily concerned with recording and accumulating accounting information in order to prepare financial statements and reports for internal users.

MARKETABLE SECURITIES
A category of current assets including stocks and bonds of large corporations and U.S. government bonds which are readily marketable and intended to be converted into cash should the need arise.

MATCHING PRINCIPLE
The principle stating that all expenses must be recorded in the same accounting period as the revenue that they helped to generate.

MATERIALITY
The principle stating that material events must be accounted for according to accounting rules, but insignificant events may be treated in an expeditious manner.

MERCHANDISE
Items intended for resale to guests. Merchandise may include food, beverages, gift shop items, gum, cigarettes, candy, and snacks.

MINORITY INTEREST
The equity interest in a subsidiary that is not owned by the parent, or the portion of a subsidiary's net assets owned by outsiders other than the parent.

MODIFIED ACCELERATED COST RECOVERY SYSTEM
An accelerated depreciation method in which the book value of an asset is fully depreciated down to zero.

MODULE
A distinct and identifiable program unit.

MONEY MARKET FUND

A mutual fund that invests primarily in commercial paper, U.S. T-bills, and other financial instruments offering attractive interest rates. Investors in money market funds may redeem their holdings directly through the mutual fund or a broker.

N

NET INCOME

The excess of revenue earned over expenses for the accounting period.

NET INCOME TO SALES RATIO

A ratio computed by dividing net income by net sales. It gives the amount of net income on each sales dollar and is expressed as a percentage. The net income to sales ratio is also called the Profit Margin Ratio.

NET LOSS

The bottom line on an income statement that occurs when expenses exceed revenue.

NET PAY

Gross pay less all payroll deductions. Net pay is the amount of the payroll check. Also referred to as net earnings.

NET PURCHASES RECORDING METHOD

A method of recording cash discounts that uses the invoice amount *minus* any potential cash discount as the basis of a journal entry. If the anticipated discount is realized, then no later adjustment is required. If the anticipated discount is not realized, it may be recorded to an expense account called Discounts Lost.

NET REVENUE

The result of sales less any allowances; also referred to as net sales. See also Allowances.

NONCURRENT ASSETS

Assets that are *not* to be converted to cash within 12 months of the balance sheet date.

NONCURRENT LIABILITIES

Long-term debt.

NORMAL ACCOUNT BALANCE

The type of balance (debit or credit) expected of a particular account based on its classification; asset and expense accounts normally have debit balances, while liability, equity, and revenue accounts normally have credit balances.

NOTE AMORTIZATION SCHEDULE

A report that provides management with information regarding a loan, detailing the periodic interest and the amount of the loan outstanding at the end of each payment.

NOTES PAYABLE

An account that includes any written promise (promissory note) by a business to pay a creditor or lender at some future date.

NOTES RECEIVABLE

An account for recording promissory notes made payable to the hospitality company.

NUMBER OF TIMES INTEREST EARNED RATIO

A solvency ratio expressing the number of times interest expense can be covered. Calculated by dividing earnings before interest and taxes by interest expense.

O

OBJECTIVITY

The principle stating that all business transactions must be supported by objective evidence proving that the transactions did in fact occur.

OCCUPANCY PERCENTAGE

A ratio indicating management's success in selling its "product." (1) Among lodging properties, occupancy percentage is also referred to as the occupancy rate and is calculated by dividing the number of rooms sold by the number of rooms available. (2) In food service operations, occupancy percentage is referred to as seat turnover and is calculated by dividing the number of people served by the number of seats available.

OPERATING EXPENSES

Expenses (other than the cost of goods sold) incurred in the day-to-day operation of a business.

OPERATING LEASE

A lease similar to a rental agreement without any appearance of present or future ownership of the leased property by the lessee.

OPERATING SYSTEM

A system that orchestrates the hardware and the software within the computer system. It establishes the system's priorities and directs its resources to effectively accomplish desired tasks.

ORGANIZATION CHART

A visual representation of the structure of positions within an operation, showing the different layers of management and the chain of command.

ORGANIZATION COSTS

Costs incurred before a business is incorporated. These costs include state incorporation fees, attorneys' fees, costs of printing stock certificates, and other costs related to the formation of a corporate entity.

ORGANIZING

The management activity that attempts to best assemble and use limited human resources to attain organizational objectives. It involves establishing the flow of authority and communication among people.

OTHER INCOME—FOOD AND BEVERAGE

An account representing sales other than food and beverage items. This account is used in the food and beverage department to record sales of candy, popcorn, postcards, and other nonfood or nonbeverage items.

OTHER OPERATED DEPARTMENTS

A term used to represent incidental operating departments not including those departments operated by concessionaires.

OVERTIME PAY

A term that indicates a premium paid for hours worked in excess of a specified total of hours as stated by the FLSA, state, or contractual provisions.

OVERTIME PAY METHOD

A method for computing overtime pay in which overtime hours are excluded from regular hours (straight-time hours). The overtime hours are multiplied at a rate which is one and one-half times the regular hourly rate. This overtime pay is added to regular pay to arrive at gross pay. This method results in the same amount of gross pay as the overtime premium method.

OVERTIME PREMIUM METHOD

A method for computing overtime pay in which overtime hours are included in the computation of regular pay (straight-time pay). The total of the regular hours and overtime hours are multiplied by the regular rate to arrive at straight-time pay. Then the overtime premium is computed by multiplying only the overtime hours by a rate that is one-half the regular hourly pay rate. The straight-time pay added to the overtime premium is the gross pay for the employee. This method results in the same amount of gross pay as the overtime pay method.

OWNERSHIP EQUITY

Financial interest of the owner(s) in a business.

P

PAR VALUE

An arbitrarily selected amount associated with authorized shares of stock; it is also referred to as legal value.

PARENT COMPANY

A company that exercises control over another company through ownership of all or a majority of the other company's voting stocks.

PARTNERSHIP

An unincorporated business owned by two or more individuals.

PATENT

An exclusive right granted by the federal government to use, manufacture, sell, or lease a product or design. The right is granted for 17 years.

PAYROLL JOURNAL

A special journal that basically serves as a check register for recording all payroll checks issued.

PERIODIC INVENTORY SYSTEM

A system of accounting for inventory under which cost of goods sold must be computed. There are no perpetual inventory records, so a physical count of the storeroom is required to determine the inventory on hand.

PERMANENT ACCOUNTS

Accounts that maintain a perpetual balance, i.e., they are not closed at the end of the fiscal year; permanent accounts are also called real accounts.

PERMANENT DIFFERENCE

Occurs when a revenue or expense appears on the income statement but does not appear on the income tax return.

PERPETUAL INVENTORY SYSTEM

A system of accounting for inventory that records the receipts and issues and provides a continuous record of the quantity and cost of merchandise in inventory.

PLANNING

The management task of creating goals and objectives, as well as programs of action to reach those goals and objectives. Planning should be completed before other management tasks are undertaken.

POM

An abbreviation for property operation and maintenance.

POST-CLOSING TRIAL BALANCE

A trial balance that is prepared after the closing process is completed. Thus only the balance sheet accounts need be listed since the revenue and expense accounts have a zero balance at this stage of the accounting cycle. The purpose of the Post-Closing Trial Balance is to verify the equality of the debit and credit balances of the permanent balance sheet accounts. This is a critical step because these balances become next year's beginning balances.

POSTING

The process by which journal entries are ultimately recorded in the bookkeeping accounts. Posting also refers to the process of transferring charges to a guest's account.

PREFERRED STOCK

Stock issued by a corporation that provides preferential treatment on dividends, but may not give the stockholder the privilege of voting.

PREOPENING EXPENSES

Costs associated with certain business activities that occur before a company is operational. They are sometimes called start-up costs. Generally, preopening expenses are amortized over a five-year period (60 months).

PREPAID EXPENSES

Unexpired costs that will benefit future periods but are expected to expire within a relatively short period, usually within 12 months of the current accounting period; examples include prepaid rent (excluding security deposits) and prepaid insurance premiums.

PRESENT VALUE OF A FUTURE AMOUNT

The present worth of an amount to be received at a future date. Determining the present value of a future amount answers the following question: how much money must be invested today at a given rate of interest in order to yield a desired amount at a specific time in the future?

PRICE EARNINGS (PE) RATIO

A profitability ratio used by financial analysts to show investors the relative value of an investment; calculated by dividing market price per share by earnings per share.

PRIME COSTS

The cost of food sold plus payroll cost (including employee benefits). These are a restaurant's largest costs.

PRINCIPAL

The amount borrowed or loaned.

PROCEDURE MANUAL

A document that informs employees how to carry out the duties listed on their job descriptions.

PROFIT MARGIN RATIO

See Net Income to Sales Ratio.

PROMISSORY NOTE

A written promise to pay a definite sum of money at some future date, generally involving the payment of interest in addition to the principal (amount of loan); promissory notes may be characterized as negotiable instruments (legally transferable among parties by endorsement).

PROPERTY AND EQUIPMENT

A noncurrent asset category including assets of a relatively permanent nature that are tangible (such as land, buildings, and equipment) and are used in the business operation to generate sales; this category may be referred to as plant assets or fixed assets.

PROPERTY MANAGEMENT SYSTEM

A computerized information system designed to carry out a number of front office and back office functions. System front office applications integrate such functions as reservations, rooms management, and guest accounting within a hotel's information network. System back office applications typically include such functions as accounts receivable, accounts payable, payroll accounting, check writing and bank reconciliations, fixed asset accounting, financial reporting, and the general ledger.

PROPRIETORSHIP

A form of business organization referring to an unincorporated business owned by one person (sole proprietor).

PURCHASE ORDER

An order for supplies or products, prepared by the operation and submitted to the supplier.

PURVEYOR

A firm that provides or supplies merchandise to hospitality operations.

Q

QUICK RATIO

A more refined version of the current ratio. The denominator is the same (current liabilities), but the numerator is made up of only those current assets that are relatively liquid: cash, marketable securities, and net receivables. The quick ratio is often called the acid-test ratio.

R

RATIO

The mathematical relationship of two figures.

REALIZATION PRINCIPLE

The principle stating that revenue resulting from business transactions should be recorded only when a sale has been made *and* earned.

RECEIVING

Accepting delivery of merchandise that has been ordered or is expected by the firm and recording such transactions.

RECEIVING REPORT

A report on items received, prepared at time of delivery.

RECORDING

The procedure of actually entering the results of transactions in an accounting document called a journal.

RENTALS AND OTHER INCOME

This report shows revenue not associated with any particular department. Examples of revenue accounts appearing in this report are: interest income, dividends income, rental of store or office space, concessions fee income, commissions income, cash discounts, salvage sales, and other similar revenue items.

REPORT FORMAT

An arrangement of a balance sheet that lists the assets first, followed by liabilities and owners' equity.

RESPONSIBILITY ACCOUNTING

The principle by which each department reports revenue and expense data separately from other areas of the organization; a given department is directed by an individual who is held responsible for its operation. Responsibility accounting provides financial information useful in evaluating the effectiveness of managers and department heads, who should be judged on the basis of revenues and expenses directly under their control.

RETAINED EARNINGS

The portion of net income earned by the corporation that is not distributed as dividends, but is retained in the business.

RETURN ON ASSETS (ROA) RATIO

A ratio that provides a general indicator of the profitability of a hospitality operation by comparing bottom line profits with total investment; in accounting terms, ROA is net income divided by total assets; in finance terms, ROA is the rate of discount that makes the weighted average cost of capital approach to net present value (NPV) equal zero.

RETURN ON SHAREHOLDERS' EQUITY RATIO

A ratio that measures the profits generated on funds provided by investors. This ratio is often computed by dividing net income (less preferred dividends) by an average of the common shareholders' equity. It is also known as the return on investment (ROI) ratio and is stated as a rate of return.

REVENUE

Revenue results from the sale of goods or services and is measured by customer or client billings. Revenue also includes items such as interest, dividends, and commissions.

REVENUE ACCOUNTS

Income statement accounts used to record sales activities such as food, beverage, and rooms sales.

REVENUE CENTER

An area within the hospitality operation that generates revenue; a facility that sells goods or services to customers. It can also be a data collection report in which miscellaneous revenue is listed.

REVERSING ENTRIES

Beginning-of-month entries in the general journal that may be required due to certain types of adjusting entries recorded in the previous month; a reversing entry is the exact opposite of the adjusting entry to which it relates.

REVIEW

An opinion as to the fairness of the financial statements and an expression of limited assurance that no material changes to the financial statements are necessary for them to be in conformity with generally accepted accounting principles.

ROG (RECEIPT OF GOODS)

A modification of discount terms that specifies that the ending period for the cash discount is computed from the date goods are received—not the invoice date.

ROOM RACK

Usually refers to a card index system that is constantly updated to reflect occupied and vacant rooms. When a guest registers, part of the multi-part form prepared may be a room card which is then inserted in the room rack. In the evening, the room rack contains forms for only those registered guests remaining for the night who are to be charged for rooms. A daily room report can be prepared from the room rack.

S

SALARY

A term that usually applies to payrolls paid monthly, bimonthly, biweekly, or annually. Generally, qualified supervisors and executives who receive a fixed amount each pay period (regardless of the number of hours worked) are considered salaried employees.

SALES AND CASH RECEIPTS JOURNAL

A special journal used to record sales activity (cash or on account) and the cash receipts for the day.

SALES CONTROL

The set of controls and forms designed to enable management to monitor the revenue of a business. Sales control makes certain that all sales are recorded and that all sales are made at the correct prices.

SCHEDULE

A report that gives supporting detail to the financial statements. Examples include departmental income statements, note amortization schedules, and depreciation schedules.

SEGREGATION OF DUTIES

A characteristic of internal control that involves assigning different personnel to the functions of accounting, custody of assets, and production. Additional segregation of duties is designed within the accounting function. The major objective of segregating duties is the prevention and detection of errors and/or theft.

SHORT-TERM LOANS

Loans for a period of one year or less.

SIMPLE INTEREST

Interest computed only on the original principal.

SKIPPER

A hotel guest who leaves the hotel without paying or checking out.

SLEEPER

A room that appears occupied, although it is really vacant. This often occurs when the front desk fails to change the room status in the room rack.

SLIDE ERROR

An error caused by moving the decimal point of a number to the left or right of its correct position.

SOFTWARE

Programs and application routines that provide instructions to the computer.

SOLVENCY

The extent to which a hospitality operation is financed by debt and is able to meet its long-term obligations. An operation is solvent when its assets exceed its liabilities.

SOLVENCY RATIO

A ratio that measures the extent of a business's debt financing and ability to meet long-term obligations.

SPECIAL JOURNAL

A multi-column journal designed to record each major repetitive activity or event; a special journal is usually composed of separate columns for each type of transaction likely to occur repeatedly during the month, along with a sundry area for recording infrequent transactions.

SPECIFIC IDENTIFICATION APPROACH

A method of costing inventory by identifying the actual cost of the purchased and issued units.

STATEMENT OF CASH FLOWS
Explains the change in cash for the accounting period by showing the effects on cash of a business' operating, investing, and financing activities for the accounting period.

STATEMENT OF RETAINED EARNINGS
A financial statement reporting on the accumulated earnings retained by a corporation. These earnings are the net income of the business less any distribution of these earnings in the form of dividends to the corporation's stockholders.

STOCK DIVIDENDS
Dividends typically involving the issuance of common shares to existing common stockholders in proportion to their present ownership in the company.

STOCK SUBSCRIPTIONS
A stock purchase plan that may allow the investors to pay for the stock over a period of time. A subscriptions receivable account is used to record the purchase as well as an owners' equity account called common stock subscribed. When the full contract price is paid by the stockholders, the stock is issued.

STOCKHOLDERS
The owners of a corporation, also referred to as shareholders.

STOREROOM PURCHASES
Food items that are purchased for delivery to the storeroom.

STRAIGHT-LINE METHOD
A depreciation method that allocates an equal amount of a depreciable asset's cost over the asset's estimated useful life.

SUBSIDIARY COMPANY
A company that is controlled by another company.

SUBSIDIARY LEDGER
A separate ledger that provides supporting detail of an account in the general ledger; examples include the accounts payable subsidiary ledger and the accounts receivable subsidiary ledger.

SUM-OF-THE-YEARS-DIGITS METHOD
See Accelerated Depreciation Method.

SUMMARIZING
The actual process of preparing financial information according to the formats of specific reports or financial statements.

SUPPORT CENTERS
Areas of a hospitality operation that are not directly involved in generating revenue, but instead provide supporting services to revenue centers. Support centers include such areas as Administrative and General, Marketing, and Property Operation and Maintenance.

SUPPORTING SCHEDULES

Schedules providing additional detail for the general ledger or the financial statements. For example, an accounts payable schedule lists all the vendors to which the company owes a balance on open account; the total should agree with the balance in the general ledger accounts payable account.

T

T-ACCOUNT

A two-column format (resembling a letter "T") in which debits are posted to the left side and credits to the right side.

TANGIBLE ASSET

A business's assets that have physical substance; for example, land, buildings, and equipment. Land is the only tangible asset not subject to depreciation because it does not wear out in the normal course of business.

TAX ACCOUNTING

The branch of accounting relating to the preparation and filing of tax forms required by various governmental agencies.

TAX EQUITY AND FISCAL RESPONSIBILITY ACT OF 1982 (TEFRA)

A federal act that established regulations affecting food and beverage operations with respect to tip reporting requirements. The intent of the regulation is for all tipped employees to report tips of at least 8% of the gross receipts of the hospitality establishment.

TEMPORARY ACCOUNTS

Accounts that begin the new accounting year with zero balances, accumulate balances during the accounting year, and return to zero by means of closing entries at the end of the accounting year; they are also referred to as nominal accounts.

TIMING DIFFERENCE

Occurs when revenue or expense amounts on the income statement differ from the amounts entered on the income tax return for a given year. Over a period of several years, the totals of these amounts will eventually be equal.

TIP CREDIT

An amount that effectively lowers the amount of gross wages payable by the employer while still meeting minimum wage standards. Provisions of the Fair Labor Standards Act establish conditions that allow employers to apply a tip credit to the minimum wage of tipped employees.

TIP SHORTFALL

The amount by which the total reported tips falls short of 8% of the gross receipts. A tip shortfall must be allocated among directly tipped employees and reported to the IRS. Tip shortfall allocations must be reported to each affected employee.

TRADE DISCOUNT

A reduction on an item listed on a vendor's price list. The discount is not dependent on the date of payment.

TRANSPORTATION COST

The cost of getting merchandise to the place of business. This cost may also be called shipping, freight, or simply transportation. In theory, transportation costs should be allocated between inventory and cost of sales. Since these costs are not generally considered significant, a typical practice is to ignore their effect on inventories in the interest of convenience and economy in the accounting system. This accounting treatment includes transportation costs in calculating cost of sales.

TRANSPOSITION ERROR

An error in which two digits in a number have been mistakenly switched.

TREASURY STOCK

Stock which has been reacquired by the company and is no longer considered issued and outstanding.

TRIAL BALANCE

A list of accounts showing account names, titles, and balances. Its sequence is generally identical to that of accounts in the general ledger since the trial balance is copied from the general ledger. It verifies the equality of debit and credit balances in the general ledger and is the first step in the worksheet process.

U

UNCOLLECTIBLE ACCOUNTS

Accounts receivable that are determined to be uncollectible. Uncollectible accounts may also be called bad debts, uncollectible receivables, or uncollectibles. A business that sells goods or services on credit will usually incur expenses due to uncollectible accounts regardless of how effectively its credit department evaluates guests and customers. See also Allowance Method and Direct Write-off Method.

UNCOLLECTIBLE ACCOUNTS EXPENSE

An account in which the periodic charges for bad debts are recorded. If the allowance method is used, the estimated bad debts are recorded in this account; when a bad debt is actually incurred, a charge is made in Allowance for Doubtful Accounts. If the direct charge-off method is used, only the actual bad debts are charged to Uncollectible Accounts Expense. Also called the bad debts account.

UNEARNED REVENUE

The offset for cash received for services before they are rendered.

UNIFORM SYSTEM OF ACCOUNTS

A manual (usually produced for a specific segment of the hospitality industry) that defines accounts for various types and sizes of operations. A uniform system of accounts generally provides standardized financial statement formats, explanations of individual accounts, and sample bookkeeping documents.

U.S. TREASURY BILLS

Securities issued by the U.S. government, for fairly short periods. Usually considered riskless.

USEFUL LIFE

The time period an asset is expected to be useful in the process of generating revenue for a company. An asset's useful life may be shorter than its actual life expectancy in terms of economic value or utility.

V

VENDOR

A firm that sells wholesale merchandise. See Purveyor.

VERTICAL ANALYSIS

See Common-Size Analysis.

W

WAGES

A term that usually applies to payrolls computed on an hourly, weekly, or piecework basis. However, a fixed weekly pay may be called a salary.

WEIGHTED AVERAGE APPROACH

A method of costing inventory using an average cost per unit. The costing average is computed by dividing the total cost of goods available (cost of inventory on hand) by the number of units available (units in inventory).

WITHDRAWALS

A temporary account (specifically, a contra-equity account) used to record personal withdrawal of business assets by an owner (proprietor or partner); it is sometimes called a drawings account.

WORKING CAPITAL

The excess of current assets over current liabilities. The change in working capital for an accounting period is determined by subtracting the amount of working capital at the beginning of the period from the amount of working capital at the end of the period.

WORKSHEET

A multi-column working paper used as a preliminary to the preparation of financial statements. The typical worksheet has five sections, each with debit and credit columns; these include Trial Balance, Adjustments, Adjusted Trial Balance, Income Statement, and Balance Sheet.

Z

ZERO BASE BUDGETING

An approach to preparing budgets that requires the justification of all expenses; this approach assumes that each department starts with zero dollars and must justify all budgeted amounts.

The
Educational Institute Board of Trustees

The Educational Institute of the American Hotel & Motel Association is fortunate to have both industry and academic leaders, as well as allied members, on its Board of Trustees. Individually and collectively, the following persons play leading roles in supporting the Institute and determining the directions of its programs.

Steven J. Belmonte, CHA
President & COO
Ramada Franchise
  Systems, Inc.
Parsippany, New Jersey

John Q. Hammons
Chairman & CEO
John Q. Hammons
  Hotels, Inc.
Springfield, Missouri

David J. Christianson, Ph.D.
Dean
William F. Harrah College of
  Hotel Administration
University of Nevada,
  Las Vegas
Las Vegas, Nevada

Arnold J. Hewes, CAE
Executive Vice President
Minnesota Hotel & Lodging
  Association
St. Paul, Minnesota

Caroline A. Cooper, CHA
Dean
The Hospitality College
Johnson & Wales University
Providence, Rhode Island

S. Kirk Kinsell
President—Franchise
ITT Sheraton World
  Headquarters
Atlanta, Georgia

Edouard P.O. Dandrieux, CHA
Director
H.I.M., Hotel Institute,
  Montreux
Montreux, Switzerland

Donald J. Landry, CHA
President
Choice Hotels International
Silver Spring, Maryland

Valerie C. Ferguson
General Manager
Ritz-Carlton Atlanta
Atlanta, Georgia

Georges LeMener
President & CEO
Motel 6, L.P.
Dallas, Texas

Douglas G. Geoga
President
Hyatt Hotels Corporation
Chicago, Illinois

Jerry R. Manion, CHA
President
Manion Investments
Paradise Valley, Arizona

Joseph A. McInerney, CHA
President & CEO
Forte Hotels, Inc.
El Cajon, California

William R. Tiefel
President
Marriott Lodging
Washington, D.C.

John L. Sharpe, CHA
President & COO
Four Seasons-Regent Hotels
   and Resorts
Toronto, Ontario, Canada

Jonathan M. Tisch
President & CEO
Loews Hotels
New York, New York

Paul J. Sistare, CHA
President & CEO
Richfield Hospitality Services
Englewood, Colorado

Paul E. Wise, CHA
Professor & Director
Hotel, Restaurant &
   Institutional Management
University of Delaware
Newark, Delaware

Thomas W. Staed, CHA
President
Oceans Eleven Resorts, Inc.
Daytona Beach Shores, Florida

Ted Wright, CHA
Vice President/Managing
   Director
The Cloister Hotel
Sea Island, Georgia

Thomas G. Stauffer, CHA
President & CFO
Americas Region
Renaissance Hotels
   International, Inc.
Cleveland, Ohio

Index

UNDERSTANDING HOSPITALITY ACCOUNTING II

REVIEW QUIZ ANSWER KEY

The numbers in parentheses refer to the learning objective addressed by the question and the page where the answer may be found.

Chapter 1	Chapter 2	Chapter 3	Chapter 4
1. T (LO1, 5)	1. T (LO1, 40)	1. T (LO1, 74)	1. F (LO1, 91)
2. T (LO2, 8)	2. T (LO2, 40)	2. F (LO3, 76)	2. T (LO2, 92)
3. F (LO3, 9)	3. F (LO3, 48)	3. T (LO4, 78)	3. F (LO3, 94)
4. F (LO7, 22)	4. F (LO6, 57)	4. T (LO5, 81)	4. F (LO5, 99)
5. c (LO1, 4)	5. c (LO2, 46–47)	5. a (LO2, 75)	5. c (LO4, 96)
6. b (LO2, 7–8)	6. b (LO2, 46–47)	6. b (LO2, 75)	6. d (LO5, 100)
7. a (LO2, 7–8)	7. d (LO3, 48)	7. d (LO3, 76–77)	7. d (LO6, 102)
8. b (LO2, 9)	8. c (LO6, 53–54)	8. d (LO4, 79)	8. b (LO6, 102)
9. c (LO3, 9)	9. b (LO6, 57)	9. b (LO5, 81)	9. d (LO8, 103)
10. d (LO5, 16)	10. b (LO7, 60)	10. a (LO6, 82)	10. c (LO8, 104–105)

Chapter 5	Chapter 6	Chapter 7	Chapter 8
1. F (LO1, 125)	1. F (LO1, 152)	1. F (LO2, 220)	1. F (LO1, 251)
2. T (LO2, 126)	2. F (LO1, 152–153)	2. T (LO2, 223)	2. F (LO4, 254)
3. F (LO3, 126)	3. F (LO3, 156)	3. F (LO5, 224)	3. T (LO5, 255)
4. F (LO6, 131)	4. T (LO5, 161)	4. T (LO10, 230–231)	4. F (LO10, 258)
5. b (LO2, 126)	5. d (LO1, 153)	5. b (LO2, 220)	5. c (LO1, 252)
6. c (LO3, 126)	6. b (LO3, 156)	6. c (LO4, 224)	6. d (LO2, 253)
7. a (LO5, 129)	7. b (LO4, 158)	7. b (LO5, 225)	7. d (LO3, 254)
8. b (LO5, 130)	8. a (LO5, 162)	8. d (LO7, 226)	8. b (LO6, 255)
9. d (LO5, 130)	9. a (LO8, 170)	9. a (LO14, 235)	9. c (LO7, 256)
10. d (LO5, 130)	10. c (LO9, 174)	10. b (LO15, 236)	10. a (LO9, 258)

Chapter 9	Chapter 10	Chapter 11	Chapter 12
1. T (LO2, 269)	1. T (LO1, 287)	1. T (LO2, 316)	1. T (LO1, 343)
2. F (LO4, 272)	2. T (LO1, 288)	2. T (LO3, 318)	2. F (LO2, 344)
3. F (LO5, 275)	3. T (LO2, 293)	3. T (LO4, 326)	3. F (LO3, 346)
4. T (LO7, 278)	4. F (LO2, 297)	4. F (LO5, 327)	4. T (LO6, 349)
5. c (LO1, 266)	5. c (LO1, 287)	5. b (LO2, 315)	5. a (LO1, 343)
6. d (LO1, 266)	6. b (LO1, 288)	6. c (LO2, 315)	6. b (LO2, 345)
7. d (LO2, 268)	7. d (LO1, 291–292)	7. a (LO3, 319)	7. c (LO2, 345)
8. b (LO3, 271)	8. c (LO2, 296)	8. b (LO4, 323)	8. d (LO3, 346)
9. b (LO5, 275)	9. d (LO3, 301)	9. d (LO4, 325)	9. a (LO6, 353)
10. a (LO9, 281)	10. a (LO3, 302)	10. c (LO5, 331)	10. b (LO6, 355)

Chapter 13	Chapter 14	Chapter 15
1. F (LO1, 367)	1. T (LO2, 387)	1. F (LO1, 418)
2. T (LO2, 370)	2. F (LO4, 389)	2. F (LO2, 419)
3. T (LO3, 371)	3. T (LO4, 390)	3. F (LO4, 422)
4. F (LO8, 375)	4. T (LO7, 396)	4. T (LO6, 426)
5. a (LO2, 370)	5. c (LO1, 385)	5. d (LO1, 418)
6. d (LO7, 373)	6. d (LO2, 387)	6. b (LO4, 422)
7. b (LO8, 374)	7. d (LO7, 396)	7. d (LO5, 424)
8. d (LO10, 376)	8. b (LO7, 396)	8. b (LO6, 428)
9. d (LO10, 377)		9. c (LO6, 429)
		10. d (LO6, 429)